D0209395

THE PARAS

The Inside Story of
Britain's Toughest Regiment

John Parker

metro

First published in hardback in Great Britain in 2000 by Metro Books (an imprint of Metro Publishing Limited), 19 Gerrard Street, London W1V 7LA

All rights reserved: no part of this publication may be reproduced, stored in a retrieval system, or transmitted in any form or by any means, electronic, mechanical, photocopying or otherwise, without the prior written consent of the publisher.

© 2000 John Parker

John Parker is hereby identified as the author of this work in accordance with Section 77 of the Copyright, Designs and Patents Act 1988.
ISBN 1 900512 89 0

Typeset by Wakewing, High Wycombe, Buckinghamshire
Manufactured in the USA

CONTENTS

ACKNOWLEDGEMENTS

As will be evident, this book does not take the form of a conventional military history. The story of the Parachute Regiment is told, as far as possible, through the recollections of those who took part in some of the most outstanding events and actions since the formation of Britain's airborne forces. These memories include numerous vivid, outspoken and very personal accounts of courageous, controversial and ultimately tough times. It is, in effect, 'the Paras on the Paras', with some interventions and observations on the surrounding history by the author *en route* through this journey.

I am deeply indebted to a large number of people for their time, cooperation and effort in the process of gathering material for this book. All the recollections presented here are the result of more than 50 lengthy tape-recorded interviews with men of all ranks, from privates to knighted generals, and wives too. Some of the tapes were made personally with myself or my colleague Alastair McQueen, who assisted as a researcher, while many others were provided by the Sound Archive of the Imperial War Museum; and in this way I have obtained memories of almost every major campaign in which the Paras have been involved. Sadly, several of those whose words are used are no longer with us. A debt of gratitude is also due to Rosemary Tudge and her colleagues in the Imperial War Museum's Sound Archive, who went to very great lengths to meet my aspirations and deadlines.

John Parker, January 2000

Parachute Regiment Battle Honours

Bruneval, Normandy, France (27 February 1942)

Soudia, Oudna, Tunisia (29 October 1942)

Djebel Azzag, Djebel Alliliga, El Hadjeba, Tamera, Tunisia (1943)

Djebel Dahra, Kef el Debna, North Africa (1942–3)

Primosole Bridge, Sicily (13 July 1943)

Sicily (1943)

Taranto, Orsogna, Italy (1943–4)

Normandy landings (6 June 1944)

Pegasus Bridge, Merville battery, Bréville, Normandy, France (12 June 1944)

Dives crossing, La Touques crossing, southern France (15 August 1944)

Arnhem (17 September 1944)

Ourthe, Rhine, eastern France (24 March 1945)

north-west Europe (1942, 1944–5)

Athens (12 October 1944)

Greece (1944–5)

Goose Green, Mount Longdon, Wireless Ridge, Falkland Islands (14 June 1982)

Prologue

WIVES AND WIDOWS

H, as he was universally known because he hated the name Herbert, was at the Army's United Kingdom Land Forces HQ in Wilton, Wiltshire, when he learned that he was to command 2 Para: the 2nd Battalion the Parachute Regiment, with its renowned history, including the famous Second World War exploits at Arnhem portrayed in the film *A Bridge Too Far*. As the Falkland Islands were invaded by Argentina in April 1982, H – Lieutenant Colonel Herbert Jones – learned that it was unlikely his battalion would be sent. He lobbied furiously, and at home his wife and the mother of his two sons, Sara, watched as he burned the phone lines to anyone who could help get his unit included in the Task Force bound for the South Atlantic. H was hell-bent on going to war. He eventually made it and never came back.

Today H is one of the revered heroes of the Parachute Regiment, and as with anything that stands out in that regiment, he became, posthumously, a controversial figure. Sara herself – so close to him in those ambitious days that she could read his thoughts – stood up for him and his Regiment. Unusual though it may be for a woman's words to lead into a story which delves into the innermost thoughts and recollections of some of the world's toughest soldiers, there is no doubt that those who knew him will appreciate the reasons, which in the ensuing chapters will become more apparent to all.

Any realistic Army wife knows that is what her husband trains for. The reality of war is never very pleasant but if somebody is trained to do the job he wants to go off to see if he can do it and what it will be like for him. Although you mightn't like it in your heart, you have to accept it and recognize that is the type of man you are married to. It is what he wants to do. And I always knew it as far as H was concerned. We first met when I was 15 and married when I was 23 and he was 24. He was on operational service in places like Northern Ireland and had been decorated for his work there. Worry about him? Well, I suppose you worry less about him as the colonel than you would if he was a platoon commander. You pretend to yourself that as he is the CO he is likely to be safer. But you don't sit down and imagine things, see in lurid Technicolor what is going on. And the other thing is that most of us are optimists anyway.

When H went off to the Falklands it was a funny situation because we didn't know what was going to happen, if anything. There was all sorts of political toing and froing and it might have all turned into a damp squib with them all going off to sea then turning round and coming back again. Being optimistic I told myself: 'Well, it won't come to a landing...' When it got to the stage when they were getting closer – they were in the South Atlantic and it was getting rougher and they were on a North Sea ferry – then I did begin to worry. In the early stages he had flown to Ascension Island for the planning meetings and I thought he would be coming back before finally leaving but he rejoined the battalion at Ascension. So I never saw him again. He was pretty good at writing letters but they were very slow in getting through to us. I got quite a lot of his letters after he died.

But what was really sad was that all ours were returned, too, unopened. It is sad to think that all those letters were written by the boys and me and they never got to him. When H was killed, Graham Farrell, the regimental colonel, came to tell me. When I saw him I thought he was coming to take me off to see someone else to give them bad news, but he was coming to see me. We knew the night before that Goose Green was to happen and it was all in the newspapers and on the news that there had been a battle. The boys were home for half-term. I had collected David from the train from Sherborne. Rupert was with me and when we got back we were talking about it. H's name was in the newspapers as the commanding officer, but we did not know he had been killed. We knew the regiment had been victorious but we also knew there had been casualties. We did not know who the casualties were.

I remember ringing one of the officers at the Para Depot and saying that it was great that we had been victorious or something similar, and he said: 'We must guard against over-optimism.' I didn't realize at the time what he was saying. He knew there had been casualties and he must have known the names and was awaiting confirmation before breaking the news. At that time we had a set-up within the battalion, a wives' club and various other things which involved both the officers' and soldiers' wives. We also had a very good families officer. I was 40 at the time, probably one of the oldest women 'in the regiment', so to speak. Some people saw me as the Mother of the Battalion. Everybody was worried, but there was not a lot of crying on my shoulder. The Parachute Regiment produces a higher quality of soldier, a better-educated soldier in the ways of the world, a more independent type of person, and that quality is reflected in their wives and they are more able to cope. An independent soldier tends to marry an independent wife. The wives of 2 Para were used to coping with things because of the time the men spent away on exercises or Northern Ireland tours.

About 24 hours after H was killed I was told. And it was then I realized why they had said we must guard against over-optimism. I couldn't believe it even though I knew I had to. I don't think anybody who is given a shock like that actually appreciates what they have been told at the time. It is like a sort of bad dream and it isn't for weeks, months, that you actually accept that it is for real, that it is true. We were lucky in a way because it was half-term and the boys and I were together. They told me first and I told the boys. In a way, it was easier because we were together and my mother was there and the wife of the commanding officer of another Para battalion. About a week afterwards we had a families day. And I remember going to that. I don't know why I felt I should go but I just knew I had to go. I suppose I felt that as I was the colonel's wife I had a duty to the battalion he commanded. I was very proud of the regiment and with that comes all sorts of attachments and duty is one of those attachments.

The wives of the senior officers and senior NCOs had a fair weight of responsibility in looking after the younger ones. You have to remember we were just wives – we were not trained social workers or anything like that. I had to go to the families day because I thought that the sooner I got back to doing things that were everyday and normal the sooner things might get better. There was no point in digging a big hole and climbing into it. Although at times I was there as a shoulder to cry on, I myself was lucky because I have always had a very supportive family. I remember sitting in Geraldine Chaundler's sitting room after her husband, David, flew off to replace H as CO of 2 Para. He was parachuted in [see Chapter 16] and I remember sitting with Geraldine and watching the television film of H and the others who were killed at Goose Green being buried in the temporary graves at Ajax Bay.

H is still there, buried in the War Cemetery at San Carlos. We assumed that everyone who died would be buried where they fell. I have a brother-in-law in the Navy and their dead are traditionally buried at sea. It was quite a time afterwards that Maggie [Prime Minister Margaret Thatcher] decided that those who died could be repatriated. I didn't like the idea of him being dug up and transported all that way back again. To me it seemed more dignified to have him buried where he fell. Even after all these years I sometimes have dreams that he did not die, that he was badly wounded and that he is coming home again. I suppose it is part of the inbuilt defence mechanism. I was never bitter about him being killed, but I suppose in a way I was a little angry with him at one stage for dying and leaving the boys and me.

But you marry a man, the person you love, and you have to accept the nature of the beast. I wished he had done something else, but if he did what he felt was right then I have to accept that.

We can all look at the if onlys in life... If only he had commanded another battalion... If only the Falklands hadn't happened... You could go on and on. But the reality is that he did what he thought to be right at that moment and that is all that matters. I do not believe his life was lost in vain. We were right to support the Falkland Islanders, who are fiercely British, against the might of Argentina. Maggie was right to go in, to send the troops there and we won a great victory – which I don't suppose we could nowadays because we wouldn't have the ships to get there.

Since the campaign, as always happens, people have been examining the way it was conducted and H's role in it. There have been some stinging things said about him. You don't like the criticism and I think you would be pretty unfeeling if you did, but if you have faith and believe in the person, then that is what is important. You don't like it being said, so you try to rise above that. In this country it is inevitable that anybody who is held up as a hero or held in high esteem will be targeted by people looking to see if they have feet of clay, looking to bring them down. I think it is a shame because I think people in this country wish to have people to look up to, and always looking for a downside, a bad side, is a shame. Most of the criticism has come from people who were not there, the armchair strategists who sat safely at home and from the comfort of their armchairs began to analyse H's strategy, to find fault with it. But unless you were on the ground and in the throes of war, which is a pretty disorganized business, how can you say what people were doing was wrong?

The criticism made the boys cross but it did not shake their faith in what H did. They believe he did what he felt he had to do at the time. They had reached a difficult point in the battle and H would not make somebody else do something he wouldn't have done himself. He led from the front. There is an argument that a CO should not be doing that, but when it got to that point of the battle where he felt things were becoming bogged down he felt that if nobody else was going to do it he would have to. He did it and, I would argue, that was the turning point. There had been many rumours that he was going to be awarded a posthumous Victoria Cross. When it happened we were all very proud, terribly proud, but he would not have been impressed with himself; he would have been impressed with his battalion and what they had achieved. Even though the boys were proud they also had to live with it. It is quite tough having a famous father who, on the one hand, is a national hero and on the other is criticized from time to time. It is all very difficult to take on board. It is then even more difficult when you follow your father into a career, which they both did: both joined the Army.

Luckily, with a name like Jones, people don't always know who they are. It is very difficult living up to your father's reputation and people's expectations based on his reputation. Then there is the criticism. They either have to stand up for him or take it on the chin or whatever. It is not easy. It was no surprise to me that they were going to go into the Army. It was not because of what H did. It was always destined. Before H died David was going in. The only thing I didn't know was what regiment they were going to join. I thought David might join the Parachute Regiment and Rupert the Devon and Dorsets. In the end they both joined the D and Ds. I never tried to stop them. You support your children in whatever they want to do and as far as joining the Army is concerned, I think it is a marvellous tradition and a marvellous occupation for those who want to do it. I always loved the spirit of the Army, I loved everything it stood for. I still do. It gives me a buzz, but I think I have an old-fashioned vision of it now. The Army has moved on.

When David graduated from Sandhurst there was a great feeling of pride and one of regret that H was not there to see it. I shed a tear, but I think H could well have been there in spirit. Rupert toyed with the idea of going into the Paras but then decided against it. David, in his uniform, was the spitting image of his father and terribly like him in a hundred and one ways. All the ways he acts and behaves are H all over again. They served together in Northern

Ireland and that was a little worrying, but I was more worried when Rupert went to Bosnia. I was worried more then, I don't know why, but I was. He was terribly involved in what was happening around Mount Igman and I remember being dreadfully worried then. I got myself in a real state about him. It was probably because it was always on the news and they kept saying that they were going in to do this, that and the other, and I thought: 'I've been here before... I don't think I can take it again.' As far as Northern Ireland is concerned I had been there before, I had lived there during one of H's tours of duty and I could understand it more. Bosnia I couldn't understand and I didn't enjoy him being there at all. By this stage I was no longer an Army wife, but just an ordinary Army mum.

I got involved with the Falklands Families Association about two years after it was formed. A group of relatives formed it on the Cunard *Countess* on their way back from visiting the graves in the Falklands the year after the fighting. Sadly we are now a much smaller band than we used to be: some people have died, others' lives have moved on and they don't want to know any more. But I think it has given a lot of people support and friendship and for all of us – particularly myself – it has shown that there are other people out there who have the same experiences, the same emotions, the same problems you have, and you know that you are a band of people with a common understanding, a comradeship, and that is very important. The vast majority of those who joined were parents because the vast majority of those killed were young people who were not married. Some have never recovered from the loss of their children. It is very hard for women and children to be widowed and left without a father, but I think it is toughest of all on parents because you never get over the loss of a child. I always feel that your child is your investment in the future. It is a little bit of you you leave behind and to lose one is a shattering blow.

H's VC is at the National Army Museum in Chelsea on what they call permanent loan. It still belongs to the family and we can get it back any time we want. The reality of it is, what is the point of me having it here in the house or having it in a bank? There is no point. It is much better having it somewhere where people can see it, and there aren't many places where it can be properly looked after. I go to see it occasionally, but it doesn't bring back any particular memories of H as it came to us after he died. He never held it, it was never part of him. We are proud of the ethos and all that goes with being a Victoria Cross holder.

1

WARRIORS FROM THE SKIES

Even in this age of high-speed air travel, nerves jangle for most mortals at the very thought of boarding a plane, let alone jumping out of it when it is in the clouds with only a flimsy canopy to stop one's body crashing back to earth with potentially fatal consequences. The idea had been around long enough, from Greek mythology to Leonardo da Vinci's sketches of a man dangling from a hollow pyramid. So let us go back in time for a few moments to recall the origins of the Paras.

As early as 1783, statesman and scientist Benjamin Franklin, then the American minister in Paris, had some sort of vision of airborne armies being dropped into battle after hearing news of the first manned flight in a hydrogen balloon by the Frenchmen Jacques-Alexandre-César Charles and Nicolas Robert on 1 December of that year. They took off from fields on the outskirts of Paris, rose about 600 metres and drifted more than 40 kilometres from the city. These early developments in balloon travel immediately began to attract the attention of forward-thinking military men and others fearful of invaders from the skies. Within the year a French balloonist, Jean-Pierre Blanchard, and an American doctor, John Jeffries, made the first balloon flight across the English Channel. They took off from Dover and landed near Calais two hours later. Blanchard also made the first balloon voyage in the United States in 1793 and before the end of the decade another Frenchman, André-Jacques Garnerin, made the first parachute jump from a balloon over Paris, using a canopy with rigid spokes. Those early experiments of jumping from balloons would remain a pertinent, if precarious, part of the training of the pioneers of modern parachuting from the early days of the Second World War, serving as a prelude to actually diving out of aircraft. Colonel Alan Wooldridge remembers his own experiences in the 1950s:

My first jump from a tethered balloon was an absolute horror – four trainees in a cage suspended beneath it rose into the air to a height of around 800 feet. It was deathly quiet. When it reached the tethered height, the Parachute Jump Instructor would oversee each man as he jumped out. The guy in charge of us liked a joke – just as I went, he yelled, 'Come back!' But then the parachute opened and down I floated to a safe landing. It was a frightening initiation. Balloon jumps were the worst part of our training.

These jumps were universally hated by the men who took up this challenge, not least because the stomach-churning experience could be worse going up than it was coming down. The silent balloon made its slow rise, often swaying wildly even in gentle air currents, until the rookie recruits, usually a 'stick' of four men suspended in a cage slung below it, reached the jumping height. They were usually already feeling sick to the stomach when it was their turn to exit the cage through an aperture in the floor, to tumble an initial 120 feet in freefall before the canopy opened and then having to manage the downward spiral with instructions being hollered through a megaphone by another instructor on the ground. What they had just experienced was a frightening test of courage that had been around since the eighteenth century.

In the late eighteenth century the French had begun a serious study of using balloons to drop troops, and by 1794 they were employing tethered balloons in warfare, as observation platforms to report the location and movement of enemy soldiers, although not to transport troops. During the American Civil War (1861–5) an American balloonist named Thaddeus Lowe formed and directed the first-ever balloon corps in the Union Army, while the North used observation balloons to direct artillery fire and to report Confederate troop movements. France returned to the thought of using balloons to drop troops during the Franco-Prussian War of 1870–71, its military scientists producing many drawings of large balloons carrying baskets laden with troops who could be airlifted into the war zones. Once again the plan never came to fruition, although when the German armies laid siege to Paris the French remained in contact with the outside world by launching more than 60 balloons carrying almost nine tonnes of mail.

The event provided a signpost for another age and from then on futuristic writers, prophets of doom and adventurous military thinkers were all predicting the possibility of airborne soldiers, although exactly how these troops would descend from the heavens was at the time unknown. For years it seemed that at best parachuting would remain a carnival attraction, used by balloonists to thrill the crowds as they dived out of their tethered craft, using canopies which would be pulled open by ropes attached to the balloon's basket. The arrival of powered flight in 1903 provided a fresh impetus, and in 1912 the first true parachute jump from an aircraft, a Benoist biplane, was made over Jefferson Army Barracks in Missouri by Albert Berry of the US Army. He used a parachute housed in a container slung beneath the aircraft, precariously reached by crawling between the wheel struts before jumping. Intrepid fairground parachutist Charles Broadwick took the experiment a stage further in 1913 when he demonstrated his own invention, a parachute folded in a pack worn on his back, which was opened by a line attached to the aircraft when he jumped out.

By the time of the First World War (1914–18) both the Germans and the Allies had air forces and were experimenting with various forms of parachutes. Given impetus by a proliferation in the use of observation balloons, the concept of parachuting from plane or balloon taxed the minds of both sides. Initially, however, the use of parachutes was confined to their role as a lifesaver. Balloon crews were suicidally vulnerable to gunners from the ground and needed a fast route to earth when attacked before the hydrogen gas in the capsule above them exploded in a mass of flames.

Parachutes were slung around the balloon in canisters and when the crew felt they were in imminent danger of being shot down they clipped them to a harness around their bodies and jumped. In the latter stages of the war the French and the Russians pioneered the use of parachutes for purposes other than saving lives, dropping agents behind enemy lines or supplies to beleaguered troops. The British and the Americans were slow to exploit the use of parachutes and even their pilots were not issued with them until September 1918 because it was felt that they would encourage cowardice in the face of enemy attacks by allowing men to jump from their aircraft rather than staying on board to fight.

The British and the Americans both formed experimental parachute groups after the war, but there was little enthusiasm for the idea and much of the early progress was made in the USSR, which benefited from technology brought by German 'advisers' who were prohibited under the Treaty of Versailles from developing their military capabilities in their own country. In 1931 the Soviets gave an impressive demonstration to German observers of a parachute drop by the 1st Parachute Landing Unit, based at Stalingrad. Within four years the USSR had raised and trained 30 battalions of paratroops organized into three divisions, and these were so impressive that a demonstration of their skydiving skills was staged for an audience of military men from throughout Europe.

General Archibald Wavell, then with the British Army's General Staff (and later Supreme Allied Commander in the Pacific), was among those present at the demonstration. It was a real eye-opener. The airborne manoeuvres included a mass drop by 1500 Soviet parachutists. 'If I had not witnessed it, I would not have believed such an operation possible,' Wavell wrote on his return, full of enthusiasm. But in 1930s Britain, where warnings of Germany's expanding military might well have been largely unheeded, Wavell's suggestion that the British Army should begin training an airborne force also fell on deaf ears. No one took the slightest notice, save perhaps for Winston Churchill, who was at the time in his wilderness years and listened to by few in high office.

Also present at the Soviet demonstration in 1935 was Hermann Goering, who had just been appointed head of the Luftwaffe. He returned to Germany determined to press ahead with the formation of his own airborne regiment, the 1st Fallschirmjäger, in complete contravention of the tattered remains of the Treaty of Versailles. Its importance in the burgeoning German military machine would be made apparent to all by his insistence that it should have the honour of bearing his own name in its formation title. As British military intelligence and MI6 would soon report, Soviet airborne skills had reached impressive levels and Goering's new outfit was in training by January 1936, with its first battalion of 600 men commanded by an air force major, Bruno Bräuer. The German Army also formed its own airborne unit in that same year and a parachute school was founded at Stendal, west of Berlin. The British took no action – an attitude that was to cost them dear in the early stages of the Second World War.

By then the Luftwaffe had established Germany's first parachute division, consisting of highly skilled, élite troops trained to perfection and later to be admired by their eventual British counterparts. Poland and France also formed parachute units and members who escaped before the German occupation of those two countries were to make a significant contribution to Allied parachute operations when these came into use. Meanwhile Goering's Air Ministry had pressed ahead with its demands for round-the-clock production of aircraft and gliders, and as war edged closer it became clear that airborne troops were to become an integral part of the early advances across western Europe and Scandinavia.

In Germany there were two distinct training patterns, one preferred by the Luftwaffe and the other by the Army; both were later copied by the British. The Luftwaffe planned to train clandestine operatives to parachute into enemy territory in small numbers, ranging from individuals to around a dozen men, trained as spies, fifth columnists, saboteurs and general troublemakers. The Army's methodology was quite different: it would drop large numbers of crack troops ahead of the main ground force to seize key objectives and so smooth the arrival of the armoured divisions. German military planners accepted that both proposals were brilliant additions to the overall concept of the Blitzkrieg, or lightning war, which they would soon launch against most of the rest of Europe. Goering continued to recognize the importance of an airborne approach, insisting in early 1939 that all of Germany's airborne troops and paratroop forces should come under the auspices of the Luftwaffe. The extent of the country's parachute capability was kept largely under wraps until the time came to unleash it.

The moment was not far off. By the end of the year the Nazis had two full parachute regiments under Luftwaffe control, kitted out in their blue-grey uniforms, and one Army infantry division trained in the techniques of airlandings. The Nazi invasion of Denmark and Norway in April 1940 marked the end of the phoney war. It was the prelude to spectacular German airborne raids across western Europe. As German warships appeared off the Norwegian coast, the airborne invasion began inland. Within 48 hours the Germans had landed seven divisions and captured all the main ports, while the airborne troops secured their positions at Oslo airport and Norway's other major airports. In fact, the weather had halted planned parachute drops at Oslo airport and infantry troops were landed in a succession of Junkers 52s to take possession. However, five companies of paratroops did drop at other key airports. The Germans established a firm hold on the southern half of Norway, and their control became complete when, less than a month later, the British and French withdrew their forces from the country in response to surprise attacks by the Nazis across western Europe, again spearheaded by airborne troops.

At dawn on 10 May German troops were carried forward in 42 gliders towed into the air by Ju 52s from Cologne and released into silent flight over Holland and Belgium to seize vital airports and bridges. Meanwhile, along a 150-mile front, 28 German divisions were assembled to move into action. Thus the Blitzkrieg, launched without warning, came to the Low Countries, and the British Expeditionary Force began its desperate retreat to the coast. The British nation went into shock, not least its military analysts when, in the aftermath of the huge operation, they pieced together the elements of the German invasion strategy: the lightning speed of the Panzer divisions which overran Dutch and Belgian defences, backed up by the fearsome accuracy of the airborne artillery provided by the Ju 87 Stukas and the devastating – and totally unexpected – arrival of airborne and parachute troops.

The latter had a particularly unsettling effect on the British public for many months afterwards, when, during the mounting fear of a German invasion of Britain, the nation was gripped by a kind of 'para fever'. The arrival of troops from the skies or the clandestine landing of fifth columnists, spies and saboteurs (probably dressed as nuns) was expected daily.

Alongside the humiliation and anguish resulting from the vast number of casualties suffered by the British Expeditionary Force, there was a salutary lesson for the British war planners: airborne troops were essential to meet the type of warfare the Germans were planning, although there were quite a few detractors from this view, not least among the upper echelons of the Royal Air Force. A hasty conference was summoned at the Air Ministry, but nothing happened apart from an announcement that 'it has been decided to establish a parachute training centre'. Major John Rock of the Royal Engineers was placed in charge of the 'organization of British Airborne Forces'. His instructions were vague and equipment scant and ill-suited to the job. 'It was impossible,' Major Rock would say later, 'to get any information as to policy or task.' The attitude of the Air Ministry was nothing short of obstructive and it remained so until Winston Churchill, who replaced Neville Chamberlain as Prime Minister on the day of the German invasion of Belgium and Holland, took a hand.

On 22 June 1940, the day the French formally capitulated and therefore the threat of invasion of Britain heightened, Churchill issued a clear instruction in a note to General Sir Hastings Ismay, head of his Defence Office:

We ought to have a corps of at least 5000 parachute troops including a proportion of Australians, New Zealanders and Canadians together with some trustworthy people from Norway and France... I hear something is being done already to form such a corps but only, I believe, on a very small scale. Advantage must be taken of the summer to train these forces who can nonetheless play their part meanwhile as shock troops in home defences ... let me have a note from the War Office on this subject.

The Central Landing School, sited at Ringway Airport on the outskirts of Manchester, which formally if tentatively came into being on 21 June 1940 as part of the Air Ministry's reaction to the German invasion of western Europe, now became the focus of great activity. John Rock was joined by Wing Commander Louis Strange, Wing Commander Sir Nigel Norman and Squadron Leader Maurice Newnham, and the boost from Churchill provided the necessary support for a strong offensive force at a time when thoughts were generally directed towards the defence of the British Isles. This very fact caused dissent from some, in both RAF and the Army, for their shared priority at that moment was the defence of Britain rather than the creation of a new offensive force. There was already a mad scramble going on for more aircraft and decent equipment to meet existing needs, let alone engage in some new and alien form of warfare in which the British had no previous experience whatsoever.

The first recruits for the first-ever British parachute units were all volunteers from the Commandos and specifically from the newly formed 2 Commando, which was given a new base at Knutsford, in Cheshire, so as to be close to the Ringway parachute school. B and C troop arrived on 9 July and the number of men who had parachute experience could be counted on the fingers of one hand, with some to spare. They faced a rapid programme of training, and were placed in the hands of a joint team of parachute instructors made up of 14 men from the RAF (under Flight Sergeant Bill Brereton) and nine from the Army Physical Training centre under Regimental Sergeant Major Mansie. They faced the mammoth task for which the words 'silk purse' and 'sow's ear' rush to mind. It was virgin territory – no equipment, no training modules, no pre-plane jump apparatus of any kind; just a few hundred parachutes and six very old and already obsolete Whitley Mk III bombers.

Enthusiastic staff at Ringway worked around the clock to cobble together some sort of training programme and organize parachute simulation gear to get the project off the ground. They had just six months to achieve what had taken the Germans six years; an impossible task. Nor were the top brass and their underlings at the Air Ministry falling over themselves to help – despite Churchill's personal intervention.

Those entrusted with the nation's defence also went through much the same deliberations as the Germans as to who was in charge – the RAF or the Army – given that the paratroops were strictly a fighting unit while the aircraft and school itself were operated by the RAF. It took several months to work out the lines of demarcation, the duties of the training personnel and which of the two services was responsible for what. A compromise was reached, with the RAF taking charge of parachute training and all matters concerned with the aircraft, while the Army kept a secure hold on the training for and planning of airborne warfare.

The lines of responsibility were only part of the problem in this race to equip and train an effective force of fighting men whose method of deployment was totally unlike anything previously undertaken in the British armed forces. The fledgling group had neither aircraft nor supplies of good, reliable parachutes, and because of the newness of it all, they were totally lacking in real-time experience. Even the instructors were deficient in that area, their knowledge having been gleaned from post-war training in the use of parachutes for survival when bailing out of a crippled aircraft.

Few instructors had trained for – or even witnessed – the procedures for depositing a heavily armed, battle-ready military unit on the ground. Whereas the Germans had been close at hand for the Soviet parachute trials in the early 1930s, every department of the British unit had to be constructed from the ground up. The order of the day was the wartime philosophy of make do and mend that dogged so many areas of Britain's military capability. Bits of old aircraft were propped up in hangars for practising aircraft drills. A DIY parachute tower was built and sandbags were used as a counterweight to simulate speed of descent, but it was a slow process because each man had to be weighed separately.

The old Whitley bombers, boneshakers of the first order, were barely suitable for the task, and the basic requirement of finding the best way to drop parachute soldiers from them took many hours of trial and error, and not a few injuries. At first the rear gun turrets were removed to provide a jumping platform. Recruits stood on this and one of the instructors pulled the ripcord and the slipstream took hold and opened the chute. It was a very unsatisfactory and unsafe method, because the men tumbled wildly in descent. Then the instructors tried cutting a hole in the floor of the aircraft, but this was not much of an improvement because unless the recruits made an impeccable exit, they were likely to bash their head and face against the rear edge of the hole. Later a third method of exiting, through a door cut in the fuselage, was tried.

The hastily prepared training programme, geared to producing a skilled unit of men brought to the peak of physical fitness in the shortest possible time, was nothing short of a baptism of fire for the volunteers, most of whom had never even been up in an aircraft, let alone jumped out of one. Experienced soldiers they may have been, but everything they encountered from now on was new. Their first experience of flying was in clapped-out old bombers that rattled and banged as they trundled down the runway, which did not fill them with confidence. Only four days after their arrival at Ringway, the trainees were given a live demonstration of parachuting by the parachute jump instructors, or PJIs as they were later known. By August 1940, 290 trainees had progressed to regular training jumps from aircraft and, in little more than a month, completed almost 1000 jumps between them. Given the shortage of reliable equipment and aircraft, the speed of training and the number of jumps undertaken, the failure rate was low: 30 refusals, 13 injured, two deaths when parachutes failed to open properly and 13 trainees deemed unsuitable for the course and given an RTU (an order to 'return to unit').

One of the initial problems the trainees confronted was the bulkiness of their padded clothing and so, after early experiments, they began using normal fighting uniform together with the parachutist's smock. Another development was the ditching of standard parachutes, used for bail-outs, and the subsequent use of the X-Type 'statichute', which opened automatically and provided a limited degree of control in descent. There were also extensive trials on the amount of equipment that a parachutist could carry – problems long ago resolved by the Germans, who indeed were already moving on to advanced training for massive and spectacular parachute operations that would shock the world. The small-time bunch who were intended to match the German paratroops were now being put through their paces on a wing and a prayer at an airfield in the north of England.

At the end of the first six months 488 men had completed parachute training at Ringway and the unit was renamed 11th Special Air Service Battalion and divided into a parachute wing and a glider wing, both managed by Headquarters Company. Even so, Winston Churchill was not happy: only 500 – must do better, was his reaction. There was also some discontent among the trainees. It had been an adrenalin-pumping few months, and by the turn of the year they were so primed for action that the lack of it – given their awareness of the war raging across Europe and in North Africa and the increasing intensity of the Germans' bombing blitz on London and, now, provincial cities – caused many of them to become impatient with incessant training for raids that never seemed to come off. Desperate to make a contribution to the effort, they began applying to return to their original regiments. Their fears were, to some extent, allayed around the beginning of the new year by rumours that plans were being laid to drop the first-ever British troops into action by parachute; it appeared that a task had been found for them to satisfy the increasing impatience of the Prime Minister.

Applications for RTUs declined and when, in January 1941, volunteers were called for as planning was being finalized for the first paratroop operation, every officer and man of the 500 in the battalion stepped forward. In fact, only seven officers and 31 other ranks were required for this trial operation, a sabotage project in southern Italy for which the group would be code-named X-Troop. It was hardly a full-blown para attack, but more like the burgeoning special operations conducted by various groups to insert raiders into enemy territory by air or sea to disrupt Italian and German land forces and blow up vital installations, bridges and railway lines. Such missions were to come thick and fast in the wake of Winston Churchill's call to 'set Europe ablaze' following the formation of the Special Operations Executive (SOE) in July 1940 after Italy came into the war. SOE's establishment was followed by the rapid growth of the empire known as Combined Operations, which eventually burgeoned even further under the command of Lord Louis Mountbatten (following his appointment in 1941) into a vast, if controversial, panoply of small, medium and substantial inter-service raiding operations, some of which were spectacular failures and led to heavy losses. As airborne tactics blossomed, parachute and glider-borne units would play an increasing and costly role.

In this period many of the now famous raiding groups and virtual private armies emerged, each with the same objective but with a very different *modus operandi*. The first, and certainly the most successful in those early days, was the Long Range Desert Group (LRDG), founded in the summer of 1940 by Major (later Colonel) R. A. Bagnold at the behest of General Sir Archibald Wavell, then Commander-in-Chief of Allied Forces in North Africa. This would be manned initially by New Zealanders. Over the next five years the LRDG conducted more than 200 operations behind enemy lines – more than any other Special Forces group. Then there was Lieutenant Colonel Bob Laycock's commando group known as Layforce, Major Roger Courtney's Special Boat Service, Lieutenant Colonel David Stirling's 1st Special Air Service and Major H. G. 'Blondie' Hasler's Royal Marines Boom Patrol Detachment, which spawned the 'Cockleshell Heroes' – to name but a few such groups. All shared one aim: to hit the Axis troops behind their lines, which called for the insertion of daring young men deep into enemy territory to cause as much mayhem as possible.

Many of the early operations of these special forces groups were swashbuckling in style and met with varying degrees of success – or failure, sometimes to the point of fiasco. Months of trial and error and not a few casualties forced war managers to press for more subtle ways to carry out clandestine work against the enemy. There were many who thought special forces and their fanciful operations were a waste of time and manpower. Sending out small groups of men to blow up railway lines or pillboxes, killing a few enemy soldiers and as often as not losing half, sometimes all, of their own team in the process – for what? Enemy morale was barely touched and damage to installations quickly repaired. There were much more cost-effective ways, it was argued, to use ships and aircraft and highly trained men. Even so, there were many good results and quite a few heroes.

The risks involved in special operations were invariably heavy and extremely evident. The fact that a good proportion of the men might not return was generally not mentioned, although there was always that plaintiff cry at the end of the briefings on all of these operations: 'How do we get home?' The escape route back to base was usually meticulously worked out, but in effect rarely ran to plan, and as the war progressed, hundreds of men sent covertly behind the lines were captured, shot up in firefights or executed.

In those early months after Churchill's call for special operations – when few of the above-named groups were fully operational – the eyes of the top brass fell upon the new parachute formation, although its original remit was certainly not as a supplier of small-party raiders. Churchill wanted the parachute troops to serve as a major airborne invasion group. But the slowness of the build-up in strength and the dire lack of equipment had meant that the formation of an effective parachute force had in fact been disappointingly inept – a point already made by the troops themselves.

At last, however, there was to be some action – even it was for only a few of the men – and in January 1941 those selected began intensive training for their first live drop. The timing was vital. They were to contribute to a wider plan to attempt, by whatever means possible, to disrupt the flow of supplies and reinforcements to Mussolini's vast armies amassed against the Allies in North Africa. The Long Range Desert Group was already doing its bit in the great Libyan Desert. Two-man teams of the Special Boat Service, launched in canoes from submarines, were to operate around the coasts. And a select group of the Special Air Service Battalion was to strike on the Italian mainland. It was very much a journey into the unknown, experimental in every respect.

The objective of the airborne unit in what was to be known as Operation Colossus was a major aqueduct in southern Italy. As part of a pipeline, this carried fresh-water supplies all the way down to the towns of Bari and Brindisi on the Adriatic coast at the very heel of the Italian boot and to Taranto on the sheltered Gulf of Taranto. These ports were the main embarkation and supply centres for the Italian campaigns in North Africa and Albania and they relied for their water on the pipeline running through the Apennines. The target aqueduct lay around 50 miles inland, at Tragino near Monte Vulture, and an airborne raid was the only option for the attack. The mission had the makings of a severe test not only of the men selected but also of the RAF's ability to put them down in a specified position in hostile surroundings, at night over countryside that had few landmarks to guide the pilots. It would be judged a success if the aqueduct was blown up; the secondary elements, such as the men achieving their goal with a minimum of casualties and going on to a successful RV (rendezvous) with the recovery craft, would provide essential information for future reference. In this instance recovery was to be made by a submarine, HMS/M *Triumph*, which would be waiting for them off the west coast of Italy.

X-Troop was hand-picked: seven officers and 31 other ranks under the command of Major Trevor 'Tag' Pritchard, whose parent regiment was the Royal Welch Fusiliers, with Captain G. F. K. Daly of the Royal Engineers in charge of demolitions. Three Italian-speakers, including a civilian named Fortunato Picchi, were attached to the troop, to help get them out of any trouble

15

they might encounter on the long march from the attack site to the coast. Training and work-ups for the operation continued through to 6 February 1941. The planners hoped they had covered every eventuality, having constructed a full-scale mock-up of the part of the aqueduct to be attacked. Aerial reconnaissance photographs and maps of the region were studied; routes from target to RV were worked out in fine detail; and one of the planners, Lieutenant Anthony Deane-Drummond of the Royal Signals, flew out to Malta to make the final preparations for X-Troop's onward journey to Italy.

On 7 February the group was transferred to Malta in eight Whitley bombers from 91 Squadron, six of which were to be used to put the men on to their DZ (dropping zone), while two were designated to make diversionary bombing raids on railway yards at Foggia at the time of the attack on the aqueduct. Once the mission was completed, X-Troop would split into groups and make their way to the coast, guided by the River Sele to its mouth in the Gulf of Salerno. There they would rendezvous with the *Triumph*, which was to gather them up and speed them back across the Mediterranean to Malta. It was an ambitious first raid that had more to do with testing the effectiveness of such operations than the safe return of the men. Nor could it be said that the operation, if successful, would be anything more than a bee sting to the Italians. No great military advantages would be won.

At dusk on the night of 10 February, Operation Colossus was launched from Malta under clear skies and perfect visibility. The eight Whitleys took off for their night flight and aimed to reach the DZ at around 21.30 hours. Two of the aircraft carried bombs to drop on the railway yards at Foggia. The remaining six carried sticks of six or seven men who would be dropped with canisters containing their weapons, food, equipment and explosives at given sites around the target. The first Whitley reached the aqueduct at 21.42 and zoomed in low to drop the troops and their equipment within 250 yards of it. By 21.50 the next four aircraft had dropped their men within 400 yards of the target, but release mechanisms on two of the Whitleys had iced up, with the result that the canisters of weapons and equipment failed to drop immediately and only one was recovered by the force on the ground. The Whitley which was carrying Captain Daly and five sappers missed the DZ entirely and put the men out over the wrong valley, 20 miles away.

The remainder of the force, now with only 800 pounds of explosive, less than half that needed for the mission, had to pare down their original plan to blow up the main supports of the aqueduct, built of tough reinforced concrete, and instead set their charges around a smaller pier and bridge. Despite this setback, the charges blew out the pier and a huge chunk of the aqueduct came down with it, causing water to pour through the gaping sides. X-Troop had done its work. Now all that remained was to get the hell out of it and make their way back to the Gulf of Salerno by the night of 15–16 February, across rough, mountainous terrain.

They split into three groups, commanded by Major Pritchard, Captain C. G. Lea of the Lancashire Fusiliers and 2nd Lieutenant G. Jowett of the Highland Light Infantry. The plan, as always with clandestine missions, was to lie up by day and travel at night. Sometimes the soldiers were lucky, sometimes not. In this case they were not. Each of the three groups was spotted and captured on the first night of their return journey, 12 February. Captain Daly and his sappers, having missed the target, fared better. They travelled for three nights and got within 20 miles of the coast before they were surrounded by Italian troops. Their interpreter Fortunato Picchi tried to talk his way out of the situation with the prearranged cover story that they were German troops on a special operation. He almost managed it, until the Italians insisted on seeing his papers. Daly and his men were taken prisoner. Picchi was tortured under interrogation but apparently gave nothing away. He was court-martialled and executed by firing squad. And so, by the end of the third day, the entire X-Troop had been captured. They were transferred to prisoner-of-war camps, from which several eventually escaped and made their way to England and back into service. It was only then that they discovered the devastating irony: that even if they had reached the Gulf of Salerno, the *Triumph* would not have been there to collect them

By a cruel quirk of fate, one of the returning Whitley bombers had suffered engine failure and was forced to ditch over the very area of the rendezvous at the mouth of the River Sele. Since his radio message to Malta may have been picked up by the Italians, it was decided that it would be too risky to expose the submarine to possible detection and the rendezvous was cancelled. The men of X-Troop would have been left high and dry to make their own way home as best they could.

And so ended the first-ever parachute mission into enemy territory, costly in terms of manpower and of little value because the water supplies to the three key Italian ports were soon repaired. Nevertheless, lessons were learned and morale boosted and it became the forerunner of and model for many operations by land, sea and air that followed in its wake. Winston Churchill was reportedly not impressed. This was not why the paratroops were brought together. Where was his corps of 5000 men? And where were the gliders to carry them and their machines? The Prime Minister was getting rather angry.

2

GET A MOVE ON!

By the early spring of 1941 the British had made little progress towards establishing a fully fledged parachute brigade. There were still some doubters who worried that much-needed aircraft and men would be diverted to a dubious cause. But all that was about to change. On 17 April Yugoslavia buckled to the Nazis in the face of a massive Blitzkrieg. That disaster was followed almost immediately by the fall of Greece, where the Allies were forced to retreat after ferocious battles which overwhelmed Australian and New Zealand forces. By then the Enigma decrypts supplied by the British code-breakers at Bletchley Park revealed that the Germans were planning a massive invasion of the strategically important island of Crete.

Churchill ordered General Wavell to send reinforcements and more guns to Crete, but the commander wired back that he could spare only six tanks, 16 light tanks and 18 anti-aircraft guns. After the fall of Greece, however, Allied manpower on the island was bolstered to around 30,000 men, with British, Australian and New Zealand troops under the command of General Bernard Freyberg. Even so, Churchill, having viewed the Germans' precise order of battle – courtesy of the Enigma decrypts – clearly had doubts that the Allies had sufficient firepower to hold on. Freyberg was desperately short of heavy equipment, much of it having been abandoned during the retreat from Greece.

Churchill's worst fears were realized on the morning of 20 May, when, as predicted by Enigma, German Stuka dive-bombers and artillery aircraft roared and screamed over the horizon and began pummelling the Allied troops' positions. They were followed by wave after wave of stinging aircraft attacks and landings, including Ju 52s towing huge DFS 230 gliders packed with troops, vehicles and guns. Suddenly the skies were filled with the greatest airborne invasion force ever assembled in the history of warfare. By late afternoon almost 5000 men had been dropped or landed on the island and one of the most costly battles of the war to date was under way as more German paratroopers and mountain troops were delivered to the island hour after hour, eventually to total 22,040. They met unexpectedly spirited resistance, the Allies' strength having been hugely underestimated by German intelligence. Even so, Freyberg was in dire trouble from the outset owing to his shortage of heavy artillery and, the greatest weakness of all, an almost total lack of air power to meet the Germans' massive aerial bombardment.

After five days of unrelenting attack, Wavell pleaded with Churchill to allow an Allied withdrawal from Crete. It had been impossible, he said, 'to withstand the weight of enemy air attack which had been on an unprecedented scale and has been through force of circumstance practically unopposed'. Churchill reluctantly agreed. The cost was high: 4000 Allied troops killed, 2500 wounded and more than 11,000 taken prisoner. The Germans also took heavy losses, particularly among the parachutists, who were shot from the skies as they came down: 3500 dead and the same number wounded.

The pull-out began on 27 May. Churchill's thoughts turned straight away to Britain's own airborne capability. In a personally written minute of that same day, he demanded immediate action towards the formation of an airborne division 'on the German model'. Seething at the failure to provide him with that force, he commented to Ismay: 'Thus we are always found to be behind-hand by the enemy.'

The dramatic impact of the German paratroop landings on Crete, combined with Churchill's anger, gave the military managers what one of their number later described as 'a veritable kick up the arse'. Within three days the Chiefs of Staff issued an edict for the immediate formation of a Parachute Brigade and called for volunteers from across the whole Army. The 11th Special Air Service (SAS) Battalion, which so far had deployed for just one operation – from which not a single man returned – was to be incorporated into the new organization, thus leaving the title of SAS vacant for the inception of David Stirling's new force, which would operate against Axis forces in North Africa and the Mediterranean. Stirling, a young officer with the Scots Guards, had been engaged in commando operations with Layforce, now about to be disbanded after heavy losses in Crete. Stirling harboured the idea of airborne raiders on a much grander scale than the operations of Major Roger Courtney's Special Boat Service, which was running sea-borne sabotage and clandestine reconnaissance missions behind enemy lines.

Stirling had never attempted a parachute drop himself and on his first attempt his canopy failed to open properly and he came down to earth with a bump. In hospital for several weeks, he used the time to set down his proposals and as soon as he had recovered, presented them personally to General Sir Claude Auchinleck, Commander-in-Chief in the Western Desert. Auchinleck liked the sound of it and so did Winston Churchill, who needed little persuading after he visited North Africa and asked to see Stirling personally. Thus the SAS was born and given a base at Kabrit, near the Suez Canal, in July 1941. Initially it went under the grandiose title of L Detachment, Special Air Service Brigade, in an apparent attempt to fool the Germans into believing that the Allies had a new airborne brigade.

To some extent, this supposition would have been correct. For back in England that same month, recruiting teams began visiting British Army regiments to select volunteers for the new Parachute Brigade that was forming under the overall command of Brigadier Dick Gale and had its headquarters at Hardwick Hall, near Chesterfield in Derbyshire. Alastair Pearson, a future brigadier and a stalwart and hero of the Parachute Brigade, eventually becoming one of only two soldiers to be awarded a DSO and three bars during the war, had already seen service in France in 1939–40 and in Suffolk during the invasion scare as a junior officer with the 6th Battalion Highland Light Infantry when he volunteered for special duties. The Parachute Brigade was not quite what he had in mind:

I had volunteered for the Special Forces and was eventually called for an interview for what I hoped was going to be a place with the Special Boat Service. One of my friends had joined them and told me it was very good. I had an interview with Dick Gale, which went quite well and I was told I would be accepted. I had no real idea of what I was letting myself in for until just as I was leaving. Gale said, 'You know, you will have to make parachute jumps.' Well, I didn't know, but anyway I had been accepted and I began my training course. It was, shall we say, interesting. The discipline was much harder than in normal Army regiments. The men tended to be slightly older, at least 60 per cent were drawn from regulars, experienced soldiers. It was a different kind of discipline to that when dealing with conscripts or temporary soldiers. The training was tough and we began preparing immediately for a series of operations across the Channel, but most never came to anything because the Navy could not guarantee to get us off and back.

Another Scot, Macleod Forsyth, was, like many of the early volunteers, a regular soldier. He had been with the Argyll and Sutherland Highlanders since enlisting at the age of 19, and in 1941 he read the notice from the Army welcoming volunteers for special duties. It contained a note at the bottom, he recalled, which specifically stated that all applications had to be forwarded so that there could be no question of company commanders keeping back their best men. Forsyth applied and was accepted, and soon discovered that although the training was as 'keen as mustard', the methodology was still somewhat primitive:

I went down to Chesterfield and was put into C Company, which was going be made into a Scottish company – Seaforths, Black Watch, KOSBies [King's Own Scottish Borderers] and Royal Scots. The CSM was a Black Watch man. We realized then what training was; everything had to be improvised. Training was being invented as we went along. In the gym, they had tables and chairs stacked 14 feet high and you climbed up and jumped off. The corporal had a foil and when he said jump you jumped; otherwise you got a whack across the arse. Other things we did [included] jumping from the back of three-ton lorries – jumping off backwards with the lorry travelling at 20 miles an hour. C Company was the first to go up to Ringway to begin a programme of jumps there. The first was the balloon jump. There were four of us in it, with an RAF corporal in charge. We sat in a basket staring down this hole in the middle. As it soared skywards … one of the others said, 'This is daft – we're hanging on here like grim death and in a minute or two we're going to bloody well jump out.'

And then, before you know it, the first jump and you don't have time to think. You land and you say to yourself, 'I've done it.' The feeling you got was tremendous; you felt so good. In those days, damn few had done it. Then we went on the aircraft – first a familiarization ride, and then up for the jump. They told us that if you didn't want to do it, nothing would be said and you would simply be returned to unit. I remember one chap refusing. He'd done two or three jumps and then suddenly he couldn't do it any more and just crawled away. It was understandable, but I said to myself, 'My God, I'll never do that! I'm going to stick it out.'

They told us that once we had our 'wings', we couldn't refuse. To refuse then would be a case of refusing to obey an order or, if we were on an operation, cowardice in the face of the enemy. In fact, that was the only refusal we had in our unit. The other thing I remember about those early days: we discovered that because we were on special training, we could get second helpings in the mess. Well, second helpings – the boys went back again and again. I once ate three Army dinners. After all that training, you could eat a horse – shoes as well. From morning to night, you were on the gallop, so you needed sustenance. And the RAF boys used to come in and there was nothing left for them. In the end, the Army had to increase the rations to fill them up.

The 1st Parachute Brigade was initially to have four Parachute Battalions, an airborne troop of sappers from the Royal Engineers and a signals team. The old 11th Special Air Service Battalion became the 1st Battalion, 1st Parachute Brigade, under the command of Lieutenant Colonel Eric Down. By the end of the summer the 2nd and 3rd Battalions were in place and the 4th was fully recruited by the end of the year. The latter was to form the nucleus of the 2nd Parachute Brigade, which came into being early in 1942. To give the new force an immediate strength, in view of the shortage of suitable volunteers, the 7th Battalion the Queen's Own Cameron Highlanders and the 10th Battalion the Royal Welch Fusiliers were transferred *en masse* to the 2nd Parachute Brigade to train as parachute troops.

At last Churchill's dream of an effective force of paratroops was beginning to take shape. There was still much to be done in terms of training, building purpose-made equipment for simulated jumps, assembling all other essential gear, exercises, delivery of the gliders, training of pilots and so on – all of which needed the input of a large amount of expert knowledge from RAF fliers and technicians. To establish a single cohesive management, Headquarters 1st Airborne Division was formed under the command of Brigadier Frederick 'Boy' Browning, DSO, MC, who was commanding a Brigade of Guards at the time. Although he had no hands-on experience of airborne warfare, he too accepted the challenge, was appointed commanding officer of Paratroops and Airborne Troops and became the father of Britain's modern airborne forces.

Browning took the whole operation by the scruff of the neck, cut through the red tape, stamped on petty jealousies and inter-forces rivalry, ditched the uncommitted and acquired equipment and services that had been earmarked for other units. A regimental tribute records that 'despite a multitude of difficulties and disappointments, there was no looking back. Airborne forces were now an integral part of the British Army, and presently wore on their heads the maroon-coloured berets soon to become famous, and on their shoulders Bellerophon astride winged Pegasus.'

In addition, Browning streamlined the training schedule yet still insisted upon quality rather than quantity, and even in those dire, dark days many men faced rejection as unsuitable. This procedure was conducted initially at Hardwick Hall, which became the combined home of the 1st Parachute Brigade and the Airborne Forces Depot. As training and exercises became more sophisticated, volunteers – as every aspiring paratroop had to be – were put through a gruelling programme of exercises to test both physical and mental stamina. It was tough; the toughest military preparation in the entire British Army, driven by the certain knowledge that airborne troops would often have to hit the ground running, often under fire from ground troops, fight their way forward from a DZ against well-hidden or heavily armed enemy formations, and survive that ordeal until they were able to link up with their own infantry or armoured troops; or, in some cases, perform their own predetermined assault and make what they hoped would be a successful exit.

However, theory and practice were seldom in harmony, and training had to be of sufficient calibre to meet all eventualities. Recruits were tested on their ability to jump from mocked-up fuselages, swinging from trapezes like circus performers and taking an air-sickness test by swaying back and forth for a quarter of an hour in a suspended boat. The physical training schedule was intensive and considered a hurdle for all who entered – and failed here. Out of it was born the dreaded P Company training unit. According to Alan Wooldridge, whose 35 years of military service included three years with 3 Para, this was:

designed to push you to the very limits of your physical endurance – and beyond it. They eventually introduced some favourites in this test of human endeavour, including the log race, where your unit carried a very heavy log over a long distance and you had to prove you were carrying your share. And then there was a test called milling where everyone went into a ring and flogged away at each other for a minute or so and the ones left standing were the winners. It seemed bloody stupid at the time – but it was all part of the overall scheme of things to get the right people. After that, you moved on to the jump instruction – how to land, how to fall and roll, and then jumping off towers high in the hangars against a large fan which slowed the body down, acting like an air brake. Finally they unleashed you in the cage beneath a barrage balloon, and you got to jump with a parachute from around 800 feet before an aircraft drop … it was nerve-racking and then exhilarating. Some, however, did not find it so. One officer who volunteered from my regiment [the Royal Warwickshire Regiment] completed the toughest part of the course with flying colours – and then decided he could go no further. He simply could not face the fact of jumping from an aircraft.

The finer arts of parachute training were instilled at Ringway and as the early months of 1942 passed a good deal of progress was made in improving both tuition and techniques, although mishaps causing quite serious injury and occasionally accidental death were not uncommon. Part of the problem lay with using bombers which had been converted for the task of parachuting troops. This usually meant exiting through a hole in the floor – and in many cases it was literally that. A bad exit could lead to a trainee taking a nasty knock as he left the aircraft; but in addition his rigging lines might become twisted together, the parachute canopy would not fully open and the rate of descent to earth would be dangerously swift and uncontrolled, although the worst malfunction was the 'streamer', in which a canopy failed to open at all. Local hospitals had a regular supply of patients 'injured in training'. The causes were kept secret. The majority would have completed seven descents in the final two weeks of training, thus qualifying for their highly prized parachute wings. They were, however, in desperate need of another test. As Alastair Pearson recognized, the work-ups and training for operations across the Channel were never-ending: 'We were put on alert and then stood down so many times, it became frustrating to all concerned. None of the operations ever came off and as I understood it, the problem then was that the Navy could never guarantee to get us back once we had dropped for our mission, completed the task at hand and were ready to come back.'

That was about to change, if only to a limited degree – but it was a successful change for all that. In October 1941 Commodore Lord Mountbatten was appointed Chief of Combined Operations with instructions from Churchill to breathe life into the raiding programme across the board, to insert sea-borne and airborne parties into sabotage and general troublemaking operations whenever and wherever possible. Mountbatten's appointment was treated with open derision by many in the military and naval hierarchy, and he was dismissed by one commentator as a 'vain and mendacious hustler'.

Over the following months his lordship personally pressed into action a number of highly risky ventures, anxious as ever to promote his own standing as well the department he was running. Some, like Mountbatten himself, were overambitious and even disastrous – the most controversial being Dieppe, where 3000 troops were lost. Some of the smaller operations – such as Operation Frankton, more popularly known as the Cockleshell Heroes' mission – also ended in tragedy without doing any real or lasting damage to the enemy, nor much to boost the morale of the British nation. And yet many lessons were to be learned from the techniques and innovative equipment devised by swashbuckling team leaders and their scientific advisers who arrived at Combined Operations in those early months under Mountbatten, and these were to be adopted for mainstream Allied operations in the coming months.

In fact, Mountbatten began his programme under the Combined Operations banner with a series of smaller raids, the second of which was to be an attack on a German radar station near Le Havre. It was one of a number of such stations strung along the Channel coast by the Germans, and RAF intelligence had pinpointed these as the main cause of increasingly heavy losses to British Bomber Command aircraft over Europe. One of the keys to the increasing effectiveness of Luftwaffe fighters and ground-based attacks on the bombers was identified as a radar system known as the Würzburg. This vectored German night fighters on to individual bombers, and RAF aerial reconnaissance had taken photographs of a dish used by the system, on a cliff top near the village of Bruneval, 12 miles north of Le Havre. The RAF and Mountbatten's communications experts at a special unit in Hertfordshire were anxious to get their hands on one of the radar sets and this was the key object of the mission.

The radar stations were all heavily defended against attack from the sea – which was the only direction in which the Germans suspected a raid might be mounted. In fact, the initial plan had been to launch a sea-borne attack using Commandos, but this was eventually ruled out as being too risky. The Army's new parachute troops, now straining to be let off the leash, might prove the answer. In January 1942 Mountbatten called in 'Boy' Browning, who needed no persuading at all to accept, realizing that this was a great opportunity to provide his men with some real action at last.

C Company of the 2nd Parachute Battalion, under the command of Major Johnny Frost, who had come to the Paras from the Camerons, was selected for the operation. The raid was pencilled in for late February, for it had to coincide with favourable moon and tide conditions and these allowed a four-day window of opportunity. Another reason for this schedule was that many of the men were still in training and the work-ups for the operation would take time. Aerial and ground intelligence had provided an excellent visual plan of the area, and allowed analysts to assess that the stations were guarded by 30 full-time guards, with a garrison of around 40 men based in the village of Bruneval itself, half a mile away. Another 100 men – operators, signallers and coastal defence troops – were housed in farm buildings around the station, and at a villa called La Presbytère, and the shore was under constant observation from the pillboxes.

It was planned to drop the Paras in groups named after famous sailors. Nelson group, for example, under Captain John Ross and Lieutenant Euen Charteris, would hit the coastal defence troops and the Bruneval garrison. Drake group included Major Frost and an expert radio mechanic, RAF Flight Sergeant C. W. H. Cox, and would take the radar station. Rodney group, under Lieutenant John Timothy, would take on the troops and off-duty staff housed at La Presbytère. No. 51 Squadron, under Wing Commander P. C. Pickard, would provide the necessary aircraft and the Royal Navy would arrange their evacuation with a flotilla of gunboats and landing craft under Commander F. N. Cook, RAN, who would have with him 32 officers and men of the Royal Fusiliers and South Wales Borderers to cover the final withdrawal.

For Lieutenant John Timothy and most of those around him at the time, the operation would provide the first opportunity of the war to see some real action as paratroopers. Born in Tunbridge Wells, educated at Skinner's School and a Marks & Spencer management trainee when the war broke out, Timothy volunteered, went to Sandhurst and was commissioned into the Queen's Own Royal West Kents before volunteering for the Parachute Brigade. Like his colleagues, he was eager for action and recalls the elation of the moment:

I was on a small-arms course at Bisley and halfway through, some of us were told to report back to Hardwick pronto. There, we were told that the company had been given the chance to go on a raid. Johnny Frost was adjutant at the time and he took over C Company. Something was on, but I don't think even Frost was aware of the details then. We began intensive training down at Tilshead, night after night, and we did one practice jump with 51 Squadron, who were flying Whitley bombers. Then it came to the time when we got the impression we were about to go on the raid. We were sent up to Scotland, to the Combined Operations base at Inverary for more training, and exercises involving landing craft. Mountbatten came up and blew the gaff, as it were, although we still did not know exactly where we were heading or what we would be doing. There were medics and all kinds of people there for the planning. It turned out to be the Bruneval raid. We went back to Tilshead and prepared to wait.

C Company was just about 100 strong, plus two or three sections from the rest of the battalion, Para medics and Para sappers. Eventually we were shown models of our target and were briefed extensively on what was required of us and we did a couple of rehearsal exercises. We knew very little about radar, but they brought a chap in who did – Flight Sergeant Cox, a very brave man who had never jumped before. They sent him up to Ringway and he did one or two jumps. Captain Dennis Vernon from the sappers was given a bit of training to act as number two to Cox.

Cox, an RAF radar mechanic, had been summoned to the Air Ministry on 1 February 1942 and was ushered into the office of Air Commodore Victor Tait, Director of Radar, who opened the meeting with the words: 'So you've volunteered for a dangerous mission?'

A surprised Cox replied, 'No, sir.'

Tait persuaded him that he had, and went on: 'I can't tell you what it is but you'll have a pretty good chance of survival.' Cox, small and slightly built, was posted to C Company to train with the rest of the men and immediately became aware that his pre-war employment as a cinema projectionist had hardly equipped him for such an adventure. On the night of the raid he was fitted up with a revolver on his belt, a knife strapped to a leg, a concealed hacksaw blade and an escape kit that included currency. His tools – metal-cutters, screwdrivers, hammers and other burglary accessories – were packed in a metal container which would be dropped separately. The company was divided into parties of around 40 men. It was a very clear night and everyone was in great spirits when they headed off to Thruxton, in Hampshire, for take-off, scheduled for 22.30 hours.

Piper Ewing played the regimental marches of the several Scottish regiments represented among the ranks of the company as the sticks of men lined up to march out on to the runway and board their respective aircraft. Twelve Whitley bombers were lined up to transport them and one by one they soared into the sky, flying low towards the French coast. RAF dispatchers on board made the final checks and, as they neared the DZ, removed the cover from the aperture in the floor of the aircraft fuselage through which the men would drop. Within minutes of appearing over the French coastline, the aircraft came under heavy anti-aircraft fire and swung and swayed and dropped violently as their pilots dodged the flak.

The men were already on alert when Action Stations! was called and they sat with eyes glued to the red light, waiting for it to change to green and... Go! Go! Go! They tumbled through the aperture one after the other to begin the operation that would go down in history as a first drop into action for Britain's newly trained and much-vaunted parachute troops. John Timothy recalls:

It was a very good exit and landing, but when we came down, the first thing I noticed was we were minus some bodies and also some containers. Both were important. They had gone a bit adrift. It was easily done; one stick was stopped. The light changed from

31

green to red because the pilot had given the signal over the wrong place. Another went down two miles out of position and had to make a mad dash to get there and link up. The DZ was clear and the rest of us landed unopposed. The main party moved up to attack the radar station, which they achieved virtually without opposition. My group was in the rear for clearing operations, mopping up pockets of German resistance, which entailed some pretty heavy skirmishes. We lost a few wounded and some were left behind, wounded and captured.

Meanwhile Frost's group had come under heavy fire at La Presbytère, while at the radar site itself one soldier opened fire as they burst in and was shot. The key radar set was quickly located and the German technician working there at the time was taken prisoner and later brought back to England. Cox and his assistants started to take apart the radar set before the Germans realized what was happening. As a battle developed around the station, he and his fellow dismantlers found that screwdrivers were inadequate and instead they had to rip parts of the set out of their housing. This proved easier than he had dared hope because the equipment was made in prefabricated sections so that parts could be sent for repair or replaced.

The withdrawal was not as easy. As the raiders left the station, machine-gun fire whistled by Cox's ears and one bullet scraped the toe of his boot. There were more heavy exchanges and they began taking more casualties. Timothy's mopping up was not yet completed and nor were the coastal defences quelled because of the delayed arrival of Nelson group under Lieutenant Charteris, who had been dropped short of the DZ. The group arrived in the nick of time and joined the battle. Heavy exchanges ensued, but by 02.15 hours the Paras were scrambling down the cliffs towards the shore, to await pick-up by the Royal Navy. One other hitch was already apparent, as Macleod Forsyth, who was in Timothy's group, explains:

It seemed our radios had gone kaput and we couldn't get a response from the Navy to pick us up. Johnny Frost fired a flare but got no response and it looked as if we were going to have a battle on our hands. [In fact Naval communications had been silenced to avoid discovery by a German destroyer passing less than a mile away at that very moment.] There was a lot of heavy fire coming down on us by then from German reinforcements massing on the cliff tops.

It was some time before a shout informed Cox that the Paras had secured the beach. He descended to the shore and after hiding the radar equipment under the cliff, crouched beside it. Major Frost, fearing that the rescue fleet would not arrive, spotted a beached fishing boat and made a contingency plan to put Cox and his booty into it and launch them into the Channel. But as mortar and machine-gun fire resumed, the six landing craft appeared through the mist. Even then, all was not plain sailing. Cox and his equipment were safe, but his boat, overloaded with wounded, ran aground. Forsyth continues:

The Germans were piling mortars and grenades at us by then. The men began wading out to the landing craft under our own cover firing. I was in the last party to leave and our landing craft was shunted by a wave on to the rocks and it took us an age to get it off. The naval officer in charge of the boat yelled at us, 'Get out and push!' Terrific, I thought.

Five hours after leaving England with six officers, 113 NCOs and soldiers of C Company, plus nine sappers, four signallers and the RAF technician, the Para raiders were heading home. They had lost three men killed in action, seven were wounded and six had been taken prisoner, including two signallers who had become lost in the dash for the beach and arrived there only to see the landing craft vanishing out to sea. Three prisoners of war, including the radar technician, were also brought back.

By 03.30 they were all clambering aboard motor gunboats waiting off the French coast to carry them back to Portsmouth, with the landing craft in tow. 'The Navy gave us some rum to warm us up,' says Forsyth:

And one of our section was blind drunk by the time we landed back home. But I suppose we could celebrate. We were in mid-Channel when it was announced on the radio that there had been a raid in France, and we grumbled about it. They might have let us get home first. But then soon afterwards we heard the Spitfires up above to accompany us home. When we got back we were given leave, and the chaps found they were being treated like heroes in the pubs. Every pub you went into: 'Have a pint, mate' – even for Paras who weren't on the raid. It was a great morale-booster not just for us, but the whole country. And we needed it. At the time we were losing everywhere and the papers picked up on it and gave us all a good boost. And it was right – the papers had been full of the Germans doing this and that and now we had caught them with their trousers down. It was one of the best-organized raids of the war.

That fact was rammed home by Mountbatten's PR machine, which would become familiar to all who worked with him over the course of the war. He arranged for Johnny Frost and his men to get a hero's welcome and for Frost to give an account of the raid in a radio interview for the BBC, which was broadcast on 2 March 1942. Briefed in advance by Mountbatten, Frost gave an enraptured interviewer a dramatic but carefully worded and unrevealing summary to provide the British public with a much-needed fillip:

We had a certain amount of worry about the weather and we were waiting for quite a few days before it was perfect. Then the day dawned and we felt it was now or never. We fed ourselves as we went along to the aerodrome and got into an aeroplane. We had never been so comfortable in an aeroplane before. Usually when we do our practice dropping we are fairly uncomfortable and worry about getting out. But this time no one worried at all and in fact every aircraft had its own little concert party going on the whole time. Even when we got to the French coast and opened the hole in the bottom of the aircraft, everyone looked out and had a good view of the coast and the sea and I rang up the pilot and made quite certain we weren't dropped in the water because that's the one thing we didn't want. We were all dropped by our air force pilots in exactly the right places and we could see as we came down the landmarks that we'd been trained to look out for.

Once we arrived in France it was just a question of taking off our parachutes and forming up at a prearranged place which every man in the company knew in advance. It was quite perfect. There was snow on the ground but we could see everything we expected to see, by moonlight. Everybody in the company made a very good landing. Once we'd formed up, we then went on to do the job. At this time there were a certain number of shots going off. The Germans were prepared for something to happen. There was a certain amount of shots coming at us, but we couldn't quite see where from. The Germans didn't seem to know who we were or what we were. Altogether, I think they were quite astonished and very frightened too. We got exactly what we wanted and destroyed everything we could and once we'd done that, we noticed a certain number of German reinforcements forming up behind the woods not very far away.

We then thought that, having done everything we set out to do, we'd better withdraw to the beach. During this time part of our company were fighting the Germans who were holding the beach defences and they very successfully overcame them and held the beach for us. We then came down and made our signal to the Navy and we were very glad to hear their engines coming in. Once we were with the Navy again, our troubles were over.

The Parachute Regiment, which officially did not come into being until August 1942, had won its spurs – and its first Battle Honour. Needless to say, Winston Churchill did not apologize for stating when next the War Cabinet met, 'I told you so!'

The vital piece of radar equipment, carried safely into the laboratories of RAF scientists, gave up its secrets. First-hand knowledge was gained of the state of German radar technology, particularly as applied to the enemy night-fighter system. Charles Cox, a modest man who died aged 84 in 1999, delivered his prize for scientific investigation in what had been one of the most remarkable exploits of its kind. Back in England, some time later, wearing RAF uniform and parachute wings, he went into a shop to buy a Military Medal ribbon. This somewhat surprised the shop assistant, since the MM is normally an Army decoration. 'What have you been up to?' he asked. 'Not much,' was Cox's reply.

Much later Cox learned that he was lucky to survive the raid. At a reunion, one of his former colleagues on the raid revealed that the radar mechanic had been given orders, if he was captured, to shoot him. Thereafter he served at Air Ministry experimental establishments. After the war he opened a radio and television business in his home town of Wisbech, Cambridgeshire, and in 1982 was among the surviving Paras who attended the unveiling of a plaque at Bruneval by the Prince of Wales, in the presence of President Mitterrand of France.

3

INTO ACTION AT LAST

In Churchill's view, one of the significant areas still lacking in the development of Britain's airborne forces was the key to the whole operation: the military glider. The Germans, as the Prime Minister had forcefully pointed out on numerous occasions, were well ahead of the game and had used gliders effectively in all their airborne operations. The enemy had been testing their use as a potential military tool since the end of the First World War. Prohibited from developing military aircraft under the Treaty of Versailles, German engineers turned instead to the study of glider flight, and by the early 1920s they had developed gliders with advanced designs.

The first gliding school in the USA was established at South Wellfleet, Massachusetts, by German pilots in 1929. When, ten years later, war came again, the Germans were ready with large gliders towed by Junkers to transport soldiers, artillery and light vehicles. In 1940 Germany became the first country ever to use gliders in war. Britain was years behind and even when its designers began to catch up, production was a slow business, partly because all factories capable of building gliders were already working full time on other wartime projects.

Churchill was given a demonstration of Britain's first prototype glider during a combined airborne exercise on 26 April 1941, but the first would not come into service until the end of the year. Without gliders, the airborne brigades' hands were tied. At that time only a limited amount of weapons and equipment could be dropped by parachute, and gliders were needed to supply such essential items as jeeps, light tanks and light artillery as well as acting as personnel carriers taking troops direct to battle fronts. The glider was a relatively fast and economical way of flying in reinforcements in support of parachute landings, the scale of which was limited by the carrying capacity of the old Whitley bombers. Stripped out, this aircraft could carry a stick of only ten men, and that at a pinch. As the Bruneval raid demonstrated, it was a hugely expensive business to carry such a small number of men in a single converted bomber: in that instance, 12 aircraft to move 125 men to the target in very cramped conditions. Even now, two years into the war, RAF resource managers maintained that they could not justify releasing decent planes for the purpose of large-scale deployment of airborne troops, and for the time being it was unthinkable to move a whole battalion by air and drop it into the target area in the way that the Germans had done in taking Crete.

Nor was Britain's first glider, the Hotspur, any better than the Whitley in its carrying capacity – and it was certainly no match for the German gliders. It could carry eight men but not heavy loads such as a jeep, or even small artillery. The Mk I had been designed as a true glider, capable of soaring. It was quickly superseded by the Mk II, whose wingspan was clipped so that it glided directly to its target once released from its towline. Only the Horsas and Hamilcars, which came into use in late 1942, would be capable of carrying cargo as well as troops. Four hundred Hotspurs had been ordered, and although there was still a shortage in the latter part of 1941 and early 1942, it hardly mattered because at first there was also a shortage of pilots to fly them. As luck would have it, the 31st Independent Infantry Brigade was on its way back to England from India. On their arrival on 10 October 1941, the officers and NCOs of the brigade were informed that, as of that moment, they were all glider pilots. This came as something of a shock because few of them had ever clapped eyes on a glider, let alone flown one. They were trained infantrymen, not fliers. But they accepted the challenge with not a little apprehension and henceforth would be known as the 1st Airlanding Brigade.

The raising of airborne units was not the sole preserve of the Parachute Brigade. Several other regiments had volunteer parachute and airborne companies, many of which were used on specialist operations in the Far East and Burma. One group of 750 volunteer officers and men was selected from infantry regiments in India in 1941 to form what was then called the 151st Parachute Battalion. They trained in extraordinarily primitive conditions, using cotton parachutes and, equipped with a handful of antiquated aircraft, they took quite a few casualties in training. Although temporarily trapped by the war in India, they moved with the Indian Army contingents to the Middle East in 1941, picked up additional recruits and became the 156th Parachute Battalion. This was eventually incorporated into the 1st Airborne Division as part of the 4th Parachute Brigade, commanded by Brigadier (later General Sir) John Hackett. It was a battalion largely composed of tough regular soldiers who had not seen England for years, veterans of Indian Army campaigns on the North-West Frontier and desert campaigns in the early part of the present war. Many were on the point of returning to England at the time war was declared, having been abroad for seven or eight years, and so never got home. One company commander, through a succession of circumstances, was away for 13 years before he returned to see his family.

Even the Gurkhas, who were never the best of fliers, took up parachuting. There is a famous story which alleges that when a Gurkha battalion was first asked to provide volunteers for an airborne unit, the Gurkha officer, having listened quietly to his British counterpart giving a short talk on the need for their assistance, went into a huddle with his riflemen and came back to ask apologetically: 'Would it be possible to drop the men from a lower height so as to reduce the risk of injury?' He had missed a vital part of the talk, and it was then hastily explained that each one of the men would be equipped with a parachute and taught how to use it. They all breathed a sigh of relief. The story may have been true, sometime, somewhere in the jungles of Burma, but one similar incident actually happened, at Imphal in May 1942. The Gurkhas, who had already suffered heavy losses during the Allied retreat from Burma in the face of a massive invasion by the Japanese, were asked to volunteer for parachute duty for raids in preparation for a new offensive. Shown a short silent film, the Gurkhas were fascinated, until a caption in Gurkhali came on the screen that sparked loud murmurs and worried looks. If they did their job well, this informed them, 95 per cent of them would be dead before they hit the ground. The captions had been wrongly placed: this one should have appeared with the film that demonstrated how to repel a Japanese parachute attack.

When the mistake was explained, they roared with laughter. To a man, they volunteered for parachute duty and went on to make some courageous airborne attacks as part of the 14th Army's return to Burma, as well as in Malaya and Borneo after the war. There was, however, another side to this story, as many would later discover: Japanese and German infantrymen were no doubt being shown similar movies about how to kill parachute troops as they floated down to earth and no one, whatever side he was on, could think too deeply about it or he would never have set foot outside the aircraft that was carrying him and his fellow soldiers to the DZ.

Humorous stories abounded among the Paras, leading a regimental chaplain to suggest that the laughter was, if studied closely, of the nervous variety and simply a cover by tough guys to mask the reality of a deadly serious business. It was frequently argued by the Paras that, compared with infantrymen, their chances of being hit by enemy fire were several times greater because:

(a)   the aircraft carrying you into battle may be shot down or the powerless glider may hit an unforeseen landscape (as often happened) before it got there;

(b) even if you make it through the ack-ack fire, the parachute might not open properly and you will crash to earth and never get up again;

(c) even if the parachute functions properly, you might break your neck, or a least a leg, landing on rough terrain, be speared through the heart by a broken tree branch or electrocuted by uncharted high-power cables (not uncommon);

(d) you might be shot coming down or possibly eaten by wild animals on landing if the pilot has dropped you in the wrong place.

All of which might occur even before the Paras went into battle. But, with a couple of daring, spectacular and costly operations behind them, British airborne forces still being put through their paces over the English countryside were finally called upon to take part in a major campaign in the autumn of 1942. They were judged to be ready and able for what was to become the classic role of the Paras, jumping into the battle zones ahead of the herd, capturing key positions and 'unlocking the door' as the ground forces moved forward. The Parachute Regiment, working in conjunction with the other airborne elements, now had a clearly defined operational objective. What was more, the big new transport gliders were coming on stream.

In two years the regiment had grown from nothing to a well-trained, well-briefed force whose first major test had yet to come. In the autumn of 1942, this lay dead ahead. There were still problems: a lack of recruits of the right calibre and a serious shortage of transport. Powered aircraft assigned to airborne troops still tended to be of the wing-and-a-prayer variety. The RAF, heavily committed in all the war theatres, struggled to provide even those needed for the airborne operations pencilled in for the coming months.

The situation was eased somewhat by the arrival of the USAAF's No. 60 Group, who brought with them the newer

American Dakotas. Though these were not perfect for British Paras' needs, they were welcomed – initially at least – because paratroops could make their exit through a door instead of through a hole in the floor of their own converted bombers. Nevertheless, this very facility caused problems and deaths in early jumps. British Paras, who used different parachutes from those of the Americans, were forced to retrain to use the Dakotas after a tragedy during the first trial drop of 250 men on 9 October 1942. Four men were strangled when their canopies snagged the aircraft's tail wheel. The static line on the British X-Type parachute was too short for use on the Dakota, and after some trial-and-error tactics, pilots found that raising the tail of the aircraft made the soldiers' exits less prone to accident.

Most of these problems were overcome by the end of October, as indeed they had to be. The rush was on and the 1st Parachute Brigade was already on standby for 'the big one' – immediate mobilization – ready to move out at any moment for operations for which they had had no real time to prepare. In addition they had to borrow men and equipment from the 2nd Parachute Brigade and other units of the 1st Airborne Division to get them up to strength and in good order. Many had guessed that they were on their way to the North African coast as 1000 guns of General Bernard Montgomery's Eighth Army thundered into action against the Germans' Afrika Korps at El Alamein on 30 October. One week later the second phase in the Allies' reclamation of the region, Operation Torch, would be ready to start. For the invasion of North Africa, the largest-ever number of Allied ships and aircraft had been assembled. The Paras had been invited to the party, although they were few in number compared with the overall strength of the landings, which consisted of some 65,000 men in 670 ships, 1000 landing craft and a planned build-up to around 1700 aircraft to attack a 900-mile front. The command team included men soon to become famous, among them America's Lieutenant General Dwight D. Eisenhower and

Major General George Patton and, on the British side, Admiral Sir Andrew Cunningham, hero of Matapan and many a Malta convoy, and Vice-Admiral Sir Bertram Ramsay, who had masterminded the miraculous evacuation from Dunkirk.

The Operation Torch battle plan called for the landing around Casablanca, in Morocco, of 25,000 US troops who, with 250 tanks, had sailed directly from their home ports in America. Another 18,500 men with 180 tanks sailed from Britain via Gibraltar to land around Oran, in Algeria, and it was intended that these two forces would combine to form the 5th Army. A joint US force of 20,000 men would simultaneously secure the Algerian capital, Algiers, and, as the 1st Army, this would move swiftly to capture four key ports of Bône and Philippeville in Algeria and Bizerta and Tunis in Tunisia.

On an operation of that scale there were bound to be problems, and the Paras seemed to encounter quite a few of them. First, there were not enough aircraft to convey them, alongside their partners the 503rd US Parachute Infantry, to their eventual destination on the North African coast and to inland DZs. The payload of the Dakotas had to be reduced to accommodate extra fuel tanks. Two battalions, the 1st and 2nd, along with the 3rd Battalion's Headquarters Company, two companies and the mortar platoon, were rushed to Greenock on 29 October to join a convoy of ships *en route* to Gibraltar and onwards towards North Africa. Their immediate strategic objective was northern Tunisia, and the plan was to cut the line of retreat of the Axis troops, who were fleeing from the advancing British Eighth Army in the Western Desert. With Axis power decimated along the southern shores of the Mediterranean, the way would be open to invade Europe through Sicily and Italy.

The remainder of the 3rd Battalion were delayed for two days by fog but eventually flew from RAF St Eval in Cornwall to Gibraltar in the early hours of 10 November. Almost as soon as they arrived they were on alert to move out for a parachute assault on the vital airfield at Bône, an operation that was to be launched from an airfield at Maison Blanche, near Algiers. By then the bulk of the Allied beach landings had forged ahead, with some hefty losses of manpower and machinery on both sides. The Vichy French commander, with 120,000 troops spread across the region who had put up a token defence, was already seeking ceasefire terms. The Germans, meanwhile, were sending in reinforcements from Europe.

The 3rd Battalion's assault party took off from Maison Blanche at 04.30 hours on 12 November and were over their target at Bône at 08.30. Unbeknown to them, the Germans had the same idea, and a battalion of Fallschirmjäger arrived in their Ju 52s just as the Paras were making their drop. The Germans abandoned their own operation and were redirected elsewhere. The 3rd took their target with little trouble, and more casualties were caused by landing on hard ground than by enemy fire. One man accidentally killed himself with fire from his own Sten gun during the drop and several sustained broken legs. The heaviest enemy fire came from marauding Stukas but the Paras held their position until they were joined by No. 6 Commando, with overhead support from a squadron of Spitfires. The mission successfully completed, the 3rd Battalion pulled out after three days and travelled west to its new position, the village of St Charles, where it was reunited with A Company and the rest of the unit, which had travelled by sea.

Meanwhile the 1st Battalion had made successful drops near the airfield at Souk el Arba and was now given orders to move north to take the town of Beja, 90 miles west of Tunis. There was a dash to prepare for the move. The battalion's stores, which had come with it by ship, were slow to be unloaded and then had to be broken down and repacked into containers, and parachutes had to be inspected and ammunition sorted. Nor was there much in the way of transport vehicles because ship space had been at a premium owing to the amount of personnel and stores. Even so, as Harold

'Vic' Coxen, then a young officer, 2iC (second in command, and later Brigadier) of the 1st Battalion's T Company, remembers:

The operation was fairly straightforward. If there was a problem, it was that we had no great knowledge of the ground and the only maps available were for tourists travelling by road. The commanding officer rode in the cockpit of the aircraft in front, searching for a flat piece of ground. We had a fairly good drop [there was one fatality: a soldier strangled by rigging that snagged the Dakota's tail]. We commandeered motor cars and trucks and began our move up to the border between Tunisia and Algeria.

As they reached a strategic crossroads towards Beja, which was the first of their objectives, the battalion was confronted by 3000 French troops heavily dug in around the main approaches and for a while there was an uncomfortable stand-off. 'We hadn't taken the French completely by surprise,' said Coxen, 'but they had not really decided whose side they were on and were holding a line there largely with their colonial troops.' Delicate negotiations were pursued and it was clear that the French had been threatened with reprisals by their German-controlled masters if they allowed the Allies to get past them and enter Beja. Lieutenant Colonel (later Brigade Commander) James Hill lied and told the French commander that they were the advance party for armoured divisions advancing towards them at pace. The French stood aside. 'We stuck ourselves in the middle of them,' Coxen recalls:

and every time the Germans came close we attacked and the Germans attacked the French and so eventually they put their helmets on and joined us, although a good many of them were somewhat reluctant. We were dropped 400 miles ahead of our ground forces. The objective of our company was to move to confront the Germans, to be a thorn in their side. We were coming

45

in on the flank of them behind their lines; we were there to be a nuisance, which we were in spite of a fairly light weaponry. Our heaviest weapons were three-inch mortars, Vickers machine-guns and Bren guns. The mortars and the machine-guns were difficult inasmuch as that we could only carry a certain amount of ammunition and we had to get resupplied very quickly otherwise we were in trouble.

The first of their operations came in the first 24 hours, when Hill discovered that a German convoy was coming through, as it did most evenings, on its way to Bizerta on the coast. The battalion's S Company laid a classic ambush and knocked out the entire convoy, killing many of the German soldiers and capturing the rest. Several similar disruptive operations followed against both German and Italian parties, although one of them did not go quite according to plan. Hill had moved the battalion towards a position north-east of Sidi N'Sir, in hilly country beyond Medjez al Bab, where a force of around 350 Italians with a few tanks had been located. Hill's second in command, Major Alastair Pearson, was to organize a blast of heavy fire from the three-inch mortars while the rest of the battalion and a company of French and Senegalese troops advanced towards the Italian position. Meanwhile a detachment of 27 sappers from the 1st Parachute Squadron Royal Engineers, accompanying Hill's unit, were to move around and mine the exit roads with No. 75 Hawkins grenades. As the sappers were about to mine the road, there were three explosions – one of the grenades, which were being carried in sandbags, had accidentally detonated, setting off the others in a chain reaction. All but two of the sappers were killed.

The blast also alerted the enemy troops to the advancing British battalion, and what turned out to be a mixed force of Germans and Italians was engaged on a hillside position. Meanwhile Lieutenant Colonel Hill took a small group of men towards the tanks – there were just three – below the main battle position.

Leading the section himself, he crept alongside the first tank and stuck the barrel of his revolver into the observation slit and immediately the Italian crew surrendered. He repeated the procedure with the second tank, this time rapping on the turret with the walking stick he always carried and shouting, 'Come out with your hands up', which they did. At the third tank, three Germans jumped out, guns blazing, and shot him four times. His adjutant, Captain Whitelock, was also wounded, hit by shrapnel from grenades thrown by the escaping Germans, who were shot or captured. Hill and Whitelock were immediately dispatched to the medics in Beja by a motorcycle and sidecar driven by a team from the 16th Parachute Field Ambulance along a rail track leading to the town. Later, recovered from the wounds, Hill returned to the fray.

Alastair Pearson took over as battalion commander and pursued an equally aggressive policy of assault patrols on enemy positions throughout the regions before they were relieved by the main force and sent back to base to rest and stand by for further orders. Meanwhile the 2nd Battalion under Johnny Frost – now a lieutenant colonel – along with other recent heroes of Bruneval, had been given a much more difficult sector. Whereas the 1st Battalion was moving mostly in hilly terrain, Frost's group was in open country that was alive with German tanks and a fair amount of heavy artillery. After several false starts he was finally given orders to gather up his battalion, a troop of 1st Parachute Squadron Royal Engineers and a section from the 16th Parachute Field Ambulance, and drop into action, close to a German airfield 40 miles south of Tunis, and blow up any aircraft on the ground.

They were then to advance to Depienne and perform a similar operation, and finally move to a third airstrip at Oudna. Just as they were about to board the 44 USAAF Dakotas revving up on the runway at Maison Blanche, Frost was told that two of the target airfields had just been abandoned by the Germans. The new orders were to drop at Depienne and to destroy enemy aircraft on the ground at Oudna. Then the battalion was to march to a location 30 miles north, towards Tunis, to link up with the 1st Army. Because there had been no time to perform a new recce for a DZ, Frost flew in the cockpit of the lead Dakota with the rookie American pilots, many of whom had never flown on military missions before, to select a new location. He chose a decent site near Depienne and the battalion came down unopposed, though scattered over a couple of miles, and suffered only seven casualties, one of which was fatal.

Frost sounded his hunting horn – a familiar sound to all who travelled with him – to call his men together. They set off on the thrust from Depienne towards Oudna, across difficult terrain and with the soldiers laden down with ammunition and equipment, all of which had to be carried on their backs. The only transport they managed to acquire were some donkey carts. Four miles down the road, a recce team reported a heavy force of Germans blocking their path, so Frost and his men laid up until the early hours, in bitterly cold conditions, and then made a detour.

The objective was to attack the airstrip, not engage a German unit; but in the end they had no choice. The following day, moving *en masse* through a valley, they came under heavy and prolonged machine-gun fire. Even so, A Company managed to reach the airstrip, but even as they arrived, they were met by an onslaught from six German tanks, strafing attacks from Messerschmitts and finally a bombardment from six Stuka dive-bombers. The spirited response by the battalion and excellent camouflage allowed them to withdraw without great loss, and Frost directed his men towards a good defensive position on the hillside. A recce of the area determined that it was swarming with German units. Frost decided to lie up and try to hold out until the arrival of the 1st Army, which, if all went according to schedule, could surely not be far away.

Unbeknown to him, that plan had already been scrapped and the news was eventually relayed to him over the radio – the 1st

Army would not be coming his way; the advance on Tunis had been postponed for two days. Frost blew his top. Macleod Forsyth remembers:

We were really dropped in it. We were constantly told that the 1st Army would be coming up to meet us. But it was the old story: they didn't and we had to fight our way back to our own lines. The Americans thought they could plant the US flag and the Germans would run away. But the Germans hadn't read the script. They [the 1st Army] hadn't moved a damned inch. The Germans were harrying us all the while.

The 2nd Battalion was marooned 50 miles or so behind the enemy lines, virtually surrounded by German heavy stuff, lightly equipped, short of ammunition, food and water and facing a long march to the nearest Allied positions. As the Paras began the journey back to safer territory, Frost decided to head for higher ground, but almost immediately they came under heavy artillery and mortar fire in a fierce battle for the summit of Djebel Sidi Bou Hadjeba. They took positions in rocky terrain, but even before they had a chance to dig in for battle heavy fire was raining down on them. Losses mounted and included the commander of B Company, Major Frank Cleaver, and one of C Company's platoon commanders, Lieutenant the Hon. Henry Cecil. At nightfall, during a respite, Frost performed a head count: 150 killed or wounded. His force was depleted to such an extent that he decided the only way forward was for each company to move independently towards a village called Massicault, where they would lie up and plan the next stage. He ordered the destruction of the three-inch mortars, for which he now had no ammunition, and the radio sets, whose batteries had expired.

The journey ahead threatened to be so hazardous that Frost decided he had no alternative but to leave the wounded behind and rely upon their being able to make contact with the 1st Army when it eventually arrived. A section of the 16th Parachute Field Force was left behind to attend them, along with a platoon from B Company under Lieutenant Pat Playford for protection.

Frost and his men pressed on, coming under constant enemy fire. They took ten-minute rests wherever possible, but starving and without water, they were soon in bad shape and almost dying of thirst. Macleod Forsyth:

Our battalion commander used his hunting horn when we were ready to move off. That was the signal. And my God, it was a real haul. We lost men simply through exhaustion. We didn't have much water. I had hallucinations. I looked up at the sky and I could see this big bar and a man pulling pints of beer. Then we came to a river [the Medjerda] and we just marched in and sat down in it. Unfortunately the water was pretty awful, and when we got on the march again, people were vomiting and really suffering. However, we carried on. Frost picked the spot where we would rest up. The Germans knew we were around and were searching for us. We were resting up once when a couple of German soldiers on a motorbike and sidecar pulled up at a farmhouse ahead, questioning the people there if they had seen the British. The coincidence was that after the war, when a group of ex-German soldiers came to a Chesterfield reunion and we were discussing these incidents, one of them said, 'That was me. I was on the motorbike.'

The force having been split to move in companies, by night, Frost found that his own group, now down to 200 men, was once again confronted by a ring of German forces. He decided to send three men on ahead, led by another Bruneval veteran, Lieutenant Euen Charteris, the 2nd Battalion's intelligence officer. Charteris was to attempt to make contact with the nearest Allied land force to get help. Frost never heard from the three men again; they were spotted and shot by the Germans before they reached their objective. He decided the only way forward was to try a mass breakout under cover of darkness and to rendezvous on a ridge two miles away. They eventually made it out of the hot zone and, spurred on by Frost's hunting horn, they arrived at Medjez el Bab two days later with only five rounds of ammunition each. As the remnants of the remaining companies straggled in, the final cost of this appalling excursion was high: overall the 2nd Battalion lost 16 officers and 250 men. The Oudna operation had been a disaster from the start: badly planned by the war managers and doomed from the outset by faulty intelligence which stated that enemy aircraft were parked on the three landing strips they had pinpointed yet overlooked the fact that, in the meantime, these planes might be moved. They were, and not a single enemy aircraft was attacked. Thus a whole battalion was mobilized against a non-existent target and those in command compounded this blunder by demonstrating a complete lack of interest in its fate, effectively leaving it abandoned far behind enemy lines.

Out of this totally unnecessary decimation of the 2nd Battalion came many stories of outstanding bravery, especially by those captured, some of whom managed to escape and return to the fold in dramatic style. Others distinguished themselves in the attempt. Among them was the battalion's redoubtable Padre MacDonald. He and Lieutenant Jock McGavin, after touching down at Rome *en route* to their POW camp, set fire to an aircraft while they were momentarily left unattended by their captors. They were about to be shot by angry Italians when a Luftwaffe officer intervened. It was the second time that members of that party of POWs from the 2nd Battalion were saved by a German officer – and as on the first occasion, just in the nick of time.

One of the outstanding stories from that period focuses on another instance where a group of British Paras were saved from execution. This event became something of an obsession in post-war years with one of those who was saved, a tough professional soldier named Gavin Cadden. The author makes no apology for breaking the general narrative to publish Cadden's recollections here in full for the first time. He had joined the Army in Scotland, signing on with the King's Own Scottish Borderers in 1931. He saw service in India, was demobbed in 1938 and returned home, got married and, when war broke out shortly afterwards, was recalled to the colours. He was in the British Expeditionary Force evacuated from Dunkirk and, kicking his heels in the aftermath, he and some chums decided to volunteer for the newly formed Parachute Regiment. He was on the Bruneval raid and was with Johnny Frost again when they set off for Algiers on Operation Torch and were dropped at Depienne at the end of November 1942.

Cadden told his story calmly and quietly, to the point of nonchalance, his tone belying the drama experienced by the party of wounded Frost had reluctantly left behind after the first major confrontation with the Germans:

We were a small platoon because some of our boys never managed to take off from Algiers for Depienne and we were detailed by Lieutenant Colonel Frost to stay behind and guard the wounded until the elements of the 1st Army came up. But, of course, the 1st Army cancelled their advance for 48 hours and that left us out on a limb, 60 miles behind the German lines and they had no way of getting back with our wounded. So we had to stay there, and took up a defensive position. Next day we saw a column coming, advancing towards us about a mile or so away. We knew we were in for it. We took up a position around Depienne village, and our wounded were in the school there – with one dead body. Anyway we were attacked by the tanks and the 5th German Parachute Regiment, and in charge of them was a Lieutenant Colonel Koch and his second in command was Major Jungwirth.

After a short battle – and some of us were wounded, including myself – we were forced to surrender for the sake of the wounded. They'd have all been annihilated. German paratroopers collected all the wounded and with their help we bandaged them as best we could. Lieutenant Colonel Koch meanwhile made off in pursuit of

Lieutenant Colonel Frost and his party. They knew all this had been going on. They were watching our drop from two miles away. We actually saw them – three Arabs with a donkey. Little did we know then they were three Germans in disguise and on the donkey's back was a radio set through which they were giving details of our drop and the number of men. I had chased them away and they were quite happy to get away without a scratch.

And so now we and our party of wounded were left with Major Jungwirth while Lieutenant Colonel Koch attempted to catch up with our battalion, or what was left of it. Jungwirth, in turn, jumped on a tank and left us with a group of Italian soldiers. In due course a German staff car drew up from the road to Tunis and an SS officer got out and surveyed our forlorn group and decided there and then that we should be executed although we had Parachute Regiment regulation dress on. We were marched into a farmyard and lined up against a wall and a machine-gun was placed ten yards from us, and a German or Italian got down and took aim at the first man – which was me – and was going to sweep right down the line.

At that moment, one of our officers, Lieutenant Buchanan, stepped forward and asked the German officer for permission to shake hands with us all before we were executed. Permission granted. So he shook hands with us all and he said: 'Don't forget, when I step back into the ranks, give them the V sign and let the bastards see that we're not afraid of them.'

When he went back into line, we all gave the V sign and the German officer lost his temper and shouted at the gunner to fire. At that very moment Lieutenant Colonel Koch reappeared on the scene, to find out what had happened to his adjutant and the rest of the party. He saw immediately what was just about to happen and even before his armoured car stopped he jumped off, ran across to the execution party, kicked over the machine-gun and pushed the gunner aside, and turned round to the SS officer and shouted at him in German. He turned round to us and said: 'You've no need to be afraid, gentlemen, you are paratroopers and brave men and we'll look after you safely.'

Lieutenant Colonel Koch put us all on to a German lorry and he got on the top along with us and told the driver to drive into Tunis. We left the dead body behind in the school with the French schoolmaster. But we drove back into Tunis with the wounded and we were put into a fort there. General Nering came out to inspect us. We all stood in line and then we were put in a cell for that night. There were no windows about, so actually we were beginning to think that we were going to be gassed. But in fact the ventilation came through the big door. And after about an hour or so a German came down with a big container of food for us and we settled in for the night.

In the morning they took us in parties of five upstairs for ablutions and we washed and shaved the best we could. The German paratroopers' sleeping quarters were up there. And the first party were away so long that we began to wonder what had happened to them. The Germans came down for another party of us, the last of us and the officer, Buchanan, and as we walked up and we looked through into the barrack room here were our friends sitting round one of the Germans' beds – all the Germans were round them – talking about how many jumps they'd done. The Germans were boasting they'd done as many jumps as us. They were giving them cigarettes, they lent us their shaving gear and everything to get cleaned up. They treated us like honoured guests.

The next day we were taken on to an airport in Tunis to be flown to a prison camp in Italy. And while we were sitting in the plane American Lightning bombers came over and bombed the airport and the plane that we were in was raised right off the ground about ten feet and crashed back down again. Some of the ammunition boxes strapped to the side of the fuselage inside fell down on some of the lads and split open their heads. A German medical officer came rushing out in a car and asked if any of us had been wounded or hurt. Anyway, he bandaged some of their heads up and before we took off they gave us life-preservers, life-jackets; they were just fitted on like a waistcoat.

The pilot told us that if we did get attacked by the Americans, which he expected, he would fly low over the water at the first sign of attack and pancake. We were to swim around until we were picked up by rescue launches. The day before we were doing our damnedest to kill one another and now they were doing their best to save our lives. We landed safely in Italy and went to a prison camp nearby called Capua. It was a small tented encampment and the fellows already there were out sitting in the sun, had their shirts off. I went up to one of them and I says, 'What's that you're doing?' He was delousing and he said, 'Don't worry, Jock, tomorrow you'll be out doing the same as me.' And as sure as God, the next morning I was. The camp was lousy, in the truest sense.

Fortunately we were moved from that camp after a week and we were put in a top-security place, a new camp that had been built about 500 yards up the road. This place, we noticed, had a big drainage system which started inside the camp. It had an iron grating over it so that you couldn't get down. We had already formed an escape committee with the officers in charge. We soon found a way of breaking through the grating and pulling it up. It had been newly laid and it led right away out to the main road. Six of us paratroopers decided that we'd get into this drain and crawl along the piping and come out at the main road and make our escape. Little did we know that the piping ran right under the sentry's box and the sentry heard the scraping of our boots on the concrete pipe above and he gave the alarm. They were waiting at the other end and we were marched back, and sent into solitary confinement.

When we came out, we were kept in a wired compound. We decided that the only way out was to volunteer for a working party. There were about ten of us – and we were to go away to a place called Bergamo, outside Milan, to work in a large factory. It was terrible work, cleaning up old Italian uniforms taken off the dead and wounded in the Abyssinian war. So you can imagine the stench that was coming off the cloth. Civilians would not touch them. We got extra food for it … and it gave us the chance to look around for a new escape route.

Every Sunday we used to get marched out to go to church. I got friendly with the Italian sentries and with the officer in charge – we called him Colonel Pappi. The Germans killed him when they took over the camp because they believed he had been too friendly with the British. The colonel asked if any one of us wanted to go to confession and he gave us a wink. Being a Catholic, I went in and soon discovered that the priest was in the Italian Resistance. I made several visits, over time, and used them to plan an escape.

He promised to give me and one other soldier refuge – he could only take two of us at the church. Several of us planned to escape – to climb the compound wall at the first opportunity and make a run for it; this we achieved on the night of a bombing raid on Milan. The Italian sentries were running about like blue-arsed flies, so it was quite easy to make a break for it. Some of the boys made for Milan and they were caught by the Germans the next day at the cathedral. They were brought out and they were shot just in front of the main doorway of the cathedral. We were told about it by the priest who was hiding us at Bergamo. We were up in the belfry. He brought us up food and water and we stayed there for three weeks. Every night we used to look out of the bell tower and we saw a big glow in the sky – which was Switzerland, 60 miles away. We decided we would try to reach the border and told the priest.

On the following Sunday he brought us down to a café and then took us to a school and he showed us what the Italian Resistance were doing. There were a lot of girls in the cellar of this school. They all had typewriters, copying propaganda against the *fascistas* and the Germans – young schoolgirls and boys risking their lives every night, distributing their leaflets. That very afternoon a German lorry drove up to the school. A *fascista* spy had given away their headquarters; we sat, meanwhile, in the café not far away, planning how to get to Switzerland. We heard shooting and there was a panic. The place cleared and I couldn't get out the front way because of the Germans who were swarming all over the place. I ran to the back door and in panic, tried to bash it open ... if I'd looked down I would have seen the bolt. Then, one of the women at the café came and lifted up the bolt and I just flew out into an alley, into the toilets, and closed the door. Within a minute or two there was a knocking, and the Italian woman was saying, 'Come, come, come!' We ran into her house, where she told me to get into her bed. I was to be her husband, home from the front and wounded. The houses were being searched and I nearly died when a German officer came in with two soldiers. I was laying in bed, eyes closed. She explained that I had just returned home. They hovered and I was saying to myself, 'I wish to God that they would give me a burst of bullets.' You see, the tension was so high I was only hoping he would kill me. But then I corrected myself: it would have meant the woman would have been killed too for sheltering me. Anyhow, the German officer saluted me, saluted the bed and left.

The woman who saved my life wanted me to stay there. She said she would hide me until our troops arrived. Her next-door neighbours were not so helpful. They got to know I was there and they made her send me away; they were right, too. If I'd have been caught there the whole row of buildings would more than likely have been blown up and all these people would have been killed.

Gavin Cadden made his way back to the church and the priest at Bergamo arranged for some clothes to be brought in and eventually for him to be taken to Milan's main railway station. They got him as far as Lake Como without incident. There he was met by another priest and two young boys and a girl. He was dressed in an old civilian suit which needed some attention because it had become ripped. They took him to a house and the girl patched it up. He stayed the night and the next morning an Italian Resistance man came in and told the priest that they were going to attempt to walk Cadden to the border and get him into Switzerland. Two young girls and two young boys were to go along with him, the girls either side of him, holding each hand as if they were related. They walked boldly up a mountain track to a point where they could see the barrier and border checkpoint. On the other side was Switzerland. Cadden continued his story:

I said to myself, 'My God, will I ever make it?' The nearer I got the worse I got… 'I'll likely be shot now.' And here down the path came an Italian *sergente*. He stopped. Well, he knew right away what it was – and they pleaded with him to let us go on. He looked at us very sternly and it seemed to be touch and go whether he was going to call the sentries and escort us back to the village. But I pulled up my shirt and I showed my tattoo [of the crucifix] and the Italian Resistance member said, '*Cattolico*.' The Italian sergeant nodded and gave us a sign to carry on. We walked away, up a dirt track, and it came right to the wires; there were sentry boxes 100 yards away. If you touched the wire rather roughly it set off a bell in the sentry box. The two young boys crawled up and dug a hole under the wire and made enough room for me to get through, and they crawled back again. The two girls had been sent back home in case anything happened at the last minute. They kissed me on the cheek and said something about God. The two boys, they risked their lives again … but it didn't seem to worry them. All they wanted to do was to help the British. They dug a hole big enough for me to get through without touching the wire, and they said, 'Right, go now.' I managed to squeeze through without touching the wire. And I was ready to run away and he called me back, this fellow, the head one. What he wanted to do was to shake my hand, and what I wanted to do was to run like hell out of it as fast as I could. But that's what he wanted to do, shake my hand. So we shook hands all round and I made for the valley.

As I did so, the sentries opened up with their guns. I don't know if they were aiming at me or making me run faster, but they couldn't do that; I was already running as fast as I could. I ran down into the valley and there was a Swiss soldier. He took me to a nearby farm and the woman there made me coffee while he called his headquarters. Two armed sentries came up and escorted me down into the town. They were very rough about it. I was put in a cell and still I was not right sure I was in Switzerland until someone came from the British consul and asked me where I'd been. He interrogated me just to make sure I wasn't a plant. Eventually he said, 'You've done well.' I replied, 'Now, how can I get back to my regiment?' He told me I'd need a good rest before I could think of that. Anyway that was me in my heaven, and looking all round and the people all smiling and walking about the street and not worrying about bombers or shooting.

It was several months before Cadden's evacuation to England could be arranged. By that time there were a lot of British and American troops coming in and they were all worrying about getting back. He finally made it back to his regiment in early 1944, just before Arnhem. He asked to see his old company commander, Lieutenant Colonel Frost, and to get back among the action. But after debriefing and medical, he was told: 'You've had enough action.' He was soon taken to hospital and eventually discharged with a full war disability pension, because of wounds to the head and neck and major operations on his ulcerated stomach caused by bad prison-camp food. 'My gall bladder went missing too, so I came back just a shell of the man and my wife didn't know me when we finally met up. She just cried.'

But that was not the end of the story, and to complete Cadden's account we must jump forward momentarily to the post-war years. He could not get out of his mind the bravery of the German officer who had saved him and his colleagues from the firing squad. Determined to try to make contact with Lieutenant Colonel Koch, he made enquiries, only to discover that Koch himself had been shot by the Gestapo for countermanding the order of a senior officer, so allowing British Paras to escape the firing squad despite the fact that Hitler had personally ordered that raiding parties should be shot. When he found out about this, Cadden laid a wreath at the Cenotaph in London and became the first British soldier, or indeed British man, to lay a wreath there in memory of a German officer. For years afterwards he sent anonymously a wooden poppy cross to the West German government to place on Koch's grave. Cadden never signed his name, but eventually the Germans identified him as the sender through one of the German soldiers involved in the original incident.

The German Embassy in London got in touch with Cadden. Koch's brother and sister visited him and in 1987 he was a guest of honour at a reunion of the German 5th Parachute Regiment, where he met some of the soldiers who had helped save him. Later he went to visit Koch's grave in Bonn.

Throughout those years Cadden also worked to establish and maintain contact between German, British and French ex-soldiers and, partly as a result of his efforts, British and German paratroopers initiated an annual meeting of friendship. As he quietly continued these efforts, he learned that he had been selected to receive the Order of Merit, one of Germany's highest awards, as well as the European Peace Cross for his work since the war in establishing a bond of friendship between the soldiers who had once fought on opposite sides. He refused both honours: 'I asked them to withdraw my name. I didn't want any honours. All I wanted was the satisfaction of laying a wreath at the grave of an officer who gave his life for us, and that was a German officer.'

4

LIGHTING THE TORCH

Although the Allied landing in North Africa had evicted Axis troops from a vast swathe of territory and diverted Hitler's attention from other pressing theatres, the follow-up to Operation Torch's initial success faltered. The Germans had not been dislodged from their footholds in Bizerta and Tunis – two of the original objectives of the 1st Army – and the campaign quickly became bogged down by a long, very wet and miserable winter. The 1st Army, short of men, was opposed by an enemy reinforced from Europe and Rommel's retreating Afrika Korps. The failure by the Allies to grasp the two key Tunisian ports in the immediate wake of Torch meant that their eventual capture was delayed by six months, which in turn put back the projected start of the Normandy landings by a whole year. With the weather preventing airborne operations, troops of the 1st Parachute Brigade were placed in infantry positions, and with little time to rest and replenish after their ferocious introduction to the North African campaign, they were soon back in the thick of the action.

Reinforcements were needed across the board. There was not a Para battalion that did not need topping up, and the 2nd more than the rest, for two of its companies, B and C, had been wiped out. Gordon Mitchell, who had joined the Parachute Regiment from the Argyll and Sutherland Highlanders only a few months earlier, was, by late 1942, on standby to go to Algiers. He couldn't wait to get there:

When I was accepted into the Parachute Regiment, I loved it. It was like a drug, you just kept wanting to go on. It was a fairly uneventful training, apart from the lad who dreamed one night that he was jumping out of his aircraft and kept seeing flying coffins. He told the course instructor and was sent back to his unit the following day. The *esprit de corps* was brilliant. That Christmas, we had a dinner in a little barracks on Salisbury Plain and the commanding officer gave us a promise that he would get us into action as soon as possible. The whole place erupted with cheers and banging on the tables and so on, with sheer enthusiasm to get going.

The time came when we were to go to Tunisia. I was in the 5th Scottish Battalion, which found the first draft of reinforcements for the 1st Parachute Brigade. The fighting was still going on, of course, and some big battles were on the cards. We went by sea to Algiers and transferred to Maison Blanche, and from there [it was] a five-day journey by train to reach the battalion, who were in the line at the time, fighting as infantry. We travelled in cattle trucks. We moved up to the front close to the Tamera Valley in a night move, reaching a gunnery battery and bedded down in the open. Periodically the guns went off and we were up close; it was the first time I had heard artillery fire so close and realized that the shells were going over my head. Over the next few days we were shelled, we were mortared, we were machine-gunned. Then there would be a quiet spell. You had a tendency then to want to get out of your trench and stretch your legs, but in fact it was the most dangerous time; it was difficult to realize you were being observed and could be a sitting target.

The enemy was prodding and probing the Allied defences for a weak spot, and if they found one they came in with a charge, heavy guns blazing. The Para battalions found themselves being used as a fire brigade, plugging the holes and holding the line and, in consequence, they were often in the lines that experienced some of the heaviest fighting. Mitchell goes on:

We were on the front for around ten days before we were relieved and then back again for ten days. Though not strictly infantry, we were being used as such because of the shortage of manpower. We were moved around the whole of the front, reinforcing positions under heavy fire or in the push forward in counter-attacks and fully fledged attacks. You'd sort of go forward, get pinned down, lose some men, advance again, lose more men, get pinned down again, make a charge, lose more men, but eventually get on top of your position. Having done all that and having lost a lot of friends, you found that the German was quite prepared to stand outside of his mortar pit and shout, 'Comrade!' There was a realization that it was a good soldier you were fighting and if we took his surrender, there was often an exchange of cigarettes and a cup of tea if there was one going. In the meantime, we had suffered a good many casualties, many killed or wounded, and the figures remained high until this phase of the battles finished in April. It was interesting to discover that the Germans were taking a particular interest in us – as Paras. Among the captured German documents was one which assessed our early battles and classed us as being very brave but not very good on tactics. They were probably right.

Nevertheless it was the Germans themselves who gave us [the 1st Parachute Brigade] the name of 'the Red Devils'. Later, when the fighting was over and we were being inspected by General Alexander, he stopped in front of me and he said the words in German and asked me what it was. I said, 'I don't know, sir.' And he replied, 'Well, you ought to be very proud – it is the name the Germans have given you – Red Devils.'

The remaining operations in North Africa engaged the 1st Parachute Brigade until the very last gasp of the conflict, which ebbed and flowed, first in favour of the defender and then, eventually, the Allies as they pushed harder and ever onward and drove the Axis troops towards the sea. The Paras were engaged in some massive and often costly battles, and the flavour of the action and the feeling of the men can be judged from these random comments from some of those who were in the mud and wet at Cork Wood, which was one of the longest engagements and brought the 2nd Battalion once more to the brink. Reduced to 160 men at one point, it received reinforcements from the 3rd Battalion but was still well under strength for the job at hand. Among the men who were in the thick of it was Macleod Forsyth:

We were here, there and everywhere and finished up at a place called Cork Wood. We arrived during the night, relieving another unit. Our company commander told us to spread out, form a circle and get dug in. But we didn't have time for that. Just before dawn the Germans attacked, thinking it was the unit we had just replaced, and they got the surprise of their lives. What a battle! The attacks kept coming but we held them. During the day we were in a clearing, and we looked up and there was a plane coming straight at us. We dived for a trench and two of us finished up in one trench with me on top. I didn't get hit but the other chap did. It's just luck. The battalion took a hell of a bashing during that time … mortaring, shelling, bombing – they threw everything at us except the kitchen sink. There was a mule train coming up to us with ammunition and rations and it took a direct hit. God almighty, what a mess. What a bloody mess. Mules and bodies everywhere. One poor chap had no arms and no legs, and was still alive. I pumped him full of morphine and then watched him die. The fighting at Cork Wood went on for days until the 8th Argyll Battalion came through. We lost quite a few men. We were burying some of the boys – one of them was hit in the face. It was just a mass of maggots – one or two were so shocked they threw up. An order had come out earlier not to use a blanket to bury your dead. I suppose they were short of blankets. Anyhow, we ignored it – sod 'em, we said – and we wrapped this boy in a blanket and buried him along with the others. Then the adjutant came on the blower asking for our report on casualties and ammunition. What a fool! I said, 'We're in the middle of a battle here. We've had no bloody time to do that.'

We withdrew to an iron mine, and everything you touched, you were red. The Germans thought they'd given us such a bashing that we couldn't get organized quickly enough to attack again for three or four days. But we did, and gave them a right hiding.

John Timothy, Forsyth's company commander when they were at Bruneval together, rejoined the 2nd Battalion at Christmas, and was shipped out to Algiers with reinforcements after a spell on secondment to American 503rd. He had previously been in Algeria at the time of the Torch landings, to help set up landing sites for American airborne troops, and was now back with his old commander, Johnny Frost:

There was very heavy fighting when I arrived and by then finding reinforcements was becoming very difficult. A platoon might be 30 in number but you were probably down to 18 or 20. We could only be reinforced by Paras and that restriction came not just from the top brass but the men themselves. A Yorkshire lad came up to me and asked if he could have a word. I said, 'Yes, what's the problem?' He said his corporal, who he was with 24 hours a day, wouldn't speak to him. Every time he attempted conversation, the corporal replied, 'Get some hours in under shellfire before you speak to me.' It wasn't very helpful, but nevertheless I arranged for this lad to go out on patrol a few times, night-time patrols, laying mines, and so on, and eventually he was accepted. The sad side of this story was that they were both dead within the month, but the incident demonstrated the strength of feeling within the battalions about reinforcements; it was an élite regiment, felt itself élite, and that was that.

Losses were fairly substantial. The Paras were being used for plugging or attacking. Either you were rushed into a position to fill a gap or you went into attack in what were all usually high-risk situations. At Cork Wood we had two or three weeks in appalling weather, attacking from everywhere. Stephen Spender's brother, Dickie, was with us. He was also a poet and had these expressions which he came out with as we were going along which kind of summed up the situation, such as 'Thud, in the mud; another dud. Thank God.'

After Cork Wood, we went wading down a river. Next day we counter-attacked and opposed German para engineers. They were a good crowd. We took their position. We found what was left of a company of the 1st Battalion; bodies everywhere. By the end of the Algerian campaign the 2nd Battalion was down to about 90 and Johnny Frost called it a company not a battalion. That was the total strength. We were being heavily hit and taking a few reinforcements, and at the end of the day that's all we had left – 90 men. We had been up against it pretty well the whole time we were there – blocking here, attacking there. 90 men!

The 1st Battalion had also suffered, notably at a feature known as Djebel Mansour; one of a succession of operations in the region in which Captain Vic Coxen had led the way with mine-marking tape. After three days of continuous activity the battalion was low on ammunition and severely hit by losses. It was forced to withdraw under covering fire from the Grenadiers and the 3rd Parachute Battalion, having lost 35 men killed in action, 132 wounded and 16 missing. The battalion regrouped, took reinforcements and went back into the fray, although on one occasion, after a long spell of assault tasks, Lieutenant Colonel (as he now was) Alastair Pearson was forced to take issue with his own commanders, and insisted that the 1st Battalion was exhausted and needed to be rested. The commanders of the 5th Corps, under whose auspices the 1st Battalion was operating, promised a rest after one more action – to capture an important hill feature from which the Germans were causing trouble. Pearson agreed and took his battalion into a surprise attack on the site under dark skies at 22.30 hours on 23 March 1943. By 03.00 they were in possession. But the promised respite never came.

In the morning Pearson received orders to join the 36th and 138th Infantry Brigades in an advance on enemy positions at Tamera, a mission which entailed a long march to the start line. The operation was highly successful, and Pearson's men set the seal on what would prove to be the last gasps of any concerted German opposition in the campaign, which had by now entered its final phase. The 1st and 8th Armies were about to link up, and the job was all but done. In the final Allied offensive, it was the 1st Parachute Brigade that opened the main coast road with an attack on 28 March. So tight was the Allied blockade of Tunisia that the Germans had no place to go. On 12 May all organized resistance by German and Italian forces halted when the German Commander-in-Chief, General Sixt von Arnim, was captured, together with his entire staff, by a reconnaissance patrol of the 1st Army. He ordered an immediate surrender and 110,000 Germans and 40,000 Italians came in with their hands up. Fewer than 1000 Germans escaped by sea.

During their North African adventures the Parachute Brigades had performed, with their three airborne assaults, the first major airborne operations of the war by British parachutists. They had fought for five and a half months as infantry, taken part in more battles than any other formation in the 1st Army, captured 3500 prisoners and inflicted over 5000 casualties for a loss of 1700 to themselves.

The nickname given to the 1st Parachute Brigade by the enemy in recognition of their exploits in North Africa was accepted as a compliment, and this was made clear in a signal: 'From Major General Browning to All Para Units: General Alexander directs that 1 Para Brigade be info that have been given name by Germans of "Red Devils". General Alexander congratulates the brigade on achieving this high distinction.'

The name was thus set in stone and remains the unofficial title for Britain's airborne forces.

Yet, even as the last German units were being booted out of the North African theatre, preparations were being made for the next major date in the Allied calendar: the invasion of southern Italy using Sicily as a stepping stone. The attack would again be led in by the Paras and airborne units, both by now substantially augmented under the expanded umbrella of British and Allied airborne forces. For the first time the vast stock of new heavy-duty gliders and their pilots would also come into their own. The depleted 1st Parachute Brigade was reinforced and joined in June 1943 by the 2nd and 4th Parachute Brigades. The latter was newly formed out of the 156th Parachute Battalion, which had been created in India in 1941, and the 10th and 11th Parachute Battalions, which rose from volunteers in British units serving in the Middle East and had most recently seen service in Palestine. The glider-borne 1st Airlanding Brigade also arrived from England and this was to combine with the 1st, 2nd and 4th Parachute Brigades to make up the operational strength of the 1st Airborne Division.

Gordon Mitchell, of the 1st Parachute Battalion, recalls that his unit was withdrawn as the 1st and 8th Armies made their final advance and the North African campaign drew to a close. His battalion was to join with incoming units from the UK and American airborne forces with whom they were to combine in the invasion of Sicily. Together they would be part of the massive armada of ships, aircraft and soldiers soon to assemble off Tunisia, ready for the short hop across the Mediterranean. The bulk of the airborne forces gathered in tented compounds and began immediate training for parachute and glider landings. Mitchell recalls the scene:

There we came into contact with Americans who were going to fly us on the invasion of Sicily. My platoon – as with others – was to undergo very intensive training for a particular operation. We were to be dropped to make a 2000-yard dash from the DZ to a bridge – which we later learned was Primosole Bridge. We trained and trained and trained. We were being timed for the 2000-yard dash, which we did every day loaded with full kit, and then it was discovered we were getting slower for no apparent reason. We had received some new recruits but everyone was very keen, training hard. The slowness was a mystery. Then the 2iC of the battalion identified a possible cause. Since we had joined the Americans, we had gone on their rations. They had everything – tinned chicken, turkey, chocolate, etc. – compared with our bully beef and biscuits, of which we were heartily sick. So we'd been gorging ourselves on this. The 2iC suggested we were put back on British rations. We were – and our times began to improve again. Whether it was psychological, no one will ever know. We trained from April to the end of June. Then the battalion was moved by air from Morocco to our staging area for the invasion of Sicily, at Sousse. The whole invasion fleet lay off the coast of Tunisia, well protected by barrage balloons. It was an incredible sight – ship after ship after ship. And for us, line upon line of Dakotas. The whole of the 1st and the 8th Armies also linked up there and, like ourselves, were swimming in the Mediterranean in the afternoons; incredible scenes, really.

The capture of Sicily was planned as a rapid pincer movement. With General Eisenhower as Commander in Chief of the Allied forces, the Americans were to advance from the west while the British 8th Army, under General Montgomery, moved in from the east coast to block the enemy's escape route across the Strait of Messina. The task of airborne troops was to capture key bridges, and high ground on the approaches to them, ahead of the arrival of the main force. Three specific targets were vital for the progress of the sea-borne assault, which began at dawn on 10 July. On the day before that massive movement of men and machinery, the 1st Airlanding Brigade was assigned to capture the Ponte Grande and clear the way into the port of Syracuse and then the harbour itself. On the evening of 9 July 2000 men piled into Hadrian and Horsa gliders towed by American Dakotas and a small detachment of 38 Wing RAF, and took off from North Africa. The weather was unusually brisk, with winds of up to gale force. This caused a problem for the inexperienced American aircrews, especially as each section had only one navigator, who travelled in the lead plane. If that aircraft didn't make it or got lost, there was no navigator. Half the gliders were released too early and 78 landed in the sea, leaving the men to swim ashore; many did not make it. Several others were shot down and those which managed a landing were miles apart on difficult terrain. Only one glider in that operation managed to reach its designated LZ (landing zone). Despite the chaotic beginnings, parties of men formed up under the most senior ranks among them and began attacking Axis troops wherever they came across them.

The enemy commanders, totally surprised by the assaults, were given the impression that a whole airborne corps had been dropped, and this helped the sea-borne arrivals, who landed virtually unopposed. Nor did the initial target go unattended. A single platoon of one of the glider-borne battalions, the 2nd Battalion the South Staffordshire Regiment, captured the Ponte Grande and held it for several hours before they were forced to withdraw under heavy enemy fire. The action was sufficient to hold the Axis troops at bay, and by the afternoon of that day the bridge was retaken with the aid of the 2nd Battalion the Royal Scots Fusiliers, fresh from their beach landing. Around 300 men were lost, most of them drowned in prematurely released or shot-down gliders, but the road to Syracuse was secure for the Allied advance.

With the 8th Army now ashore and advancing across the coastal plain towards Catania, the 1st Parachute Brigade was tasked with taking other vital targets, especially the point where the main road crossed the river via the Primosole Bridge. After two postponements the operation was launched on the night of 13 July, when 113 parachute aircraft and 16 gliders carrying 1856 men took off from North Africa. Vic Coxen was in the first aircraft:

We were going over the coast near where the river joined the coast. In my aircraft were two men who were going to set up the Rebecca Eureka devices which guided the gliders in. They went out first. I was looking out of the window and saw the river; came back and hooked up. At that moment the aircraft banked and went out to sea again. I unhooked and went forward and asked what was the matter. The pilot said we were ten minutes early. I said, 'That doesn't matter a bugger; they know we're here – they're already firing at us. Get in!'

They turned back and I took my place in line as we headed for the dropping zone, when suddenly the aircraft bent sideways and climbed sharply. He'd overshot and there was a bloody great hill in front of him. Everybody went arse over apple cart. I went out on my knees. All of my stick got out except the last three, who were tangled up at the back of the plane somewhere. When I came down, it was on the top of a hill; we were in the wrong bloody place. My batman landed below me and broke his leg. We assembled quickly and started marching towards the south side of the river. I didn't want to be caught in the open. We ran into a German coastal battery, which we knocked out, and captured 40 Italian prisoners, who were a bloody nuisance, quite frankly. In the end I told them to bugger off after we'd disarmed them, but they stayed with us, even though we had no guards on them. Shooing them away didn't work and eventually they were handed over to the British ground forces.

The close formation of aircraft and tugs with gliders followed close behind and met heavy anti-aircraft fire. A combination of inexperienced US pilots, lack of navigators and fear of running out of fuel meant that few of the gliders came down in the right place for the attack on the Primosole Bridge. Only 295 officers and men of the 1st Parachute Brigade came down close enough to the designated DZ to form up for the operation. The bridge itself and the high ground overlooking it was the objective of companies of the 1st and 2nd Battalions. The northern approach was the 3rd Battalion's target, but not enough of them landed to even make the attempt. Gordon Mitchell was with the assault platoon of the 1st Battalion:

We were to land 20 minutes before the main force. I remember the briefing by the battalion CO, Alastair Pearson, a great officer and fellow Scot. He sat us down in an olive grove and gave us an encouraging send-off, promising bloody overwhelming air support. He couldn't have been more wrong, of course, because we didn't have bloody overwhelming air support. By the time we took off, the sea landing was already under way. Our job was to capture and hold Primosole Bridge until relieved by the 8th Army, which would open up access to the Catania plain. The brigade was assigned 90 Dakotas, with my platoon taking off ahead of the rest to spearhead the assault. Incidentally, our American pilots had never been into action before. They were all civilian airline pilots who were just put into uniform to fly these aircraft. We'd trained with them, of course, but they'd had no operational experience.

We were to head north-east over Malta and then change direction to north-west and fly up the Sicilian coast and literally turn left at the location of our dropping zone. Well, the first thing that went haywire was as we flew over Malta. The British Navy, who weren't expecting aircraft at that time, mistook us for the enemy in heavy weather and opened up at us with ack-ack fire. It was pretty terrifying, especially for those like myself (and the pilots!) who had never experienced anti-aircraft fire before. The American planes were also carrying a kind of onboard chief whose job it was to see that everything went according to plan at the door. Well, when the ack-ack started, he put on his steel helmet and grabbed a tommy gun, which he fired out of the open door. He seemed to think we were being attacked by fighters!

Anyway, we carried on relatively undamaged and eventually reached the Sicilian coast, where again we were met by heavy ack-ack fire, and frankly I had never been so pleased to jump out of an aircraft in my life. There's always a little bit of fear before you jump, but on that occasion I felt I could have jumped without a parachute. Twenty years later I did a tour of that very spot with the artist David Shepherd, who had been commissioned by the Parachute Regiment to paint a picture of the drop, and I found, going over the ground again, that we had landed exactly on the DZ – which was very good; many were not so lucky. But we had a senior pilot because they had to be sure they dropped us in good order ahead of the rest. One of the things I remember about arriving in Sicily was that as we were landing in one field German paras were landing not very far away, coming in as reinforcements against us. In fact, some of our chaps got mixed up with them and there were a few running individual battles.

An armoured car also gave us a bit of trouble soon after we hit the ground, but we sorted that out and made it towards the bridge. There we found that, instead of being this great assault that we had trained weeks and weeks for, with all those 2000-yard dashes every morning, we had been beaten to it. Brigadier Bellamy and two or three men from Brigade Headquarters were already there; they had knocked the sentries out and captured the bridge themselves, although it was a short-lived success. The bridge soon came under heavy attack by a far, far superior force of Germans and Italians than we could muster at that time.

In fact, very few of the incoming Parachute Brigade had actually dropped. Many planes had been unable to find their DZ and, short of fuel, turned back. On the first roll-call of the 1st Battalion, only 90 answered their names. A few others, who had been dropped astray, straggled in later. These few men held that bridge for two days and two nights under severe shelling and machine-gunning. It was non-stop. There was a hell of a lot of noise and we lost around 23 men. The shelling put farm buildings at the side of the bridge on fire and I went in and released a number of horses which were tethered inside. We were being covered by the British Navy, who were pouring 15-inch shells into the forces attacking us. They were so large, you could hear them before you could see them – a long, whining noise. We had some Italian prisoners and they were screaming, 'Mamma mia, Mamma mia.' Eventually we had to withdraw from that position. Alastair Pearson himself occupied one of the pillboxes and covered the withdrawal. We marched for two or three hours until we reached the forward elements of the 8th Army. The password for the whole of the 8th that day was 'Kill all Italians', which Montgomery invented. But they didn't challenge us; the Durhams just let off a burst of fire at us until we shouted out our identity. From there, we moved back to a town, where we were able to stop for a respite, have a brew-up and a meal. One of the great sights at this time, for me, was a Highland division coming up – I think it was the Gordons – in company groups led by their company piper. It was the most stunning thing. And just beside us was this store of oranges, in a barn, and we gathered up as many as we could and gave these chaps oranges as they passed. They looked surprised and couldn't make out what we were doing there.

Another incident which comes to mind was the arrival of a glider; much of the heavy equipment, the six-pounders towed by jeeps, came in by Horsa gliders. We were lying on the river bank at night, under a moonlit sky. Suddenly, for an instant, the moon seemed to be blotted out. It was a very large glider, flying very close above us. It reached the river, where one bank was higher than the other, and it hit the opposite bank; you could hear the chaps shouting, but the glider just sank out of sight. There was nothing we could do. The divisional commander, Major General

Hopkinson, also had a watery landing. He came over by a glider which had been cast off early and landed in the sea – an awful lot of them did. Eventually he came to see us and asked us what had gone wrong; why hadn't it gone according to plan? He was very concerned.

We then motored back to the 8th Army at Syracuse, carrying wounded with us. We came under attack several times and had to bail out and run for cover to return fire. I always felt sorry for the wounded, who had to be left on the wagons while gunfire landed all around them. Anyway, we eventually made it to 8th headquarters and lay down outside a big house in large grounds. We were all staked out and clapped out; this American officer came round and put a blanket over each of us. Next morning, we washed and cleaned up, marched down to Syracuse harbour and were put on a tank-landing ship to return to Tripoli, taking with us our wounded and 1400 Italian and German prisoners of war. That night, we were very heavily bombed – terrifying when you are below deck – and they let off smoke as a screen. Half of it came down on us. There we were, huddled together, lights out, choking on the smoke.

It was the Germans' 4th Parachute Brigade that had counter-attacked the tiny British 1st Parachute Battalion contingent as they briefly held the Primosole Bridge, and under heavy fire from three sides the British force had to slowly withdraw south, where they took up a position for a last-ditch stand. The handful of airborne troops held the bridge for longer than was believed possible and it was retaken by the 9th Battalion the Durham Light Infantry on 16 July after a ferocious battle lasting two days. Despite some horrendous miscalculations by the pilots and chaotic landings, the paratroopers eventually reached all of their objectives and were withdrawn to North Africa to prepare for the next stage of the operations – the invasion of Italy, leaving Sicily in the capable hands of the ground forces. By 17

August all opposition on the island crumbled with the fall of Messina, the last major city to succumb to Allied bombs, which left it in ruins.

By then Allied warships were already pounding the coastal regions of southern Italy and bombers and fighters were harrying targets along the length of the country. As with the invasion of Sicily, the Paras and airborne troops of the 1st Airborne Division would lead the way, joined by a sea-borne assault, to take and hold Taranto and begin the move north without delay. The 2nd and 4th Parachute Brigades were moved across to the southern Italian port by sea from Bizerta on 8 September. During the crossing, news of Italy's surrender became known, and in the event the landing took place unopposed, although it was not without incident. HMS *Abdiel*, carrying the 6th Battalion – known as the Welsh battalion because they had recruited almost entirely from the Royal Welch Fusiliers – hit a mine in the harbour and was cut in two, leaving 58 men dead and 154 injured.

The invasion of Italy did not go altogether smoothly either; supplies to the 2nd and 4th Parachute Brigades were slow arriving and there were shortages of both manpower and communications. Even so, some very worthwhile tasks were performed ahead of the main troop landings. It was soon after the armistice that John Timothy found himself at the helm of an unusual parachute mission. He had missed the invasion of Sicily, having just spent several weeks in a military hospital in North Africa – 'with ingrowing toenails of all things, dammit' – and caught up with his unit, the 2nd Parachute Battalion, at Taranto:

We pushed on up to Barletta, just below the heel of the boot ... and by then a number of prisoner-of-war camps were being opened up. Some had already been deserted by the Italians and a large number of British and Allied POWs just came out and dispersed into the countryside and in the woods, fearing that the

Germans would simply take over – as indeed did happen in a number of cases. All kinds of different operations and schemes were launched to try to locate these escaped POWs who were milling around the countryside. At Barletta, I was to select eight men and launch a search party. Other battalions were doing the same in different areas. My section was dropped around a place further north, near the coast. We took off in a bomber which was not a Para aircraft. It simply had a rectangular hole through which we made our exit by bunny-hopping towards it and down and through. It took a fair while, especially as we had one non-jumper, an Italian-speaking American who was going to act as interpreter. The RAF coastal command were flying this thing and unfortunately they dropped me, the last out, about 20 miles from the DZ. Our plans went somewhat awry and I found myself alone. Next morning I searched for the chums; no luck. They had obviously gone on their way, doing the job we had all been briefed to do. They had their maps, RV locations, escape money and so on. Meanwhile I carried on alone, tripped around looking for these escaped POWs. Contact was made surprisingly quickly, usually in twos and threes, hiding in barns and what have you. I gave them packs of cigarettes and maps giving them the location of a beach RV from where they were to await pick-up. There were a couple of odd experiences.

I reached one village, still very much on my own. I got quite a crowd, about 40 or 50 POWs. So I got them together and began addressing them, trying to convince them I was who I said I was – bearing in mind that some of these chaps had been in the bag for a long time. Some of them didn't even believe there was such a thing as a British para. So I had to sell the idea of what I was doing – talking about home, Marks & Spencer and what have you. Some still didn't believe me; and one can appreciate their apprehension. Many of the escaped prisoners were by now working with the local resistance. One chap asked me, 'When was Crystal Palace burned down?' and I said, 'The beginning of the war.' This immediately destroyed their confidence because of course it burned down before the war; it was my error. I was thus invited to a farmhouse to meet leaders of the local resistance. They sat around a big table; there were one or two British POWs. The leading officer of the group, who spoke reasonable English, got up and said they knew very well there was no such thing as a British para, that I must be a German spy and they were going to shoot me. I wasn't very happy about this. I looked around the table and it appeared to me that there was no one on my side. I was racking my brains what to do. I said I had been personally sent by General Montgomery and that others were doing the same elsewhere. I was there to see what was happening and in particular what resistance forces there were and whether they were worth helping or whether they were traitors. The officer dithered. They all looked unsure, but eventually I was escorted out of the area.

At another village I came across six or eight British chaps playing cribbage. I stopped and had a couple of games with them and told them I was seeking escaped POWs. There was obviously some form of underground network going on because one of them remarked, 'You'd better be careful. There was a chap named Captain Timothy doing what you're doing and he was shot yesterday.' I told them I was definitely Captain Timothy and I hadn't been shot.

I carried on, on the move all the while. I had been on my own for about a fortnight now, living off the land, sleeping rough and occasionally getting food and shelter from the locals. There was no hardship or real danger. Then I had a stroke of luck. Moving around, I came through a clearing and there, waiting for me, was a chap wearing a red beret – he was a sergeant named Smith from 2 Para who had been captured only recently. We joined forces and this was a great help, because having been a prisoner of war himself he could convince others of our mission. He was a good chap and a great help. We proceeded on our way, directing people to the RV and in due course we got to a point overlooking the RV itself and discovered there were between 400 to 500 people gathered. An SAS unit was organizing them at the side of the coastal road and at the appointed time on the appointed day for the RV, a signal was flashed from the shore and amazingly a signal came back from the Royal Navy, who had a boat there, ready and waiting.

The operation to collect the POWs was going to take some time. The Navy began sending boats over to collect them. Unfortunately, while we were waiting, a group of POWs broke into a nearby farmhouse. The farmer opened up with a shotgun and blazed away and within minutes a German armoured car appeared on the scene, also blasting away, and the chums we had rounded up quickly vanished into the ether. Well, to cut a long story short, myself and Sergeant Smith and the SAS men searched around afterwards, but they had all made a run for it. We got back about 40 or 50. So the whole operation was shattered by these fools trying to break into the house.

For John Timothy and the rest of the 1st Parachute Brigade, the war in Italy was over. Other pressing matters were awaiting back home.

Meanwhile the Germans were still managing some solid resistance to the invasion of the British, for whom the push north was no easy task. The Allies had to fight their way forward against some strong Nazi fortified positions and the 2nd Parachute Brigade was among those units called upon to remain behind and fight as infantry while the rest of the 1st Airborne Division returned to England to prepare for the invasion of western Europe.

The 2nd Parachute Brigade, under the command of Brigadier C. H. V. Pritchard, was made up of the 4th, 5th and 6th Battalions and was strengthened by the addition of the 2nd Parachute Squadron Royal Engineers, the 127th Parachute Field Ambulance Squadron, a REME (Royal Electrical and Mechanical Engineers) light-infantry detachment and a Corps of Military Police. The new grouping was given the *ad hoc* name of the 2nd Independent Parachute Brigade Group and ordered to bolster the British line north of the River Sangro, where it came under the auspices of General Sir Bernard Freyberg's 2nd New Zealand Division.

In dire weather and heavy snow, the Allies began concerted attacks on the German positions, while the 8th Army advanced on the Adriatic coast towards Orsogna – almost in line with Rome on the opposite side of the country – with the 2nd Independent Parachute Brigade playing a vital role in both attacking manoeuvres and patrols. The brigade was especially used to take prisoners in an attempt to discover information on battle orders. Para patrols would go out in the snow covered in white sheets for camouflage, laying ambushes and grabbing enemy soldiers when and where they could. They achieved some startling and cheeky successes in this objective. However, as far as the general advance was concerned, appalling conditions and surprisingly tough enemy defences brought the three battalions to a grinding halt. They spent more than three months of intense, taxing and at times exceedingly frustrating battles, suffering heavy shelling from both sides of their positions. One company headquarters took 17 direct hits in a single day.

Similarly, the US 5th Army had been kept at bay around Monte Cassino, scene of the famous battles of the Allied campaigns in Italy, costly and heroic. At the end of March the 2nd Independent Parachute Brigade was summoned westward to the Cassino front to relieve New Zealanders and British Guards units, and once again it took leading positions in probing missions. The Parachute Battalions' logs are filled with tales reflecting their mixed fortunes, of good days and very bad ones, of comrades lost and of heroes surviving great odds. Two episodes stand out:

A reconnaissance patrol commanded by Lieutenant J. Pearson of the 6th Parachute Battalion was given the task of finding a way through a minefield close to enemy positions in the Cassino sector. They were proceeding well until one of the mines exploded, injuring four of the men. Pearson ordered his group back, carrying the wounded with them, and they began to retrace their steps as best they could, with Pearson in the lead on all fours and the rest following suit. Unfortunately he knelt on a mine, which blew off both his legs beneath the knees. He ordered his men to go on without him. They refused, of course, and carried him out of the minefield with the other wounded and then took him across the difficult terrain on the back of a mule to the nearest medical station, a journey which took almost four hours.

Conversely, there was a story of sheer luck, involving Sergeant Tucker of No. 2 Platoon of A Company, 5th Battalion. The platoon was part of the 2nd Independent Parachute Brigade Group's contribution to Operation Dragoon – a parachute assault launched from Italy on a target near St Raphaël, in the south of France, on 14 July 1944. In this operation, in support of the US 7th Army, men were dropped from 126 aircraft. Owing to a faulty Rebecca Eureka beacon, several pilots missed the DZ and the sticks of men they were carrying were scattered far afield, up to 20 miles away from the rendezvous point. Among these was Sergeant Tucker's company. He himself landed on the roof of a building containing a large number of German soldiers, who, hearing his boots hit the tiles, immediately rushed out and loosed off in his direction. He returned the fire with his Sten gun and then signalled as if he was giving himself up. But instead he managed to convince the German commander that his patrol was completely surrounded by two divisions and that they might as well surrender or be cut to bits. They did, and he marched out with 80 German soldiers marching at the point of his Sten gun.

By then, Rome had been liberated and the Germans were in retreat across what was known as the Gothic line – between Pisa and Rimini – destroying bridges and other installations as they went. General Sir Oliver Leese, 8th Army Commander, ordered that the airborne troops should now be used to avert the German demolition attempts. Only 60 men could be spared from the 6th Parachute Battalion. Under the command of Lieutenant L. A. Fitzroy-Smith, the party was dropped in three Dakotas, while a second wave of aircraft carried dummies which were thrown out with parachutes to make the landing force look much larger. The DZ near Torricella was identified without mishap and the drop was impeccable. The raiders spent a week harrying, prodding and diverting the attention of an entire German division at a crucial time in the Allies' final push north. A dozen men were lost and half the survivors were captured as they tried to return to Allied lines. It was the last action by the 1st Airborne Division in the Italian campaign before the German armies in Italy capitulated. Vic Coxen, who had moved from the 1st Parachute Battalion to take command of the 4th when the latter moved over from North Africa, sums up those difficult months in Italy:

It had not been an easy task because Italy had a mass of natural defensive positions, valleys and good cover. The same applied to us inasmuch as we could get dug in and took fewer casualties unless a shell hit directly. One of the last we did was Salerno, to which we came up through the mountains, while the main attacking force came in by sea. We then moved up to Rome and were there for the liberation. I was invited to go and see the Pope and I said, 'Yes, but I'd like to bring the whole battalion', because there were many Irish in the 4th Battalion. Not all were Catholics, of course; some were good Ulstermen and naturally they did not come along. We were ushered in and went through, passing the Pope six abreast. It was a bit of a crush and because of it, I went past the Pope backwards. One of my Ulster sergeants stopped me when we got back.

'Did you see the Pope?' he asked me.

'Yes, I saw him,' I replied.

'Did ya get him?' he said sternly but with a flicker of humour in his eyes.

'No, I did not.'

After that, we were on standby to do any one of 12 different operations in support of the Army on the Po. We had carried out practice drops around Rome in readiness. Eventually we were flown out to be dropped on southern France, although even as we took off we knew that it was already on the cards that we might be pulled back to go to Greece, where the political war was stirring.

5

THE LONGEST DAY

The Parachute Battalions freed from engagement in North Africa had leapfrogged Italy and headed straight back home to the UK at the end of 1943 and went *en masse* into intensive training for the D-Day landings. The Allied invasion of Hitler's Fortress Europe, three years in the planning, was on the brink of realization. By April 1944 the United Kingdom had become a huge armed camp, with hundreds of ships and aircraft, thousands of tons of military hardware, millions of rounds of ammunition and 2 million troops being pulled in from their positions in the war theatres as they became available to take their place in the hugely complex invasion plans that were now emerging.

It would soon become clear that once again the airborne forces and parachute troops would spearhead the Normandy invasion. Existing units were enlarged, new ones created and by the late spring a second British airborne division, the 6th, was fully operational under the command of Major General Richard Gale, one of the great pioneers of the Parachute Brigades, with Brigadier James Hill's 3rd Parachute Brigade as the core unit. His three battalions were to be joined by a Canadian parachute battalion, along with Britain's 5th Parachute Brigade and the 6th Airlanding Brigade. Incidentally, the '6th' in the new airborne division's title was there for no other reason than to confuse the enemy, for in reality there was only one other such British division in existence. Brigadier Frederick 'Boy' Browning was appointed General Officer Commanding (GOC) of both divisions and promoted to the rank of lieutenant general.

The 6th Airborne Division went into immediate rehearsal for Operation Overlord – the D-Day landings – at airfields and training grounds all over England, along with troops from many other regiments. A vast panoply of huge military exercises were taking place across the country in the run-up to the invasion of Normandy's beaches. By the time of D-Day, 6 June 1944, the members of General Gale's 6th Airborne Division – including the 7th, 8th, 9th, 12th and 13th Parachute Battalions and the 22nd Independent Parachute Company of the Parachute Regiment – knew their parts: they were assigned the task of protecting the flank of the sea-borne invasion. Their area extended from Ouistreham to Caen and included the double water obstacle of the River Orne and the Caen Canal. While their operational strength was overshadowed by the extent of the amphibious landings, it was nonetheless absolutely crucial to the success of the whole operation, especially in the initial stages.

In the greatest sea-borne invasion ever staged, 156,000 British, American and Canadian troops would go ashore in the first 24 hours, followed over the coming weeks by an army of more than 2 million. On the other side of the Channel, Field Marshal Erwin Rommel, lately Montgomery's opposite number in North Africa, was entrusted with the German defence of this long-anticipated onslaught and made the historic observation: 'for the Allies as well as for Germans ... it will be the longest day.'

In the preparatory period the airborne and parachute units were still under strength in terms of both men and aircraft, with the result that many young, some would say green, recruits were being given rapid parachute training. It was well into the new year before sufficient aircraft from eastern Europe and North Africa came into service to provide realistic capability for the movement of so many men. On 24 April 1944, with all available aircraft by then more or less in position, the whole 6th Airborne Division was airlifted for an exercise in what was in reality a dress rehearsal for Normandy, though none of them had been officially informed of this and in fact, right to the last, every possible precaution was taken to keep the invasion plans under wraps.

It was necessary for several key operations to be rehearsed down to the finest detail. One of these would engage the talents of the 9th Battalion the Parachute Regiment (3rd Parachute Brigade) under Lieutenant Colonel Terry Otway. This unit was charged with knocking out one of the key German coastal defence positions, in darkness in double-quick time before the sea-borne troops began to come ashore. Eventually they discovered that the target was the Merville battery at Franceville Plage, which would immediately confront troops of the 3rd British Infantry Division when they made their beach landing. This was a brilliantly designed emplacement, positioned so that it could sweep the entire landing area of any invading force and knock down incoming soldiers by the hundred.

Aerial reconnaissance photographs and ground intelligence established that the battery possessed four 75mm guns built on 12-feet-high concrete ballast, surrounded by six-feet-thick concrete walls and covered with 13 feet of earth. Every access to the battery itself was through impregnable steel doors protected by 20mm guns and machine-gun posts. If that was not sufficient to keep out marauders, the 400-yard-square structure was surrounded by a 100-yard-wide minefield and a 15-feet-thick barbed-wire barrier. All land approaches to the battery had also been mined and were dotted with machine-gun positions, manned 24 hours a day, and on the seaward approaches deep anti-tank trenches had been built.

In all, it was believed that around 200 men manned the defences of this seemingly invincible fortress and the Paras had to put it out of action before the first Allied assault vessels appeared on the horizon. But how? The assault on the battery could not be left to one single attacking proposition. An ingenious network strategy which would set up attacks in waves was proposed and, if all else failed, HMS *Arethusa* would attempt to come in alone and pound the battery with her heavy stuff.

Training men for this vital assault was also a problem, in terms of both scale and approach, and it was felt that the only way to give the battalion any real chance to assess what it was up against was to assemble a mock-up as near as possible to the real thing. The site chosen was at Newbury, Berkshire, where earth-moving plant cleared an area equal in size to the battery and its immediate surrounds. A full-size model was built which included all the obstacles the assault force was likely to meet. Then the 35 officers and 600 soldiers of the 9th Battalion who were to take part in the raid rehearsed their various roles until they knew them perfectly. When it was considered that they had reached the ultimate in their proficiency, live ammunition was introduced for the last five days of rehearsals. Long briefings, reaffirming every minute detail, were held and every man was asked to draw a sketch of the battery from memory and write a brief summary of his own role on the night of the attack.

Security for this mission, as well as for numerous other special operations planned for the early hours before the dawn arrival of the invasion force, was at its highest and was tested to make sure that details were not leaking out. In this case, a number of specially trained young women, selected for their looks as well as their investigative skills, were employed to try to extract information from the troops, although the exact manner in which this was done has never been disclosed. The final piece of the jigsaw was also withheld – the name and location of the battery, which were not made known to the men until the operation was under way.

Elsewhere the units of airborne and parachute troops were being trained to protect the flanks of the invading Allied forces as they hit the beaches of northern France, attack command and communications centres and harry the German forces and cut off their movement towards the beachhead. The British 6th Airborne Division was to go in ahead of the invasion force, dropping around Ranville, north-east of Caen, to cover the landings of the

British 2nd Army coming ashore on their designated beaches, code-named Gold June and Sword. The US 82nd and 101st Airborne Divisions were to perform similar operations for the US 1st Army, landing at the beaches code-named Omaha and Utah.

The area to be taken by the 6th Airborne Division included high ground on the eastern sector around the River Orne and the Caen Canal. The 'must achieve' targets for the Paras and airborne forces on the British side of the invasion plans therefore included the Merville battery, the high ground overlooking the route forward for the advancing British troops and the bridges across the canal and river to halt an immediate counter-attack by enemy forces while the beach landings were proceeding. For this purpose, the 15th Special Service Brigade (Commandos) would provide additional firepower for the 6th Airborne Division after landing by sea.

There were additional hazards for the Paras: spiked poles and a nasty selection of other obstacles erected by the Germans on likely DZs and glider landing sites. Companies of Pathfinders would have to be dropped well in advance to guide them in with Rebecca Eureka beacons. As was always the case, the Parachute Battalion commanders gave intense briefings to their men so that every one of them – not just their company commanders – knew what was expected. This ensured that if the men were dropped in the wrong place, or became separated from their company, they would at least have a basic knowledge of the area, and could attempt to link up with one unit or another. Brigadier Hill's words of encouragement before they left were prophetic: 'Gentlemen, in spite of your excellent training and orders, do not be daunted if chaos reigns. It undoubtedly will.' Prophetic indeed: he himself dropped into six feet of mud and slime and struggled for four hours across ditches full of deep water to reach solid ground, and many of his men drowned in the attempt.

And so the final stages of this massive military transaction began to shuffle into place, like a giant game of chess, and on 5

June the convoys of ships, aircraft and gliders packed with the first instalment of men, vehicles, guns and tanks were ready to begin their journey to the coast of Normandy.

At midnight, under a cloudy, moonless sky, Pathfinders of the 22nd Independent Parachute Company took off ahead of the rest and within an hour or so they became the first troops to land in France, planting their Rebecca Eureka beacons to guide in the first wave of airborne forces. Apart from the Merville battery, the Paras were given key targets, such as the crucial bridges over the River Orne and the Caen Canal, to foil any German rush towards the landing areas. The two Parachute Brigades began their drops half an hour after the arrival of the Pathfinder Company, followed through the night by gliders carrying the Divisional HQ and the 4th Anti-Tank Battery of the Royal Artillery.

Heavy cloud made it pitch-dark down below and visual contact with ground features was difficult. Wind and air currents also caused trouble, and troops were widely scattered and had no choice but to set out on foot to try to find the rest of their chums. For some, it would be the end of the war – dozens were captured, wounded or shot as they came down. And despite all the planning the first and most crucial raid on the Merville battery, which fell largely to the 9th Battalion, did not run to the plan, which called for two parties to be dropped in advance for rendezvous and reconnaissance tasks, and a third group to create diversionary fire, while the rest of the battalion, with a contingent of Royal Engineers, formed the main assault force. Five gliders were packed with anti-tank guns, jeeps, ladders for scaling the anti-tank ditches and explosives. Demolition parties carried Bangalore Torpedoes: long metal pipes designed to blow a safe route through minefields and other enemy defences. Three other gliders were piloted and occupied by men who had responded to calls for volunteers for a specific task, well knowing the dangers, and these were trained to perform the high-risk venture of crash-landing on top of the battery. The 50 soldiers in the gliders would, in theory, then leap out and attack the battery from within while the remainder of the battalion blasted its way through the perimeter.

Unfortunately, the weather upset these meticulous plans, even before the Germans opened up their defence. High winds played havoc with the drops, scattering troops from all the battalions involved over several miles, and one batch – as will soon be seen – came down near the River Dives, which the pilot had mistaken for the Orne. The three gliders to be crash-landed on the Merville battery never made it. One came adrift from its towing plane and ditched, the second, blown off by the wind, landed in an orchard 50 yards outside the perimeter of the battery and the third was released too early and came in on a nearby village.

By 02.50 hours, when the attack operation should have been under way, the 9th Battalion could muster a mere 150 men out of the 35 officers and 600 other ranks who had been training for weeks for the Merville project. It was able to field only one sniping party, it had no six-pounder guns and just one machine-gun, no jeeps or trailers, no sappers, no mine detectors or glider-borne stores. Those remaining faced the seemingly impossible task of putting the battery out of operation ahead of the land forces coming ashore. One further setback almost had tragic consequences when an aerial bombardment on the battery by Lancaster bombers missed the target area completely and hit the battalion's forward contingent.

Even so, the group managed to get through the battery's outer fences and blew a path through the minefield with Bangalore Torpedoes. The battalion commander decided that his hugely depleted and lightly armed force should make an immediate assault on the target as best they could, regardless of the cost, and as they edged forward they came under heavy artillery and machine-gun fire. Three of the enemy machine-guns were miraculously silenced by the battalion's own solitary machine-gunner. And another stroke of good fortune came when the party aboard the glider which crashed into the orchard disembarked to confront a German platoon being sent to reinforce the battery and engaged them in a battle lasting almost four hours. This enabled the remainder of the battalion to make an heroic charge on the battery through two breaches in the outer perimeter and force themselves into the very heart of the compound despite strong German resistance, until they reached the point of virtual hand-to-hand combat – at which the Paras excelled.

Fierce running battles ensued for three hours, their ferocity evident from the casualty figures – five of the battalion's officers and 65 men were killed or wounded and only 20 of the German defending force were still standing when the latter finally surrendered. And so the Merville battery was won with just 45 minutes to spare before the deadline when the HMS *Arethusa* was to have begun a bombardment of the compound unless a signal to abort had been received from the 9th Battalion. Although losses had been heavy, the Para assault force undoubtedly saved hundreds of lives among the thousands of British troops who would soon be wading ashore.

The battalion was down to just 80 men at the end of the task, yet it reorganized, picked up other stragglers and moved on immediately to take its second objective that night, which was high ground near Le Plein, where once again it was heavily outnumbered by a defending force, but managed to hold out until reinforced later that day by the 1st Special Service Brigade. From a position of near desperation, in which almost everything that could go wrong had gone wrong, the battalion completed its objectives in magnificent style.

Elsewhere the remaining battalions of the 3rd and 5th Brigades had similarly mixed fortunes, many being dropped far from the designated DZs. Brigadier Hill, leading the 3rd Brigade and a large number of Canadians, came down in treacherous and watery terrain near the River Dives and the brigadier was himself wounded once again, although he struggled on to his RV. The 1st

Canadian Battalion also mustered enough men to proceed with their action, blowing up the bridges at Varaville and Robehomme virtually under the noses of the defending forces. And so, despite the widely scattered airborne landing, the objectives assigned to the two Parachute Brigades and their comrades in the 6th Airborne Division were being achieved as the night progressed, ahead of the invasion of the greatest assault yet mounted against Hitler's forces. As the thousands of troops and their massive armoury came ashore, along with the remainder of the air-landing troops, the great saga of D-Day gradually began to unfold. Nor was the 6th Airborne Division able to pull back once the beachhead was under control, as had been planned. Pulled into the general defensive actions, it added one more famous addition to its battle honours – an outstanding performance around the town of Bréville, overlooking the strategically important Ranville area.

The battles around Bréville had raged for 48 hours when, early on 10 June 1944, the Germans succeeded in penetrating the Allied line between the 1st Commando Brigade and the 3rd Parachute Brigade. In an attempt to capitalize on the manoeuvre, the enemy launched a dramatic fresh assault aimed at splitting the divisional area – the area assigned to the 6th Airborne Division – in two and breaking through to the invasion beaches. This attack was repeatedly beaten off by the 13th Battalion over the next 36 hours, with great loss to the enemy, and a counter-attack by the 7th Battalion restored the situation, leaving 200 enemy dead and 150 prisoners on the battlefield. The Germans, however, still maintained their position at Bréville and a further attack by the 153rd British Infantry Brigade was beaten off with heavy casualties on both sides.

By 12 June the position was critical. The Germans launched two major assaults with infantry and armour on the positions of the 9th Battalion, which managed to fight them off but was reduced to just 200 men. A counter-attack by a company of the 1st

Canadian Parachute Battalion led by the already wounded Brigadier Hill, turned the tide once again, but by then the only divisional reserve was a weakened 12th Battalion and the 6th Airborne Division was growing weaker by the hour. Bréville had to be captured and placed firmly in Allied hands.

On that day, after ten hours of battle, General Gale made his decision: the 6th would go back into the attack immediately and hit the Germans as they took a brief respite. At 10.30 that night the 12th Battalion, now well below half its strength, was joined by a company of the 12th Devons, a single squadron of tanks and the 22nd Independent Parachute Company for a last-gasp assault. Disaster struck at the outset when their own shellfire fell short of their start line, killing the Paras' commanding officer and the Devons' company commander and seriously wounding many others. The British troops then faced intense enemy counter fire, but they rallied under their platoon commanders and non-commissioned officers. In what turned into a bloody, bitter scrap, with much hand-to-hand fighting, they finally forced the Germans from the town. At the cost of eight officers and 133 other ranks, Bréville was finally and firmly in Allied possession after what proved to be the decisive engagement of this sector in defence of the beachhead.

Thereafter the badly wounded 6th Airborne Division remained in position, protecting the left flank, troubled only by minor attacks although called upon for some aggressive patrolling. Then after a brief period of consolidation, it formed part of the general advance forward and across the Seine. By the third week of August, the 6th had fought its way ahead over 60 miles of defended countryside, largely on foot because of the shortage of vehicles, had taken 1000 prisoners and had freed 400 square miles of French territory from Nazi occupation.

Once again, the sheer guts and fighting skills of the Paras had been proved beyond doubt, especially since they started out from such a weakened position, with so many of their troops scattered

93

across the countryside and their specialist skills lost from their units. As for the men themselves, isolation from their own units could be traumatic as they scrambled across hostile terrain behind enemy lines to reach designated positions. In the first two days of the D-Day landings alone, the 6th Airborne Division suffered 786 casualties and another 1200 men were dropped or landed in the wrong places, cast adrift in enemy territory.

These may have been modest figures, amid the wider picture, but they conceal dozens of stories of inspired heroics and bravery and most, from the point of view of the individual concerned, were considered 'not unusual – just an exercise in self-survival for which we had been trained'. Douglas Baines from Goole was one of the thousands in the 'missing' category of Allied troops after the Normandy landings. He was a young rookie paratrooper on the D-Day invasion and one of the many for whom the drop into action did not go according to plan. His account provides a suitable link between the Normandy invasion and the next and most famous of the Paras' contributions to the war effort: the attempt to form a bridgehead over the Rhine.

Baines had volunteered for the Army as soon as he was 18, joining the West Yorkshire Regiment. He remembers that the pay was 14 shillings (70p) a week. After sending his mother seven shillings, he was left with very little. He heard there was an extra two shillings on offer for joining the Parachute Regiment, and applied. Volunteers were being sought to make up the new 6th Airborne Division, but even so it still wasn't easy to get in. There was to be no cutback in standards just because there was a shortage of men. On completing parachute training, he went on a mortar and then a machine-gun course. Still in his teens, Baines found himself among those engaged in the preparations for D-Day and in the section who were to be dropped near the River Orne:

We were well briefed and I carried 200,000 francs escape money, rifle and ammunition. We were supposed to meet in Ranville, at the brickworks, but the RAF pilot missed the River Orne and dropped us miles away, right in the middle of the River Dives. When I came down, I thought it was a road I was landing on in the darkness. But it turned out to be a river. The descent was fine, but I came down with a big splash. The tide was out on the Dives but it was very deep in mud and slime. I sank up to my waist and thought I was going to drown in it. I freed myself from my kitbag [which was attached to a paratrooper's leg for the drop] and chute, but even so it was a real struggle to get out. I managed to hang on to my rifle and about 50 rounds of ammunition. I lost everything else. It was pitch-black. I couldn't see any of the others. I called out but got no reply. It took me an hour and a quarter to pull myself to the bank. It was heavy going. However, one of my unit who was on the same plane came up. We commiserated with each other about the cock-up. We had no idea where we were. There were no others around. The landscape was totally unidentifiable because the Germans had swamped the area by opening the sluice gates when the tide came in, to make it impossible terrain for tanks. It was pretty impossible for us too.

We could see nothing and had to tread very warily as we set off to make our way ahead; there was noise in the distance, guns and screams, but no way of telling how far away it was. As we set off, we soon hit anti-tank ditches dug by the Germans which were filled with water. We fell into several; they were anything from four to six feet deep; you could lose a man in there with no problem.

We made our way in the direction of the noise, again not really knowing what we were walking into. We discovered we were between the River Dives and the Dives Canal. We were stuck there for several hours and soon after daybreak a little Frenchman came by, paddling a small boat. He saw we were British soldiers and told us to get in, and he took us back to a farm on the outskirts of Cabourg [almost on the coast at the mouth of the Dives] and hid us in a barn. He told us the place was swarming with Germans and they called there every day for milk. The farmer was very kind to us.

It was only then that we realized that there must have been many Paras in the same position as ourselves who had been dropped in the wrong place, in the middle of German lines, and were struggling to find a way out. Somehow, the farm buildings we were taken to became a haven for them. Eventually others who had gone astray on the landings were either brought in by members of the family or stumbled across the buildings as they tried to make their way across country. Very soon there were around 30 of us being hidden there – all Paras from different units. God knows how many had been wandering around, or how many were captured.

The Germans were all around and some of us decided we had to move out and try to get to Allied lines. We were also a danger for the farmer and his family. They were absolutely heroic. We heard after the war that one day not long after we left, the Germans came and searched the farm and found some .303 ammunition in the hayloft. They blew up the farm and took the male members of the family and shot them. When we left the farm, we could see barrage balloons in the far distance, and we decided to try to make our way towards the action. We came across a deserted farm and holed up there for a while. We could only move at night. During the day we could hear German troops, presumably reinforcements, coming in, quite often by horse and cart. Once, we were so close to their encampment we could hear the cooks singing in the mornings.

We discovered some RAF panniers which had been dropped and we managed to bring those in. They contained rations which lasted us for about five days. We tried several times to reach British lines. We were moving parallel to the coast and the Germans were reinforcing all the while. It was difficult to find a place to break through. We took shelter in an isolated farm building. One day we saw a German officer and two other ranks approaching, obviously to check it out, but we had removed all the wooden railway sleepers that had been laid down as footpaths and so they decided they didn't want to get wet and turned back. They shelled the barn a couple of times and took the roof off. We moved on and found a similar building. By now we were out of food and the guy who I was with, named Peacock, used to be a butcher in civilian life. He killed a cow and butchered it, so we had meat and potatoes, which we got from the fields.

We now headed out towards the coast road to see if we could get through that way, and managed to avoid the Germans up to a place called Colombelle. We were going through a forest; it didn't give us much cover because the trees had been shelled and suddenly we found ourselves surrounded by Germans and so our escapade in Normandy was at an end. We were taken to the encampment nearby where we were interrogated: name, rank and number. It became clear to us at that point that the Germans didn't actually know the precise point of the Para landings – simply because so many had been dropped in the wrong place.

As far as I could make out, there were British Paras wandering around all over the place, many of them well away from the original dropping zone. They took us to a holding POW camp; a caged compound where we joined about 150 other prisoners – all ranks, including an RAMC [Royal Army Medical Corps) lieutenant colonel, an RAF fighter pilot and many Paras. There was very little food and we were eventually moved by coach to Paris, where we were put into another cage, where the Germans more or less put us on show. Parisians came along and clapped – not because we had been caught, but because we were British. We stayed five days in Paris and then we were moved to Châlons [-sur-Marne, 120 miles east of Paris] and put into a much larger cage, which included a whole mixed bag of forces, including Americans and Canadians, until there was enough to fill a train load, and we were packed into cattle trucks to be taken to Germany. *En route*, the RAF came and strafed it, of course.

The journey across country was slow and laborious. The prisoners were cramped, hungry and thirsty. On one of the occasional stops, Baines had managed to get a look under the wagons and calculated that there was a clear way through the floor if a hole could be cut in the wooden timbers. The only tool to perform this operation was a small knife he had hidden in his sock, but it was sufficient to allow him and another prisoner from his battalion to begin gouging out an escape hole. They had been aboard the train for four or five days before they had cut a hole large enough to get through, covering it with straw every time a German guard came to inspect them.

One night, when the train slowed over an incline, they smashed out the last of the wood and dropped down on to the track and lay motionless until it passed over them. They discovered that they were still in France, near Bar-le-Duc, around 100 miles from the German border. For the rest of the night they hid, but when it was light they saw a farmer working in a field and cautiously approached him. He led them to a nearby farm building and gave them some eggs. There they remained for three days, until a French Resistance group arrived. Baines continues his story:

They knew exactly who we were and obviously we had been checked out. We joined up with them and started going out with them, hitting the Germans. It was a group of about 30. They frightened me to death. They were making these plastic bombs, which were pretty primitive; they weren't careful at all. The Germans were in the area and we used to go out at night-time to blow up a few wagons and communications, and sniping. One night we heard all these tanks moving out – it turned out the Germans were retreating and in came the Americans.

The group turned out to see the Americans coming through. The jeeps were constantly running out of gas and in one of them was General Patton, whom we approached when he stopped and suggested we might join up with him. He told us to fuck off, although he did give us some cigarettes. He couldn't be bothered with us. We moved on alone and came upon some more American

MT [Motor Transport] people. They were heading for Paris. One of them gave us a lift in a 15-hundredweight truck that was filled with boxes of KP rations ['Kitchen Police' rations to be eaten on the move]. We helped ourselves to a couple of boxes.

We had a couple of nights in Paris and discovered they had opened up what was called a Red Ball supply route to the front. No one was particularly interested in us and so we got a succession of lifts back to the coast. We managed to get on a boat back to England and ended up at Tilbury docks, and finally reported to a police station in Waterloo. We were questioned and eventually interrogated by MI5 to establish our story. One of the officers who questioned me asked how I knew that the tide was out when we dropped into the River Dives at one o'clock in the morning. I told him that if it hadn't been I would have drowned! They gave us ten shillings to get a train back to Salisbury Plain.

There I went back into the Nissen hut which I had been in before we left and reported to the sergeant major, who said, 'Where the fuck have you been?'

So I told him.

Baines was given a month's leave and then discovered that his jump pay had been stopped. He was still a Para and expected to be jumping again as soon as he was back in his unit. He complained and was summoned before Lieutenant Colonel Ken Darling, who listened to his story and was so enthralled by the account that he promptly made Baines his personal driver in Headquarters Company.

It is necessary now to leap ahead momentarily to complete Baines's story. In December 1944 he found himself back in action when the 6th Airborne Division was hurriedly moved to the Ardennes to fight off strong counter-attacks by the Germans, and once that operation was completed, it was on hold for the Rhine crossings. In the waiting period, a driver of one of the jeeps that was to be dropped by glider was killed in a road accident.

Colonel Darling asked me if I'd take his place. So I went with Headquarters Company with the jeep and trailer for the Rhine crossing. The jeep was loaded up and the trailer filled with mortar bombs. We were loaded aboard a Horsa glider ready for dropping. We had been told there would be a clear run because there was no anti-aircraft fire or artillery, but of course when we got there there were 88s all round the dropping zone and we were shot down. We weren't far off the deck when a shell hit the front of the glider, took the whole front off. We just nose-dived to the ground. Both the pilots were killed and I was wounded. I was hit in the knee and I struggled out of the glider and crawled under the trailer. Then I thought to myself, 'You're a bloody idiot – you're lying under a pile of mortar bombs.' I tried to get out but couldn't move again and the next thing I knew an RAMC stretcher party were taking me to a nearby farm, where they put me in plaster of Paris from the chest downwards. I was there for about two days before they brought me to Brussels, and then on a plane back to England. As far as I knew, I had just injured my knee – until I got into hospital and found I had a broken femur as well. I finished up at a military hospital at Basingstoke, where two surgeons from Harley Street were working.

I was in hospital, back and forth, from March 1945 to 1947, with numerous operations on my knee, until finally, on 5 November 1947, my left leg was amputated.

6

ARNHEM: THE BRIDGE TOO FAR

Before the Falklands War, Arnhem was the single most famous name in the history of parachute and airborne troops. Just as John Wayne, Robert Mitchum and co. portrayed the events, including paratroop action, in *The Longest Day*, in Richard Attenborough's *A Bridge Too Far* a galaxy of American and British stars played some of the soldiers who took leading roles in the extraordinary mission to capture the bridge at Arnhem. Many of these men have been mentioned already in these pages, and their finest hour – and for many their last on this earth – is now recounted.

Interestingly, reviewers of *A Bridge Too Far* pointed out a problem with the film: it failed to make the military tactics clear. As will soon become clear, there was a very good reason for this. Some have charitably described the Arnhem operation as a 'magnificent disaster'. It was magnificent only in the effort, courage and sheer bloody-minded spirit of the men involved. Everything else *was* a disaster, hugely costly in life and limb, hurried in its conception, ill-informed in terms of intelligence, devoid of proper communications and badly handled by both its planners and those managers who stood back from the action and watched, most often from the safety of the other side of the English Channel. Nor did anyone ever apologize for such an almighty cock-up. In the accounts that follow, largely from the mouths of those who were there, the true story of that bridge too far will unfold.

Arnhem was already more than a twinkle in the eyes of several ambitious generals as the Allied Forces pushed south and west from the Normandy landings after some stubborn resistance from German Panzer divisions. Paris was liberated on 25 August and by then the Allied war machine was planning its next major objective: to cross the Rhine and move into the German industrial heartland of the Ruhr – and, perhaps, to end the war by Christmas 1944. By the first week of September the Allies had routed the opposition, opened the Germans' Western Front and liberated Brussels, and after moving 250 miles in five days the ground forces were within 65 miles of the Rhine. But there was a problem brewing.

General Eisenhower, as Supreme Allied Commander, had assumed direct control of the Allied land forces in Europe on 1 September from Montgomery, who reverted to commander of his own 21st Army Group, with promotion to field marshal as recompense. Eisenhower's staff advised him that the rate of advance could not be sustained. With the Germans still holding many of the Channel ports, supplies had to be run from Normandy along a narrow, ever-lengthening route. As already observed by Douglas Baines during his encounter with General Patton, vehicles were running out of fuel, ammunition and rations as they moved onwards. Montgomery still wanted to press ahead towards the Rhine while the Americans covered his back; if successful, this could, he suggested, cut the war by six months. Eisenhower refused, not least because the American public would not be best pleased to see the British winning the war.

Eventually a compromise was reached. Montgomery would try to form a bridgehead over the Rhine, using the 1st Allied Airborne Army – commanded by an American, Lieutenant General Lewis Brereton, with Lieutenant General 'Boy' Browning as his number two. The group, which had been held in reserve in the UK since July, consisted of the British 1st Airborne Division, Poland's 1st Parachute Brigade and America's 18th Airborne Corps, the last comprising the 82nd and 101st Airborne Divisions. The airborne forces were jubilant, especially the British units, who between them had seen 17 separate operational plans made and cancelled since they returned from Italy and had spent their time training, all the while smarting that the 6th had been used for Normandy.

Now, they and the American units were to be dropped behind the German lines to capture and hold 12 key bridges over the Rhine, across which elements of the British 2nd Army, notably the XXX Corps under the command of Lieutenant General Brian Horrocks and led by the Guards Armoured Division, would dash and establish themselves on the north bank of the river. The last and most vital of these bridges, which were to be taken progressively, was the main bridge at Arnhem. According to Montgomery's plan, this would be the target of Britain's 1st Airborne Division – or more precisely, as it turned out, the 2nd Parachute Battalion. Once the bridge was captured, they would hold it for a length of time – it turned out to be either one or two days, depending on who is telling the story – until the Guards Armoured Division arrived to relieve them.

Market Garden, as the operation was code-named, was launched just seven days after Eisenhower gave his approval. The logistics were a nightmare. The operation involved the landing, by parachute and glider, of more than 10,000 men, along with their vehicles, jeeps, wagons, mortars, medical teams, engineers, explosives, headquarters staff, general supplies and so on. And once on the ground, they could be resupplied only by air. The sheer weight of men – amounting to three and a half divisions – would require a vast number of aircraft if they were to be shifted in a single day and thus achieve the vital element of surprise.

It was calculated that to get them on the ground in one lift would call for 3790 aircraft: around 2500 to drop the parachute troops and the remainder to tow gliders bearing the infantry and hardware. As there were only 1545 available, two-thirds of which were American Dakotas, it would be necessary to make three separate lifts, spread over three days. The RAF were ready to consider a quick turnaround and, by making night drops, complete the movement within the space of 24 hours. But the proposal was quashed by Lieutenant General Brereton because of the inability of the American troop-carrier aircrews to fly at night, and because of the experiences in Normandy, when night-time landings left so many men scattered and adrift.

Given those restrictions, it was necessary to make a progressive landing of the force, which somewhat negated the principal aim of their arrival on German-held territory: to take the enemy by surprise. The US divisions elected to drop all their parachute troops on the first day and bring in the heavy equipment and glider-borne infantry during the following two days. This proposal worried many of the US battalion commanders who were to lead the men into action, since it meant that their assault would be totally reliant on the lightly armed paratroops, with no artillery or transport for at least 24 hours.

The British commander, Major General Roy Urquhart, decided to split his force, so that battalions of the 1st Parachute Brigade and the bulk of his 1st Airlanding Brigade would go in on the first day. The 4th Parachute Brigade would land on the second day, and the remainder of the air-landing troops and the 1st Polish Independent Parachute Brigade would go on the third day. This arrangement threw up its own problems for the British in that the only suitable DZs and LZs were up to eight miles from the Arnhem bridge, and the troops would face a long and exposed march to reach the target in the required time. There was considerable concern among the British battalions that priority would be given to the two American drops – even though the British objective was farther away.

It was also noted that the American troops would be nearest to the approaching 2nd Army and therefore would be relieved first at the bridge at Nijmegen. British Service cameraman Mike Lewis, who was at the briefings for Market Garden because he was going along to take an official record of the operation, could not help feeling that when this was explained to those present, the British officer imparting the information sounded almost apologetic. Lewis explains:

That staff officer was going as far as he could to express his criticism, his doubts about what was taking place. Had anybody protested? To be dropped over two days, the furthest drop away from the land army, put the British in the most vulnerable position. It was perfectly obvious they'd be out on a limb. We should have had all the aircraft on day one, gone in mob-handed first. As we came out, I said, 'This is going to be a disaster.' Others with me agreed.

Even so, the British commanders – publicly at least – seemed to believe that the undertaking was not beyond them, a belief based upon the intelligence concerning the likely opposition. And therein lay another major error. Reports submitted by the 21st Army Group and the 2nd Army in the days leading up to the Arnhem assault suggested that the areas in question were held only by a thin scattering of German troops. A report from the Dutch resistance that a large contingent of heavily equipped SS troops had arrived close to Arnhem was discounted as being unreliable. Forty-eight hours before the operation was due to be launched, however, further reports pointed to the presence of the 9th and 10th SS Panzer Divisions resting in the area on their way back from Normandy. This information came from Allied intelligence and was reported directly to Eisenhower's chief of staff, Lieutenant General Walter Bedell Smith. Eisenhower was informed immediately, but passed the buck to Montgomery, who dismissed the reports with little more than a wave of his hands. Yet there was already confirmation available. A major in the 1st Airborne Corps' intelligence section produced Dutch resistance reports and aerial photographs which he claimed supported the theory of large concentrations of German forces. The reconnaissance photos showed tanks and heavy armour. He sent them directly to Lieutenant General Browning. There was no going back, however, and the major who had produced these photographs was relieved of his job in Brussels and sent back to the UK, allegedly suffering from nervous exhaustion. Operation

Market Garden went ahead as planned. A huge scale sand model, 12 feet wide by 20 feet long, was quickly built from aerial reconnaissance photographs, showing every one of the bridges, every house and copse, and all possible DZs in the area.

Major General Urquhart's key men in the British strategy were the Parachute Battalions, whose commanders included veterans of previous operations, including Lieutenant Colonel Johnny Frost (of Bruneval, Oudna and Sicily fame) who became a crucial figure as the disaster of Arnhem began to unravel. Frost recalls:

The briefing [for Market Garden] was at Brigade Headquarters, near Grantham, two days before the operation took place on 17 September. I and the 2nd Parachute Battalion were to take three bridges over the Rhine; first the railway bridge, which was outside the town [Arnhem] by about four miles, then a pontoon bridge which was right inside the town and finally the big main bridge. I was to have some part of my force on the south side of the main bridge but the bulk inside, on the north side. By the time we had this bridge we hoped that the rest of the brigade would have got into Arnhem and we would be holding a perimeter north of the bridge.

It seemed perfectly feasible because the information we were given about the enemy was such that there didn't seem to be very much opposition. We were told that there was no question of any enemy armour, that they would probably consist of a few SS recruits and a good many Dutchmen who were being trained in the vicinity of Arnhem, and otherwise Luftwaffe personnel actually manning the anti-aircraft guns. I did think that having to take three bridges was asking rather a lot. I wasn't at all happy at having my force split by the river. I would very much have preferred if we had been given the task of taking the north end of the bridges and somebody else had been told to take the south end of the bridges by dropping south of the river. There was really very little time to raise it. There was a great sense of emergency... The briefing took about an hour and I just drove back to my headquarters, got the maps out and had a look at the thing and decided on a rough plan and then ordered the company commanders and everybody to present themselves at a certain time.

The final countdown went very much according to plan. By this time the American aircrews who were dropping us and all the marshalling personnel knew their stuff very well. The weather was perfect – clear, fine, cloudless, very little wind, ideal parachuting weather. We began taking off from a group of airfields in Lincolnshire which looked after the American Air Force. I was very optimistic. The German Army had taken the most tremendous hiding in Normandy. All the information was that they were a beaten force, retreating more or less in disorder back to behind the Siegfried Line and into Germany, so I was expecting a fairly easy battle. We knew that the whole of the British Army was coming up to cross over the bridges after we'd taken them. They were fresh, they had been rested, re-equipped; one could see absolutely no reason why the thing shouldn't go according to plan…

Ahead of the main body of troops were the Pathfinders of the 21st Independent Parachute Company, under the command of Major B. A. 'Boy' Wilson, who were to mark the dropping and landing zones for the first lift. Their numbers included Private John Stanleigh, until recently a German citizen, whose father had served in the German Imperial Army and was wounded at Verdun, for which he was awarded the Iron Cross. They were a Jewish family and with the arrival of the Nazis they were persecuted, lost their business and were sent to concentration camps. John managed to get out and into Britain, where he had relatives in Liverpool. He changed his name, volunteered for the Army in 1940, went into the Pioneer Corps and eventually moved to the 21st Independent Parachute Company:

We had been on standby for weeks in Oxfordshire, training for several plans that were raised, discussed and dropped. We'd been back from Italy for nine months and really done nothing but training and exercises with the Americans and the RAF in all sorts of places, and we were getting a bit fed up. After all, we were disappointed that on D-Day the 6th Airborne Division had been used instead of the 1st; we felt let down. This inactivity was difficult to cope with. Ours [the Pathfinder Company of the 21st Independent Parachute Company] was a specialist unit: we used special equipment to bring in gliders or other airborne divisions at a certain place at the right time, day or night. We had special infrared lights and during the daytime we used coloured panels which were laid out on the ground which helped the pilots to release the gliders or the airborne troops in a certain position, allowing for the wind direction. We used to get there, as we did at Arnhem, four or five hours before the Division got there. That was our normal routine to be there well ahead of the combat units. So the provisions that were made were no different from what we'd done throughout the exercises which took place in the UK prior to the real thing, in 1944.

We had, in a section, a Sten gun, two-inch light mortar, a sniper and the normal issue of ordinary 36-percussion grenades and special phosphorus grenades, number 38 and Very pistols, marking equipment and that sort of thing. We took off about eight o'clock in the morning from Burford in Oxfordshire and two and a half hours later we landed outside of Oosterbeek, east of Arnhem. It was a lovely morning and as we came down we could hear the church bells ringing. It was a routine drop. All our containers arrived in good order and we set ourselves up in the wood very close to the first DZ. We weren't very far from the GHQ dropping zone where Major Wilson, our commanding officer, spotted some Germans. One of the Germans was firing at him, so in a typical Hussar manner he walked up to them and started to shout at them, 'What the bloody hell do you think you're doing, firing at British officers?' And they put their weapons down. He said to one of our corporals, 'Arrest these men and take them away.' And that was it. They were firing at us as we came down, you see. After all, they were having a picnic or something in a field and suddenly there were parachutes coming down that weren't their own. They were a bit elderly, I must admit, but still I thought it was typical British officer. I don't suppose that's been recorded before.

He just used sheer psychological pressure. The Germans were very frightened of him – he didn't even pull his revolver. Apart from that one episode things went absolutely according to plan. We laid out our panels, the right colours in the right place. There were three platoons in the company and each platoon worked on the DZ allocated to it. And two hours later the first gliders started to arrive. We also worked a radar set which receives from the aircraft a signal on a certain wavelength and sends it back on another wavelength. It's called a Rebecca Eureka [beacon]; it gives the pilot, normally, a clear idea on what course he is and what he's heading for. So we turned on the Eurekas at the right time on the right code and the gliders came along. There were only one or two accidents on the part of the gliders and then they disembarked. They opened the back and out came the jeeps and the guns, anti-tank guns. And they just set off and we had to wait until they were out of the way.

I would say there must have been 50, 60 gliders at my particular DZ. The Horsas came first, each held about 20 men. Some had fewer men than jeeps; some had 17-pounder guns with ammunition. They were light artillery, parachute artillery. We lost two gliders; that's to say they didn't land properly, they buried themselves in the ground and I think there were two or three casualties straight away. But for such a large number of gliders coming down it wasn't surprising. It was quite a good average anyway. The area was flat and fortunately there were no dikes.

Back in England, the progressive take-off of a vast fleet of aircraft and tugs with gliders went ahead more or less as planned over the coming hours, each wave surrounded by a protecting force of fighters. Bombers went ahead to give the Germans some diversionary harassment. John Frost and his 2nd Parachute Battalion were among the leading formation:

We had all the Sunday papers, which we used to read avidly. Of course one could smoke and eat and so on. Then, when we got over Holland, we gradually began to see the details that we expected to see and finally the series of rivers. I always used to jump number one, so I was in the door and could make quite certain that we were going to land exactly where we expected, and we did. A large number of fighters and fighter-bombers were escorting us and all the known flak positions had been attacked. I don't say they had been taken out but they had been attacked, so we expected no opposition.

Descent and landing went well and I had a good look round to see what was happening to everybody else before we headed off to our rendezvous where I was to meet my Battalion Headquarters. Immediately I became aware of how badly the wireless sets were working. On the dropping zone itself it was easy enough to see; I could see my companies forming up in the places I expected them to form up so I had no worries then. The terrain was very flat and open, but once we left the dropping zone and got into the country it was very heavily treed and, after a very short time, built-up as well. This had a very unfortunate effect. All our training had been taking place in Lincolnshire, which was much more open country. With these rather small wirelesses you almost need visual contact to have really good reception. This was very much limited by the trees and the buildings.

Another problem was that we started meeting civilians straight away, people on bicycles and people welcoming us. They were crying out, 'How lovely to see you, how nice, we've been waiting for so long.' The one thing that did worry them was: Were we many? Were we going to have enough chaps to deal with the enemy? As we marched on there were many little villages and settlements. The Dutch all came to their gates to give us what they could, mostly milk and apples. Some offered their cars, but we did not take them up on that.

It was very nice but it became a little bit of an embarrassment in a way. The whole thing seemed a little bit incongruous, I think that's the word. We were marching on our journey toward the bridges three-quarters of an hour after landing... One little party of Germans turned up in a lorry and an armoured car and they were speedily dealt with and taken prisoner. We were around seven miles from the first of our target bridges ... at Oosterbeek. We did meet pockets of resistance, which we dealt with as quickly as we possibly could without deploying. We were not seriously held up at that stage – not until my first objective, which was the railway bridge. My C Company had been briefed to get on to the railway bridge fairly quickly, with covering of machine-gun fire and mortar fire. This they achieved without much trouble but when the leading platoon was about halfway across, the bridge was blown up and they were forced to come back and unable to cross.

I left C Company to deal with that problem and we moved on, but when we gradually got into the outskirts of Arnhem opposition became stronger. There was no doubt that we would have to deploy one company to try and get round. This I did. My B Company was told to move up on the left on to some high ground called Den Brink. This manoeuvre was enough to allow the A Company, the leading company, to squeeze on down the road past them, then past the Rhine Pavilion Hotel, which was rather a landmark, and down the edge of the river and into the town.

Frost's arrival at the main target seemed almost too easy. So far, everything had gone according to plan. Resistance had been light and they had marched speedily on to their objective. Even so, he was worried that he was now short-handed although, of course, he expected that other units from the brigade would follow on and join him. The remainder of the troops in the first lift were still landing and forming up at their designated rendezvous to march forward. The 1st and 3rd Battalions were also to head for the bridge, but taking separate routes from that taken by Frost's 2nd Battalion. The 1st Battalion, held initially in reserve, was to bring up the rear. Frost's battalion – minus B and C Companies, now otherwise deployed – began to take up its position at its objective, but the euphoria of a relatively easy approach to the target was soon to be challenged:

We all arrived at the north end of the main bridge with what was really just one company, A Company, my own Headquarters Company, Brigade Headquarters and the support company, B Company. The last-named had been detached to take the high ground at Den Brink and C Company was involved at the railway bridge, so it would be some time before they could disentangle. We had gone on as hard as we could. Once we got to the main bridge it was getting dark and so we, as quickly as possible, occupied buildings which dominated the approaches to the north end.

There was one big old government building and a sort of factory building. We had been told that the Dutch underground had been very much penetrated and it would be very unwise to rely too much on any offers of help that they gave us in the town. By this time, although we'd managed to occupy the buildings fairly quietly, our main aim was to get across the bridge to the far side. So one of the A Company platoons started to move across. It's a horribly dangerous thing to do even in the half-light, because you only need one machine-gun on the far end to cause very heavy casualties and indeed that is what happened. Before they'd gone very far machine-guns from the far end opened up. Bullets were splattering off the road and on to the girders beside the bridge, and that leading platoon had quite a few casualties and had to come back.

The platoon was led by Lieutenant A. J. McDermott, whose 15 men repeatedly tried to force their way across until ordered to withdraw. A second attempt was made soon after by Lieutenant

Jack Grayburn and his platoon, one of several attacks he led over the next 48 hours that demonstrated his courage and steadfastness but which sadly culminated in his death in the attempt to hold the bridge. He was awarded a posthumous Victoria Cross, one of five which were to be won at Arnhem during the next nine days. Frost continues his account:

It was obvious to me that it was unlikely that we were going to be able to get across the bridge with the resources I had available to me without having unacceptable casualties. Enemy opposition had been rather sporadic. It now began to be very much more in evidence. The other companies still hadn't emerged yet and I wanted to get to the other side ... so I sent my chief engineer down to where the pontoon bridge was. This, he discovered, had been dismantled by the Germans and was no longer going to be a means of getting across the river. That made me all the more certain that there was no possibility of our getting across the river that night. Anyway, we had few enough people as it was to hold the north end, let alone bothering with the south. So I then determined to make as tight a perimeter as we could to hold that north end because as long as we held that north end, if the British troops came up from the south – which is what they were meant to do – we could deal with any anti-tank guns that could have thwarted their moves across the bridge subsequently.

We made one more attempt to see if we could feel our way across the bridge but illuminating flares were put up by the enemy and very heavy machine-gun fire was brought down on us. At about this time too three German lorries came over the river from the south. These we set on fire. They were full of ammunition. They made a furious noise for the rest of the night. Heat from burning lorries meant that you couldn't physically get on to the bridge.

I was expecting the whole of the 1st Parachute Brigade and the entire 1st Airborne Division, the next day and we had been told – and it always gets lost sight of – that the British Army would be up within 24 hours. During the last few years this has become 48 hours, but my recollection was that they were expected to be up within 24 hours. Gradually we tidied up and I began to feel quite happy about being able to hold the north end of the bridge and bring fire to bear on the bridge if the enemy tried to come across it. That was really the situation at dawn.

But at dawn the whole Arnhem operation exploded.

1. Kosovo, 12 June 1999: the noise, dust and swirling air make for a surreal scene reminiscent of *Apocalypse Now* as 1 Para waits to embark on Puma helicopters of 33 Squadron RAF on the road to Pristina (Kevin Capon, Crown Copyright)

2, 3. The Bruneval raid, the second major operation by Britain's parachute troops in the Second World War. The object: to drop on to the château (Crown Copyright), capture secret German radar equipment and dash home, courtesy of the Royal Navy, waiting offshore (Airborne Forces Museum)

4. *Above:* Bound for battle: their first action as a brigade in the Second World War took the Paras to North Africa in 1942 (Airborne Forces Museum)

5. *Left:* A casual stroll after honours were won, in Soudia, Oudna, Tunisia, in October 1942 (Airborne Forces Museum)

6. In training for the next big one: Sicily, where the Paras again took accolades for their contribution and the capture of Primosole Bridge on 13 July 1943 (Airborne Forces Museum)

7. The D-Day landings: emplaning for the great offensive, 5 June 1944 (Airborne Forces Museum)

8. Mixed fortunes met those who came by glider. Note how the glider splits on landing to facilitate unloading of men and equipment (Airborne Forces Museum)

9. Ready for the off: the Paras with a message on their Dakota (Airborne Forces Museum)

10. 'So good to see you': Dutch civilians welcome airborne troops to Arnhem before the great battle (Airborne Forces Museum)

11. *Left:* Arnhem: the spectacular sight of landings at dropping zone 'X' at 14.30 on Sunday 17 September 1944 (Airborne Forces Museum)

12. *Above:* The Arnhem target, and what proved to be the Bridge Too Far (Crown Copyright)

13. *Left:* Arnhem: the charred remains after the British force had been beaten back and captured by German Panzers who, according to intelligence, should not have been there (Crown Copyright)

14. *Right:* The Rhine crossing, 1945: one of the many casualties hit by German flak (Airborne Forces Museum)

15. *Below:* Earlier in the war, General Eisenhower meets Lieutenant Colonel Johnny Frost, leader of the Bruneval raid, who was captured at Arnhem after his heroic stand

16. A hero's welcome for the Paras as they enter Athens and chase the Germans out of Greece

7

THE PANZERS MOVE IN

Shortly after dawn on the second day there were some unexpected arrivals at the Arnhem bridge as Frost and his depleted battalion set themselves up to await the arrival of the rest of their own airborne division. They expected them to start filtering in at first light, followed towards the end of the day by the Guards Armoured Division. Still positioned on the north side, they busied themselves laying mines and preparing for what they believed to be an 'at worst' situation, an assessment which proved to be well wide of the mark. First a trickle of German administrative vehicles came over and these were blown up and set on fire. Not very long after first light a great column of enemy armour crossed from the south. Frost's men had laid mines on the bridge for this eventuality. Some of these vehicles were destroyed by the mines and the rest were blown apart by anti-tank guns covering the bridge and the PIAT hand-held weapons. Frost described the outcome as 'a good execution job on this squadron'. The vehicles turned out to be from the reconnaissance squadron of the SS's 9th Panzer Division, a discovery which astounded Frost:

I'd been given absolutely no information at all about the presence of SS Panzer troops of any kind. It wasn't very easy to pick up the German wounded because the whole area was swept by fire, but gradually the German wounded were carried or staggered into our own buildings and were then put down with our own wounded. It was at this stage that we realized from their badges that these were troops from the SS Panzer Division…

If a Panzer reconnaissance squadron was out, then the rest couldn't be far away; nor were they, and Frost would never get the reinforcements he was expecting to arrive at any moment. The 1st and 3rd Battalions had been halted by unexpected opposition after their perfect landing and were immediately engaged in heavy fighting that prevented them from reaching the 2nd Battalion at the bridge that night – and then not at all. The 1st Battalion advanced along the railway track and met an enemy which was indeed reinforced with tanks and armoured vehicles from the 9th Panzer Division. In bad light and torrential rain, fierce fighting continued throughout the night against a German force seemingly well prepared for this encounter, and British casualties were heavy. John Timothy, a past stalwart of the 2nd Battalion, was with the 1st Battalion's R Company, an infantry unit:

We were doing advance guard for the 1st Battalion and we were hit straight away. I lost two officers within about ten minutes. Out came German armoured cars and then we were faced with tanks. You could hear them milling around. We settled down and put our anti-tank equipment out and waited for a bit of light. There was no signals communication at all. The wireless sets weren't working. We had no communication with the battalion. The only contact we had was during the night when the second in command of the 1st Battalion came across from their camp from the other side of the woods in pitch-black. We were to join up with the main body as soon as possible. We'd got to get to the bridge and link with the 2nd Battalion at any cost. My company was asked to do a bayonet charge with the rest following on to break out... [We] were down to pretty dodgy numbers. The company moved off through a valley with enemy troops facing us and positioned on high ground. The advance party was badly hit and down to about eight men. Eventually we made it to within about 1000 yards of the bridge. I was down to six men in my company, another had eight, another had about a dozen and there were about ten in Battalion HQ – and that was the 1st Battalion. That didn't mean to say the rest were all killed or wounded; many were dispersed during actions. We headed for some houses for cover but the Germans had tanks followed by flame-throwers out, hitting houses and buildings. And that, basically, was the end of the 1st Battalion. Those of us who weren't killed went into the bag. I, among many, became a prisoner of war. We were taken for interrogation by a Luftwaffe officer. It was friendly enough. He asked me what Boy Browning looked like and I didn't tell him – just repeated my name, rank and number. Then, interestingly enough, he went to a file index and threw down a card with my name on it – 1st Lieutenant Timothy – which obviously dealt with the Bruneval raid. He said, 'What about this?' I repeated name, rank and number, and he just crossed out '1st Lieutenant' and wrote 'Major', and that was that.

Timothy, along with many others, was eventually taken to a permanent POW camp in Germany, from which he eventually escaped two weeks before the end of the war.

Back at the dropping and landing zones, John Stanleigh and his crew from the Pathfinders were preparing for the second instalment of the British 1st Airborne Division to arrive on the morning of 18 September:

The second drop was going to be quite different because the Germans had woken up. They were strafing the area and sent in Messerschmitts. It thus became an opposed landing and quite a few gliders caught fire in the air before they could land safely. There was no response from any Allied troops at all and that really worried us. We were expecting Mustangs to come across from Holland but apparently the weather wasn't good enough. Even so, morale was still high; some even thought it was a lark, good fun, but as we hadn't found any Germans yet we felt somewhat cheated. It was our mates that had gone off to fight the Germans and we were what we'd call miles behind pottering about on the landing zone and felt it was time we were in business ourselves. That happened after the second day when they'd all come down; we just became ordinary airborne infantry…

We marched [the four miles] towards the objective along the railway and took up positions in the Oosterbeek suburbs. After all, the progress had not been as was expected. By rights, there shouldn't be anyone left and we were puzzled that we were still playing about in the suburbs of Oosterbeek whereas we should be almost within sight of Arnhem by then.

Anthony Thomas came in with the second wave, the 4th Parachute Brigade, made up of his 156th Battalion, along with the 10th and 11th Battalions and other elements of airlanding troops who dropped just north of Wolfheze and immediately discovered that things were not as they should have been. Thomas joined the Durham Light Infantry in 1937, was with the 3rd Commando Brigade at Dieppe and joined the Paras in 1943. In the previous few months he and his mates had been briefed, debriefed and stood down on eight different occasions, and by now they were getting a little fed up. However:

Finally it happened and we were bound for Arnhem. But we had a bad time because we dropped into an area laden with ground troops. The DZ was almost surrounded. The number of German troops on the ground had been vastly underestimated. There were two Panzer divisions who were actually resting on their way back to Germany and we dropped right in the bloody middle of them. They were shooting us out of the sky. They turned everything into the air as soon as they saw the drop. We lost a lot of our dead on the DZ itself. I was with C Company then, a colour sergeant. We got badly shot up. We parted and headed for the bridge but ran straight into SS troops, who opened up on us. By that time we had already lost two patrols … the 156th Battalion lost more men at Arnhem than any other battalion.

The next step was to try to get into Wolfheze and so on to Oosterbeek and again we hit resistance, but finally we made a dash through a railway tunnel into Oosterbeek, where the main battle erupted. We held the northern circuit. The southern circuit was held by what was left of the 11th Battalion and the rest of the circuit by remaining troops. Steadily, however, more and more German armour was coming in and they were knocking us out systematically. By then the 11th Battalion was almost gone, the force cut down or captured. We had a large party of glider pilots with us at the time and they were actually fighting as infantry. By the time we got down to the old church we were 100 yards from the Rhine and still continuing to fight, hoping to reach the main bridge and the 2nd Battalion, but had very little to fight with. We had lost all our supplies because they had been dropped in the original DZ, where we had encountered so much trouble, and they were far behind us...

Jeffrey Fraser Noble, then a 20-year-old lieutenant with a platoon in the 156th Battalion of the 4th Parachute Brigade, was among the last of the second lift to drop and was hit by catastrophe even before they reached Arnhem. His platoon had split into two aircraft loads. His own aircraft had been forced to crash-land even before leaving British airspace. One of the parachutes on the two containers carrying machine-guns and ammunition, which were slung under the Dakota, had started to open. The aircrew was told to ditch it, pronto, but it wouldn't release and they had the bizarre situation of men being dangled out of the aircraft door, floating in the slipstream, trying to prise the chute loose. It wouldn't budge. The only alternative was to land, because no one could jump in case they were hit by or caught up in the tangle of ropes and the container, which normally would have been dropped first. But then they realized that this tangled mess meant they would have to crash-land. They came down with a bump at the Americans' Flying Fortress base. There some tough mechanics came out with sledgehammers and bashed the aircraft back into shape as best they could. The American pilot said there was no way he was going to take the plane back into the air, but Noble and his men insisted. They didn't want to miss Arnhem.

After much persuasion, the pilot agreed and the Dakota limped precariously off the runway. Once airborne, they managed to make up time and could see the tail end of the formation well ahead, but since they were a lone aircraft without protection they took a lot of flak. But they came through relatively unscathed, although the rest of the platoon in the plane ahead was not so lucky: they were brought down by flak and all but one of them were killed. When Noble's plane came in, the DZ was on fire. 'It was thick gorse,' he said:

set ablaze by mortars and with smoke bombs. Germans guns were all around the DZ as we landed. Half my stick landed in woods occupied by Germans [and were captured or shot]. I stood up and was immediately shot in the thigh, but the bullet hit my map case. One officer, one of our rifle platoon commanders, was hit in both legs and, finding himself surrounded by burning gorse, shot himself because he didn't want to be burned to death. Surprisingly, quite a lot of civilians came out to the DZ and were very helpful, giving us drinks of water and wine. Even so, when I got to Battalion HQ, I only had about a third of my platoon.

Flak and the fact that the Germans had overrun the supply zones turned out to be among the key factors that hampered the troops on the ground. Supplies dried up almost immediately. The RAF were dropping containers accurately enough, but the supply zones had been changed in the light of events on the ground. Messages from divisional headquarters concerning redirection of supplies had apparently not been received in England. Consequently the RAF were doing their utmost to get the supplies in through a wall of tracer, totally unaware that they were dropping in the wrong place. On the ground, desperate attempts were being made to attract the pilots' attention with signals and coloured panels, but from the air these were invisible through the trees, smoke and general mayhem.

The pilots were taking terrible risks, some dropping their load as they headed towards the earth on fire. As they came in they were being shot out of the sky by both the mass of flak and by attacking fighters. Over the next few days the supply situation became absolutely desperate, not least for the RAF crews who were trying to get through. Army cameraman Mike Lewis reckoned that many men on the ground must have been in tears as they watched the pilots' extremely brave efforts:

They were coming in so low and there was so much flak that the ground shook beneath our feet. And I could see planes, black through the trees, large as houses, pilots fighting to hold their course … and bursting into flames – one of the few times in the war I nearly wept. I really did. To see Dakotas and Lancasters going into the Rhine through the black trees – and all for what? And from one of them came fluttering down a sheet of paper. One of the men ran over to it. It was that day's newspaper, the Daily Express. And the headline read, 'Siegfried Line Crumbling – Hitler On The Run.' No one could speak at that. Here we were, having all kinds of shit knocked out of us, and according to this newspaper it was the other way around.

On the worst day, the RAF lost a fifth of its aircraft on what were courageous yet hopeless sorties. Those that did get through were unwittingly providing the enemy with sustenance and starving their own troops, as John Stanleigh recalls:

We weren't told what had gone wrong, but we knew something was a bit odd. We dug in near some houses on the edge of a little wood. It was very pleasant. The next day we went nearer the other end of the wood and we saw supply drops coming in and at the same time we realized that with every supply drop the Germans were simply waiting for our Lancasters to come down low and then shot them down. I think I personally must have seen at least eight or nine Lancasters being shot down in a very short space of time, just like flies, plucked out of the air, burning, coming down into that area where we'd been waiting. It was terrible. I mean, I can't describe it to you now how we felt to see these boys being shot down. Some [aircrews] escaped and these people were given rifles and just helped to man the line … and [eventually] we had to count our ammunition because we had virtually none left. We'd got a few odd containers, but most containers dropped in the German lines. I went out one day under cover with my section sergeant to bring a container in. And when we opened the container we found battledress and red berets in it. And he got wounded for that.

We began to take heavy casualties. We were 200 when we set out and our casualties were about 55 per cent, although [that was] quite good in relation to the rest. We also had no food. Our supplies all got dropped in the German lines. We could see them coming down and the Germans loved it. They had feast day after feast day with the food, which was better than theirs. Dropped them right into their lap. And we couldn't understand what was going on. We weren't dejected, we were just puzzled. We thought there'd be a change and the containers would come down in our lines, but they didn't. We didn't know it then, but there was no radio communication whatever between our unit and HQ in London – not a single message got through.

Lack of communication was also a major problem with the beleaguered 2nd Battalion troops on the bridge. They simply did not know who had landed, where they were, when they were expected, why they hadn't made it through – and, worse, they couldn't establish why the British Army ground reinforcements from XXX Corps which were, according to Johnny Frost, supposed to arrive within 24 hours, were nowhere in sight. Frost takes up the story again:

The one message I got rather worried me, saying that the rest of the brigade were going to give up trying to get to the bridge during the night and would renew their attempt in the morning. But during the night the enemy made quite certain we were sealed in. Anybody who was trying to get through in daylight would find it much more difficult than trying to continue to get through at night. By then we must have had about 50 men killed or wounded. There were huge great cellars underneath the government building and all the wounded were put in there. I wanted reinforcements ... but I realized by now that things weren't going very well for the rest of the brigade. I managed to get a message to B Company, under Major Crawley, who was by what remained of the pontoon bridge. He came up and strengthened the positions by the head of the main bridge. I could get no word at all to my C Company...

Gradually the enemy pressure increased in the way of infantry attacks, closed in to our positions and enemy armour approached, but mainly there was terrific bombardment, both of artillery and mortar. That went on all through the Monday and the Monday night, the Tuesday, the Tuesday night and Wednesday. By late Wednesday we were in a pretty bad state and running out of ammunition. We were limited to the amount of ammunition we were able to bring into the town with us and there had been no replenishment whatever. When you're fighting at close quarters like that one thing you have to have is ammunition. Orders had to be given to the men only to fire when one was absolutely certain of having a kill, but that does allow your opponent to improve his position as you simply dare not scatter ammunition about.

We did get a certain amount of support from our own light regiment, which was near the church at Oosterbeek, three or four miles away, but that was the sum total of the support we could get. We still hoped that the other battalions would come up, although we did have one welcome reinforcement that first night – one company of the 3rd Battalion which managed to march mostly up the railway line and came to join us. They were less one platoon but at least they were fresh men and very welcome.

They were deployed north, on the most northern approach to the bridge. The worrying thing was, though we could hear quite a lot of fighting going on from where we expected the division to come from, we could hear absolutely no fighting at all from the area of Nijmegen, where we were expecting the Guards Armoured Division to approach from. We'd done our stuff and the plan had been OK and we were getting a little bit annoyed that nobody else came.

The following morning, Wednesday, I was wounded, blown up by a mortar bomb. I was having a discussion with Douglas Crawley, one of my senior company commanders. We were actually discussing then whether there was anything we could do and a mortar bomb or shell landed right in the middle of our little group and blew us all over, backwards. We were all wounded and bemused by the thing. My batman, Wicks, managed to survive that because he was with me. I was hit in the leg and ankle, not very badly but extremely painfully, so after a time I was given morphia and went down to the cellars. My second in command had been killed on the first night and another officer, Freddie Gough, leader of the reconnaissance squadron, who by then had no troops to command, assumed the overall command at the bridge, while still referring any problems to me...

The fight for the Arnhem bridge, which Boy Browning, parroting Montgomery, had decreed must be taken at all costs, was all but lost. Frost and the last 147 of his men still standing had been literally blown off it, but enough had regrouped to keep up some form of resistance for a few more hours. Those still trying to fight their way through were unaware of these developments because of the lack of radios. Meanwhile the Germans were pouring more troops into the area. The 503rd

Panzer Battalion, with King Tiger tanks, and the 171st German Light Artillery Regiment, along with a number of companies of Luftwaffe formed into infantry, raced to the scene; all would be in action within 24 hours, by 4 p.m. on 20 September.

The fight raged on, and into it, adding more confusion, had stepped the 1st Polish Parachute Battalion, who had no more success than the British units, already at full stretch. According to Anthony Thomas of the 156th Battalion:

They arrived a day late, having been delayed by fog. Some dropped in the wrong place and because few of them could speak English, some of our chaps thought they were bloody Germans and there was a lot of inter-fire among them and us. Half of the Poles dropped [as arranged] on the southern side of the river and couldn't even get across. A year later we found there was a ferry bridge across the Rhine which we could have used and could have got across.

The 156th, the 10th and the 11th Battalions of the 4th Parachute Brigade were taking a pounding. Jeffrey Noble says that the 156th had been split apart:

We sheltered in Wolfheze and took up a defensive position with remnants of the 10th Battalion. At dawn an attack came in with Tiger tanks and all sorts of SS. Our officer commanding shouts, 'Every man for himself' and we scattered into the woods. I managed to gather about 20 men with me from all sorts of units. We got away, clambering over fences, through houses – a mad scramble in fact. We had no idea what was happening or where the rest of the people were. We decided to lay low for a bit and at that moment a company of the King's Own Scottish Borderers came through the woods and had not met any enemy by some fluke. I put myself under the command of their company commander as a scratch force and we headed towards the river. Very soon, we ran into opposition. We were completely surrounded and the company commander decided to surrender his whole company. I personally didn't agree with it and took to the woods with some of my parachutists. But his was probably the right decision because 130 men lived to see the end of the war. My batman, Private McCarthy, stayed with me. We made a run for it, but unfortunately I was subsequently wounded, partially blinded for a while, and we were surrounded. McCarthy said, 'Right, this is it...' And we were in German hands.

The 21st Independent Parachute Company's Pathfinder Company, the last group to join the fray as infantry, came up to the main battle arena still unaware of the catastrophe at the bridge and the fate of so many of the men they had helped to land safely behind the enemy lines. They took up position alongside the surviving soldiers of the remaining units, who included remnants of the 4th Parachute Brigade, another company from the 7th Battalion the King's Own Scottish Borderers, some pilots and gunners from the 1st Airlanding Light Regiment the Royal Artillery, the 1st Battalion the Border Regiment and the 2nd Battalion the South Staffordshire Regiment – all greatly reduced in numbers.

None of them, apart from that single company from the 3rd Battalion, managed to get anywhere near the bridge, which Frost's men held for three days and four nights until finally they were overwhelmed. Frost himself was still lying wounded in the cellars of the government building beside the bridge. He and his senior officers had the previous day discussed doing a northwards sortie but agreed that it was much more important to remain in position at the north end of the bridge for as long as possible so as to give the maximum cover to anybody trying to cross from the south. Soon it was painfully evident that no one was coming up from the south, or at least not yet, and Frost had no alternative but to call it a day:

We were absolutely sealed in by a ring of enemy infantry and armour. We were being bombarded with self-propelled guns which you could actually see firing at us. This had the effect of just setting more and more buildings on fire until finally this big government building, where Brigade Headquarters had been, and was an absolutely key place, caught fire. There was no means of putting the flames out, so the head doctor came to see me and said, 'I'm afraid unless we can put the flames out your 200 wounded men are going to be burnt alive, including you, sir.' By this time we'd almost ceased to be a fighting force because of lack of ammunition etc.

So the doctor said, 'Can I go out and try and make contact with the Germans so as to evacuate the wounded?' This he did. The Germans agreed to a truce to get the wounded out. Everybody available, including the Germans, and I may say, the SS, laboured with might and main to get everybody out of the building, by which time it was blazing quite fiercely. After they'd got almost the last man out, including the German wounded and prisoners, the building collapsed. But from that time on, really, our own men were just in little groups of people dotted about without any co-ordination. When the morning came completely superior numbers of German soldiers were able to round them up. I myself was taken out of the building and laid on the embankment the other side.

The battle had ceased for quite a time and everybody was moving about quite freely. Then we were put on to German half-tracks and the stretchers were laid across them and driven into the St Elizabeth Hospital, which is on the western approaches of the town. There we were put into beds. I knew then that as soon as possible the Germans would evacuate us further. I'd taken off my badges of rank and hoped that I would somehow or other be able to escape as a private soldier, but early next morning we were put into ambulances and driven right into Germany. Once they know you're the commanding officer, special measures are taken to make certain you don't escape. Anyway they were very interested in interrogating you. I don't think they did know who I was all the time; even when I got to a German prison hospital they didn't seem to know I was a lieutenant colonel. I got no different treatment to anybody else, nor was I interrogated, ever, though funnily enough, it was ridiculous because the Germans, I could hear them asking for me when we were taken outside the building.

It was just as well that Frost gave up when he did. The progression of any effective fighting force from his own division to the bridge was well and truly blocked and the Guards Armoured Division was still miles from Arnhem. The battles raged on and Pathfinder John Stanleigh remembers some classic moments:

The major part of Arnhem for us was really spent holding particular houses and streets. No. 2 Platoon held four or five houses in that area. We had been progressively decreasing in numbers, people being shot, or blown to pieces or wounded. So one by one, the truth sort of came over that we had got fewer and fewer numbers. But it didn't seem to matter to us; we felt, 'We'll get through somehow, there'll always be somebody else.' On the other hand, it was terrible to hear of people, our own mates, being killed off. And just a memory afterwards – 'Oh, it can't be true.' It's only years afterwards, when we went back to the cemetery and we saw all the graves, [that] it suddenly dawned on us: 'Yes.' And we, of course, remembered them as they were many years ago.

Meanwhile the German loudspeaker vans were touring around, telling us that Montgomery had abandoned us. And the best thing, if we wanted to see our wives and sweethearts again and our families and mothers, [was] 'Give yourself up now and at least you have a chance, otherwise you'll be obliterated.' We shouted obscenities back at that. And then suddenly, one day, a piper appeared from nowhere, in the middle of the battle. It seemed like the First World War. I don't know, he must have been from the KOSBies ... and [during] all the hoo-ha that's going on there, he suddenly appeared with his pipes and walked up and down over the parapet. It was really like a film. And he disappeared again – I'm sure he was real.

The Germans were shooting at him but he was quite unconcerned, but we didn't see him again. The KOSBies suffered terrible casualties. We had the KOSBies on our left for quite some time and the South Staffordshires on the other side. It was a miniature First World War battle except it only lasted seven days. It was a question of who had ammunition. Machine-guns suddenly stopped firing because they had no ammunition. There was very little coming through. One night, with a gun patrol I became cornered in a Dutch house somehow. I was just by a back door looking out sideways and couldn't see any Germans. So I went back into the house to light a cigarette. The moment I had cleared the path, there was a burst of machine-gun fire hitting just exactly the spot I had been. It shook me quite considerably. We realized that we were cut off from our own position although it was only half a street away.

Fortunately, I had some phosphorus grenades. We went into the back garden and we knew roughly that the German machine-gunners were only about 20 yards away and I threw one of my precious phosphorus grenades at them. It hit the tree above them and the phosphorus was pouring down on them. And there was an almighty noise and we looked. Two Germans were absolutely on fire, absolutely on fire, trying to beat out the flames. So we put them out of their misery, which was the only humane thing to do under the circumstances.

We did lose one of our men there, unfortunately. So there were all sorts of episodes at Arnhem. Like a call of nature: I had my trousers down in a front garden when suddenly I saw a German walk in with his Schmeisser [sub-machine-gun] on his shoulder and as yet he had not seen me. And I could do nothing. I thought I'd really reached the end because the next moment he'd see me and fire and kill me. At that very moment Val Allerton, my sergeant, walked down the other side. He saw me and saw the German and shot him on the spot.

These emotions you can't put into words. And things happened every day. There was a Dutch chap who came round with apples and sweets; he was a really nice man. He always wanted to know how we were getting on, what we were doing, he was a great guy. But one day the owner of the house we were in came in and he saw this man. After he'd gone he told us that this chap was a Dutch Nazi even though he was also a member of the local police. We discussed it among ourselves and felt that something had to be done about it if he came again, which he did.

We asked him what he was doing, questioned him about his association with the Germans, which he denied and then we searched him and we found German papers on him, German letters and messages that he'd written for the Germans giving information about our location. Well, we decided that we had no choice. We held a little trial among the three of us. It was very late in the proceedings, almost on the last day. And we felt if we let him go he'd go back to the Germans. He'd probably given them information already which must have helped them to locate some of the houses which we were in. He was definitely a spy. So we decided to shoot him. We drew lots for it. We told him we were going to shoot him, told him why. He went to pieces, admitted it and begged for mercy. We said, 'No' and shot him.

The fighting continued in this hellish cauldron into the following weekend and beyond, with numbers rapidly declining. During the night of 24 September a final effort to help the traumatized survivors of the 1st Airborne Division was made from the south side of the river by a battalion from the Dorsetshire Regiment. Trucks were sent carrying assault boats with which to begin the crossing. The bad luck continued: two trucks took a wrong turn and ended up in German hands, two skidded off the wet road and two others just got lost. Only nine boats turned up. As the Dorsets piled in, the Germans opened fire. Of the 420 British soldiers who set off, only 239 reached the other side and most of those were captured. A mere handful reached the 1st Airborne Division's ever-shrinking perimeter. It was the last straw.

Major General Roy Urquhart, the divisional commander, who had himself been missing for four days, trapped by German gunfire after visiting one of his units, gave the order to withdraw in the early hours of the 24th. All equipment was to be abandoned; the troops would make their way to the river and try to get across into the south as best they could, and meanwhile the XXX Corps was to pull back to Nijmegen. Anthony Thomas was with a few stragglers from the 156th Battalion:

My group had only two alternatives: to give ourselves up or try to get to the river. The only direction we had was from guns firing star shells on the other side. But the Germans, of course, twigged what the bloody star shells were for and bombarded both banks with heavy fire. We pulled back and under darkness made our way downriver for about half a mile. We left the wounded on the banks, and walking with the water up to our necks to begin with, I managed to get across with two other chaps. We discovered two Canadian craft on the other bank and thank goodness there was an operator in one of them. We tied them both together, got back across the other side, loaded our wounded in and that's how 28 men and one officer got out of Arnhem. In the end, by people coming back through the underground and various other routes, we finished up with 47 out of 820 of that battalion. We had gone into that operation with high expectations, and to do what Montgomery had expected us to do – thus shortening the war. It could have happened. It could have worked. If two units could have got to the bridge, it could have worked.

The fight for the bridge had, by Monday 25 September, turned into Escape from Arnhem or, to give it the official title, Operation Berlin: the evacuation of all remaining troops from the north of the Rhine, sanctioned from London. John Stanleigh recalls those final hours:

We were told during the night that we were going to pull out. About ten o'clock somebody came along and said, 'In half an hour we're going to move down to the river and we're going to get out because it's the end.' Until then we thought we'd just go on and on. We didn't really think that we'd have to retreat. We felt, 'We're doing well on our particular front.' We hadn't given an inch away. The nearest Germans were about 100 yards away. It was very patchy and many of them, I think, just wanted to be out of the war. When we did get away we moved towards the river. I found myself marching next to a chap who was wearing a German tin hat.

I said to him, 'Why are you bringing this tin hat home?'

And he said, '*Wass?*'

So I looked at him, said to him, 'Are you German?'

He said, 'Yes.'

I said, 'What are you doing in this column here?'

He said, 'I've had enough of the war, thank you. I want to be a prisoner.'

So he got evacuated out.

It was pitch-dark and bucketing with rain. The nearer we got to the river the worse it got, not so much with the Germans firing – they were firing somehow across the area but [they] did not know what was going on. We had a point to make for ... every 60 seconds a tracer round was fired to get our bearings. We got to the river in the end. There was a queue, several queues, and nobody knew what was going to happen. Canadians came along in amphibious vehicles. They picked up a certain number every time and the rest had to wait. And some of them got waterlogged, some got shot to pieces. When they came to the end, there were no boats for some of us, those who were left behind. Those of us who could swim tried to swim across. It took me nearly an hour. The currents were very strong, and I lost all my clothes.

On the other side, I began walking, naked. And I came to a Dutch farmhouse. Some of our chaps were there and the Dutch were talking to them. They gave me some old clothes and I joined the rest. We walked for about a couple of miles until we came to a sort of staging place. I think we probably had an hour there. It seemed much longer because I went to sleep. Somebody woke me up and said, 'If you don't come now you'll be left behind.' So we got on to this lorry or God knows... I was too sleepy to care much. And we were taken to Nijmegen to a school and fitted out with new uniform and whisked back home, flown back to Melton Mowbray in Leicestershire.

* * *

Market Garden was a failure and a tragedy. Of the 10,000 of the 1st Airborne Division who fought at Arnhem, only 2163 returned under Operation Berlin, and that is not counting the losses suffered by the Polish 1st Parachute Brigade, which were also substantial. The remainder were killed, wounded or captured. Montgomery would never admit to total failure; instead he liked to refer to Arnhem as 90 per cent successful. Johnny Frost made this assessment of an outstanding display of human courage in an attempt to sustain an operation which, like Dieppe, was severely flawed:

On reflection, I don't think our performance could have been bettered. A lot of people said that it was part of a greater risk and never should have happened, but there are certain items which I think ought to be fully noted:

(1) The information about the enemy. It was apparently well known to the airborne corps commander, General Browning, and to Army headquarters, that this SS corps had been put north of Arnhem to recuperate after their battles. They'd had tremendous casualties and had a terrific pasting in Normandy, but they'd had this before and come back. They were an extremely experienced fighting unit; they'd been

right through the Russian campaign and brought back to fight in Normandy. So there it was; it was terribly wrong of our own intelligence people to have written off those troops and then not to have accepted reports that they were in the Arnhem area before Operation Market Garden. But we did not know, nor did the actual corps commander know, or says he didn't know. But certainly my general didn't know and I certainly didn't know. I think it was very dubious that we could have succeeded against that type of opposition. We went on the understanding that there were a few SS recruits and Luftwaffe personnel.

(2)   The biggest nonsense was the Air Force's only flying the one sortie on that first day when weather conditions were perfect, and I'm not blaming the RAF because I think they wanted to do it. It was a comparatively short lift and to say that they couldn't do it is absolute bloody nonsense. A lot of the airmen that I know, experienced airmen, said, 'Yes, we could have done it' and Air Marshal Hollingshurst was very keen to do it. The man who was against it was the American overall airborne force commander: he was the man who said it was asking much too much of the crews. It's ridiculous, and because of this split lift only one brigade, of our division, was available that first day to guard the drops of subsequent lifts, so all surprise had gone and all the momentum had gone. So I maintain that the worst thing that ever happened was this failure to drop the two lifts on that first day and I'm absolutely adamant about that.

(3)   We were very unlucky in the failure of our radios. I think this was vital – for an ordinary army advancing it is quite simple because your sets are tuned in and 'netted' [hooked up to the network] and you just walk forward with them actually in use. We were also very unlucky to find Field Marshal Model in Oosterbeek. There was the one man in the German Army able to galvanize the opposition, right on the spot. He was very

much a Hitler man and able therefore to ask for support and get it. I was later told by General Harmel, commanding the 10th SS Panzer Division, that he was up and down the German positions like a caged tiger and put the fear of God into them. So that was the kind of leadership which was being used by the opposition. Reading the memoirs of Field Marshal Montgomery, as far as I can see most of the time during this period he was battling with Eisenhower for the next stage, and General Dempsey, the Army commander, may have been an excellent man but there didn't seem to be any reports of him coming up and trying to put a bit more pressure on our own ground troops to get on a bit further.

I think the most dreadful thing about the planning was the very low priority given to the Nijmegen bridge. Browning said to Roy Urquhart, 'Take Arnhem bridge and hold it.' He said nothing of the same sort to Gavin, the commander of the [US] 82nd [Airborne] Division. There was no question of that being just as important, and in reality it was. Arnhem became a fixation and to some extent remained so. Montgomery apparently said, 'In years to come it will be a great thing for a man to be able to say I fought at Arnhem.' On that point I agree.

The history of war is full of what ifs? and no episode more so than Arnhem. In the years that followed, the men who were there met at their memorials and social gatherings and chewed the fat. Names were named: Montgomery was arrogant; Urquhart was naive and not fully experienced in airborne warfare; Browning wasn't honest with himself or his corps officers; Horrocks had been sick and not fully effective. But then, what if, asked Jeffrey Noble of the 156th Battalion, it had succeeded? His view is that 'it would have shortened the war and, what we didn't know then, changed the face of Europe ... we would have been in Berlin ... the Russians would have been back in Warsaw ... Britain would not have sustained so much V1 and V2 attack ... and so it would have been wonderful.'

Instead the memorial to the operation is to be found in cemeteries. The Arnhem-Oosterbeek War Cemetery contains the graves of 3328 British and Commonwealth soldiers and, like many such sites, became a place of pilgrimage for survivors and relatives. German losses at Arnhem were estimated at 3200.

8

'MY WIFE WILL KILL ME!'

In the gloomy aftermath of Arnhem, the thoughts of the men who made it home were with the thousands killed or wounded and the many left to be gathered up by the Germans. However, the spirit of those men hauled off to Germany was not broken, and there was even some dark humour along with the tales of continuing courage even in the hands of the enemy. One of the RAF personnel, as they were being marshalled for the journey to the POW camps, kept moaning to the others that his wife would kill him when he got home since he'd arranged to meet her at the cinema and, of course, hadn't turned up. His name was Flight Sergeant George King, and he had been a rear gunner, but on this occasion he had found himself working as a dispatcher for the resupply aircraft. He told everyone who would listen, including Lieutenant Jeffrey Noble, who relayed this story, that he wasn't even supposed to be on duty that particular day but someone went sick and he was called in.

He had already arranged to meet his wife at the local cinema at 7 p.m. and because the take-off was scheduled for late morning he hadn't told her he was going, assuming that it would be a quick flight to Arnhem and back in time for tea. Over Arnhem, however, while he was busily dispatching containers, he heard the Dakota pilot cry, 'Abandon aircraft. Abandon aircraft.' Following the instruction, he went through the door. He hadn't taken the precaution of strapping on his parachute and grabbed it as he went out, getting his arms through the harness so that it was half on and half off. He managed to land with only a few very black bruises – and shoeless. In the rush, he was still wearing his civilian shoes when he left; they were whipped away in the slipstream. Furthermore, he landed between the German and the British lines and because he was wearing a grey uniform unidentifiable in the mêlée, his own side fired at him every time he moved because they thought he was a German and the Germans fired at him because they thought he was British. So he lay in no-man's land all evening and all night worrying about his wife waiting at the cinema.

The following morning he identified himself to a British patrol. They gave him a Sten gun, took a pair of boots off a dead German and told him to tag along behind. Unfortunately the patrol was immediately engaged in a fight and everyone was captured. George King, in German jackboots and an RAF uniform, was an object of suspicion and was given a rough time by his captors because of the *Terrorbomben*. Many RAF personnel were badly treated because of the heavy bombing of German cities. In the POW compound, King was suddenly pulled out by a German commander, along with a British artillery captain, to deal with some unexploded bombs. The Germans were sure that he would be an expert on such matters and refused to listen to his denials of such talent. Neither man knew what to do when confronted with the bombs sticking out of the ground, and did not attempt to disarm them but simply dug them out and rolled them into the Rhine. And when Jeffrey Noble met the RAF sergeant as they were on their way to Germany, King said to him, 'My God – all this in 24 hours and my poor wife waiting in the cinema queue wondering where I've got to.'

Morale among the prisoners was quite high, and attempts to escape were frequent. One of the most audacious was made by John Potts, a company commander of the 156th Battalion. He was badly wounded in the leg and taken to hospital. After treatment and despite being on crutches and still wearing remnants of his British uniform, he climbed out of the hospital window and hobbled off down the street. Meeting some German soldiers coming in the opposite direction, he thought he'd had it, but they just said good morning and walked on by. He managed to get to the Dutch frontier, where he saw a farmhouse in the distance and stumbled up to it, thinking he was safe. He wasn't: the occupants handed him over to the Dutch SS.

Others did not live to tell the tale, as Jeffrey Noble well knew: 'One of my friends, Mike Gambier, who was injured in the ankle, recovered and managed to get away from the train. He was caught by the German SS with another young officer from a Parachute Battalion and put against a wall and shot. We found out where that was and we found out that the SS man who did it was captured by Dutch civilians at the end of the war, and was court-martialled and hanged.' Meanwhile Noble himself was taken to Oflag 79 at Braunschweig. Inside there were about 3000 officers, who were soon to be joined by a trickle of new prisoners captured during the next airborne assault launched from Britain: the Ardennes campaign.

As the decimated remains of the 1st Airborne Division took their rest and began to re-equip, reorganize and replenish, the 6th Airborne Division – itself now revitalized and re-equipped after the substantial losses during the Normandy landings – was placed on alert in mid-December 1944. On the 16th Hitler began his last-ditch effort to save the Third Reich from defeat by launching a new offensive on its western front into the Ardennes forest towards the port of Antwerp in what became known as the Battle of the Bulge. It was the Germans' biggest gamble, aimed at cutting the Allied supply, halting the build-up for the invasion of Germany itself and surrounding four Allied armies in the region, thus forcing a second Dunkirk evacuation.

The German attack was launched with a spearhead of V-1 rockets against Liège and Antwerp, while 2000 guns were ranged against the southernmost positions of the American forces. A massive wall of firepower from five Panzer divisions came up behind, followed by four powerful Waffen-SS armoured divisions. With 13 infantry divisions and five armoured divisions now moving on Allied positions, Hitler expected his troops to be in Antwerp within four days and it seemed possible that they might achieve this, given that the Americans had clearly been surprised and were retreating from such a strong attack. In fact, few of his generals believed the plan could succeed, but they carried on out of loyalty and fear.

The Allied commanders quickly recovered and their defences remained solid, despite the huge German assault. On 20 December, the day Field Marshal Montgomery took command of all Allied forces north of the German push, with General Patton commanding troops to the south, Britain's 6th Airborne Division was mobilized to Belgium and was deployed along the apex of the 'bulge' of the German advance between Dinant and Namur. The weather was appalling, with deep snow, frozen ground and then mud and slush, as once again parachute troops found themselves as infantry in a cauldron of heavy and bitter fighting. The 3rd and 5th Parachute Brigades had joined the move to rebuff German advances, fighting house to house through village after village. The 6th Airborne Division was a relatively small cog in what was now a very large wheel, rolling inexorably against the concerted might of the German forces. Before the Battle of the Bulge was over, the Allies were to move in the equivalent of 35 divisions.

Even so, casualties were heavy in what, for the 6th Airborne Division, became a short, sharp campaign. The 13th Parachute Battalion was among those particularly hard hit during their attack on the village of Bure, when they met a strong infantry force backed up by tanks. After a two-day battle the battalion managed to fight its way through, at the cost of 200 men, 68 of whom were killed. The 6th's effort was part of the Allied strategy to push the Germans back to their start line, and close off, by the end of January, the salient which they had achieved. The division was then withdrawn to Holland, and returned to its base in the UK in mid-February to prepare for the next major operation: the second attempt to cross the Rhine. This time the groundwork had been done, although the cost had been high: 120,000 enemy troops, 80,000 Americans and 1400 British. But the way was now clear. With the Russians advancing from the eastern front to within 50 miles of Berlin, the defeat of Hitler's last major offensive ensured that the collapse of Nazi Germany was now only weeks away.

* * *

Meanwhile a group of Paras who had been exceedingly active in the invasion of Italy temporarily disappeared from view, overshadowed to some extent by the high-profile activities of British airborne troops in western Europe during the D-Day landings, Arnhem and the Ardennes. But this almost forgotten army was battling away in eastern Europe in what developed into a crucial and at times delicate political situation. To recap: when the 1st Airborne Division returned to the UK in November 1943 to prepare for the above operations, the 2nd Parachute Brigade remained in Italy, where it was formed into the 2nd Independent Brigade Group, comprising the 4th, 5th and 6th Parachute Battalions, the 2nd Parachute Squadron Royal Engineers, the 127th Parachute Field Ambulance group and a REME unit. Our narrative left them, it will be recalled, as the 2nd Parachute Brigade fought as infantry in the last major sweep through Italy, where it was used in 'fire-brigade' roles, deployed to bolster the lines in numerous points, including the Cassino sector. Withdrawn from the lines in June 1944, it was eventually moved to Rome to begin training for operations in the south of France, in the follow-up to the Normandy landings. Having been tasked with capturing an area around St Raphaël, the brigade took off from Italy in the early hours of 15 August and within ten days completed all its objectives after only sporadic and fairly weak opposition. With American troops arriving to bolster the ground force in the south of France, the brigade was returned to

Italy at the end of August to prepare for a more demanding deployment. Its presence was now required in Greece, where the withdrawal of German forces of occupation was already under way to provide troops for other fronts. Five weeks after returning from France, the Paras had sufficient supplies and aircraft to begin a full-scale airdrop timed to coincide with a sea-borne landing by the 23rd Armoured Brigade. Vic Coxen, by now a lieutenant colonel commanding the 4th Battalion, remembers:

Even as we took off for France we knew that it was already on the cards that we might be pulled back to go to Greece, where the political war was stirring at the end of 1944. Anyhow, we went on with our French operation, being dropped to join British and American troops … anyway we were quickly pulled out and the whole brigade was to be dropped in Greece, 15 miles west of Athens.

The drop was hazardous. The wind speed was 35 miles per hour, well beyond the normal maximum for a drop and there were a large number of casualties coming down.

I could see that the DZ was immediately beneath us. I said to myself that we were in danger of actually coming down on the designated dropping zone if we were not careful – which would have been a first! But the plane swung around and one of the airmen came back and complained that there was a strong wind; I said there was nothing I could do about it. We had to drop. If I had been more sensible, I might have said don't drop us on the DZ, which was an old airfield; beside it there were olive groves and I might, with hindsight, have selected that area to drop. But no, we went ahead with the original plan to hit the DZ, but with the wind, when you landed, the chute went straight on blowing because it wouldn't collapse and unfortunately several chaps were killed and about 30 or 40 were injured – broken legs and arms. I was lucky; I was blown across the field, bumping across very hard ground until my parachute caught on a barbed-wire fence which brought me to a halt. The Greeks came to help and looked after the wounded very well. They were put into private houses and cared for. We commandeered what vehicles we could and moved into Athens and took over everything. There was no resistance whatsoever.

The brigade was given a rousing welcome in Athens, where it was joined by sections from the SAS Special Boat Squadron under the command of Lieutenant Colonel Lord Jellicoe and the RAF Regiment. These units formed up to chase the remaining Germans and capture as many as possible before they reached the border. 'They were already on the way out when we landed,' explains Coxen:

and we attempted to head them off to stop them getting back to Germany itself. We were only partially successful. There were a couple of major battles, and we pretty well cleared them out of Greece and chased them towards the border with Yugoslavia, where I received a signal which I wish I'd kept but didn't: 'Churchill to Coxen. On no account do you cross into Yugoslavia.'

It was obviously not a British zone and on the borders between the two countries I met Russians and had a glass or two of vodka. We only managed to capture around 600 German troops and they were mostly Caucasian soldiers, poor buggers, who had been promised their freedom by the Nazis if they joined up. Now they were in the bag and some curious shenanigans followed about what to do with them. Finally they were shipped back to Russia, around 400 of them. I think they were all eventually killed. With Greece cleared of Germans, we were put on standby to move back to Italy. I was called in ahead of the battalion to plan an operation on the [River] Po. When I arrived, I made my feelings known that there was not a snowflake in hell's chance of pulling the brigade out of Greece because the political situation there was on a knife edge and the internal struggle for power could blow at any moment.

Coxen was right. Even during the German occupation, the country was bitterly split between royalists (the EDES) and communists (ELAS), the latter wishing to ensure once and for all that the Duke of Edinburgh's family did not return to the throne after the war. The departure of the Germans instantly fuelled this internal strife. In addition, the Greek communists were requesting support from the Russians – who were already in Yugoslavia and Bulgaria – so that the whole situation looked likely to erupt into a full-scale civil war: the 6th Battalion alone was confronted by an organized unit of some 5000 communist guerrillas in central Greece. The prospect of confrontation between British troops and the communists was already a reality when, in November, it was decided to withdraw the brigade and deploy it in support of the 8th Army. Coxen, then back in Italy to discuss the withdrawal, offers a forceful summary of the situation:

Eventually they agreed with me and I was ordered to return to Greece that afternoon. In fact it had already gone sour when I arrived back and they had to send two jeeps with machine-guns to get me back inside the headquarters in Athens. In the weeks ahead we suffered around 100 casualties to the rebels – including my doctor, who was shot close to our base in Athens. Our troops were pretty fed up about that. They had come over to save Greece and now found they were being shot at by these bastards. We responded in kind, working with nationalist battalions, cleared Athens of the communists, block by block, searching every house for arms and insurgents. One had to move rather carefully; some of these chaps were suicide soldiers as young as 14 who had been brainwashed to die for their country. They used to sing songs about democracy and then shoot the bloody soldiers who had come to free them from the jackboot.

The brigade's duties were defined predominantly as maintaining law and order, but the strong ELAS forces were no pushover and the Paras were eventually forced to take a much heavier stance. There were full-blown battles in several areas before the 5th Battalion, supported by elements of the 23rd Armoured Brigade, attacked the main ELAS force, killing 70 and capturing 400. Further heavy fighting in January 1945 cost the brigade dear. The 5th Battalion lost more than 100 men while the 6th lost every one of its company commanders, killed or wounded in action against the communists. However, the uprising was quelled in the second week of January, when the brigade led an assault on the main ELAS forces, killing almost 200 and capturing 520. The guerrillas withdrew and on 16 January the Paras began to disengage from this bitter confrontation by handing over a more peaceful region – for the time being at least – to the Greek National Guard.

After returning to Italy to await orders, the brigade faced a frustrating three months during which it prepared for 30 separate airborne operations which were subsequently cancelled, including five for which all the men were emplaned ready for take-off. They returned to the UK in the first week in May without further call on their talents, which General Alexander had personally applauded in a letter to the brigade praising its record of successes completed with 'dash and fighting efficiency'.

* * *

By then the war in Europe was over. The 6th Airborne Division became part of the final operations, and in this role it was sent once again to the place where its colleagues in the 1st Division had taken such a pounding: the Rhine crossing. This time, the 6th was better prepared, better briefed and had sufficient transport to drop all the men in one lift and within close range of all the targets. Indeed, since the criticisms over the split movement of the 1st Airborne Division at Arnhem and the long march to the bridge, much work had been done to improve the planning of delivery of troops and heavy equipment right to the heart of the matter.

A totally fresh strategy had been developed, largely at the behest of Brigadier Chatterton, commander of the Glider Pilot Regiment. This would ensure that an entire brigade could be landed in tactical groups close to its objectives. Battalion platoons and companies were segmented and flown in together by planes going in almost single file, so that each stick of men dropped on to their DZ and could muster at their rendezvous quickly and efficiently. Troops bearing the heaviest equipment would get priority landing closest to the target.

Since the 6th Airborne Division would almost certainly face an opposed landing, tactical solutions to reaching its objectives were worked out in detail in advance. The lessons learned at such great cost at Arnhem could now be applied with substantial benefit, though it was not possible to eliminate the grave risks to life and limb that were posed by such a massive deployment of troops by air. The 6th was to join the US 17th Airborne Division, both linking up with the British 2nd Army on the left of the two fronts of the attack, while the American 9th Army moved from the right. The airborne troops' objective was to capture and hold key terrain north of Wesel, then establish and defend bridgeheads for the assault crossing of the Rhine by ground forces with whom they would link up on the first day of operations, scheduled for 24 March 1945. The 6th would land in broad daylight in the northern area of the Wesel sector. This part of the sector, like most of the target zones, was heavily populated by German Panzer Divisions and infantry, as well as a hefty deployment of anti-aircraft artillery, estimated by intelligence reports to be close to 1000 guns.

In the 48 hours before the planned attack, 5561 bombing raids were launched by Allied aircraft which pounded Germany with 15,100 tons of bombs while fighter-bombers hit ground positions, gun batteries and convoys. Further attacks on enemy positions were scheduled to be carried out by ground batteries and Allied fighter and fighter-bombers in the two hours before the first parachute troops and glider landings commenced. The first takeoffs were planned for 07.30 on the 24th, and that morning the weather in both England and around the Rhine was fine and clear. Packed with gear, guns, vehicles and supplies, the huge gliders were now awaiting only the men. The parachute aircraft, 242 planes in all, were lined up on their runways to begin the lift. Among those thousands of souls straining at the leash was Jim Absalom, from Liverpool, a communications officer with the 12th Parachute Battalion:

We really did want to get going. After the Ardennes, it had been back to parachute training, weapon training, night marches and the rest. All the sort of things that you'd expect soldiers to do when they are training to get to a peak of perfection ready for another action. And then eventually, on 24 March, we flew off from somewhere in Oxfordshire. The Dakotas were all lined up on this airfield. Ours was number 137. I noticed there was sticking plaster over all the bits that jutted out, like handles and things. And I said [to one of the crew], 'What's the idea of doing that?' He said, 'Don't you remember the other day there was a chap being towed round the sky underneath a Dakota hanging on the end of his static line?'

I said, 'Yes, that was our chaplain.' We knew him as Holy Joe, a first-rate bloke. And he'd gone out of his aircraft on a practice jump, failed to break away from the static line and he'd been towed round the sky... Eventually they lowered a kitbag on the end of a rope and he got hold of it and was pulled back in. Holy Joe Jenkins then went down, drank half a bottle of whisky and did another parachute jump. Well, they were sticking plasters on all the jutting-out bits so that it didn't happen again. The Rev Jenkins held a drumhead service for us before we flew away.

We flew over Belgium and Holland and we saw all the craters below us and so on. Eventually we moved into formation with the huge armada of aircraft of which we were in the vanguard, until there beneath us was the Rhine, majestic and calm... We got the red light to stand by and we all hooked up, and then we all moved down the aircraft shuffling with your left foot forward because you had a kitbag on that leg with your equipment in. And I'd got parts of an SCR 300, which was a Canadian radio with which I was to establish contact with brigade and army as soon as we landed.

The green light came on and we started to shuffle out. And all of a sudden [with ack-ack fire all around)] one chap stood at the door and couldn't go any further. I shouted, 'Boot him.' I heard him say, 'Oh no, oh no.' I shouted again, 'Boot him.' And they booted him out and he went down. So we were all out, and dropping, and I remember lowering my kitbag so that it hit the ground before I did and at the same time I realized I was passing people at a fast rate of knots, whereas we should all be going down at the same sort of speed. They were doing about 18 or 20 miles an hour; I must have been doing about 30. And looking up I saw my batman above my head, waving and pointing down to my parachute, trying to tell me exactly what I knew was happening anyway by then. The front three panels of my parachute had been hit by flak from air bursts that were being fired at us from 88mm guns. So I'd got a big hole in the front of my parachute. Well, I hit the ground with a thump but I was very fortunate; just bruises. Others weren't so lucky.

We moved across the dropping zone to a rendezvous in a copse of trees. Our gliders were coming in; there were three to each battalion loaded with quartermastering stores. And soldiers in each of those. Our three gliders were all shot out of the sky as they landed, with only one survivor, a young chap named Doug Baines. Having been captured once and escaped during Normandy [see Chapter 5], he could easily have backed out of this, but he, being the sort of bloke he was, came anyway and he was in one of those gliders; and he lost a leg.

As we went across, so I was trying to get the blokes spread out a bit so they wouldn't get damaged by the air bursts that were flying around us. What the Germans used to do was to shoot 88mm guns above your heads so that the shells exploded above you and then pieces of the shell dropped down, killing or wounding anyone below. As we went across I saw a tank or armoured vehicle coming towards us. I couldn't make out what sort it was. I'd got my pistol drawn and I was shooting at this thing. And it was only 40 years later that my pal told me it was British who had landed from one of the gliders. Not that the pistol would have done much good, as he pointed out. We got to the rendezvous. And it was my job then to set up communications as fast as I could. And I'm glad to say that because we'd packed our radio sets very carefully there was only one damaged…

In spite of the softening up of enemy positions in the previous 24 hours, anti-aircraft fire had been heavy as the incoming troops reached their dropping and landing zones. Eighteen of the parachute aircraft were shot down before they reached the DZ and another 115 were damaged by ack-ack. Of the rest, several units suffered casualties on landing, especially the 5th Battalion, who overshot the DZ and took heavy ground fire as they came down. So did the 1st Canadian Parachute Battalion. Nine of its men were shot as they came in; among them was their commanding officer, Lieutenant Colonel Jeff Nicklin, who was unfortunately caught up in a tree immediately above a German machine-gun nest and was killed by a burst of fire as he hung helpless in his parachute harness. One of the Canadians' aircraft burst into flame as it was hit by flak immediately over the DZ. Even so, by mid-afternoon all the parachute troops were on the ground, having cleared their rendezvous, and were heading for their assigned roles and targets.

The 6th Airlanding Brigade probably had the most difficult time of all the units and performed incredible heroics, coming in last with its great, lumbering gliders in tow, packed with men and machines. It struggled to find its landing zones in the fog of war – the dust, smoke and haze caused by the activity on the ground. As was usual with such raids, the brigade was an easy target, and lost around 30 per cent of its incoming flights, either before or after making their drops. However, preparations for this mission had accounted for such eventualities, and tragic though the losses were, they affected neither the start of the operation nor the outcome. By 11.00 that night, all the objectives assigned to the 6th Airborne Division had been achieved and contact with the 17th US Airborne Division had been established to the south.

Activity continued throughout the night of 24–25 September, the airborne troops beating off some strong counter-attacks by German infantry and Tiger tanks which continued even as they made their rendezvous with ground armies. The scene was set for the breakout from the bridgehead which would go ahead the following day, and this would be followed by a thrust into the heart of Nazi Germany. Major General Ridgway gave this assessment of the operation at that point:

The airborne drop in depth destroyed enemy gun and rear defensive positions in one day – positions it might have taken many days to reduce by ground attack. The impact of the airborne divisions at one blow shattered hostile defence and permitted the prompt link-up with ground troops. The increased bridgehead materially assisted the build-up essential for subsequent success. The insistent drive to the east and rapid seizure of key terrain were decisive to subsequent developments, permitting Allied armour to debouch into the North German plain at full strength and momentum.

From that time the 6th Airborne Division played a continuing role in the Allied advance across Germany and on to the Baltic which it had helped to make possible. The parachute and glider troops made a journey of some 350 miles largely on foot in under 40 days, halting on the way to fight many a tough battle and a lot of running skirmishes with marauding German units. They trudged all the way to the River Elbe and onwards until they met the incoming Russian Army's advance guard on the Baltic coast. On the way, Jim Absalom recalls, they saw the sights that Nazi Germany had to offer:

There were many things we didn't like and a lot of incidents on the way whose seriousness was lessened by the humour of the blokes around you and the way they reacted in emergencies. Some were amusing in themselves – years earlier, when I was a young soldier, I'd been at a Brigade of Guards depot for a drill course and had dealings with this drill sergeant, the biggest man I've ever seen in my life. He filled a door. Drill Sergeant Evans. And now all this time later, I was a lieutenant signals officer on our march through Germany and the Guards Armoured [Division] vehicles came along just as we had stopped for a brew-up. They stopped and jumped down off their vehicles and from one of them, I heard this voice scream out at me: 'Take your hands out of your pockets, that man.' It was Drill Sergeant Evans.

At one place – Celle, I think it was – we came across a prisoner-of-war camp full of Americans – except for one Grenadier Guardsman. And as we went past they flocked out to see us. They made way for this Guardsman, who marched through the middle of the Americans, who all looked a bit untidy. But he was immaculate in his old service dress with brass buttons. He'd obviously been a Dunkirk man: his cap badge was shining and what remained of his boots were polished. He marched up to the CO, saluted and said, 'I'm very glad to see you, sir.' And we all gave him a cheer and he joined our convoy.

The troops were nearing the end of their journey but even then, in those last few miles, there was still loss of life:

We were moving along quite fast towards Wismar – by then we'd got transport and I'd got a jeep. The CO was in his jeep just behind me and there was another jeep in front with a trailer and a few other vehicles with equipment. As we went along some Typhoons, our own aircraft, came down and strafed us. Anything that moved over a certain line they shot and we carried no identification marks on our vehicles – the phosphorescent material that goes on the roof. We simply hadn't expected any aircraft then. One of the rocket-firing Typhoons hit the jeep in front of mine and the chap sitting next to the driver was blasted out of his seat. We laid him by the side of the road, but there was nothing we could do for him and he just died.

They call it friendly fire these days... Our blokes were screaming all sorts of language at them. It was sad because we were not far from our final destination, just a few miles away. Anyway, we continued on and finished up eventually at the end of our journey, at Wismar in the province of Mecklenburg. We had stopped at a little village not far away when the CO said, 'See if you can get England on the radio, Jim, and we'll broadcast it.' My signallers were excellent blokes and we managed to tune into London – and picked up Winston Churchill's speech announcing the end of the war. And so it was over.

9

SHOT IN THE BACK

The euphoria of Victory in Europe was tinged only by the unfolding horrors of the Nazi death camps and the apprehension of unfinished business in the Far East, where the Japanese had refused to follow Germany and come out with their hands up. And so, even as the men of the 5th Parachute Brigade were heading home from Wismar, they were being earmarked for deployment in a theatre of war that was totally alien to them. They were to fight alongside Field Marshal Bill Slim's 'forgotten Army' – the 14th – which was still heavily engaged across Burma and beyond. Lieutenant General Browning had been poached by Lord Louis Mountbatten to become his lordship's Chief of Staff in the South-East Asia Command (SEAC) in November 1944. In his new capacity, the former commander of Britain's airborne forces recommended his erstwhile chums for immediate action in the vital task which now seemed to lie dead ahead: an airborne operation to wrest from Japanese control the Singapore causeway into Malaya.

A whole new mode of attire and range of equipment was hastily being prepared for the Paras, including tropical uniform, jungle boots and the new No. 5 Jungle Carbine, which none of them had seen before. A battle-ready brigade was to be assembled, re-equipped and keyed up for action within six weeks of their return from Germany, consisting of the 7th, 12th and 13th Battalions the Parachute Regiment, 22nd Independent Parachute Company, 4th Airlanding Anti-Tank Battery RA (Royal Artillery), 3rd Airborne Squadron RE, 225th Parachute Field Ambulance RAMC and detachments of Airborne RASC (Royal Army Service Corps), REME, RAOC (Royal Army Ordnance Corps) and

Military Police. For those expecting early release from the traumas of war, and especially those hoping for demobilization, there was to be something of a rude awakening, as Jim Absalom, with the 12th Battalion, explains:

I came back from Germany with an advance party to get the barracks ready at Larkhill. As I stepped off the plane a very tall beautiful WAAF lieutenant came across and gave me the best kiss I've had for years and said, 'Welcome home.' I said, 'Thank you very much.' Then we went and had a pint. The chaps eventually came back and we got 28 days' leave, having discovered our next assignment was as part of the British Liberation Army [BLA] – otherwise known as 'Burma Looms Ahead'. Sure enough [on returning from leave] we were put on a troopship and sent out to India, where we did a very short period of what was fondly called jungle training. It wasn't really. We were billeted in a place called Kaliar in army huts outside Bombay in quite a different sort of area and atmosphere than we'd experienced before. We were told all about the dangers of sex and about the dangers of mixing with the wrong people and the dangers of drinking the wrong water. We were shown films about it. By the time we got there, we weren't going to go out of those barracks if we could avoid it because you never knew what might happen outside.

However, a group of us did manage to get to Bombay a couple of times. I arranged with a market trader to send a carpet home, which was there when I arrived back a year later. We had a meal at the Taj Mahal. Then we did this jungle training in the Ghats, in the hills up above Poona. That was interesting; different country entirely, all new to us – except the food. When we went out, we had haversack rations, British-style corned-beef sandwiches – which we couldn't eat because they were covered with huge bluebottles. All the chaps were shouting in disgust at these things. You simply threw them away. Indian drivers took us on another bit of training and they went down the Ghats at about 900 miles an hour and no brakes. Often you peered over the side of tremendous drops, ravines.

Finally we were put on the [P and O liner] SS *Chitral*. The original plan was that we were going to drop on Singapore as an independent parachute brigade... We found out later there were about 80,000 Japanese there and we thought that was pushing our luck a bit. That would have been about 20 to one, and in a way when the Bomb was dropped we were rather pleased. It's a terrible thing to happen and a rotten thing to say, but the fact remains that it saved our lives.

The atom bombs dropped by the Americans vaporized the cities of Nagasaki and Hiroshima and, on 14 August, Emperor Hirohito surrendered. The 5th Parachute Brigade was thus diverted to make what was expected to be an assault landing on the Morib beaches of northern Malaya, although when the Paras stormed ashore in early September not a single bullet was fired in anger. They began what was supposed to be a swift march towards Kuala Lumpur, but they had gone about 15 miles when the monsoon season broke and unleashed the heavens upon them – which was just about the sum total of the opposition they faced. By then Kuala Lumpur was already in Allied hands, so they turned around, marched back to the *Chitral* and headed for Singapore, arriving in mid-September for an operation somewhat aptly entitled 'Fiasco'.

The Allied troops who had regained control of the British colony had removed Japanese troops into POW camps, and the Singaporeans, stunned by almost three years under the brutal occupying regime, were ready to break loose in a variety of ways, not least on the wrong side of legal. The 5th Brigade was given the task of installing some order into the chaos of regions now devoid of civil administration, or at least lacking administrations whose politics and resistance to corruption were acceptable to the Allied commanders. The Paras and their associates were to become involved in all kinds of community-based rebuilding activity, including schools, hospitals, transport and sport. Jim Absalom and others in the battalions found themselves seconded temporarily into the police force:

In fact, I became acting superintendent... Singapore was a bit wild; it was an old colonial place which had been knocked about a lot. The people were so delighted we'd come back. When I took over the police station in our sector, I got our own battalion medical officer to look at the policemen first of all. We found a lot of them had VD and so on. The families were in a shocking state. They lived in barracks at the back of the police station. We managed to put them in some sort of order. The situation was naturally very bad, yes – all kinds of lawlessness, not least of which was the illegal booze. Before the war there were two or three distilleries, breweries. When we arrived, there were about 42 ... a lot of illegal drinking and bad liquor. I sent bottles to the city analyst, but before I got the report back 28 British soldiers were either killed or blinded or their stomachs had burned out by drinking some of that stuff, which was being laced with methyl alcohol that they were stealing from Changi airport. That was what Singapore was like then. And of course we had taken into custody all the Japanese [including civilians]. When the Japanese had taken over Singapore and moved into the Alexandra Military Hospital, they'd killed nurses and doctors there. It was our chaps, based in Alexandra barracks, who found the bodies of many of these nurses and other staff who had been bayoneted by the Japs...

The 5th Brigade remained in Singapore for several weeks, until the civil administrators had formed themselves into viable groups. They were then ordered to proceed at once to the north-east coast of Java, first at Batavia (later Jakarta) to perform a similar task – in an area rife with heavily armed political extremists and criminal elements from the tripartite population of Indonesians, Chinese and Dutch nationals, all of whom were fighting with each other as the Japanese laid down their arms. The region was in dire straits. With the surrender of the Japanese, law and order had completely broken down, as had virtually all the public services. Communist-backed Nationalist guerrilla forces were forming up everywhere and because the Japanese had given themselves up to local forces, there was an ample supply of weaponry, which, in many cases, was immediately turned on the Japanese prisoners.

As they entered this mêlée of social disorder the men of the 5th Brigade found themselves hard pressed to assert any effective control over the so-called Indonesian Freedom Fighters, who, for the most part, were simply mercenaries and bandits out for the kill and the profit. The Paras were also called upon for other tasks, and Jim Absalom, having left his post as a superintendent of police in Singapore, was appointed, among other roles, acting local magistrate:

We did our best to re-establish law and order there. But it was a Gilbert and Sullivan sort of a place with headquarters of different organizations all up and down the main street: Dutch Army, British Army, Indian Army, local forces of one sort or another. And if there was a shot fired at night they all shot at each other. I was then put on provost duty in Batavia and did my best to keep blokes, our own fellows, out of trouble. You see, there were brothel areas set up in no time at all and we had to steer them clear. It was a dire situation and from what I could make out, our chaps got restless and our brigadier then went to see the General Officer Commanding and we got moved to central Java, at Semarang. I was then given a job reorganizing the civilian police in one part of the town. I was also the magistrate for that area and also had the prison. If anybody got picked up they came and stood before me and it was like dealing with a soldier. You either told him off or gave him five days in the lock-up. I think the fact that we were there served to hold the peace a lot.

We also had a Japanese battalion under our command, the Kedo Battalion, which had surrendered. Mountbatten had given the order that they could be used and armed if we were under pressure – which we were – and the brigade put them on the outer perimeter of Semarang while we sat inside. So whenever there was any trouble out there our chaps could go out and sort it out and then get back. If the rebels decided to attack us, then the Kedo Battalion would hold them off. They served us very well. There were a few incidents. One of the Japanese who had deserted, he'd run amok in the town and was found in the middle of Semarang by one of my acting Para policemen. He shot the policeman in the stomach and the policeman shot back with his Sten. But then this Japanese went missing. We found him dead in an outhouse about a mile and a half away; he'd dragged himself over some fields. And my Para policeman was in hospital for quite a while.

The first anniversary of the Rhine crossing had passed when it was assessed that the 5th Brigade could withdraw, having restored order to a reasonable degree with a Civil Affairs Bureau, although many areas of local life remained chaotic and a breeding ground for all the unrest that was still to come. The brigade's engineers had helped to revive public services and the 225th Parachute Field Ambulance RAMC had helped to establish a medical service. However, food supplies remained a problem and at one stage the brigade was feeding 5000 children a day.

Before the brigade left in April, it was applauded by the locals for the work its men had undertaken and completed, a fact recorded by the local newspaper editor, who wrote laudatory words about the fair and precise manner in which the British Paras had established law and order in their topsy-turvy country and had done much to help to re-establish community life. It was hoped, he added, that the incoming Dutch administration would do as well. They didn't, but that's another story.

* * *

While the 5th Parachute Brigade was deployed in the Far East, the 6th Airborne Division as a whole was assigned to the Strategic Reserve based in the Middle East, where temperatures were rising in the wake of the end of the war. The new Labour government had made no secret of the fact that it wanted to relieve the financially challenged United Kingdom of the overseas commitments of its armed forces. This, Winston Churchill furiously pointed out in the House of Commons, would in no time at all lead to the decline and fall of the British Empire, as indeed it did. India was already heading towards the big showdown, while the protectorates and other British interests in the Middle East – even then being courted by the Soviet Union – showed signs of trouble. The situation was particularly tense in Palestine, the Holy Land to Christian, Jew and Muslim, over which Britain had been granted a mandate following the carve-up of the Ottoman Empire by the League of Nations after the First World War.

Since the late 1800s oppression of Jews in Eastern Europe had caused emigration of Jewish refugees to the region. Some of the more militant formed the Zionist movement, promoting the belief that Palestine was the God-given home of the Jewish nation, while others felt that Jews were international and had no specific homeland. During the First World War, when Turkey sided with Germany, Britain and its Allies pledged to give the Arabs independence from the Ottoman Empire after the war. In the event, Britain proved to be two-faced in dealing with the joint claims of the Arab and Jewish populations of Palestine. The Arabs claimed that Palestine was included in the area promised to them, but in an attempt to gain Jewish support for its war effort, the British government confirmed that it favoured the establishment of a Jewish 'national home' in Palestine without violating 'the civil and religious rights of the existing non-Jewish communities'.

The region's peoples were immediately put on to a collision course that would continue to threaten its stability throughout the remainder of the twentieth century. The Jews took the British mandate to mean the establishment of a Jewish state. The Arabs, meanwhile, pointed to what they considered to be a built-in safeguard, namely that the Jewish presence would not be expanded without their prior approval, and throughout the 1930s responded to the increasing Jewish immigration with a violent campaign of harassment that culminated in bitter fighting in the years leading up to the Second World War. In 1939, with so many Jews fleeing from persecution in Germany and Russia, the British government put a limit of 75,000 immigrants into Palestine over the next five years and declared that no further expansion would be permitted without the say-so of the Arabs. During the war the dispute was more or less put on hold and both Arab and Jew joined the Allied forces. Afterwards, however, with the 1939 immigration quota already used up, the Zionists, fired up by the discovery that 6 million of their brethren had died in the Holocaust, naturally wanted the British to allow entry into Palestine of the vast numbers of European Jews who had been displaced by the war. The 'national home' promised after the previous world war by Lord Balfour now became not merely a place where these lost souls could rest their heads, but one which was also a profound and imperative ingredient – the focal point – in the spiritual and psychological recovery of the battered Jewish nation as a whole.

But Palestine was just one of many areas demanding the attention of the Allied governments of Europe, whose cities, countryside and national economies lay in ruins, at the same time as their colonies and protectorates were disrupted and in revolt. For the time being, Palestine was not high on the list of priorities, but the Zionist movement was determined to intensify the focus on the international political agenda by using organized violence. By the end of 1945, encouraged by the Zionists and other Jewish groups, refugees were pouring into Palestine in ever-increasing numbers. The British government remained firm in its resolve to limit immigration despite calls from the Americans to relent and begin talks on the formation of an independent Jewish state. The

Prime Minister, Clement Attlee, angrily rejected this suggestion, while Whitehall pointed to the delicate balancing act required to maintain Arab oil concessions in the Middle East. Meanwhile thousands of Jews were already heading to their promised land aboard ships from Europe. The answer was to pour in battle-weary British troops and gunboats to keep them out.

By mid-September 1945 the entire 6th Airborne Division was preparing to move out to Palestine to join the large number of other British forces ranged across the entire region who had been called upon for a variety of duties but mostly to deal with internal security. Now that the 5th Parachute Brigade was committed in the Far East, it was replaced in the division by the 2nd Parachute Brigade, which was to link up with the 3rd Parachute Brigade and the 6th Airlanding Brigade. Most of the Paras went by sea and initially took up residence six miles from Gaza, in a series of tented encampments around the divisional headquarters, the staff of which had gone on ahead. According to the War Office, the Paras were flown to the Middle East as part of the Strategic Reserve for the whole region and Palestine had been selected as the base for this because of the country's airfields and training facilities. In theory, the Paras were not to be engaged in internal security; but it didn't work out that way and they sailed straight into controversy.

Even before they arrived in Palestine the Paras were unwitting pawns in a political power struggle, derided by Jewish newspapers as the 'Gestapo', whose mission was to 'perpetuate Nazi anti-Semitism'. The Palestinian Jews – or at least the Zionists – treated them as an enemy invasion force, there to lay the heavy hand of oppression upon them at the behest of a duplicitous British government. The Paras were surprised by the viciousness of these verbal attacks. After all, many Jews had served in their ranks in various operations against Nazi Germany. Furthermore, the Parachute Regiment could boast of a number of recent battle honours which, it was felt, hardly deserved this propaganda onslaught.

As the Paras entered Palestine, Jewish paramilitary groups were already forming with gusto. Many of these had a membership well trained through recent activity on behalf of the Allies, and with so many weapons now available from a variety of sources, they were soon to be well equipped with the latest firepower and explosives. Furthermore, they were backed by wealthy Jews, notably Americans. Over the coming months the names of the armed groups would become well known to newspaper readers around the world, and indeed the men who led them were to become international figures in Israeli politics. There were 'official groups' who had the support of the Jewish Agency and were made up of highly trained, well disciplined soldiers under experienced commanders. In addition there were several violent extremist groups who answered to no one but their own leaders, including the Irgun Zvai Leumi (IZL) and the even more notorious Fighters for the Freedom of Israel, also known as the Stern Gang.

The Arabs, meanwhile, had been rearming since the end of the war and had garnered the backing and support of several of the major Arab states. And so, by the end of 1945, the three-pronged situation had re-emerged of Arab versus Jew while extremists on both sides were pitted against the British. With an explosion in the number of Jews arriving in Palestine, mainly from Europe, the tension rose to breaking point. Along the coast the British were attempting to hold back the flood of refugees, who were classed as illegal immigrants. Many of those who got ashore were arrested and placed into large compounds, ready to be transhipped to other holding camps out of the country and away from the trouble zones. It seemed, to the outside world, that Britain was on the brink of building its own form of concentration camps, and the Jewish extremists made much of this dramatic turn of events.

The 6th Airborne Division, supposedly in Palestine only as part of the Strategic Reserve, was now to be widely deployed on internal security. The 3rd Parachute Brigade was sent to the

Lydda District, which included Tel Aviv, the 6th Airlanding Brigade went to Samaria and the 2nd Brigade, the last unit to arrive from the UK, remained for the time being near Gaza before moving out to the regions of most disquiet. The situation was developing into a fiasco and a public relations disaster for both the British government and the parachute troops themselves.

The forced repatriation of immigrants yielded pitiful photographs and highly descriptive accounts published in the world's media, especially in America, where the substantial Jewish population held such sway over vote-hungry politicians, made much of British 'brutality'. This was all being played out against the backdrop of events in Germany, where retribution for the death camps was being sought in the Nuremberg trials and daily reports of the Nazi crimes were unfolding in horrific detail. The airborne troops, deployed in some of Palestine's worst areas of violence and pursuing their command policy of 'cordon-and-search' for terrorists and weapons in the settlements and enforcing the curfews imposed in the cities, were given the Jewish nickname of Kalanyot, which referred to a red poppy with a black heart. This was in addition to being spat at and taunted face to face with being Gestapo or SS. In short, the British soldier doing his government's bidding in Palestine was on a hiding to nothing.

While Alfred Rosenberg, philosopher-in-chief of the Nazi movement and one of the founding advocates of the extermination of the Jews, was explaining his theories at Nuremberg (whose judges subsequently ordered his execution), the Stern Gang was plotting its next outrage, seemingly to coincide with Rosenberg's appearance in the dock; indeed each new development in the war crimes trials seemed to herald another outrage in Palestine. On 25 April 1946 an assault unit of the highly organized gang attacked a lightly guarded military car park, killing seven soldiers of the 5th (Scottish) Parachute Battalion and although there were far worse atrocities yet to come, the Car Park Murders, as they were known, became a turning point in the confrontation between the British troops and the Jewish community. Gordon Mitchell voiced the feelings of many. He had last been in action with the Paras in 1943, for the invasion of Italy, was then transferred to the SAS – which, he said, was 'sadly and stupidly disbanded completely' at the end of the war – and was back with the 1st Parachute Battalion for the Palestine posting:

We were flown out to Tel Aviv – our job was typical internal security duties. Stopping and searching vehicles and people; cordon-and-searching areas for house-to-house inspections. It was very difficult. We had gone into Palestine feeling very, very sorry for the Jews, very sorry indeed. Then they started shooting us in the back. The gloves were on us and you could not really hit back – shall we say, very much like Northern Ireland years later. Very quickly, and almost completely, the British Army turned anti-Jewish and pro-Arab. We would then go down to the beaches, watching for illegal immigrants coming in and we had to tranship them, some to Cyprus, some to Kenya, and three ships actually went back to Germany. Some of my battalion were on those ships escorting them back. Considering it was now supposedly peacetime, we lost quite a few chaps in Palestine.

Riots in Tel Aviv, in particular, brought fresh and direct conflict between elements of the 6th Airborne Division and Zionist extremists who were now being harboured and protected by a large section of the Jewish community. In one massive search operation, the 6th, reinforced to field no less than five brigades, three armoured car regiments and supporting units, searched the city of Tel Aviv and the homes of its 170,000 people. On 22 July 1946 the King David Hotel in Jerusalem, which was being used as headquarters for the British Palestine Army Command, was blown apart, with 150 casualties. And Ben Hecht, the American writer dedicated to the Zionist cause and the vilification of the

British – as in *A Flag is Born* (1946) – wrote: 'Every time a British soldier is killed in Palestine, I make a little holiday in my heart.'

The constant searching of Jewish settlements and the confiscation of weapons held for protection against continuing attacks by Arabs, pushed the situation inexorably towards a seemingly insoluble state of affairs – very like, as Gordon Mitchell said, Northern Ireland 20 years later. The British government published a White Paper on the future of Palestine in the second week of November 1946 but once again fudged the key issues. This was met two days later, on 17 November, by fresh rioting and terrorist attacks in which eight British servicemen were killed and 11 seriously wounded. And so it went on: the murder of servicemen and civilians, usually shot in the back or blown up by skilfully laid and electrically detonated mines; the capture of hostages, including British soldiers, who were eventually hanged; explosive charges in all manner of guises, hidden to cause maximum damage inside buildings – the Jewish extremist gangs wrote the textbook on urban terrorism.

Finally the British government felt it could do no more, and appealed to the United Nations to find a solution. In the meantime one of the most dramatic Jewish attempts to break the British embargo on immigration was already on its way. In February 1946 the *Exodus*, a former US troopship previously named *President Garfield* and now owned by the Zionist underground movement the Haganah, left Baltimore, captained by an American Jew with young volunteers as his crew. It picked up its cargo of 5000 Jewish refugees waiting at the small French port of Sète, near Marseilles, and reached Haifa on 18 July 1947. There, as the packed ship docked, it was confronted by a boarding party of British troops whom the refugees attempted to deter by hurling tins of food and fighting with iron bars and tear gas. The hand-to-hand battle lasted an hour or more, before the troops gained control and herded the refugees on to three other waiting ships, bound for Cyprus.

By then the British had detained more than 20,000 would-be Jewish immigrants and shipped them out of Palestine. In the terrorist reprisals that followed, two British soldiers, Sergeant Mervyn Pace, 43, and Sergeant Clifford Martin, 20, were kidnapped by Zionists and discovered hanging from two eucalyptus trees in a suburb of Haifa with notes pinned to their shirts stating they had been executed as spies.

The United Nations' Special Committee did not reach Palestine for its inspection tour until early summer 1947. They were boycotted by the Arabs, who could not even contemplate a glimmer of cooperation. In the end the UN recommended the formation of an independent Jewish state by the partition of Palestine. Britain was pleased to accept the UN verdict and leave as quickly as possible; it had a much bigger problem confronting it – namely the withdrawal from India, where a similar solution was being pushed through by Mountbatten to form the independent states of India and Pakistan and the beginning of some of the worst ethnic violence of modern times in which 4 million of the population were to die.

In Palestine, immigration controls were lifted immediately in the Jewish sector, henceforth to be known as Israel, and the 6th Airborne Division took on a new role in the final months of its deployment there: that of interposing itself between the Jews and the Arabs. The latter were now being supported by terror gangs from surrounding Arab nations, and with the Jews' own extremist units outlawed and their forces on the defensive, the much-maligned British Paras were helping to protect those who, over the past few months, had been trying to shoot them at every available opportunity. The British troops were finally withdrawn in May 1948. Several wars and half a century later Israel and the Palestinians have still to conclude an unequivocal peace.

10

Upon Swift Horses (or Bikes)

The 6th Airborne Division and its Parachute Battalions returned to the UK in 1948 to some unwelcome news. It was to be disbanded. Cutbacks in Britain's armies, and especially those on costly overseas operations, had been demanded in the post-war years by politicians. In common with many units of the three services in the aftermath of the war, a similar fate had already befallen the other of the two heroic wartime divisions, the 1st Airborne, and, of course, their friends of the SAS, both of which disappeared as regular operational forces in 1946 and would continue in name as Territorial Army (TA) units. By the end of the war, the Parachute Regiment had 18 battalions and a number of independent pathfinder units. Three battalions had been formed in India and two in Egypt. The new, slimmed-down regiment would consist of just three battalions and associated companies.

The 16th Airborne Division (TA) was formed as a nominal replacement for the two airborne divisions – the number chosen to keep the 1st and the 6th in its title – under the command of Major General Roy Urquhart, who had led the 1st Airborne Division at Arnhem. The new formation consisted of the 4th, 5th and 6th Parachute Brigades (TA), which were made up of nine Parachute Battalions, designated 10th to 18th.

On the dissolution of the 6th Airborne Division in 1948, the 2nd Parachute Brigade would form the nucleus of the remaining battalions: the 4th/6th, 5th (Scottish) and 7th (Light Infantry) Parachute Battalions were re-formed as the 1st, 2nd and 3rd Battalions the Parachute Regiment (henceforth to be known as 1, 2 and 3 Para) while the 1st (Guards) Parachute Battalion was reduced to company strength. The remaining one brigade of the

Army's regular airborne strength was re-designated as the 16th Parachute Brigade, again to maintain the links with the dissolved 1st and 6th Airborne Divisions. With other elements of the 6th either disbanded or heavily reduced, and the virtual elimination of all other airborne links, the Parachute Regiment was transferred from the banner of the Army Air Corps to become a separate formation within the Corps of Infantry.

The Parachute Regiment was now eligible to carry colours. It had a motto – 'Fear Dispels Knowledge' – but since it had come into being, despite constant calls upon its officers and men, it had acquired none of the trappings of the more established regiments. And it certainly had none of the treasures that had been passed down the decades, battalion to battalion in the way of trophies, memorials or even mess silver. It did not even have a regimental march and even if it had, there was no band to play it. All that the Parachute Regiment possessed was a red beret and a badge. Colonel Ken Darling was placed at the helm of a small team to acquire some history for the regiment and produce a formula for future recognition. This was finally achieved two years later when, on 19 July 1950, the three remaining regular battalions were turned out in fine order on Queen's Parade, in their adopted new home of Aldershot, to be presented with their first colours by King George VI. Ken Darling ran the show when the 1st, 2nd and 3rd Battalions paraded before an impressive gathering which included the ennobled Field Marshal Viscount Montgomery of Alamein as Colonel Commandant of the Parachute Regiment; Lieutenant General 'Boy' Browning, who by then had retired from the service to become Comptroller of the Royal Household on the recommendation of his old boss Lord Mountbatten; and Lieutenant General Sir Richard Gale, one of the original founding fathers of that small group of original volunteers upon which the regiment was built.

By now the regiment also had its own band and drums – 110 bandsmen and drummers recruited from other units which were being reduced after the war – and gave the first public performance of the newly acquired regimental march, *The Ride of the Valkyries*, suggested by the Royal School of Military Music because of its airborne links with Scandinavian mythology, in which the Valkyries were 'divine maidens who rode through the air, sword in hand, upon swift horses to do Odin's bidding … presiding over battlefields to determine the course of strife or to select the bravest fighters for Valhalla.' Divine maidens they weren't, but it was the nearest the school of music could get to evoking the idea of paratroopers. The slow march adopted for the regiment was *Pomp and Circumstance No.4*, which was very fitting in view of the occasion. King George VI and Queen Elizabeth were greeted by a royal parade and the King presented his own colours and the regimental colours to each of the three battalions and gave a speech which summed up the brief history of the regiment:

I have been deeply impressed by what I have seen, and I congratulate you on your fine bearing and drill. This has been no surprise to me, for I have watched the growth of your regiment from its earliest days, and I recognize in this parade the keenness and spirit which have brought you through the perils of so many difficult operations. Yours has not been a long history. Only a short time separated your first raids on the Tragino Aqueduct and the Bruneval radar station from the fighting in North Africa and Sicily; very soon afterwards, in the 1st and 6th Airborne Divisions, you were adding your weight to those great blows which fell upon the enemy in Normandy, at Arnhem and on the Rhine, and which brought the European War to an end. There were other battles and much varied training, for you had to fight not only as parachutists but often for months at a time as infantrymen. The volunteers who came from all arms of the service to fill your ranks had much to learn; they learned it quickly and they learned it well. These colours … are the traditional symbol of a soldier's loyalty. The qualities which they represent and call forth are those which are common to, and indeed essential to, all good soldiers in all ages: they are qualities which you have shown that you possess alike in war and peace.

I am fully confident that you will maintain the high standard which you have already established, and that these colours will always be safe in your hands.

The regiment needed this ceremony, in terms of both receiving its colours and being formally established as a regiment. With such a short operational history, it had little to anchor it, save for the many awards for bravery collected by its men and the list of campaigns now officially recorded by the battle honours emblazoned on its colours. There were to be other changes too, which, some say, eventually changed the philosophy and to some extent the mindset of the parachute troops, moving them away from the original concept of volunteers and into the realm of professional soldiering of a different kind. Direct enlistment into the regiment of other ranks was introduced for the first time in 1953 and direct commissioning of officers followed in 1958, although a small proportion of the latter continued to be seconded from other corps and regiments.

The formal establishment of the Parachute Regiment as fire-brigade infantry, able to drop or land into any action, was welcomed by the military strategists and top brass currently casting an anxious eye on the unravelling of colonial ties and the disintegration of centuries of European control over lucrative lands and trade agreements throughout North Africa, the Middle East, Asia and the Far East. The Second World War had turned nationalist groups into highly efficient freedom fighters, well armed, well trained and now, having been freed from the oppression of German and Japanese invaders, they wanted the pre-war colonialist powers out too. The French, heavily engaged in Indo-China, suffered the disaster of Dien Bien Phu, where so many parachute troops of the Foreign Legion's élite were killed in the prelude to the nightmare of Vietnam. In addition, Britain and

America were unloading troops in support of South Korea's civil war with the communist-backed North. Communist terrorists, or CTs as the colonial powers called them, were embarking on a campaign of murder and bloodshed across Britain's former interests in the Malay States. India and Pakistan were still in turmoil and profoundly dangerous instability was emerging in the Middle East as the British government pulled out of the region and left the newly created state of Israel plunged in the midst of sworn enemies. Meanwhile, in North Africa the Mau Mau were running ruthless terrorist activity in Kenya.

The British government was also confronted with the worsening situation around the Suez Canal. Egypt's dissolute and bulbous playboy monarch, King Farouk, was in trouble. Rumours were rife of his imminent assassination or some other non-accidental misfortune engineered by the rising nationalist politician Gamal Abdel Nasser, who, courted by the Soviet Union, was dedicated to liberating the country from three main evils: the monarchy, imperialism and feudalism. Although Britain had withdrawn troops from Cairo and Alexandria – much to Churchill's disgust – by the beginning of 1950, it could barely contemplate losing control of the Suez Canal Zone. As a result, a large and ever-increasing military force was maintained along the west bank. Nasser wanted this out. In addition, he demanded the cancellation of Egypt's Suez Canal treaty, which had been in force since 1888, when an Anglo-French commission ratified an international convention guaranteeing all nations access to the waterway in both peacetime and war.

The British War Office, having been advised of this demand, had already dispatched troop reinforcements to Egypt to protect British citizens working and living there, as well as the many British governmental and private business interests now under threat. There was considerable unrest, with strikes and outbreaks of violence at many British-controlled establishments, and the whole situation began to look exceedingly fraught. In October

1951 the 16th Independent Parachute Brigade's Headquarters Company and 1, 2 and 3 Para were flown into the Suez Canal Zone, while the remaining elements of the Parachute Brigade and heavy equipment came in by sea, to bring British troop numbers in the area to around 70,000. On 19 October, after Egypt's formal rejection of a five-nation pact for the long-term defence of the canal, British troops, including Paras, seized key points along the Canal Zone while their Egyptian guards slept. It was an unopposed assault, with no serious British casualties and two dead on the Egyptian side.

Although Britain had secured access to the Suez Canal for the time being, tension between London and Cairo mounted. Farouk was shuddering in his pink palace, awaiting a top-secret mission from the British Special Boat Service, controlled by Mountbatten (by then Commander-in-Chief of the British Fleet in the Mediterranean, based in Malta). The unit was to be landed off the Egyptian coast by submarine, to whisk him and his entourage away to safety, pending his possible return at a later date to wrest control back from Nasser. The daring scheme was ready to be launched when Farouk changed his plans and, on the night of 26 July 1952, sailed away in his own yacht to the fleshpots of Europe, his possessions stowed in 200 trunks, never to return. Nasser became president of Egypt and promised to get the British out as soon as he could.

The three Parachute Battalions were then largely engaged on internal security duties, particularly around the docks and other British-controlled property, while the brigade's artillery unit, the 33rd Parachute Light Regiment RA, guarded the British ordnance depot at Geneifa. It was a delicate, softly-softly operation aimed at keeping control of Suez without engaging the Egyptian Army in a full-blown shoot-out, although since this was always on the cards, contingency plans were prepared. The 16th Independent Parachute Brigade joined other British forces to counter any move by Nasser's troops to take over the Canal, while 1 Para was on standby for an airborne attack on Cairo with 3 Para and a squadron of the 4th Royal Tank Regiment, should the lives of British civilians be threatened. Egyptian forces advanced towards the Canal Zone in the New Year but stopped five miles away and made no further attempt to gain control.

Gordon Burt was with C Company, 1 Para, having previously been a REME armourer. He had volunteered for a parachute course at Aldershot, and within a month of completion was on his way to the Middle East. On arriving at Port Said, the battalion was moved to the Canal Zone on emergency duties and then, after spending a few fairly uneventful weeks there unloading ships during a strike, was sent down to link up with 3 Para. Burt recalls:

We were on standby all the time, largely under canvas on a desert site between 1951 and 1953. Friction was high among the Egyptians. It manifested itself with their sniping at these locations. They never came out into the desert where our camp was; it was confined generally to urban areas. We had three locations and occasionally you'd get a motorcyclist driving by throwing a hand grenade, or sniper fire, usually at night. We did not suffer any severe casualties; our casualties tended to be in training. If we chased and caught them, we then had to hand them over to our military police and they took them to the local Egyptian police. They were Nasserite campaigners bent on taking over the Canal for themselves, although it never appeared coordinated – just terrorist activity, often involving many students. We also faced demonstrations of crowds of 50 or 60 people who were waving flags though not bent on causing great damage.

Our orders then were to control them in a defensive manner and where possible talk them out of it and try to convince them we weren't there to kill Arabs. It wasn't a particularly happy time for the brigade, especially inasmuch as we never really knew how long we would be engaged there. Initially, the brigade had gone there as an active service tour for three to six months, but it did go on for almost three years. In the latter stages, a few families were allowed [to come to Egypt] for accompanied tours, but only about 20. We lost a great number of our wartime soldiers at that time because they were not very happy to sit back in such conditions for two or three years with not much activity.

As Burt said, the British troops maintained a foothold in the Canal Zone without allowing the situation to develop into full-scale conflict or pushing Nasser to call in the aid of his Soviet suitors. Eventually the British and Nasser came to an agreement that all British troops would be withdrawn from Egypt over the next two years and evacuation would be complete by June 1956. In effect, Nasser had achieved exactly what he set out to do two years earlier: to kick the British out of Egypt after almost a century of occupation.

* * *

In the meantime other difficulties were emerging in the Middle East and Asia which would require the attention of parachute units. Not the least troublesome of these was what became known as the Malayan Emergency, a communist-led revolution against imperialist rule which had been simmering since the end of the war. This came to the boil on 16 June 1948, when Chinese communists murdered three British rubber planters. The perpetrators of the crime were Britain's former allies, then known as the Malayan People's Anti-Japanese Army. Now called the Malaya Races Liberation Army, they were still run by their communist Chinese leader, Ching Peng, MBE, who, as well as receiving a medal from King George VI, had marched in the 1946 Victory Parade in London.

Ching declared war on the British following the formation of the Federation of Malay States in February 1948 under a British

High Commissioner. He had behind him a well-disciplined organization and an army of 5000 men run on formal military lines. Britain declared a State of Emergency the day after the murders. 'The Emergency' – it was never referred to as a 'war' – was going to be over by Christmas but lasted almost 11 years. The enemy was the CTs – part of a long line of such warriors who gave Western governments a real run for their money through the fifties and sixties.

The CTs were well versed in warfare in the jungle, which British troops in Malaya nicknamed 'the Green Hell'. Stretching 400 miles between Thailand and Singapore, the Malayan peninsular had a hot and wet climate, and four-fifths of the land area was once covered in dense tropical rainforest. The forest harboured all the nasties imaginable, including leeches, ticks, scorpions, snakes, very large caterpillars which combined with the sheer effort of hacking away at creepers and vines, and wading waist deep in its mosquito-blown swamplands was a task and a half for any army. Many units of the British military had been engaged through the late forties and early fifties, notably the Gurkha regiments, who had settled in their new bases in Malaya and Hong Kong after their exit from India. In short order, the Gurkhas were massed in Malaya, their four battalions operating at various times in conjunction with other British Army regiments. But the CTs were an elusive bunch and so General Sir Walter Walker, soon to take command of the 17th Gurkha Division, was instructed to write a pamphlet on the techniques of tracking and ambush. This information formed the basis for the instruction given by the Jungle Warfare School, which was hurriedly set up at Kota Tinggi in Malaya as the Emergency began to spread. In the meantime British troops faced long and monotonous patrols which were largely a game of hide and seek; the CTs were hiding and the British were seeking.

The communist guerrillas emerged every now and again, carried out acts of savagery and vanished again. Occasionally there were skirmishes and shoot-outs but, from the British point of view, no successful conclusion was in sight. By March 1950 the CTs had taken a hefty toll: 863 civilians, 323 police officers and 154 soldiers had been killed. The terrorists had also suffered, largely at the hands of the Gurkhas, and their casualty figures were 1138 killed, 645 captured and 359 surrendered.

In Hong Kong at that time was a British staff officer who had served in Burma at the time of the Chindit operations: 'Mad Mike' Calvert, who had ended the war as commander of an SAS brigade in north-west Europe. In May 1950 General Sir John Harding, Commander-in-Chief of Far East Land Forces, sought out Calvert and asked him to make a detailed study of the problems facing troops in Malaya and to report back as soon as possible. Calvert took off for the jungle, made a 1500-mile tour, unescorted and along routes infested with terrorists. He visited villages, spoke to their headmen and then prepared a large summary of his findings. Among his suggestions was the idea, used successfully in the Second World War in Chindit operations against the Japanese, of linking ground forces with airborne troops to hit enemy supplies and to resupply the ground patrols on long search and ambush operations.

The combination of Paras and – for the most part – Gurkha infantry had worked extremely well. And now Calvert's suggestion led to the formation of an SAS-style force, to be led by Lieutenant Colonel Mike Calvert himself, enlisting former SAS men into a group of Special Forces known as the Malayan Scouts – which was itself the forerunner to the re-formation of the SAS in the form of the 22nd Special Air Service Regiment some years later. A secondary aim of Calvert's plan was to make contact with the indigenous people of the jungle regions and win their trust and cooperation. His little army, heavily dependent on parachute drops into specific areas, was initially reinforced with a squadron of Rhodesian SAS men, and when their tour ended these were replaced by a squadron of volunteers from the Parachute Regiment who became part of the SAS-led operations for the next 12 months.

The Para squadron, made up of volunteers from the three battalions, formed the Independent Parachute Squadron under Major Dudley Coventry and flew out to Malaya in April 1955 to go through six weeks of special training at the Jungle Warfare School before joining 22 SAS at its base in Kuala Lumpur. The new unit was organized and operated as an SAS squadron, as Walter Walker explains:

[John] Woodhouse [CO, 22 SAS] had perfected the highly dangerous occupation of dropping into trees during their initial involvement in the Malayan Emergency. Woodhouse was a very shrewd man and [later in Borneo] it was he who advised me to use the SAS in an eyes-and-ears role, but with a sting. He developed four-man fighting patrols which consisted of a commander, an expert in explosives, an expert in communications [and working the special radio sets they had] and a medical orderly. They went deep into the jungle, gave villagers food and medical supplies and got information in return. They had an excellent communications system through which they could get right back to Woodhouse and pass the information; he in turn passed it to me. Years later I met my opponent, who had been on the enemy side at the time, and the first thing he asked was, 'What sort of radio did you have that enabled you to tell you exactly where my troops were and when they were going to cross the frontier?' I was able to tell him the truth: that the SAS won the hearts and minds of tribespeople by arranging to protect their villages, and the villagers did some spotting for us. Their communications gear enabled the information to be forwarded on instantly. The first principle of jungle warfare, in those conditions, was to win the hearts and minds of the people, not destroy their villages or [use] scorched-earth policies as the Americans did in Vietnam.

The Independent Parachute Squadron was used in the early development of these techniques in Malaya, operating patrols which penetrated deep into the jungle. These patrols faced the constant threat of ambush by an enemy well used to such conditions. The patrols had to be resupplied by air because, along with the Gurkhas, they were pioneering the development of long-range jungle patrols, which lasted for up to ten weeks at a time instead of the more conventional four- or five-day treks. Food and fresh kit were dropped every seven days in zones cleared by hand. The clearing operation included the felling of trees to secure visibility through the dense jungle canopy, but even then, too often the containers were left hanging high and dry. Supplies of clothing were vital: boots rotted quickly in the wetness underfoot and the lightweight jungle uniforms were stinking and in tatters within a few days.

Susceptibility to extreme physical exhaustion, dehydration and sickness were major problems in addition to the sheer hostility of an environment in which, if the enemy was spotted, it might be just for a fleeting second. It was a tough 12 months for the squadron, but most of the men wouldn't have missed it. Afterwards they returned to base at Aldershot and thence to their original units, where other calls to arms were already on the horizon.

* * *

Cyprus had been a strategic launch pad for British military operations to the Middle East for decades, just as Malta was for the Royal Navy. The island had been ruled by the British since it was ceded by the Turks in 1878, and it became a crown colony in 1925. But by the 1950s, as in so many other British possessions across the globe, the population, which had absolutely no affinity with Britain, was getting restless. Neither did the native population consider themselves Cypriots: they were either Greeks or Turks, with the former outnumbering the latter by three to one.

The island became increasingly volatile in the middle of the decade during a bloody campaign by Greek Cypriot extremists fighting for Enosis: union with Greece. A Greek-Cypriot secret organization called EOKA flared into the open with guerrilla attacks against the British and Turkish populations. Its leader was the hot-blooded Colonel George Grivas, a fierce nationalist notorious for his savagery against communist prisoners during the Greek civil war of 1946–9. Archbishop Makarios, leader of the Greek-Cypriot community, made no attempt to decry the violence, and in 1955 the British Governor of Cyprus, Field Marshal Sir John Harding, declared a state of emergency. Large numbers of British troops began pouring into the island, and at various times all three battalions of the Parachute Regiment were engaged, along with many other elements of the nation's military.

The Paras moved in after Harding had failed to reach agreement with Makarios in a number of secret meetings. Although the British governor was eventually authorized to offer independence from Britain – which eventually came about in 1960 – it was not enough for Grivas, who wanted nothing less than union with Greece. EOKA's elusive bands of terrorists stepped up the concerted programme of attacks against British soldiers and the local population who supported British rule or worked for British interests. Operating from mountainous terrain which gave good cover, such as the Troodos Hills, they descended on villages and towns to conduct an appallingly ruthless campaign of murder which verged on bloodlust. All those who opposed – or were thought to oppose – the EOKA campaign were mowed down with Thompson sub-machine-guns, sprayed with petrol and set alight in front of the members of their village, or simply knifed to death.

Deaths inflicted on Turkish Cypriots by the terrorists threatened to spark a three-way conflict and raised the possibility of intervention of troops from the Turkish mainland, which in turn would have led to the involvement of mainland Greece – as indeed later happened. As the island's British governor, Harding was thus attempting to keep the lid on what the newspapers were describing as an 'explosive situation'.

Like a military Mafia, EOKA began to inspire such fear in innocent civilians that they dare not speak out. An off-duty British sergeant, out shopping in Nicosia with his four-year-old son, was shot dead in front of many witnesses. The alleged killer was apprehended and then released because no one saw anything, heard anything or recognized the accused man. Meanwhile terrorist violence of this kind continued to receive the tacit approval of Makarios.

John Rymer-Jones was with 3 Para. He was commissioned from Sandhurst into the 1st East Kent Regiment in 1953 and seconded to the Parachute Regiment in 1955 after service in Kenya against the Mau Mau. In the autumn of that year he became a platoon commander and while still a member of 3 Para, was attached to Headquarters Company of the 16th Parachute Brigade:

In 1956 we were dispatched to Cyprus, ostensibly on our way to Jordan because King Hussein – who I'd been with at Sandhurst – was facing an unstable time and wanted some assistance. Two battalions went out at the same time to Nicosia. But the Jordan deployment was cancelled and we were volunteered to Field Marshal Harding, Governor of Cyprus, for anti-EOKA operations. It was a high-profile stance with two forces committed to those duties: the Parachute Regiment and 3 Commando. The Commandos and the Paras cooperated very closely, although sadly we were not getting very close to Colonel Grivas.

However, they did arrest Archbishop Makarios. It was one of the early tasks confronting the paratroopers: 3 Para got the job, surrounded his palace and took him into custody. Without delay he was transported to the Seychelles, to remain there in exile until a solution was found.

Gordon Burt came in with C Company, 1 Para:

We were one of the first units to operate against EOKA, operating right across Cyprus. We had a number of very successful operations in which people were arrested and weapons were confiscated. At different periods, depending on how the talks to settle it were going on, our rules of engagement could vary between 'shoot to kill', 'challenge and shoot' and 'challenge and not shoot'. It was different almost every time we went out. It was tremendous training for the brigade, especially the newcomers. It was also very frustrating. EOKA terrorists were well versed and knew the area much better then we did and were able to flit in and out very quickly. We would arrive minutes after a group had moved out of their hilltop location, but generally we were not capturing large numbers. It was relearning, I imagine, the experience gained in the war, possibly in Greece. I can remember our training – of going into a place where there were suspected terrorists. There was a fire burning in the grate, a new fire, and we were able to take the fire out, lift the flagstones and there discovered a terrorist below it. We would move in the early hours of the morning, putting out a perimeter guard and then put in a unit trained in searching. Another method of finding hidden terrorists was to throw a bucket of water over the floor and if it disappeared down the cracks, you would know there was very likely hollows underneath, hiding people or weapons.

We carried on the operations right across Cyprus, although most of the time it was up in the mountains. Again, we felt we were doing a worthwhile task. Only now, looking back on it, there weren't that many terrorists to hunt down and we seemed to have a great number of troops there. This then makes us realize when we have something like the Yugoslavia situation – where Lieutenant General Michael Rose, who had at one time been Brigade Major of the 16th Parachute Brigade, called for more troops – just how many were needed for an area like Cyprus. There was virtually over a division there, all on active service at the same time.

The action tended to be sniper fire when we took up a location. On one occasion we moved into an area which the terrorists had recently vacated. The Company Sergeant Major, Jimmy Foster, took a patrol out, just after 3 Para had missed Grivas [see below]. On the borders of each battalion's areas, ambush parties were set up and Jimmy Foster was taking out one from C Company and moving along the tracks and must have reached the border area [of 3 Para's location] without realizing it – and what you must appreciate is that we were dressed much the same as what we imagined the terrorists were, with bandannas around one's head and with cam[ouflage] cream – and so as he rounded the bend he was shot straight through the chest, with the bullet going into the next guy and the next guy from a 3 Para ambush party. They weren't certain at that time if it was 3 Para and they took cover, taking the bodies with them, and then sent back one NCO all the way to our camp, which took him probably 40 minutes. He came rushing in to say that they had been ambushed by terrorists. The Company commander at the time was away and I then started to get ready a second group to go out to assist when it came out over the radio that 3 Para had made contact. Since the grid reference was the same, we were able to put two and two together and ascertained that 3 Para had fired on our patrol. Jimmy Foster was killed and the other two seriously injured.

This unfortunate incident occurred during a search operation inaptly called Lucky Alphonse, in which several battalions were deployed. It was rumoured that Grivas had a hide in the dense undergrowth of Paphos forest, and the troops were making a sweep through the area. A Greek monastery at Kykkho was searched and evidence discovered that terrorists had recently been harboured by the monks. The search operation continued and Sergeant Scott, leading a patrol of C Company, 3 Para, saw a group of terrorists up ahead, and as the patrol gathered for an ambush, one of them slipped and fell, alerting the gang of their presence. The terrorists fled, abandoning everything in their camp. Alan Wooldridge, with 3 Para, remembers:

We had been alerted by intelligence, who said they knew where Grivas was hiding – usually it turned out to be where he had been. This time, it was Grivas – and we'd missed him again. We found his diary and other possessions. I picked up his radio, my batman got his bed. We spent a lot of time chasing Grivas, and of course in cordon-and-search operations. I have many memories of leaping from one roof to another [in Nicosia] – and sadly went through one of them, landing on a breakfast table amid a shower of asbestos shards. The search operation in Nicosia was done using bicycles because there were no vehicles. It was an excellent way of getting about. We commandeered hundreds of bikes for the job and when we'd finished they were all piled up in Atatürk Square for the locals to sort out. Then, we were back in the hills, sweeping across the terrain, surrounding villages, searching, laying ambushes. There were some very successful operations... We found a lot of weapons and captured numerous terrorists. But we never caught Grivas.

Not long after the Grivas alert a nasty but accidental tragedy befell the British troops, as John Rymer-Jones recalls:

We carried out operations with a resident battalion of the Gordon Highlanders and on one occasion we had left the Bay of Morphou in a sweep up into the hills when the most appalling fire broke out. Many from 3 Para and the Gordon Highlanders were trapped. Once a fire starts, air currents lash it up the gullies and the fire leaps from ridge to ridge. The only defence was to lay down in a gully. Run for it and you're dead. Twenty soldiers perished in the fire. The mass burial at the military cemetery was one of the most traumatic events I had ever attended.

Among those trapped by the blaze were A Company's second in command, Captain Mike Walsh, and Captain Mike Beagley, who were travelling in a vehicle driven by Private Hawker. Their vehicle became engulfed and all three made a dash through the flames downhill, hoping to escape. Beagley and Hawker never made it. Walsh survived after falling into a ditch, although he had been badly burned when the flames swept over him. A formal investigation into the two deaths concluded that it was a tragic accident, although Colonel Grivas had already claimed credit for it. The British government flooded the island with posters, offering a £10,000 reward for information leading to the capture of Grivas. Informants were promised protective custody and a free passage to 'anywhere in the world'.

In July 1956 2 Para was sent to Cyprus to join the operations against EOKA. The battalion's deployment was more than just a matter of reinforcement. Hostile background activity had erupted once again around the Suez Canal. The scene was set for another slice of British history that would definitely fall into the 'unfortunate' category.

11

THE SUEZ FIASCO

It didn't need a crystal ball to predict that President Nasser of Egypt was planning to wrest the Suez Canal from international control and claim the revenues it produced for his own country. The crunch came when the British and Americans withdrew from negotiations to finance the Aswan High Dam, which Nasser was desperate to build to improve Egypt's irrigation and therefore crop production, as well as to generate hydroelectric power. Britain and the USA claimed that the Egyptian economy was simply too weak to sustain such a project. However, the underlying cause of the refusal was Nasser's recent arms deal with the Soviet bloc. He had mortgaged his nation's entire cotton crop for the next five years to finance the £200-million purchase of aircraft, tanks and artillery. When the Aswan Dam talks finally broke down, Nasser retaliated by declaring martial law in the Canal Zone, exactly one month after the last of Britain's 70,000-strong troop garrison had left under the terms of the agreement reached two years earlier, in 1954.

There, in front of him, was the massive revenue-producing international waterway from which Egypt received no direct benefit, having sold its shares in the Suez Canal Company to the British in 1875. And so he pursued the route of many other rising nationalist governments around the world: he severed ties with the 'imperialists' and nationalized their assets – in this case the Suez Canal Company – without compensation. There was dancing in the streets of Cairo on the night of 26 July – the fourth anniversary of the ejection of King Farouk – when Nasser announced nationalization of the canal. He expected that shipping tolls would pay for the Aswan Dam within five years and warned that if the imperial powers did not like what he had done, they could 'choke to death on their fury'. To this the British Prime Minister, Anthony Eden, replied that Britain would not allow a man with Nasser's record to have his 'thumb on our windpipe'.

Britain and France were fearful of the risk to oil supplies from the Persian Gulf. The French were also concerned that Nasser was supporting the increasingly violent independence movement in Algeria. Without taking America into their confidence, the two nations began secretly to plan a joint military action to depose Nasser, by assassination if necessary, and regain control of Suez. In August 1956 the British and French military went on high alert for possible action in the Canal Zone. This would eventually involve the whole of the 16th Parachute Brigade, which was still heavily engaged in Cyprus but had been ordered in mid-July to begin immediate training for the possible drop into Egypt.

The brigade's role in Cyprus, largely in internal security, cordon-and-search and hill tracking, had deprived its men of parachute experience for months, some of them having not made a drop for almost a year. Reservists were also being recalled for the first time since the Second World War, and they too were short of recent parachute experience because of the shortage – once again – of suitable aircraft. John Rymer-Jones recalls that the Para battalions were recalled to Britain from Cyprus one by one for ten-day retraining exercises before returning to the island. The shortage of aircraft was already apparent: the troops were travelling back and forth in the bellies of old Shackletons, which were also being used as long-range maritime patrol aircraft. On returning to Cyprus, Rymer-Jones was transferred to Brigade Headquarters as an intelligence officer and began three months of provisional planning for Suez. This entailed interpretation of aerial photographs, making models of the DZs and briefing battalion commanders on airborne landing sites:

Reservists had been recalled in the UK and had to be trained up because there had been virtually no reservist training. There were all sorts of preparations being made for possible military intervention. We were looking at DZs around Alexandria, Suez, Port Said and at sites around Cairo, although there was no specific planning at that stage. We were operating on a need-to-know basis and really had no idea what was going, other than that I was taken off EOKA operations.

Meanwhile the build-up of troops and equipment was under way. In the first week of August the 13,350-ton aircraft carrier *Theseus* left Portsmouth with the 16th Parachute Brigade on board. Personnel also included a large number of relatively inexperienced National Servicemen. French parachutists, from an élite Foreign Legion battalion, were also moved to Cyprus, along with other elements of the French military aboard requisitioned ships sailing from Marseilles. Gordon Burt recalls:

As the Suez situation worsened, the French airborne came out to Cyprus and we joined them for training. The sad thing was that we were jumping from their aircraft since we didn't have enough of our own for training. We were jumping from their Nords, which they in turn had bought from money loaned to them from the States. It put us to shame to see the French turn up with 30 or 40 Nords lined up on their airstrips and we hardly had any aircraft, just a couple of Hastings and a couple of Valettas, and I'm afraid that was it. The training was very successful, but come the time of Suez, it was a bit sad because lack of aircraft meant we could only parachute in one battalion group if and when we invaded.

While all these preparations were in hand, Colonel Grivas took advantage of the Suez diversion and mounted fresh terrorist actions against the British forces on Cyprus. Anthony Eden's deliverance of a new constitution which put Cyprus on the road to independence was not sufficient for Grivas. He was still insisting on union with Greece. On 27 September four newly arrived soldiers were severely injured by a bomb in a toffee tin placed in a restroom. Three days later, in the face of these renewed attacks, all three Parachute Battalions, along with the No.1 (Guards) Independent Parachute Company, began a massive sweep through the mountains of Kyrenia. It was the first of two successful operations, code-named Sparrowhawk, which turned up a number of arms dumps and led to the capture of more than 20 terrorists.

On 25 October, however, while engaged on another sweep across the Morphou hillsides and the Paphos Forest, Brigadier 'Tubby' Butler was ordered to withdraw the entire brigade from EOKA operations and prepare for deployment in Egypt. It was no coincidence when, 72 hours later, Israel amassed along its 120-mile border with Egypt a spearhead force of 30,000 troops, with another 400,000 as yet unneeded men in reserve. In encounters near the border the Israelis decisively defeated the Egyptians, who fled and were pursued across the Sinai Desert. A battalion of Israeli paratroopers was dropped at the Mitla Pass to head them off in an attack which military observers described as 'too big for a reprisal attack and too small for war'. How right they were.

The second wave of the pincer movement began as the Israeli troops swept almost unopposed to within 20 miles of the Suez Canal. On 27 September Britain and France issued a 12-hour ultimatum calling upon both the Egyptian and Israeli forces to withdraw from the Canal Zone. Israel agreed; Egypt refused. This was all a front, because there had been intelligence exchanges between the Israelis and the British and French military chiefs before the launch of Operation Musketeer, which swung into action on the night of 30 October. Without informing the USA, Britain sent Valiant and Canberra jet bombers to join French aircraft in bombing military targets and airfields in and around Cairo and the Canal Zone.

Within 24 hours the Egyptian air force was virtually wiped out. The Americans were furious about having been kept in the dark and accused the two European powers of acting in collusion with Israel – a charge which was true, although they denied it. John Foster Dulles, the US Secretary of State, went over the top in declaring that anything, 'including a major triumph for Nasser', was better than war. Meanwhile the invasion of Egypt proceeded in a somewhat bodged-up fashion.

Originally the entire 16th Parachute Brigade was to have dropped on strategic targets but – as with Arnhem and so many other missions – Britain didn't possess enough planes to transport the unit in one airlift. The RAF could supply only enough Hastings and Valettas to carry 668 men – these were to be 3 Para, commanded by Lieutenant Colonel Paul Crook – six jeeps, four trailers, six 106mm anti-tank guns and around 170 supply containers. The initial odds were expected to be five to one against the parachute force, and the task force would still be a day's steaming away. John Rymer-Jones, who had been engaged in much of the planning for the invasion, locating DZs, expected to be part of the sea-borne invasion. However:

On the night of 3 November I was with a large group from Brigade HQ, three to four dozen officers and soldiers. We had embarked with the invasion fleet being assembled at Limassol [Lemesós], only to see a launch approaching in the early hours... Captain Sid Cooper was aboard bearing the message that certain elements of Brigade HQ were to go back to Nicosia and parachute in with the 3rd Battalion the next morning. We were briefed on the night of the 4th... We of Brigade HQ were to parachute in at 5 a.m. in two aircraft of the fleet. I was in a Viking, which had a large boom across the body, and to parachute out you had to climb over the boom before launching yourself out of the door. The majority of the fleet were Hastings. The Vikings were dug out of mothballs. We were to fly in at three heights stacked at 500, 600 and 700 feet, which meant that having dropped 200 feet before discovering the main parachute hadn't deployed, then you were in trouble… We flew in with the main body of the 3rd Battalion.

First ones out at El Gamil were A Company and Brigade HQ. But what was Brigade HQ doing there? The brigadier's tasks were not only to command 3 Para but also a battalion of French paras. The drop was fairly uneventful, although there were obstacles ahead to be negotiated. 3 Para had a pretty hazardous time. They had to fight their way out of the eastern boundary across a sewerage works then into a narrow strip of land 150 yards wide between the sea and an inland lake to get into a mined cemetery towards Port Said. The Egyptians … were deployed in groups around the airfield itself. Nine soldiers were hit in the air; some landed in the sea, one descended with his equipment hanging 20 feet below him. He saw someone aiming at him only to be hit by his equipment, knocking him over and enabling the soldier to dispatch him.

The Egyptians had SU100 self-propelled artillery pieces and a lot of machine-guns, but the biggest and most upsetting pieces were lorry-mounted batteries of rockets and these would come hurtling over and land in a pattern on the airfield. We knew it was a pattern because Brigadier Butler decided to take us for a walk to see how Colonel Crook and the forward troops were doing; the rockets were coming in as we went. We walked forward and Paul Crook saw us coming, turned his back on the enemy and bravely – with an arrogance that passes itself on to raise the tails of the troops – came to meet us. There were all sorts of singular acts of bravery and heroism. [A group from this time still meets regularly: the 3rd Battalion Suez Veterans, which was formed much to the chagrin of the Army establishment.]

The French could only manage a similar drop and this was to be performed in conjunction with a high-speed naval task force which would dash across the Mediterranean to launch a sea-borne invasion to follow up the paratroops. Once through the El

Gamil airfield, 3 Para was to clear and hold the region between the airfield and Port Said, secure the native quarter and link with Royal Marines Commandos as they came ashore. The French, along with a unit from the 1st (Guards) Independent Company, dropped south of Port Said, to take control of the southern approaches to the town. They would then set off hard to the canal. Gordon Burt was with the sea-borne invasion:

...1 and 2 Para had to go in landing craft. But once again we did not have the landing craft available and they had to be borrowed back from the Far East and as far as I can recall they were manned by Nationalist Chinese crew and that meant that when we boarded them to go across to Suez every item of kit had to be secured because we soon learned that a rifle or binoculars disappeared. In fact the bolt out of my rifle was removed. We spent quite bit of time drifting around the Mediterranean because we clashed with the American 6th Fleet, who weren't in agreement with us going in, and we could not pass them for the time being. Eventually they moved on and we reached the beach, where we dug in at Port Said. It was very low-lying and as soon as you dug in, the slit trenches filled with water. Even so, morale was high initially. Like all regular soldiers, we were looking forward to some action, but it did drop a great deal as things progressed.

The Egyptians opened up with 120mm guns and mobile Russian-made multi-barrelled rocket-launchers, as well as with machine-gun and mortar fire. In these early exchanges British casualties were light, and 3 Para had captured the airfield within half an hour of their arrival and it was cleared and ready for use four hours later. After the French dropped in good order, watched by a large crowd of seemingly untroubled Egyptians, and pressed south, it was clear that the Egyptians were not keen to continue, at least not around Port Said, as John Rymer-Jones explains: 'The action didn't last long and the brigadier went off to sue for peace.

The local mayor and senior military officers were invited to sign a surrender document that night. Then some Russian consul people promised their support and by the next dawn, the Arab ceasefire was withdrawn.'

The assault force was now landing on the beaches at Port Said under covering fire from 3 Para, while the Royal Marines Commandos were brought ashore in Navy helicopters. Rymer-Jones:

The Commandos came in low-flying, observed by us, and we were wondering what the devil they were doing flying into the teeth of machine-guns and all sorts of other fire to land on the beaches of Port Said. Why our advance wasn't continued I shall never know. 45 Commando received many times the casualties that 3 Para had, and it struck me as gross stupidity and lack of appreciation that a helicopter force should fly in low over the sea at a fortified defence. However, the Marines were delighted with their performance. Port Said was quickly suppressed and we then moved from the airfield to a Brooke Bond tea factory and from there the brigade commander went to meet the first element of the sea-landed forces. Throughout the morning, in spite of reports of another ceasefire, mortaring and shelling continued.

The Egyptians were making a stand in the native quarter, a shanty town, and 3 Para patrols were met by rocket and sniper fire. The members of one four-man squad were all hit but they were quickly rescued by Captain Malcolm Elliott of the 23rd Parachute Field Ambulance group, who just happened to be passing. He was later awarded an MC. Then 3 Para moved an anti-tank gun into position and knocked out the enemy guns. Unfortunately, the shanty town was also shot to pieces, and caught fire. While these sporadic battles were proceeding, the 45th Royal Marines Commando reached its RV and 2 Para also came ashore in the afternoon and began its move forward through Port Said, facing sniper fire. After landing, 1 Para moved west along the coast and dug in to begin its own designated manoeuvres. Gordon Burt recalls another problem confronting the invaders and further examples of the somewhat chaotic state of British preparations for such expeditions:

…we faced the situation of being short of aircraft for striking. I only ever saw two Hunters and they had to go back to Cyprus to refuel and when you called for an air strike you had to wait quite some time before any action was taken. This manifested itself again where 3 Para landed and where the Commandos went on. The Marines called for an air strike and it didn't come in. They were left there for quite some time, an hour or so, and decided to move on themselves. They had just moved on the objective when the air strike came in and so that was a sad occasion. We ourselves didn't have any transport either. Each platoon in my company were told to go out and see what transport they could commandeer. One platoon came back with a bus, another had a tip-up truck and I'm afraid mine came back with a horse and buggy. Anyway, we all piled on this bus and motored down, heading to the Canal and then possibly towards Cairo.

We came under fire from snipers in a tall building and quickly got out of the bus and took cover. We laid there while rounds were going about us. I asked the commander if I could take a small group up and deal with it but he said no, an air strike had been called. So we had to wait there under fire for some time until finally the Hunter came in and blew the top off the building and we then all got back on the bus. We only went about a mile when we were stopped again. We were turned around and were sent back to the beach, where we had started from…

As evening fell, there was an unconfirmed report of another ceasefire. In truth, it was more of a cave-in by British and French politicians. The Paras, John Rymer-Jones recalls, were getting angry:

The idea was that the 2nd Battalion and armour [heavy and light arms] would head straight down the road and secure the Canal. But then, on the night of 6 November, orders came from the Commander-in-Chief and the Corps Commander that were absolutely explicit. There was to be a halt. A British community down at the Canal had turned out with goodies to greet us. There was no opposition and it would have been straight motoring to our objective. We were very disappointed and everyone was saying, 'What and earth are we going to do now?'

We knew that something that was within our grasp had been abandoned to [as they learned later] US pressure. In straight military terms, we could have achieved our objective. It was very frustrating. And, thank God, we were able to be shipped back within a week. The rest of the invasion force was left to tidy up and there was a lot of tidying up to do. There were, in my estimation candidly, huge Egyptian casualties. The shanty area to the west of Port Said was in tatters with a lot of fire and damage and I don't think the Egyptian authorities had any idea what the civilian casualties were. Or the military losses either. We had proceeded through a lot of stiff opposition and a number of Military Crosses were won from the action.

The Suez debacle – or at least the fighting – ended officially at one minute to midnight on 6 November. The whole business had been put under the auspices of the United Nations after much political wrangling and double-talk from the Americans and Russian threats of 'modern and terrible weapons' coming into play, while Cairo radio reported to its jubilant, if disbelieving, listeners that the parachute forces had been totally annihilated. The 16th Brigade *en masse* began clearing up while lookouts kept watch for snipers; the order was no firing unless their lives were in danger. The Paras were glad when, a week after their arrival in Egypt, they embarked in ships to return to Cyprus. Operation Musketeer was over and the men were smarting. Gordon Burt:

The aircraft carrier *Hermes* drew up as close as it could to the beach and we were ordered to go aboard. It moved out and we were ordered to throw all our ammunition overboard because the captain did not wish to proceed with loose ammo on his ship. That done, we were to return to Cyprus. We then spent two weeks expending all loose ammunition because it couldn't be packed up. Myself and six others from my platoon threw hand grenades till we were sick of hearing them. Then, I'm afraid, we had the reservists with us who had been called back for Suez. Their main interest then was to get home because, as far as they were concerned, the emergency they had been called up for had finished. But of course this didn't happen and we were then sent on EOKA terrorist duties. Morale was pretty low that we had been withdrawn. Word was filtering back about the political opposition surrounding Suez. We had gone there to do what we thought was a job for our country but we weren't really prepared for it. We didn't have the transport, whether it was air transport, ships or vehicles. It was a very shoddy operation.

Other British troops remained in the Canal Zone while United Nations secretary general Dag Hammarskjöld began assembling a 6000-strong internal force to go into the Zone under the UN beret to maintain a peace settlement. The British troops were formally withdrawn on the arrival of the UN force on 21 November. Hampered as they had been by lack of equipment, they had got away with so few casualties purely because of their professionalism. In fact, the handling of the Suez crisis had bumbled into chaos almost from the beginning. Eden's decision to schedule his attempt to regain control of the Canal for 5 November was doomed politically from the start, as the operation was launched on the eve of the US Presidential elections. President Eisenhower, running for a second term, didn't want to send the Americans to war – or even support his former allies in one – and certainly not on the day he was saying Vote For Me! He was spitting f-words by the mouthful in his anger that Eden and his

French counterparts had chosen this day of all days. In the event, he was elected for a second term and for some time thereafter showed great hostility towards the British and the French.

After the ceasefire had been ordered by the UN, Eisenhower blackmailed Eden into a humiliating assurance that all British troops would be withdrawn. The invasion had caused a run on sterling in the world money markets and America would not intervene to help the British treasury unless it was given a cast-iron guarantee that Britain would pull out. It did, and so did Eden, who resigned six weeks later.

It is also worth mentioning that on the same day that the British force landed in Egypt, 1000 tanks of the Red Army rolled into Hungary and crushed the Hungarian Revolution. Soon after dawn, the last words broadcast by Radio Budapest before it was silenced by Soviet troops were: 'Help... Help... Help...'

Two days after voting for an Anglo-French-Israeli withdrawal from Egypt, the UN Security Council told the Soviets to get out of Hungary. It took them 33 years to comply.

* * *

In the light of Suez, the Americans were forced to reconsider their reluctance to become involved in Middle East scraps, especially when their own interests were specifically challenged. To many in the Arab world, Nasser's confrontation with two of the so-called superpowers was an inspiration and not least to a group of young army officers in Iraq who arranged for the bloody murder of the Iraqi royal family. Although it had been smouldering away since the British withdrawal from Suez, the crisis in Iraq flared up again on 14 July 1958 when a coup by Iraqi army officers led by General Kassim wiped out the pro-Western regime of King Faisal II. The 23-year-old King and his powerful uncle, Crown Prince Abdulillah, were murdered and their loyal Prime Minister, General Nun el-Said, was kicked to death by the Baghdad mob.

The coup immediately caused concerns over the future of young King Hussein of Jordan, formerly of Sandhurst, who had come to power six years earlier after the assassination of his father, King Abdullah. His brief reign had already brought him into conflict with Nasserite politicians in his own country. Simultaneously President Chamoun of the Lebanon was facing rebel militia funded and armed by Nasser and, scared by events in Iraq, requested immediate Western aid. The day after the regicide in Iraq 1700 Marines of the US Sixth Fleet paddled ashore at Beirut – then a Middle Eastern showpiece of high-rise hotels and home to many American banks – where the steaming Marines in their war kit were greeted by bikini-clad Lebanese girls dishing out ice-cream.

Two days later, on 17 July, RAF Beverley and Hastings transport aircraft began landing 2000 British Paras at Amman airport in response to a cry for help from King Hussein, who had discovered that Syrian troops of the recently formed United Arab Republic, led by President Nasser, were massing on Jordan's border. The British force consisted of the 16th Parachute Brigade minus the 1st Battalion (which remained in Cyprus to continue covering emergencies), along with 208th Squadron RAF with its ground-attack Hunters and maintenance staff. These swift moves by the USA and Britain left Nasser and the Soviet Union fuming.

Meanwhile, King Hussein having broken off diplomatic relations with the United Arab Republic because of President Nasser's support for the revolutionary regime in Iraq, troops were on the move all over the region. Jordan became the focal point in the West's operation to retain stability across the whole of the Middle East.

Britain's advance party, consisting of the Paras' Brigade Commander, Brigadier T. C. H. Pearson, DSO, OBE, and a small Headquarters and Signals element, was isolated on Amman airfield for several hours after landing on 17 July, much to the surprise and embarrassment of the Jordanian authorities who knew nothing of the plan. Major General Michael Forrester, Brigadier Bob Flood and Brigadier Richard Dawnay, all then of lesser rank, recalled the operation on which they were engaged:

Dawnay: In June 1958 we were placed on alert to go to Cyprus once again. There were no signs at that time that there was going to be any problem in Jordan or Iraq. Life was as normal as it could be. We had no idea that we might be called upon, even when the United Arab Republic was formed in early 1958.

Forrester: But you never really knew – contingency plans were two a penny then. Joint planners had many of these plans stored away and the Parachute Regiment was by now performing well as a fire brigade.

Dawnay: Companies were turned out quite often; it was a culture. It was fire-brigade mentality.

Flood: The battalions had been in collective training before we got orders to go to Cyprus, leaving on 12 June. We were always at a high state of readiness at that time... All commanding officers were taken out to an American ship and given a very good briefing. The loyalty of some elements of the Jordanian Army had a large question mark. We were to confront all possible dangers, from internal uprising to full-scale invasion from Syria or elsewhere. On the 17th [July] we were given notice we were off the following day, the 2nd Battalion having already started. We sat up through that night redoing the load tables. We were heading for Amman.

Dawnay: We were used to changing roles, suits and everything at short notice. So it was no problem to switch from a para role to airlanding. We flew in, and my first impression was the incredible rocky, bare country, and other parts of it looking incredibly wealthy. One was terribly concerned with getting our own outfit sorted. We were well aware there was an urgent situation. We needed to set up communications and were generally lacking in knowledge when we set off. Things began to happen very quickly.

Flood: I landed in the last flight, in the middle of the night. Every aircraft was uncertain what it was going to find. It was a pleasant surprise to land fairly comfortably. Each battalion had its own piece of real estate: 2 Para was responsible for the airport; 3 Para was responsible for the King, his mother, British nationals and the British embassy. The security of Amman was the responsibility of the Jordanian Army. We were warned, however, to make sure that should anything go wrong, to take necessary action to secure the King and the British. We had a shortage of major arms and we would have to place great reliance on RAF Hunters should anything occur. There were six Hunters deployed; they couldn't send more in because of difficulties with the storage of aviation fuel. We also had call on aircraft carriers in the Mediterranean. So we did have a fair few aircraft available.

After the two battalions arrived, things relaxed somewhat. Towards the end of the month, the atmosphere changed; once again tensions mounted and the possibility of reinforcement with armour was under consideration. Nothing changed until 9 August, when there was a reinforcement from the Cameronians [1st Battalion the Camerons (Scottish) Rifles], who had arrived at Aqaba from Kenya aboard the commando carrier HMS *Bulwark*, and who came up to Amman to strengthen our position. There was a substantial movement of men and stores throughout that time. The final reinforcement, the 17th Field Battery Royal Artillery, arrived with six 25-pounders. On 11 August there was a pledging of loyalty by the Bedouins to the King. Even so, I don't think it was ever assumed that if a brigade-sized attack was launched against us, we would be able to hold out.

Dawnay: We were encouraged to maintain a low profile and were very sensitive to the various velocities of the Arabs and we were encouraged not to be seen too much. The troops were largely bivouacked and had to improvise a lot for ablutions and cooking. Brigade HQ managed to get use of some buildings. We had very little transport, although we did some field training out in the desert, but that was much later in the year, when things were less tense. The turning point to the whole business was a resolution in the United Nations on 21 August.

Forrester: By early September we had an idea that withdrawal was on the cards and indeed on 30 September the King announced we were withdrawing. The United Nations secretary general visited and it was by then all over – without a shot being fired in anger. Our being there had nipped it in the bud and probably saved King Hussein.

Towards the end of the Paras' deployment, training and recreational time was made available, including expeditions to local sights. They also helped deal with the 500,000 refugees from the border areas. King Hussein paid a ceremonial visit to the brigade to express his gratitude and there was little doubt among both military and political pundits that the Paras' excursion to Amman passed without undue drama because of the speed and skill with which they had deployed.

12

WHERE'S THE FIRE?

In the dozen or so years following the end of the Second World War – the supposed peace – there had been few months in which the Parachute Regiment was not in action; in fact it was so busy that exercises and training had taken a back seat. The regiment had continued to spearhead British troop movements into trouble zones and hot spots, mainly at the eastern end of the Mediterranean, and that situation would not change as the 1960s approached, for the Paras continued to be involved in a varied collection of tasks.

But while the fire-brigade role in which they had established themselves provided the young 'Toms' with all the action they ever wanted, it highlighted a problem for the older members of the battalions, many of whom had joined during the war or been seconded or transferred from other regiments. The nature of the tasks confronting them usually meant that they found themselves dispatched to some fly-blown desert, jungle, warren of fetid Middle Eastern alleys or other dangerous terrain, often living under canvas and surviving on backpack rations, and with few, if any, opportunities for accompanied tours – that is, with their wives. As Colonel Alan Wooldridge pointed out, parachute troops were a particular breed who had grown up on an exceedingly tough training regime with the added adrenalin rush which came from the sheer exhilaration – for such it was for most – of parachuting to earth. Few observers of military history have examined this fact, that it was something more than mere soldiering that brought the Paras together and welded them into closely knit groups who lived, worked and played together in a way that few other British Army units – apart from the SAS and the Gurkhas – were inclined to do. Nevertheless, it was a young man's game, and increasingly so. 'Everything we did in training was designed to push the man to the limit of his physical endurance,' said Wooldridge:

and as the years went by, the physical side became ever more demanding although the parachuting side was like a drug; you never wanted to stop. Later on, after a lot of messing around in various parts of the world, being sent to these curious places, one's thoughts drifted towards a more settled existence, particularly for those of us who had married and were constantly being separated from our wives and families.

That situation was never more apparent than in the late fifties and throughout the sixties, when hostilities, actual or threatened, continued to arise one after the other in the far-off places where Britain had interests it wished to protect, until finally the Paras found themselves in the most demanding of all their postings, ironically the closest to home: Northern Ireland. Before that, however, came years of postings which provided few opportunities for any kind of settled life other than that to be achieved around the home base in the UK, whenever the men could get back to it. Those who had left the service, experienced life on the outside and were then called back to colours as reservists were often not entirely happy to be back for any length of time, perhaps rightly so, because the original brief for reservists was to fill gaps in case of emergencies. Weekend soldiering was one thing, but as Gordon Burt discovered when his unit, 1 Para, returned to the hillsides and forests of Cyprus against the EOKA terrorists at the tail end of the fifties, some reservists were not terribly enthusiastic about the prospect:

We still had the reservists with us and they knuckled down to it. However, after two or three days I had an incident where I'd gone out and left a base guard and when we came back I found that our members of base who were reservists had gone to sleep. I had to then remove them back to our headquarters and had to take the action of putting them before the commanding officer; they got 28 days. It was coming to light then just how dissatisfied all the reservists were at being kept on after Suez – which is why they had been called back – and so very soon after that they were all sent home. We carried on the operations right across Cyprus, although most of the time it was up in the mountains. Again, we felt we were doing a worthwhile task. Only now, looking back on it, there weren't that many terrorists to hunt down and we seemed to have a great number of troops there.

The regiment remained hampered by the lack of decent aircraft that could be assigned to the task of carrying them to their missions and back home after these had been completed. Whenever the units were withdrawn from Cyprus, as they were from time to time, they usually faced an uncomfortable ride in battered old planes that should have been scrapped years ago.

We were told that the aircraft had become available to take us back to the UK. But these were coastal command Shackletons and I think there were 12 available and they were going to just keep coming in to land as and when they were available. Two battalion groups were to be shuttled home in these Shackletons, which normally carried a crew of 19. They cut it down to about seven and all the rest of the spaces were taken up by us, getting in the bomb bays, the rear-gunner's space, the front-gunner's space – everywhere in the aircraft that you could fit a man. You just crammed yourself into a sleeping bag and kept quiet. We were shuttled through Trieste back to the UK.

Although Colonel Grivas, who had called a ceasefire in 1958 and then revoked it, would continue to cause trouble for the time being, the Cyprus question had been moved to the United Nations after the island was granted independence in 1960, with Archbishop Makarios as its first president. Despite the existence of a three-party agreement between Britain, Greece and Turkey, the problems that arose from the attempts by the island's two nationalities to live in harmony remained unresolved. For the Paras who had already spent so many years there (and those who would see an outbreak of further troubles in 1964), it was a frustrating time, as Gordon Burt explains:

We look back at that [Cyprus] as a brigade effort because all three battalions were there. Looking back at it, I don't know … we had the information about terrorists but the likelihood of us coming across them in that way was very small, but I think we probably contained it to an extent. By being there in that great force we probably prevented a great number of others from taking up the cause. Once again, with talks continuing, as they do in all these locations, and finally finishing up with Archbishop Makarios taking over, it left a funny taste in one's mouth at that time to see these people who supported terrorists coming to power. One of those who took over the local newspaper was one of the top terrorists. But as one grows older one accepts that this has to happen and probably must happen if you are going to have peace.

The general attitude of the unit to the enemy was simply one of doing our job; this is what we were training for, this is what we joined the Army for; it was what we wanted to do. It was good training and kept us very fit and I think most of us were sorry that we did not see a great deal more action. It was a professional activity.

* * *

There was more of the same to come, and for the time being the location was once again the Middle East, volatile, unpredictable and dangerous as ever. The new regime in Iraq lost no time in rattling its sabres after Kuwait declared independence from Britain on 19 June 1961. Any intelligence officer with an eye on the history books could have predicted that before long the Iraqis would be casting an acquisitive eye over that oil-rich little patch at the tip of their country to which they claimed territorial rights. What Saddam Hussein eventually managed in 1990 – the invasion of Kuwait – was threatened that summer. Kuwait, which had been a British protectorate since 1899, was undoubtedly one of the most crucial of all the oil-producing states for Britain, which at that time was taking 40 per cent of its oil from the Kuwait Oil Company, jointly owned by British Petroleum and the Gulf Corporation of America.

The Emir of Kuwait, Sheikh Abdullah-Al-Salim, used a clause in the independence agreement to call for Britain's immediate help as soon as the Iraqis began their threatening manoeuvres. A serious situation seemed to be developing when Iraq ignored British warnings of intervention. HMS *Bulwark* was dispatched immediately to Kuwait with 600 men of 42 Commando RM, arriving on 4 July. Within a week 8000 British troops were assembled from units then based in Bahrain, Kenya, Aden and Cyprus, led in by the 2nd Battalion of the Parachute Regiment. Although they had originally been assigned to the Strategic Reserve in the late 1940s, this was the first time the Paras had been deployed under that banner. With its associated companies, 2 Para formed a brigade group, which was flown in and moved immediately to Matla Ridge, 40 miles from Kuwait City, the country's capital.

Once more the Paras were spearhead troops for the overall British deployment and, yet again, found themselves bereft of transport. The Emir gave orders that they were to be allowed to commandeer whatever they needed and they managed to acquire a good selection of both two- and four-wheeled vehicles. By the end of the fifth day they were joined by a defensive line of other British troops along the border with Iraq. But by then the Iraqis were already having second thoughts, largely because of the prompt arrival of the Paras and the Commandos, and aborted the invasion. The Paras then moved out to a base in Bahrain, already home to several elements of British forces, including the SBS, with whom they established a good working relationship.

Under blazing sun they took up residence beside Muharraq airfield in a makeshift camp devoid of any of the comforts of modern living. So began a long-term deployment of the Parachute Regiment, with each of the three battalions taking a turn at the camp over the coming three years. It provided excellent training opportunities, but the heat was a killer and for eight months of the year made exercises almost unbearable, even in what was classified as lightweight kit. On exercises the temperatures inside the Paras' Beverleys were such that the sweat from their bodies would actually run down the aircraft as it climbed skyward. They were advised to drink a minimum of 15 pints of water – repeat, water – a day to avoid dehydration. Rotational duties back at Kuwait did, however, allow for some R and R (rest and recreation) at the beach and the sporting facilities of the Kuwait Oil Company.

In October 1960 2 Para was relieved by 3 Para and returned to Cyprus. The newcomers were welcomed by a terrorist bomb planted on a Beverley parked at Muharraq which exploded as the last of 3 Para's planes came in.

Tours of eight months or so were to become the norm and a new permanent base for the resident Para battalion was rapidly built on a desert location at Hamala, with much of the work being carried out by the soldiers themselves alongside a busy programme of training exercises. The battalions arrived as a group, along with their affiliated batteries, but even when the new camp was completed there was still no family accommodation, whereas other British units were able to enjoy visits from their wives and families. It wasn't until 1964 that a limited number of families were allowed to accompany their husbands and fathers – just 80 in all, although this number was steadily increased as facilities improved. Not that Bahrain was the place to be as far as sporting and social facilities were concerned. The countryside was hostile and uninviting, so eventually limited numbers of soldiers were sent in groups for sports and relaxation to Aden, Kenya and Cyprus. This opportunity was enjoyed by most, especially the fitness fanatics.

In spite of the British presence – or, more accurately, because of it – the turmoil unsettling the region at that time did not bypass Bahrain, which suffered spasmodic local disquiet, such as riots and minor acts of terrorism, although the Paras were not called upon to intervene. They kept a close eye on the situation because the few military families who were there were being housed in the city, not far from student rioting, while the soldiers themselves were tucked safely away in their camp.

Elsewhere the campaign against the British presence was more determined, especially in regions which were on the brink of falling into Soviet-influenced hands. The domino effect of Nasser's arrival was continuing. In 1959 six tribal states within the British Protectorate of Aden formed the Federation of the Arab Emirates of the South. Britain signed a treaty with the Federation which promised its members independence. The date for independence was later set for 1967. Britain retained control of the Federation's foreign policy and provided military protection and economic aid. In 1962 the body's name was changed to the Federation of South Arabia and all but four of the tribal states in the Protectorate eventually joined this.

In the early 1960s Britain tried to form a representative government that would rule the Federation after independence but the political groups involved could not agree on who should rule. The radical nationalists began a terror campaign against both the British and the tribal leaders. Two radical groups, the

National Liberation Front (NLF) and the Front for the Liberation of Occupied South Yemen (FLOSY), also fought each other. In 1962 the hereditary ruler of what was then called the Yemen, the Iman, was deposed by an army-led coup backed by Egyptian troops. He took to the hills and hired the founder and former leader of the SAS, David Stirling, to supply him with a band of mercenaries – all ex-SAS – to form and train the nucleus of his royalist army in exile. And so began long-running battles among rival factions within the Federation, all along the coast from the Yemen through the tribal sheikdoms to the British colony of Aden. There was a confusing array of participants: some – like the unofficial SAS – were in it for the money, some for the excitement and some for the politics, while there were others who didn't really know nor care who they were firing at.

One of the centres that engaged the British Paras and the official SAS was the Radfan, an extremely inhospitable region in terms of both its terrain and its people – a fact not entirely understood by British intelligence staff when they made an assessment of the tribal troubles that blew up there between 1964 and 1966. The situation demanded the presence of British parachute troops, who went in alongside other Army units, including A Company of the SAS, whose commander candidly admitted: 'We did not appreciate the intensity of the violence or the tribal reaction to our presence. I expected a few dissidents to poop a few rounds and then go home again... So often we underrate our enemy.'

Lying 50 miles north of Aden, the Radfan was part of the British Protectorate. The area was populated by fierce tribes who ran a toll-gate system for caravans passing through their territory on the traditional supply route along the Dhala road up to the Yemen. It was also on one of the routes to Mecca. When this source of income was banned by new laws in 1963, the tribesmen began taking potshots at anyone who happened to come along and their insurrection was supported by the Nasser-backed rebels in the

Yemen, thus bringing the effects of the Yemeni civil war into the Radfan. The British decided to act to quell the tribesmen and sent in the 45th Royal Marines Commando, successive waves of Paras and the SAS. The first planned drop, of 3 Para's B Company, was to be led in by No. 3 Troop of A Squadron, 22 SAS. The ten-man SAS team was on the ground and was to mark the DZ for the Paras. However, they were forced to abort when they were surrounded by 90 tribesmen. Fighting their way out, they managed to call down some air fire from RAF Hunters. Twenty-five of the Radfanis were killed, but the SAS patrol lost their commander, Captain Rob Edwards, and communications man, Trooper Warburton, whose bodies they had to leave behind. Later the heads of the two SAS men were displayed on spikes in the Yemen.

In the end, with the element of surprise lost, the Paras came in by road. Then, each man heavily laden with a pack weighing around 55 pounds, they advanced on foot, climbing steep cliffs and gullies. The scene was described by John Rymer-Jones, who was on one of the three major operations carried out by the regiment in the Radfan between 1964 and 1966:

...it was an extraordinarily punitive expedition. It was initially a commando operation to support the move to quell tribal uprising in the hills above Aden, to the north. Then it was decided that the whole of the 3rd Battalion of the Parachute Regiment under Lieutenant Colonel [later General] Tony Farrar-Hockley should all go down to Aden to launch our drive into the Radfan ... an extraordinary happening, with a tactically deployed point company in fighting order with the whole of the rest of the battalion in very light order indeed coming up ... and we pushed forward into Radfan tribal territory which had last been surveyed by an Indian survey team in 1920 – map reading and grid references meant nothing. Gullies were 2000 feet deep and from ridge to ridge about 1000 yards in many places and there was a fortress at every entrance. The leading troops had air ID panels for recognition by the air support and when we came under fire we could call on that. There was every kind of weapon around ... from machine-guns to old-fashioned muskets from the turn of the century. It had been policy for every member of the Aden Protectorate Levy to be given a rifle on retirement, so for years these guns had been going into the tribal communities and now they were being turned on 3 Para attempting to put down a native revolt, walking miles over this incredible terrain. But we won and it became a campaign for which there was a medal.

In fact numerous medals were awarded in what began as a short, punitive operation against rebel tribesmen and became a long and grinding deployment against an enemy who were at times virtually invisible. The campaign would engage the attentions of the Paras until the spring of 1967, and involved many fierce battles until the tribesmen at last gave in, although by then Britain was, in any event, preparing to abandon its ties with Aden for good. Originally seized in 1839 to stop pirates attacking ships bound for India, the Aden Protectorate was now to be left in the hands of the Moscow-backed People's Republic of South Yemen as part of the Labour government's avowed aim to curtail British military involvement in the region and indeed to substantially reduce all of its commitments east of Suez.

* * *

Running alongside conflict in the Middle East was another equally difficult and tedious campaign, fought in conditions very different from the heat of the deserts. This time it was the wet and impenetrable jungles of Borneo, where the war that wasn't – it was merely a 'Confrontation' – flared when the beady eyes of the 'Mad' Doctor Sukarno, president of Indonesia, fell upon the British protectorates on the island of Borneo. At the time, Britain was responsible for the defence of the Sultanate of Brunei and the colonies of North Borneo (later Sabah) and Sarawak. All of these states, it was hoped, would join the Federation of Malaya to form a powerful and stable alliance. Sukarno had other ideas and backed local communists in a flare-up in Brunei which rapidly gathered pace right across Borneo.

The three British protectorates shared borders with Kalimantan, the Indonesian region of Borneo, which accounted for three-quarters of the island's land surface. Sukarno was intent on taking control of the remaining quarter, to add 7.5 million inhabitants to the 100 million he already ruled. His further ambition, inspired apparently by the Japanese in the Second World War, was to take over the whole of the Malayan States, including the prize of Singapore. In 1961 he was poised to continue, and the British government approved a hurried, if limited, military response, sending in an initial force drawn from the Gurkhas, the Royal Marines Commandos and the Queen's Own Highlanders.

Before long 28,000 soldiers would be deployed, including Australians, New Zealanders and what proved to be a very active contingent of the Special Forces. This last was represented by 22 SAS, one of whose squadrons was commanded by Major Peter de la Billière (later British commander in the Gulf War), and elements of the Parachute Regiment. The Paras were sent in to join patrols devised by the SAS, and thus encountered the jungle conditions of the Far East for the first time since the 5th Brigade's arrival in Java at the end of the Second World War.

This deployment of Special Forces – of which units of 2 Para were selected to temporarily become part – was requested by General Sir Walter Walker, who, apart from being Major General of the Gurkhas Brigade, was appointed director of military operations in Borneo, since he was the foremost military expert on jungle warfare in the British Army. Media reports spoke of him as an 'enigmatic' and 'eccentric' figure, but he largely put these down to sources at the Ministry of Defence whose noses he had put out of joint by making no secret of his indifference to some of their edicts. To use his own language, he was under sufferance from fart-arses, who, in due course, took their revenge by delaying his knighthood for several years.

Walker was the principal architect of what would become a most successful campaign, one with very low casualty figures and innovative in its use of Special Forces in conjunction with both Gurkhas and parachute units. This approach would set a pattern for the future, as well as initiating a regular working relationship between the Paras and the Gurkhas. Walker decided upon the combined use of SAS, Paras and ground forces because he went in with one hand tied behind his back. For he was governed by strict terms of engagement, specific and limiting, which had been drawn up both to comply with United Nations requirements and to assuage the British government's fear of engaging its forces in a long and costly jungle war in a terrain that was naturally hostile and, in parts, still uncharted. The overall penetration depth allowed in cross-border attacks was just 5000 yards, although this could be increased to 20,000 yards for specific operations authorized by Walker himself, who saw it as 'a ridiculous situation when you think about it – how can you expect a patrol hacking its way through dense jungle to actually measure 5000. They might need 9000 yards ... or even more.'

These actions were known as the Claret Operations. In theory there could be no cross-border operations for the purpose of retribution and the Ministry of Defence was absolutely insistent that no member of the British forces should be taken prisoner and no British casualties, dead or alive, should be left behind in case they might be photographed and produced as evidence to the world of British attacks. Initially, only the Gurkhas and the SAS – both foremost in the art of jungle warfare – were to be used in cross-border offensives. The Gurkhas had formed their own Independent Parachute Company specifically for the Borneo operations, to link up with the SAS. They were to be joined first by No. 1 (Guards) Independent Company, for operations in 1964, 2 Para in 1965 and 2 Para's C (Independent) Company later the same year. All incoming troops had first to undergo six weeks of training at the Jungle Warfare School at Kota Tinggi in Malaya, of which Walker was one of the founders.

They went through the rigours of patrolling and surviving in jungle so dense that an enemy could be five yards ahead of a patrol and not be spotted. They learned the intricate tasks of instant recognition and interpretation of human tracks and footprints, urination, crushed grass, broken twigs and so on. When they made camp no soldier was allowed to eat, smoke or unscrew his water bottle without his platoon commander's permission. At night, sentries prodded any man who snored, and whenever the company was on the move a recce section led the way, their packs carried from behind.

They learned about snap shooting – that is, at dead-ahead targets – and helicopter drill, acquired a modest grasp of local languages and received instruction in medicine. This last skill was particularly important given the way they were to operate: usually as small units who might be put into the jungle for days or even weeks at a time. Walker used these SAS-created patrols at the forefront of intelligence gathering over what was effectively an 800-hundred-mile front.

The Guards' parachute company completed two tours in Borneo, acting directly under SAS command and as effectively as the SAS themselves. This link-up was so successful that it became a permanent fixture, and in 1967 G (for Guards) Squadron was formed within 22 SAS, based at Hereford. In fact, very few Guardsmen who passed the tough selection procedures used by the SAS chose to return to their regiment and in the end the Guards became reluctant to give up their best men to G Squadron. Walker, who was assured that the Guards could 'do anything that the SAS can do', was inspired to request more parachute troopers, this time so that he could train patrols specifically in SAS methods.

The call went out to 2 Para in October 1964 to form an independent company of around 120 men for deployment in the jungles of Borneo. It was decided to base the group on 2 Para's C Company, with additional personnel recruited from the battalion itself, along with men from signals and medical units, all under the command of Major Peter Herring. A request for volunteers attracted a mini-stampede and 250 were eventually chosen for a special selection course in Wales. These were whittled down to the required number of men, who then reported to Hereford for six weeks of specialist training with SAS instructors, concentrating on demolitions, signals and medicine.

They then moved out to Brunei for jungle training in preparation for the gruelling tasks ahead. C Company was to take up long-range patrols, pioneered by the SAS and the Gurkhas, which lasted up to six weeks. They would take initial supplies of food and ammunition with them, each man carrying an 80- or 90-pound load in his bergen, and were resupplied by helicopter drops every 14 days. The company was used on Claret Operations across the border, general intelligence gathering and ambush patrols. It was these patrols, Walker said, that provided a great deal of intelligence for the main body of ground forces to pursue. One four-man patrol was required to join a Punan semi-nomadic village whose menfolk moved around the jungle armed only with blowpipes, killing wild pig and monkeys for food. Lieutenant John Winter and his team, with Lance Corporal Barker and Privates Seeney and Phelps, virtually went 'native' on one of their 12-week stints with the Punans, eventually emerging almost unrecognizable from the jungle and, as Peter Harclerode reported, they clearly 'preferred their own company and could be found muttering quietly to each other in strange languages in dark corners of various bars in Sibu'.

In January 1965 2 Para, minus C Company, was deployed to Sarawak. A, B and D companies were assigned to their own bases, usually around 20 miles apart but in communication with

Headquarters Company at its fortified base at Balai Ringin. Their combined operations were organized to try out completely new techniques for the battalion, devised by one of their own experts on the terrain in which they would be working: their commanding officer, Lieutenant Colonel Ted Eberhardie. He had been an intelligence officer with the 12th Battalion at the time of the 5th Brigade's landing in Java and was well acquainted with the conditions they faced. There was also input from another experienced jungle tracker, Captain Huia Woods, a Maori formerly with the New Zealand SAS during operations in Malaya in the early fifties.

The Paras were working in a manner totally different from anything they had tackled before. Foremost in Eberhardie's view was the need to reduce their carrying load as they set out on jungle patrols where swiftness of foot was essential to survive in a terrain that was perfect for ambushes and which, in places, rose as high as 6000 feet. They carried no backpacks, just belts with pouches containing the minimum required for survival. On patrols of longer duration they would be resupplied by helicopter. Chasing an elusive enemy, all sections of 2 Para had a busy time and engaged in numerous firefights in appalling conditions, often in pitch-darkness and teeming rain. In a confrontation in which Walker judged success by the body count, they had 'done well' – inflicting a large number of casualties on the enemy with only light losses to themselves.

The battalion returned to Britain in August 1965, although the Paras' involvement in the Borneo operations was not over. Towards the end of the year 3 Para was to provide another company, D (Patrol) Company under Major Peter Chiswell, for further specialist operations on the island. Again volunteers were sought to fill four patrol platoons, each consisting of four four-man teams on the SAS model, and once again the call was heavily oversubscribed. The patrols were needed to supplement intelligence operations, and part of the group, in addition to undergoing intensive pre-deployment training with the SAS, went to Singapore for a crash course in Malay. Officers and NCOs also attended briefings at the Army's Intelligence Centre at Ashford, Kent. They all came together for a Christmas party at a hotel in nearby Farnborough before flying out to Borneo in the first week of January. There, for the next six months, they were used on deeply penetrative surveillance work and close reconnaissance work, locating and mapping enemy positions and movements, reporting ultimately to SAS headquarters. They remained on these vital operations until July 1966, when confrontation edged towards its conclusion and the Parachute Regiment's contribution to the effort was at an end.

* * *

By then the final act in Britain's long-standing involvement in Aden and the surrounding area was being played out. Harold Wilson's Labour government wanted all British troops evacuated as soon as possible. In 1967 the government of the Federation of South Arabia collapsed. Britain announced that it would proceed with withdrawal of troops and give power to any group that could set up a government. The National Liberation Front emerged as the most powerful group and proclaimed the Federation an independent country – the People's Republic of South Yemen and violence again flared, with British troops and expatriate communities preparing for the final withdrawal, scheduled for 30 November 1967.

Months before that deadline was reached, 1 Para was posted to Aden to be part of the British force covering the withdrawal amid the chaos of gun-crazy radicals shooting at each other while both sides were attacking the British security forces. The battalion set up shop in Sheikh Othman and Al Mansura, although eventually it devoted all its attention to the first. In both towns the narrow streets were a death trap for soldiers, alive with snipers and shoot-and-run gunmen. British troops were necessarily working with the South Arabian Army, although they were deeply suspicious of their loyalties. The usual cordon-and-search operations were set in motion, but in the mêlée of activity by armed gangs the soldiers spent much of the time in firefights trying to protect themselves. Gordon Burt was among them:

The situation again was very fluid, with a lot of sniping and not knowing exactly who your enemy was because it was suspected that the armed forces of Aden at the time had taken up the cause of the terrorists. We were briefed many times that we had to be very, very careful of our approach to their armed forces [the South Arabian Army], even if we did not suspect them of anything. We had Lieutenant Colonel Mike Walsh as commanding officer at that time and again we took over certain locations and buildings from which we operated. One of them was OP [Observation Post] Golf, next to a college, and I passed to our museum a diary kept by one of the students at that college at the time of our move into that area. They all left the college and the teachers went on strike as soon as we arrived. We were regularly mortared and sniped at.

One evening I was going around the posts with the company commander when suddenly the mortars started landing; fortunately many of them didn't explode. We took cover in the slit trench post we were visiting – five of us crammed into it. When we came out we found a two-inch mortar embedded about a yard from the trench, with others around. When we called bomb disposal to get rid of them, we actually found the mortars had been manufactured in Australia. Ongoing from that, I worked out that the maximum range of a two-inch mortar was 250–300 yards and there were only certain positions they could fire from. We did a search of the college and found an area which was overlooking a garage which looked to be one of the positions most likely to have been used. We started an OP on that garage from then on, for the next two weeks, but to no avail.

While we were withdrawing from position, all the windows were shot out from the college by a passing gunman. We were building up a post at an old leper colony which was thereafter called Fort Walsh. Every company had to help sandbagging it as they moved in. The old timber building was bending under the weight but very necessary because the sniping happened virtually every night. One night when we were filling the sandbags, working like proverbial slaves, my company – in this case B Company, which had been formed from all new recruits, an excellent company but all young lads – they all began to go down with some sort of lurgy and started collapsing. One lunchtime I was saluting the company commander and as I saluted him I went out like a light and next thing I remember I was in an RAF hospital. I was a fitness fanatic and as soon as I could move I started to try some exercises, but just ended up collapsing again. It was discovered to be a form of sandfly fever, from flies buried deep in the sand which we had all been digging in. I had ten days' leave back in the UK after that, but I came back ready for action.

When I returned D Company took over from us at OP Golf and not long afterwards they had a Russian anti-tank missile fired which penetrated the wall of the Ops rooms and several received superficial wounds – very lucky. I don't think there was any doubt by then that the terrorists in Aden were getting assistance from their own army. An incident that brought this home to me one night was when a patrol had gone out and was not answering the radio. The company commander sent me out with three men to find them.

As I left the building we came under fire and several rounds went between and around my legs before we were able to dive for cover. We located the spot from which we were being fired at and made a dash down the street. As we did so, a car came around the corner at a high rate of knots and I stepped out and pointed my weapon directly at it. The car stopped and in it were two officers from the Aden Levies. We asked them to get out. They had no weapons with them and we weren't at liberty to search them. They claimed they were rushing back to base on an emergency and I had to let them go. We moved on, and around the next bend I located the house from which we were fired on, kicked the door in and found a very guilty-looking woman there, very flushed. We located the window from which we had been fired on. She was gabbling on in Arabic, but from the photograph on the sideboard we identified the two people we had just stopped in the car. If we had been able to search the vehicle we would probably have found the weapons in the boot. This was the sort of situation that confronted us.

Other incidents, within the battalions, came with the formation of an undercover group, which worked very successfully. But it was all to draw to a close very soon as we began to evacuate. While we were on operations the RAF and all the families had been able to withdraw and the containment had allowed this to happen relatively safely.

In the countdown to the final pull-out, the safe evacuation of personnel, stores, arms and equipment became the prime concern of British troops. Accordingly, 1 Para was assigned to form a tight defensive position around Khorsmaksar airfield since there remained to the last the possibility that a fighting withdrawal would be necessary. Two days before the deadline the SAA declared its support for the NFL and on the same day 1 Para came home on RAF transport, leaving 42 Commando RM to cover the last exit from Aden – and the end of Britain's 123-year rule. Those last months had seen situations requiring an alternation of diplomacy and toughness on the part of all concerned, and 1 Para's contribution was recognized with a DSO for Mike Walsh, along with a batch of other awards, including one MBE, three MCs, 16 Mentions in Dispatches and one Commander-in-Chief's commendation.

* * *

After Borneo and the Middle East, the next item on the Paras' agenda as the busy sixties drew to a close seemed like a Sunday School outing in comparison. It was certainly a curious adventure to be flying out to the Caribbean to another troubled outpost of declining British colonialism: the normally peaceful island of Anguilla. What was termed an 'insurrection' had broken out among the 6000 inhabitants of this slender, 13-mile-long stretch of paradise. They were protesting at their inclusion in the newly formed Caribbean Federation. The Colonial Office picked up a very large sledgehammer to crack a hazelnut and promptly dispatched 2 Para, minus B Company but accompanied by 120 members of the Metropolitan Police, to sort them out. And, on the basis of local intelligence, the then commanding officer, Lieutenant Colonel Richard Dawnay, had been briefed to anticipate an opposed landing. Among those who went on this excursion was Gordon Burt, not long back from those fetid alleys of Aden, who had now switched battalions:

We had 48 hours' notice to say goodbye to our homes and went to Lyneham [RAF base in Wiltshire] to fly out to an airbase on the island of Antigua. The original plan was to parachute into Anguilla from the base. But when we reached Antigua, we discovered there were no aircraft available for the drop. There were two frigates in the area and the plan was changed to go in by sea. I was left at the base with three men and the rest left on the frigates.

The next aircraft in, the following day, taxied to the end of the runway because the Antiguan government would not let us go off the airstrip. We had an area about 50 metres by 100 metres and that's all they would allow us. And on that we had to unload any aircraft that came in. We unloaded our fresh arrival and not long afterwards a civilian aircraft came in and out stepped some gentlemen with suitcases. They informed us they were the cipher team [and] asked if I had transport to take them to their hotel. I had to inform them that their hotel was the stretch of tarmac over there. That's were they stayed for the next two days until the 2iC arrived back from Anguilla to tell us what had happened: that they had been met by lots of flashes on the beach – the flashes of press cameras there to report the event. There was no gunfire or military activity whatsoever.

We then all flew over to Anguilla, where a temporary strip was set up. We were allowed to use the local school as a base. Cordon-and-search operations were set up, but all that was found was one old anti-tank rifle and a few holes in a couple of buildings. Apart from that, there didn't appear to be any justification for us being there, or for the type of operation we had carried out. What happened then was that the stores that we had been sent were two-man bivouacs, but when the company went to put them up they were found to be full of holes. There were some heavy storms about and they weren't any good at all. We carried on with our duties again, with the company doing fitness training, and then engineers arrived to build the camp, followed by the contingent of the Metropolitan Police, who all arrived on the island, much to their pleasure, because it was a very small place with just one crossroads.

We were then changed from war accounting to peaceful operations, which meant we had to quickly do up all our books from a certain date. Myself and the paymaster and the 2iC moved away to bring them all up to date. One thing I wasn't aware of was that all our rations had been taken away on the frigate, which I hadn't been able to account for. Therefore when the whole thing was ended and we arrived back in the UK, we were given a bill for the rations – and the rotten bivouacs I had sent back on an aircraft that brought in supplies. When they arrived back in the UK, they had been given a quota number which listed them as being from the Far East but they never accepted stores from the Far East because of the bugs and moths that might be in them and so they were all burned. So once again, the bill was sent to us to account for, which the CO at the time was not too happy with. I imagine that these tents had been re-routed from the Far East to us and were not in good order. I believe that the UK admin looked into this, that once again we were not ready for an overseas operation, and a great deal of work went into ensuring that in the future we forces were better equipped.

In the event, the whole operation on that scale seemed to have been hardly necessary. One company was retained there, and also the battalion band was sent there to hold the Queen's Birthday Parade in June – which must have been the largest contingent of military and police ever seen on Anguilla.

The battalion suffered from some humiliating press reaction as news hit the headlines of the beach landings on Anguilla, backed by the guns, unused, of the frigates. But in the end the Paras came out of it quite well. B Company, which had flown in to replace the rest of the battalion, remained on the island with a contingent of the Metropolitan Policemen and set about helping a number of development projects and re-establishing friendly relations with Britain. Their work was eventually recognized with the award of the Wilkinson Sword of Peace 'for their acts of humanity and kindness overseas'. However, Michael Stewart, Britain's Foreign and Colonial Secretary, went over the top in his letter to the battalion, congratulating it on 'a difficult task: to establish and maintain law and order ... this called for a high standard of discipline and impeccable conduct often in trying conditions...'. It was a politician's way of covering up a cock-up. The whole fiasco wasn't the fault of the Paras, but rather the result of a panic reaction from Stewart and his underlings in charge of the colonies – pathetic, fawning creatures that they were.

What on earth were 6000 deeply impoverished Anguillans going to do that warranted a beach invasion – let alone a parachute landing – by 850 crack British Paras with a track record of knocking all kinds of nastiness out of Nazis and other aggressors against the British crown? Fortunately, the good humour and goodwill of the Paras themselves rescued an otherwise exceedingly embarrassing situation.

13

THE TROUBLES

The 1960s was ending on a wave of protest. With the greatest peacetime revolution, cutting across so many facets of Western life, well under way, the once-great British Empire was now reduced to a few minor colonies and protectorates of no great importance. At the same time, the Army was undergoing a major shake-out, for deep cuts had been envisaged by the Labour government as the decline and fall of empire reduced the nation's commitments overseas. Careerists in the British military looked on despondently; where now to go to war, get promoted and win medals? The place was actually right on their own doorstep. In Northern Ireland the decade of protest passed almost unnoticed, the province's own affairs dwarfed by shows of popular power throughout Europe that had spread from the civil-rights campaign in the USA. These demonstrations reached a climax in 1968, dubbed 'the Year of Dreams': massive anti-war rallies in London, the students' and workers' revolt in Paris, the Prague Spring of Freedom crushed by Soviet tanks in August; the year when Martin Luther King and Bobby Kennedy were shot – and, less prominently, 100 Catholics were hurt in a Londonderry riot.

In the beginning, no one paid much heed when intellectuals, journalists and trade unionists formed a committee to usher in a civil-rights movement in Northern Ireland. The Catholics were second-class citizens in a society ruled by Protestants. Along with discrimination in housing, jobs and services, gerrymandering and the absence of one man one vote, there were firebomb attacks and, from the mid-sixties, assassination attempts on Catholics by the Protestant paramilitary Ulster Volunteer Force (UVF). The international climate provided the springboard for local protest.

The fateful 5 October 1968 march through Belfast by 800 protesters, organized by the Northern Ireland Civil Rights Association and largely made up of Catholics but with significant support from Protestant liberals, marked the start of a new era of opposition to this two-tier society. It was met with the boots and batons of the Royal Ulster Constabulary (RUC) and the dreaded B-Specials, the Ulster Special Constabulary, whose make-up was almost totally Protestant and whose partisan reputation was such that its officers were considered as bad as the so-called Loyalist gangs who had been terrorizing Catholic areas for the previous four years. In fact, Lieutenant General Sir Anthony Farrar-Hockley, former Colonel Commandant of the Parachute Regiment, has said that British troops were deployed to the province initially not just to support the civil administration, but to protect Catholics from the B-Specials.

Meanwhile the IRA, founded back in 1919, had recently been in a political backwater after some of its leaders embraced Marxism, and had more or less renounced violence. When violence erupted at the October civil-rights march in Northern Ireland, the IRA leadership in Dublin at first refused to release guns from their weapons dumps, supposedly because they feared a Protestant backlash in which Catholics would be massacred. Certainly the Protestant paramilitaries were heavily armed, and ready to turn up the heat. In the following months more than 1500 Catholic families, compared with 300 Protestant families, would be forced to leave their homes because of firebombings, looting and general intimidation by the Loyalist gangs. Before long, vociferous young Catholic political activists in Northern Ireland were demanding the IRA's protection, – as well as looking to reassert some of the original principles of Republicanism, born so long ago and boosted by the martyrdom of Michael Collins. They saw the civil-rights movement as, to some extent, a suitable Trojan Horse.

However, as the months passed, there would be no need for disguises. The evident tensions on the streets of Northern Ireland

rose dramatically towards the end of the Protestant Marching
Season in the summer of 1969. The fuse to the explosion of
violence that eventually emerged was the outbreak of the worst
street fighting the province had seen in many years. Rioting
flared in Londonderry towards the end of the Orangemen's
Apprentice Boys' March, and in the ensuing three days of battles
five people were killed and more than 700 were injured. The
Catholic population, under attack from marauding Protestant
gangs, protested at the actions of the B-Specials and the RUC,
who, they claimed, allowed the gangs a free hand. They were also
angered by the IRA's failure to protect their communities from the
nightly attacks by armed mobs hurling petrol bombs. Eventually
young IRA members in the province began to talk of forming a
breakaway movement from the official IRA and of arming
themselves to assert a Republican response to the rapidly
worsening situation.

Until the middle of 1969 there was only a small garrison of
British troops in Northern Ireland, generally at a strength of
around 500 men. In August, as the violence flared, the province's
Prime Minister, James Chichester-Clark, mobilized 8500 B-
Specials, a move which – to the Catholics and Republicans – was
a red rag to a bull. In addition, the first British troops beyond the
complement already stationed there arrived in Northern Ireland
on 19 August. This small detachment from the Prince of Wales's
Own Regiment was to be withdrawn as soon as order was
restored but, of course, it never was. From then on the number of
British troops deployed in Northern Ireland rose ever higher,
exceeding 20,000 troops in 1972, the province's bloodiest ever
year, which saw 468 killed and 5000 injured.

The Parachute Regiment was among the first troops to become
involved in the conflict in a major way, and was the unit which
would sustain the greatest number of casualties over the
following 30 years. The call came after a day of some of the worst
rioting seen so far in Belfast, on 11 October 1969, when a mob of

500 Protestants stormed down the Shankill Road, throwing stones and other missiles. As the riots spread, 69 people were arrested, dozens were injured and it was a Protestant gunman who claimed the first victim among the security forces – ironically an RUC officer – in a demonstration which began on the announcement that the B-Specials were to be disbanded and replaced by the Ulster Defence Regiment. As was feared, the UDR turned out to be the B-Specials in a different-coloured uniform, subject to few checks on their religious and political affiliations and eventually numbering many members who concurrently belonged to Protestant paramilitary organizations.

Late that night around 2000 people, including UVF gunmen, had gathered in the Shankill Road and were confronted by the RUC and troops from the 2nd Battalion the Light Infantry. There was sporadic sniper fire and as the hostilities intensified CS gas was used in a vain attempt to disperse the crowd. Soon after midnight troops of the same unit's 3rd Battalion were met by a crowd of 1000, from whose midst came automatic gunfire. By 2 a.m. 16 soldiers had fallen wounded. The riot was a landmark in that it was the first time that British troops were ordered to fire back at snipers and bombers.

'JJ' was an officer with 1 Para that weekend in October when the first unit from the Parachute Regiment prepared to move in:

We were part of the Strategic Reserve and were meant to have gone training in Northern Ireland that summer. That was halted. We had been to Canada on an exercise in New Brunswick and came back to find ourselves on standby as spearhead battalion for the Strategic Reserve. On 11 October A Company was in the Isle of Man on an exercise, another was in Somerset, training, and our commanding officer was away for the weekend. The majority of the rest were in Aldershot. I as 2iC was called out at 4 a.m. on the Sunday to be told that as spearhead battalion, 100 men were required as reinforcements for Northern Ireland immediately. I was to select a company to stand by. At 5 a.m. a second message came through. Two companies were required. And so through the morning it built up and soon it became apparent that three, perhaps four companies were to go. There was a certain amount of difficulty in contacting them; some of these who had completed their exercise in the Isle of Man had gone to ground. However, we had the required numbers there by midnight on 12 October and inside 24 hours we were all in the province, and from then on, without a moment's respite until Christmas. What did we do? Little more than hold the line … but it was the beginning of the establishment of a really solid line between the Shankill Road and the Falls Road areas… It was a very active area.

We made enormous efforts not only to keep the two factions apart but to act as intermediaries between them. It was a case of not showing excessive partiality to the Protestant community, who were welcoming us as their allies. We had to make the point that we were everyone's allies and were there to make peace.

The people of Northern Ireland had heaved a sigh of relief as more troops moved in. However, this was a temporary feeling that would soon turn to hatred in many quarters as British troops floundered, hampered by poor intelligence, inexperienced in handling trouble among their own people and led by those whose most recent experience of urban unrest was in the wild colonial campaigns launched by a nation withdrawing from the last remnants of its empire. The top brass seemed to believe that the same principles that they had used to tackle the guerrilla-packed hillsides and towns of Cyprus, and to fight running battles in the mountains and deserts of the Middle East or the jungle terrain of Africa and Asia, could be applied to the streets of their own country. In fact, there was little alternative. The momentum with which the violence in Northern Ireland had gathered pace caught everyone by surprise.

The government, the Ministry of Defence, intelligence analysts and military chiefs all failed to understand the depth of this unrest and the reasoning behind it. They based their response on the belief that the issue was religion and the solution simply the extension of civil rights, whereas it was nothing of the kind. Religion merely provided the badge of affiliation; underlying it was a complex pattern of tribal groups, including armed paramilitaries, vested interests, criminality and extreme bigotry, all of which were to shape the tragedy of Ulster and, despite the 1998 Good Friday peace agreement, remained in place as the millennium turned. The soldiers in the front line came to know this better than those in Westminster who were running them; and indeed the methods proposed in the early days by so-called specialists in military reaction to violent uprising went in completely the wrong direction and succeeded only in antagonizing everyone.

That first weekend of most severe rioting left a bitter taste. Lieutenant Colonel Michael Gray assembled his 1 Para for action, but in the event his men were not called upon; they merely stood in reserve with the Light Infantry while the 2nd Battalion the Queen's Regiment took the brunt of the crowd violence until the rioters gradually dispersed on 14 October. Gray knew he was to remain in place, however, in one of the more volatile areas and therefore needed intelligence. By the end of that first week he was to discover that there was none, not even from the RUC. In its responses to Army requests for help the RUC was bland to the point of being obstructive and remained so for some years. Gray would have to start from a blank sheet of paper in regard to information on suspected terrorists, whether Loyalist or Nationalist. There was simply nothing written down. The only orders he received were explicit in one thing, being designed as much for political expediency in the run-up to a British general election as to address the situation on the ground: work to the utmost to restore life to as near normality as possible as soon as possible, to enable a withdrawal.

The troops' first priority was SAS-style 'hearts and minds' excursions into the local communities on both sides of the religious divide to get involved with local people and try to convince them that they were non-partisan and friends. JJ was among those in 1 Para who had to combine a community-relations approach with the military one of organizing security patrols against the armed and dangerous elements of the population:

It was an extraordinary few months from October 1969 to February 1970, a period in which I learned to sleep no more than five hours a night. I would be out every night from 7 p.m. to 2 a.m., visiting company positions, guard positions, and being passed from one patrol to another, making my way to all the battalion positions. Our operations also involved some gesture of support for the local communities. We set up discos and sports clubs, which I would visit, but inevitably I ended up looking at patrols, which was ridiculously stupid, wandering around the streets of Belfast in the dead of night from one part to another.

There was, by then, a general rejection of us: people were shouting and throwing things. We had gone in to keep them apart but they were becoming increasingly militant. It was horrifying, even in those early days … the no-go areas … walls dividing roads, splitting communities, hearing from people how they'd lived happily in mixed communities – so tragic. We had the greatest sympathy for them. The general deprivation was apparent. There was a complete lack of such things as sports grounds; playing facilities were minimal. There was nothing for miles. Communities, whether Protestant or Catholic, were in two-up and two-down terraced houses containing families of six to ten people in very poor living conditions and when father came home into the living room and he wanted some peace and quiet, they were thrown out. You don't have to pick sides for cowboys and Indians. You're a side already and so it built in such an appalling way.

The Army was thus confronted by two increasingly vicious elements, which gradually sub-divided into many more. The IRA was being pressured by activists in the north to renew the avowed principles of its past heroes, to return to arms in support of a united Republic of Ireland and to protect and enhance Catholic communities. The official IRA continued to refuse the release of weapons to Ulster and a major split was imminent. The Provisional IRA (PIRA), or Provos, whose young members included Gerry Adams and Martin McGuinness, was formed in January 1970 with the intent of picking up the IRA's erstwhile armed struggle to protect Catholics, although the group had only a small number of weapons. The Protestant groups and gangs had a head start on the Republicans in the current upsurge of conflict. Notable among them was the Ulster Volunteer Force (UVF), which was formally outlawed in 1966 following a number of sectarian attacks and its declaration of war on the IRA. The UVF and other Protestant paramilitary groups made great play of their Loyalist alignment, but in those early days the nature of that loyalty was never quite apparent. And it is worth remembering that it was they who started this wave of violence, not the IRA.

Until now the two communities had been 'protected' by the B-Specials, who had a long history of anti-Catholic behaviour and sentiment, and the RUC, also largely manned by Protestants. The incoming British troops had to a steer a course through the middle of the current ferment, regardless of their own views. 'There were Protestants and Catholics among our troops,' says JJ, 'but they never identified themselves as such, then or in the past, not even to mention that they were Irishmen. We were absolutely non-partisan.'

Policy discussion about the tactics of the security forces in those early days often centred on all those hardy annuals used in Cyprus and elsewhere, such as cordon-and-search, which had been successful in the island's area of containment. But there was still very little intelligence on personalities. Similarly, methods of riot control used in Aden were hardly suitable for the streets of Belfast, and in all aspects of security new approaches had to be invented and learned by the troops themselves. Two-day courses in internal security operations were established almost immediately by 1 Para to teach its soldiers the new techniques. Here the keyword was restraint, which hadn't always been necessary in the hidden-away alleys of Aden. However, some of the lessons learned overseas were of use, particularly in unearthing possible terrorist formations and matching snipers to snipers. JJ himself devised a system for the covert insertion of patrols and observation and surveillance posts in specific areas:

We formed cadres for the battalion's snipers using the very latest night-vision sights, which had just come into our hands from America. They were nothing compared to the technology of today, but at least it gave us night vision when most of these guys were running about. For instance, if there was a sniper in a darkened window of a house or on the top of the building, it would be virtually impossible to get an accurate bead on him. These image-intensifiers helped enormously, although, as usual, they were in pretty short supply and during that autumn we were able to set up sniper units in only two of our OPs [observation posts] in the Shankill Road. As more equipment came in, these were eventually copied and followed by 2 and 3 Para as they came into the province, and other Army units. We needed all the gear we could get – in November our area was extended when we took over the sector handled by 41 Commando on top of the one we were already running, which included some very heavy no-go areas: the Peace Line, the Boyne Bridge and the Divis Flats. [The Divis Flats] were a horror story. It was an extensive block, three or four flights, a rabbit warren and a hotbed of Republicanism and known as a hiding place for IRA terrorists. The flats were searched often, and the people there developed their own warning system to alert anyone inside who might need to make a fast exit. They would bang dustbin lids or saucepans – anything metal. Or, for a silent warning, they would send their kids running across the landings ... within minutes the whole place was aware we were there.

The general level of violence actually declined for a while, and during this false dawn the Labour government, facing a general election, tried to decrease troop involvement in the province. The 39th Infantry Brigade, of which 1 Para was part, was ordered to cut its force from seven to four battalions. The result was that, at a crucial time in Belfast, troops were thinly scattered, attempting to carry out community relations as well as security patrols. By January 1970, 1 Para in particular was attempting to deal with an upsurge of mob violence and sniper fire in the wake of the formation of the Provisional IRA and its three brigades in Belfast, Londonderry and South Armagh. The fight was now on in earnest. With its membership increasing at a phenomenal rate, the PIRA announced its intention to force the British out of North Ireland with bomb and bullet, and since this objective was allied to the protection of Catholics from the increasing number of attacks from Protestants and unionists, it received a groundswell of support. This arrived in the form of home-grown succour on the island of Ireland from the Northern Aid Association (NORAID), which channelled money from the USA and assorted governments who sponsored terrorism, later to include such luminaries at Colonel Gaddafi.

By February, when 1 Para had completed its first tour, the organization of the Provos was well established, whereas the British military and intelligence response remained some distance behind. Not least of the problems at this time was that the troops coming into Northern Ireland were invariably on short tours of six months or so, which meant that their operations lacked continuity. Each new unit virtually had to start afresh in gathering intelligence such as lists of contacts, suspects and locations. Both 2 and 3 Para came in on short-term engagements – interchanging with other regiments of the British Army – until finally it was decided to bring the battalions in for far longer stays.

In September 1 Para returned for a 20-month tour, the first extended deployment of its kind, which was not at all what many had joined for; once again the battalion was under the 39th Brigade and based at Palace Barracks, Holywood, two miles from the centre of Belfast. Three of its companies were on alert to deploy to trouble spots anywhere in the city. The equipment was getting better and the four rifle companies had possession of seven one-ton Humber armoured personnel carriers, known as 'Pigs', and the Reconnaissance Platoon had six Ferret scout cars.

The Parachute Regiment had made its own assessment of film of riot scenes. The Paras in Northern Ireland adopted more aggressive tactics: rather than approaching mobs in line behind riot shields, they would, where possible, drive right up, disgorge from their personnel carriers and confront the rioters virtually eyeball to eyeball. Soldiers in the companies who were to use this approach were trained specifically to make sharp arrests, and since many of the rioters they confronted were teenagers, the Para riot-control specialists reckoned that, using these methods, they could go safely into a crowd of up to 3000 people. In time, statistics proved the claim, and within months the incidence of large-scale riots was on the decrease, although the Paras began to attract increasing criticism from local community leaders for their tactics.

There was, however, a substantial rise in shootings and bombings as the Provos became better armed and adopted their own military manoeuvres, some of which were a direct copy of what the British troops were doing – using OPs, patrolling the backstreets and running clandestine training sessions at which their own experts in rioting, petrol-bombing and arms skills were present. 'GB' arrived in Belfast with 3 Para as these developments were moving into second gear. He was 2iC of a support company, covering the Ardoyne, and later became an Operations and Intelligence Officer, directing patrols on the ground before moving on to similar work with the Special Forces:

After a period during which we had been sniped at pretty regularly with home-made mortars, nail bombs, glass bombs, I thought then that the best idea was to find out who people were and where they lived. It seems an odd thing to say, naive almost, but the fact is, we did not have a deal of knowledge in that area. I decided the best way to do this was to form my own patrol, and simply go out and do it. And so with two NCOs and another – i.e. a four-man patrol – I would go out to each street with one man guarding my left, one guarding my right, and I knocked at every door and asked them kindly if they could assist us with information, to ensure that we were not making errors or carrying out raids on the wrong houses if we were given information on weapons or terrorists hiding in the area. We needed to know who lived there. Apart from the occasional abuse, I think it rather took them by surprise and within a month I think I had covered the whole of the Ardoyne...

When I look back now, I smile at myself because some of the well-known personalities now ... their parents opened the doors and they were probably in the house at the time. But nevertheless it got us information we required. From that, I worked out with shading the maps what they could see of us and what we could see of them – i.e. they were congregating in places that could not be seen by any of our OPs. We needed empty houses where people had gone away, or left the area, and these proved very useful for OPs. [At one OP] it wasn't long before quite a large group of known players gathered right below us and there was quite an exchange of weapons. We knew that there were a number of Army patrols on the ground in this area and that they were likely to come under fire unless we did something. I informed my base location and we opened fire. We killed one and injured three. Of course, there was furore, riots and goodness knows what and it was quite a business extracting oneself from this location and getting the wounded to hospital.

We were able to do that, but the riots continued for two days. The men involved were readily identified as being wanted for questioning by the police. However, all incidents had to be thoroughly investigated and, upon return to base, all our weapons were confiscated and taken away for ballistic tests and each man in the patrol was questioned at long length by the military SIB [Special Investigations Branch]. Unknown to us at the time, this all had to come to court. There were people who were arrested and they were in hospital at the time. They were charged with taking part in several previous terrorist activities. Meanwhile we carried on with our patrols and I was able to form a special patrol which did very close surveillance of the areas and questioning and going into clubs and so on. Many's the night I spent in a club until two in the morning. [No member of the patrol was allowed to drink alcohol.] They were all Catholic clubs. What struck us at the time was that there was no real law and order about the clubs except that which the club committee kept. Therefore, if the club was not closed on time, I would call the club chairman to close it. It caused a good deal of trouble but nothing that we couldn't handle. I gained the respect of many wives in the area who used to say, 'I never saw my husband before this.' We also gained some recognition as a regiment that meant business but was fair.

In the clubs we would question people we might not recognize, ask them where they came from and what they were doing in the area. We were also able to keep an eye on known personalities, who they were conversing with or meeting, all of which was recorded. It was primitive stuff compared with what came later, but it was to work out to our great benefit. Known IRA men were recognized and, without saying it in words, we were letting them know that they were being monitored. We got to know many of the people in the clubs; the reaction was humorous to some extent, although with occasional abuse. They would tap into their televisions and pick up our radio broadcasts on our own personal radios. The dangers to us were total. Some soldiers were happy to come on my patrol but most were quite happy to avoid it because we liked to feel we were going right to the root of the problem and to this end we carried out OPs from several buildings.

One chap, who has since died, used to go on holiday and asked me to look after his house. It was very useful, overlooking one of the clubs where they used to drill junior members of the IRA on Thursday evenings. We saw them actually being formed up in a backstreet in their uniform and then go into the club. We did not interrupt them because we did not want our activities known or our OP blown. The intelligence was more worthwhile than arresting them for drilling. We could recognize them for future use.

Another situation happened a few weeks later. We were on patrol, and I was going into a corner shop, leaving the others outside, when a rake of sniper fire went straight across the wall. How it missed them I'll never know. We dived to the ground but could not see which house it had come from. So once again, it became an area we had to get an OP in. We found a likely house and moved in, and the very next morning we found everything taking place. There were young lads on street corners posted as lookouts to warn of any patrols. We saw one of them come running back and the next minute a guy appeared in a doorway opposite with an Armalite [rifle]. We were watching from our OP and took a bead on him. He seemed to fire but nothing happened; his weapon had misfired and he ran back inside, apparently to get instructions on how to operate the gun, and then reappeared. We could hear on the radio our own patrol coming up the street and I had no alternative but to order that fire be brought on him. Because of what had happened previously, where we hadn't got troops on the ground quickly enough to get the weapons used in such attacks, I had to then send a member of my own patrol to get the weapon before someone else picked it up. I think that was an awful thing to have to do, on an open street. But we were the only ones there and with the other patrol heading in from the other end of the street, we had to get that weapon. He got down there, but before he reached the spot another young guy ran out to grab the weapon. I shot at him to miss, which one shouldn't do in reality. I wanted to stop him snatching the weapon. My other man got down there, retrieved the weapon and it wasn't long before we got an ambulance on the scene for the wounded IRA man and an armoured vehicle to evacuate us. Even so, by then a crowd had gathered outside and we had to show ourselves at the window and point weapons at them to hold them at bay.

I briefed the section commander, who was on the ground, to search the house into which the young chap had run. They did not find him. Some time later the same chap was picked up by the Grenadier Guards and he told them he had been hiding under the stairs all the time... In the heat of the moment, with a group of screaming females standing in front of a cupboard, it's just a problem to get them out of the way to do a thorough search, while outside 200 people had gathered, throwing stones and bottles. My patrol was evacuated pretty fast, and soon after we left the mob began attacking the house we had been in. They took it apart brick by brick, and within a day there was nothing of it left standing, so that it couldn't be used again.

These sorts of incidents where one doesn't have the chance to get the terrorists involved – I found the whole question of terrorism in Northern Ireland was much more distasteful than anything I had experienced. This was part of Great Britain. You could rightly see it in other places, such as Cyprus and Aden, where they felt we were the intruders into their country and were not frightened to take on the Army face to face, unlike the IRA. Thereafter we began to make much more use of photographers or our film man. We were a bit slow in doing this. There was always one available, and the command 'Photographer to the front: take pictures' became familiar to all. [It was useful] having someone on the ground who could get around the side of them and take pictures of them throwing stones or with weapons.

I had to attend court sessions later in connection with various incidents, bringing with me all soldiers involved. I can remember being in the witness box for as long as two and a half days being cross-examined about how we had carried out certain operations.

This did lead, later, to IRA terrorists doing similar operations – taking over a house and shooting at our troops in the same way. This was always the danger: of information, of how we carried out our operations, coming out and being known publicly. I know one can read about them in books, but specifically this was word for word in a court, being cross-examined by counsellors who are acting for the terrorists at the time and willingly or not do pursue the situations they need to know about more than for the purpose of proving innocence.

We would appear in court in civilian clothes, and although we were Soldier A, B or C any knowledge or recognition of us became known straight away. So they were fully aware of everything we were doing and who we were…

One particular day, some time later, a contact asked to meet me in one of the clubs. I was very suspicious because, quite frankly, it looked like a set-up, so I had a patrol go on the ground in the area. I went along to the club at 10.30 in the morning … and soon afterwards this chap came in. On his heels, five other players came in. They encircled me and one of them said, 'We've got you now, you bastard,' and I did not have much of an answer for that. We were by then in a sort of a courtyard which led out on to the street. One of them suggested that a check was made to see if I had anyone posted outside and lucky for me the patrol was just coming down the street. They shoved me outside the gate and one of them said, 'There'll be another time.' Then they vanished, but here I had a certainty for recognizing five names. Conversely, they already knew mine.

That was one of the dilemmas of these 'meets'. Many is the time when you were told you were going to get information and spent hours and hours speaking to people but really you couldn't forgo it. At the end of that particular tour I returned to operations with the Special Forces which I cannot speak of. Looking back on that period, however, I was left with the view that what I had witnessed was very akin to gangsterism. These clubs were making thousands of pounds … six clubs in the Ardoyne alone. They were all allowed licences, probably because the police felt that it was better to have them in one place than on the street. However, they were used all the time specially to get rid of weapons, which could be passed around and then out. I had several incidents inside clubs, but in a place with 200 people inside it was very difficult to carry out search-and-find operations. It was akin to gangsterism on both sides, whether it was in the Ardoyne or the Shankill Road. The clubs, the taxis, the insurance policies were all a form of criminality.

It was truly an alien scenario in which the Paras found themselves and one that was again highlighted by the lack of a coherent and precise policy from local or central government around which the commanders on the ground could build a workable response. As well as finding themselves short of intelligence and lacking direction from Westminster, especially in regard to specific direct action, the troops suffered from the internecine rivalries that were building among the various agencies by now crowded into the province, including RUC, Special Branch and MI5. Into this mêlée in 1970 came Edward Heath's new Conservative government, with a philosophy that was dictated to some extent by electioneering promises and which produced a Home Secretary, Reginald Maudling, whose approach to Northern Ireland was both cynical and uncaring. In fact, Maudling made only three visits to the province during his two-year tenure, and by then the damage was done and the tone of administration for the immediate future set in stone.

Maudling's first trip to Belfast summed up his lack of understanding of the situation. He told the Army in no uncertain terms that it was up to them to 'deal with these bloody people'. The Army did not unanimously welcome this responsibility. Many among its top brass correctly assessed that a totally military-led response to the growing violence in Northern Ireland would merely be exacerbated by the 'get-tough' policy demanded by the Conservatives' Unionist allies and now advocated by

Maudling. The Home Secretary's blinkered view of the developing crisis was quite evident from his one clear declaration: that the IRA was 'the sole enemy' and had to be put down. He was simply parroting the views of the Northern Ireland Loyalists and Unionist politicians.

Within days of Maudling's first visit, however, the implementation of this new policy became all too apparent. On 3 July a riot broke out in the Lower Falls as troops searched for an IRA weapons cache of what turned out to be 19 guns. The Provisional IRA came in with nail bombs, while the Army poured in 3000 troops and fired 1600 CS gas canisters into rows of terraced streets as military helicopters warned people through loudhailers to get into their homes and stay there. Under that cloud of choking gas, a frightened neighbourhood had its first taste – literally – of what lay ahead. A night of shooting followed, with IRA snipers firing on the advancing soldiers; four civilians were killed and 67 wounded. And when the trouble calmed, troops moved in to tear suspect houses apart.

Months of escalation followed, and in 1971 the top-secret Cabinet Committee which handled Northern Ireland affairs approved the imposition of internment without trial. Around that development was built a series of undercover intelligence operations, interrogations and tough, harassing cordon-and-search techniques by the military which were all a direct hand-me-down from the colonial outposts of Kenya, Cyprus, Aden and elsewhere and now were to be implemented on the streets and in the special internment prisons in the United Kingdom. Internment became the most contentious issue in the history of the Troubles, failed to resolve anything and attracted international criticism for its brutality.

These events of the first year of the new Conservative government, an administration cosseted by muddled Whitehall thinking, put down a blueprint for the immediate future which the Parachute Regiment in particular would be expected to follow.

14

GETTING PERSONAL

Sandra Willetts met her husband Mike at a local dance, just after he had returned from Bahrain. He was, she says, tanned and handsome and a very kind and considerate sort of guy. He'd been a soldier for five years, was proud of being in the Parachute Regiment and loved the life, having previously been a miner since leaving school. Mike and Sandra married the same year. Mike was made sergeant and they settled to what was a decent style of life – until Northern Ireland began to make its calls upon the regiment.

The couple had two children, aged three and five, when Mike was with 3 Para as the battalion began another five-month tour in the province, in February 1971. Sandra, like all Army wives, dreaded the Northern Ireland posting. Mike's company was based in Belfast, working the Springfield district. He and Sandra were in daily contact by telephone and he always spoke to the children. Mike was always in decent spirits, and although he had been involved in a number of serious incidents, he kept up an outward calm so as not to alarm Sandra unduly, telling her they were all getting on with their job as best they could.

On 25 May Mike called his wife at lunchtime, as arranged. They talked about their daughter, who had started school that day, and the other minutiae that often filled their telephone calls. As usual, Mike did not say much about his work other than that it had been a relatively quiet few days. However, around eight o'clock that evening there was a knock on Sandra's front door. As she opened it a feeling of ice-cold horror swept through her. There stood the battalion families officer and the colonel's wife, who asked if they might step inside. It could mean only one thing. They said there had been an accident, but of course that was merely a way to introduce the news. It was no accident. And they came out with the truth of it straight away. Mike Willetts had been in an explosion – an IRA bomb. The details weren't clear but they wanted Sandra to go with them immediately to Heathrow Airport to fly to Belfast. She arranged for the children to be taken care of and left at once. She was ushered into the VIP lounge at the airport to await her flight and seemed to have been there for a long while when the families officer returned and gently explained that it was too late: Sergeant Mike Willetts had, unfortunately, died in the operating theatre.

It was only after the funeral a week later that Sandra could bring herself to hear the full story of how her husband died. She knew it would be bad in terms of injuries, and it was. The story was related to her by the commanding officer of the regiment: Sergeant Willetts was at Springfield Road police station, which was also the Battalion Headquarters, when a terrorist bomb was discovered in a suitcase. There were a number of people inside the station at the time, including a woman and her two children, along with a male civilian and police officers. Mike Willetts barked instructions for everyone to get out and told another NCO to dash upstairs and clear the building. He stood in the doorway of the room, ushering out the woman and her children and finally the policemen, effectively shielding them with his own body until they were safely past him and outside. It was a selfless act and one that his wife was not at all surprised to learn of. 'I wasn't surprised at all,' she recalls:

because there was no way he would have gone out of that door leaving anyone in there. He loved people. His friends and colleagues all spoke highly of him. The presence of the children and their mother made him do what he had to do, which was get them out of there as soon as possible. My own grief eventually moulded with a sense of pride, but also anger that the bombings continued. He was an example of a good British soldier... The regiment was very proud of his actions and his courage was recognized posthumously with the award of the George Cross – the highest award given in peacetime.

There was no such recognition in Belfast, and the hatred now being displayed against the British servicemen was evident when Sergeant Mike Willetts was carried out of the building on a stretcher. People pushed forward to jeer and spit on the dying soldier; he had saved a lot of lives that day, but no one there bothered about that.

There were two deaths among the Paras in Northern Ireland that year – the first of many. All three battalions were seeing longer stays and it had become clear that the Army was to some extent using them as the blunt instrument, whether they liked it or not. By the autumn of 1972, 2 Para had completed four tours totalling 16 months, while 1 Para was assigned the gruelling 20-month tour that began in September 1970, under the 39th Infantry Brigade. The foundation drills that were the basis of the original Parachute Battalions now seemed a long way off, and the many fresh recruits – 18 or 19 years old – in the three battalions must have wondered why they had been trained to jump out of aircraft.

In place of jumps they faced constant patrolling, usually on foot, being shot at, and spending hours in uncomfortable OPs or close surveillance work. They were among the front-line troops who were taking not only the bullets, the bombs and the landmines but also the interminable abuse and spittle of the local residents whose houses they might be searching (some said wrecking) or whose gardens they were turning over, or whose lofts and attics they were crawling through, hunting for weapons.

On 9 August 1971 the Northern Ireland Prime Minister, Brian Faulkner, formally ordered internment without trial. On that day 2 Para, with support companies from 1 Para and the Parachute Squadron Royal Armoured Corps, elements of the King's Royal

Hussars and a section from the Royal Artillery, formed a group to undertake Operation Demetrius. It was among the first of many major cordon-and-search operations after the introduction of internment, aimed at putting pressure on the IRA and the Provos and cautioning those who might harbour them. Although more than 300 people were arrested in this and other operations in those few days, the original intelligence gained was poor and few of those picked up turned out to be members of the IRA. Initially it had the opposite effect to what it was supposed to achieve. Most Catholics in Northern Ireland now believed that only the Republican movement could shield them from the Protestant paramilitaries and what they saw as the brutality of the British troops.

The situation worsened on the streets and in the four days after the start of internment 5000 Catholics and 2000 Protestants had their homes burned to the ground by terror gangs from both sides. The Paras also did some damage: it was now British Army policy to rip apart any house where intelligence led troops to believe that suspected terrorists were hiding, or where caches of weapons might be hidden under floorboards or in attics. In some cases earth-moving gear was brought in to dig up gardens. If nothing was found, the occupier could file a claim for damages.

Needless to record, the death toll shot up dramatically in 1971. The IRA stepped up its city-centre bombing campaign and more killings ensued. The Protestants responded with the formation of the Ulster Defence Association (UDA), a coming together of various vigilante and paramilitary groups which soon began to match the IRA, shot for shot, bomb for bomb. The introduction of internment and the rounding up of hundreds of men from both sides – though mostly IRA suspects – proved to be a totally ineffectual weapon against the violence, and merely turned up the heat.

The year ended in horrific carnage. The IRA bombed a bar in the Shankill Road, killing two people and injuring many more, several of whom were maimed for life. The Ulster Volunteer Force responded by bombing McGurk's Catholic bar in the city's North Queen Street, killing 16. A week later a Protestant shop in the Shankill Road was bombed, killing four, including a seven-month-old boy.

By the end of 1971 around 900 people, almost all of them Catholic Republicans, were in prison without trial under the internment system – many of them taken into custody by the Paras. A ban on public demonstrations and marches was also imposed. The Northern Ireland Civil Rights Association decided to ignore it and called a demonstration in Londonderry for Sunday 30 January 1972. The city, known to the Catholics as Derry, is on the north-western border between Ulster and the Republic of Ireland. At that time it had a population of 55,000, two-thirds of whom lived in the Catholic districts of Creggan and the Bogside. The latter was a Republican heartland and had been a 'no-go' area for troops and police for about two years; it was ruled by the IRA and the Provos, which both had units there and effectively controlled the district; they policed it, kept troops and Protestants out, ran their sideline businesses and trained young recruits. The British security forces were under pressure from both the Northern Ireland government and Westminster to restore such no-go areas to a 'state of law as soon as possible'.

The Northern Ireland Civil Rights Association obtained assurances from both the IRA and the Provos that the anti-internment march could go ahead unhindered by them, and that neither group would use it for its own purposes. In fact, both would have armed men on duty, some at crucial stages of the march, while others acted as stewards and some took up sniper positions. Major General Robert Ford, the new Commander Land Forces in Northern Ireland, put Brigadier Andrew MacLellan, commander of the 8th Infantry Brigade, in charge of the operation to contain the march. There would be only a token police presence and platoons of soldiers supplied by the brigade would man barriers along the route. Ford prepared Operational Order No. 2/72, dated 27 January 1972, which stated that if rioting broke out, water cannon and rubber bullets were to be used if necessary and CS gas as a last resort. 'Hooligans and rioters' were to be arrested by a central arrest force, to be furnished by 1 Para, commanded by Lieutenant Colonel Derek Wilford.

The following day Chief Superintendent Frank Lagan of the RUC contacted MacLellan and said that the only way to avoid serious violence was to let the march proceed, photograph the marchers and arrest them later. MacLellan agreed to put this to General Ford. But there was no going back. The Operational Order had been approved at the highest level: Edward Heath's Northern Ireland Cabinet Committee, known as Gen 42, of which Heath and Home Secretary Reginald Maudling were members. By all accounts Maudling in particular was in a 'crush the bastards' frame of mind, but then he had other troubles on his mind too. His good friend John Poulson was heading for bankruptcy in a scandal that would eventually lead to the Home Secretary's resignation over his connections with the corrupt architect.

The actual arrest operation was to be carried out by Support Company of 1 Para. According to later evidence, this was the only company to have fired live ammunition. No explicit orders were given about opening fire or returning fire; there were already rules in existence for that possibility. Even so, Derek Wilford, speaking in the BBC's 1992 television documentary *Inside Story: Remember Bloody Sunday*, said:

I asked the question which, in fact, for a long time has worried me. I said, 'What happens if there is shooting?' To which I got really a very sparse reply to the effect that, 'Oh well, we'll deal with that when it comes.' It's my greatest regret that I didn't actually pursue that question and say, 'Right, you know what – what do you want us to do if we're shot at?'

The Support Company was briefed. The men were warned they could expect to be shot at. They were told to keep an eye on the high ground, for snipers and bombers.

The march went relatively peacefully until it reached the junction of William Street and Rossville Street, where the lorry at its head turned right up Rossville Street, leading the marchers away from any confrontation with soldiers at the barrier in William Street. However, about 200 marchers, most of them young men, broke away and began throwing stones at the soldiers on the barricade. The troops responded with rubber bullets and water cannon. It was at this point that 1 Para was given permission to begin its arrest operation. Brian Cashinella, who was then Northern Ireland correspondent for *The Times*, said in a television interview that as 1 Para came through the barricade he was standing next to General Robert Ford: 'He was waving his swagger stick, saying, "Go on, the Paras, go and get them, go on, go and get them." And then all was mayhem.'

A violent, screaming, shouting confrontation broke out under the arid, choking cloud of CS gas and the thud of rubber bullets, to which soon would be added the sharp sound of gunfire. According to the official Brigade Radio Log, one sub-unit was ordered forward at 16.07 hours. Three minutes later, at 16.10, Support Company began firing live rounds. Within half an hour 13 young men who would be classed as 'rioters and hooligans' lay dead and another 13 injured. Bloody Sunday had made its ignominious entry into history.

Much controversy surrounds the question of who precisely sanctioned Support Company's opening fire upon the demonstrators. Lord Widgery, who conducted the government's one-man inquiry into the shootings, outlined the task which he said everyone knew was expected of 1 Para:

In the Parachute Regiment, at any rate in the 1st Battalion, the soldiers are trained to take what may be described as a hard line upon these questions. The events of 30 January and the attitude of individual soldiers whilst giving evidence suggest that when engaging an identified gunman or bomb-thrower they shoot to kill and continue to fire until the target disappears or falls. When under attack and returning fire they show no particular concern for the safety of others in the vicinity of the target. They are aware that civilians who do not wish to be associated with violence tend to make themselves scarce at the first alarm and they know that it is the deliberate policy of gunmen to use civilians as cover. Further, when hostile firing is taking place the soldiers of 1 Para will fire on a person who appears to be using a firearm against them without always waiting until they can positively identify the weapon.

According to Widgery, the order to commence the arrest operation came from MacLellan and was given to Lieutenant Colonel Wilford over a secure wireless link. The main centre of controversy would be whether or not the Support Company's lethal response was justified – and indeed whether or not it had come under fire first from IRA gunmen and bombers who were on the periphery of the fray. There was no doubt, Lord Widgery would say, that IRA guns were firing. Both wings of the IRA admitted that they sent for reinforcements when the firing started. One of the wounded, Alexander Nash, was hit in the arm by a low-velocity bullet which may have come from a gunman rather than a soldier.

The ammunition check of the Support Company showed it fired 108 rounds of 7.62mm ammunition from self-loading rifles. However, identifiable bullets were recovered from only two of the 13 people killed, so that it was not possible to say which soldier had shot which deceased. No officer above the rank of lieutenant fired any shot. Eleven privates were responsible for firing 62 rounds between them, while ten officers fired 46 rounds altogether. Only three soldiers fired more than ten rounds: Private S fired 12, Lance Corporal F fired 13 and Private H fired 22 – altogether a fifth of all the shots fired by the Paras.

In the immediate aftermath the Minister of State for Defence, Lord Balniel, put the case on behalf of the government and the British Army in spite of protests that this pre-empted the Widgery inquiry:

There has been a series of reports involving the most serious allegations against the Army's conduct... Therefore it is right for me to set out in good faith the facts as I know them. It is not right that the Army's case could go by default when bitter, intemperate, and, to the best of my belief, inaccurate or untrue statements have been made against it. It would be grossly unfair to the forces in Northern Ireland. We must also recognise that the IRA is waging a war, not only of bullets and bombs but of words. It is waging a highly skilled war of propaganda, in which corpses, the unutterable sadness of relatives, the confusion, the gullibility and the downright lies are all brought into play. Civil rights marches suit the IRA's tactics and purposes well...

By five minutes past four the crowd in Rossville Street was largely dispersing. There was clear separation between the rioters at the barricades and the remaining marchers in the area. There had, however, already been two incidents foreshadowing the terrorist violence which was to come. At 3.55 a high-velocity round was fired across William Street from the direction of the Rossville Flats, striking a drainpipe four feet above the heads of a party of soldiers. A few moments later, a man was seen preparing to light a nail bomb in William Street; he was shot as he prepared to throw, was seen to fall, and was dragged away by his fellows. Between 4.05 and 4.10, the brigade commander ordered the 1st Battalion, the Parachute Regiment, to launch an arrest operation against the rioters, who were well separated from the marchers. These rioters were flagrantly breaking the law; hurling missiles at the troops and establishing a degree of violence which was quite unacceptable. The level of their violence was highly dangerous to the police and Army.

The arrest operation was discussed by the Joint Security Council after decisions had been taken by Ministers here. Three companies of soldiers therefore came through the barriers in William Street... They fired rubber bullets when necessary. Two companies made a number of arrests. One company found the rioters it intended to arrest withdrawing towards the Rossville Flats and followed them in armoured vehicles towards those buildings. On the way, three rounds struck one vehicle, and a burst of about 15 rounds from a sub-machine-gun struck the ground just a few yards away from a group of soldiers as they got out of their vehicle. The soldiers continued to arrest the rioters whom they had chased. They arrested about 28 in a matter of a few minutes. At the same time, they came under fire from gunmen, nail bombers and petrol bombers, some in the flats and some at ground level. Between 4.17 and 4.35 p.m., a number of these men were engaged. In each case, soldiers fired aimed shots at men identified as gunmen or bombers. They fired in self-defence or in defence of their comrades who were threatened. I reject entirely the suggestion that they fired indiscriminately or that they fired into a peaceful and innocent crowd.

That was the official version of events. The Ministry of Defence issued a detailed account of the Army's tally:

Of the 13 men killed in the shooting that began after the bulk of the 3000 marchers had been peacefully dispersed, four were on the security forces' wanted list. One man had four nail bombs in his pocket. All were between the ages of 16 and 40. The shooting started with two high-velocity shots aimed at the troops manning the barriers. No one was hit and the fire was not returned. Four minutes later a further high-velocity shot was aimed at a battalion wire-cutting party. This shot also was not answered. A few minutes later a member of the machine-gun platoon saw a man about to light a nail bomb. As the man prepared to throw, an order was given to shoot him. He fell and was dragged away. Throughout the fighting that ensued, the Army fired only at identified targets – at attacking gunmen and bombers. At all times the soldiers obeyed their standing instructions to fire only in self-defence or in defence of others threatened... The troops then came under indiscriminate firing from apartments and a car park. The following is the Army's account of the return fire: 1. Nail-bomber hit in the thigh. 2. Petrol-bomber, apparently killed in the car park. 3. A bomber in the flats, apparently killed. 4. Gunman with pistol behind barricade, shot and hit. 5. Nail-bomber shot and hit. 6. Another nail-bomber shot and hit. 7. Rubber bullet fired at gunman handling pistol. 8. Nail-bomber hit. 9. Three nail-bombers, all hit. 10. Two gunmen with pistols, one hit, one unhurt. 11. One sniper in a toilet window fired on and not hit. 12. Gunman with pistol in third floor flat shot and possibly hit. 13. Gunman with rifle on ground floor of flats shot and hit. 14. Gunman with rifle at barricade killed and body recovered.

Unfortunately the subsequent Widgery inquiry did not produce witnesses to back up the soldiers' claims. There was little doubt that the IRA themselves 'doctored' the scene by whisking away incriminating materials and, it was speculated, several other bodies or wounded personnel. However, the inquiry merely fuelled the very speculation it was supposed to have answered and, in the event, simply added sustenance to the IRA's huge propaganda effort.

As to those killed, it was difficult to prove one way or the other whether they were IRA members, Provos or just young lads out for Sunday sport – baiting the troops. The dead were mostly teenagers:

Gerald Donaghy, aged 17, killed by a single shot to his stomach, fired by Soldier G, at Glenfada Park. He did not die at once, and was taken to receive medical assistance nearby, but died there. A police photograph of his body where he fell showed that he had a nail bomb in one of the pockets of his trousers. Later the Widgery inquiry was told that in fact four nail bombs were found on him. Widgery dismissed suggestions from witnesses these had been planted on the body.

James Wray, aged 22, died at Glenfada Park at the same time as Gerald Donaghy. He was one of a crowd of people running away from the soldiers. Two eyewitnesses said they saw Wray fall to the ground wounded and that he was then shot a second time from behind and killed.

Gerald McKinney, aged 35, was among the same crowd as Donaghy and Wray and was killed by a single shot from the same soldier who shot Gerald Donaghy.

William McKinney, 26, died just after Gerard McKinney (no relation) from a single bullet which came from behind, passed through his chest from right to left and then through his left wrist. (Referring to these three deaths, Widgery said that the firing by soldiers in Glenfada Park 'bordered on the reckless'.)

John Young, aged 17, died at Glenfada Park, killed by a single shot to his head. He was among a group of young men throwing stones at the soldiers. Forensic tests revealed lead particles on his left hand which, Widgery would conclude, indicated that he had probably fired a gun despite evidence that there were a number of ways in which the body could have been contaminated by lead particles, either from colleagues or the people who moved the body.

William Nash, aged 19, was with John Young and died from a single shot to his chest. Widgery again believed that lead particles found on his left hand indicated that he may have been firing a gun, probably at Soldier P, who said that he had shot four times at someone who was firing a pistol at him. No weapon was found near Nash, but Widgery once again made the point, repeatedly, that the IRA had 'cleaned up' after the shootings.

Michael McDaid, aged 20, died from a single shot to his face alongside John Young and William Nash. Lead particles were found on his jacket and his right hand. Widgery concluded that he had probably been contaminated by lead associated with firing by Young or Nash and not from the soldiers who picked him up or their vehicle.

Michael Kelly, aged 17, was shot by Soldier F in the same bout of firing that killed Young, Nash and McDaid. He died from a single shot to his abdomen. Lead particles were found on his right cuff. Widgery accepted that Kelly had not fired a weapon, nor thrown any bomb at the soldiers.

Kevin McElhinney, aged 17, died from a single shot which hit him from behind at a time when he was on his hands and knees, trying to reach the Rossville Flats. Father O'Keefe and a newspaper photographer testified that he was unarmed. Widgery believed that he must have been killed by Sergeant K, who said that he had fired on a man who was crawling along carrying a rifle. Widgery said of him: 'I hesitate to make a positive finding against a deceased man ... [but] I was much impressed by Sergeant K's evidence.'

Patrick Doherty, aged 31, was shot trying to reach the Rossville Flats. A series of photographs taken at the time showed he was unarmed. Widgery found that he had probably been killed by Soldier F in the mistaken belief that he had a pistol.

Jack Duddy, aged 17, was killed by a single shot that passed through his chest. Three eyewitnesses, including a priest, said they saw a soldier take aim at him as he fled the scene. Widgery concluded that he was hit by a bullet intended for someone else.

Hugh Gilmore, aged 17, was hit by a single bullet as he was running from the soldiers. An eyewitness, Geraldine Richmond, who was running with him, said he was unarmed; a photograph taken after he was hit confirmed it. Richmond was under the impression that he had been shot from behind.

Bernard McGuigan, aged 41, was shot through the back of the head as he went to the assistance of a wounded man in the Rossville Flats; he had a white handkerchief in his hand at the time. Lead particles were found on both his hands. Widgery concluded that the forensic evidence 'constituted grounds for suspicion that he had been in close proximity to someone who had fired'.

In his own report on the dead, Lord Widgery said that some of them were wholly acquitted of complicity in handling firearms or bombs, but that there was a strong suspicion that others had been firing weapons or handling bombs that afternoon. He also found that none of the dead was proved to have been shot while handling a firearm or bomb.

It was a significant point. Later the government – while confirming that the troops acted lawfully in self-defence – said:

by reason of this finding of Lord Widgery, all of the deceased should be regarded as having been found not guilty of the allegation of having been shot whilst handling a firearm or bomb and in a spirit of goodwill and conciliation towards the relatives and friends of the deceased and on an ex gratia basis Her Majesty's Government have agreed to pay to the relatives of each of the deceased the respective sums...

The compensation payments ranged from £250 to, in one case, £16,575.35. Payments were also made to the 13 wounded by Army bullets and no charges were laid against any person arising out of events on Bloody Sunday.

The Widgery inquiry ended up satisfying no one and, in the end, not even the soldiers who were there to perform the Operational Order approved by the Northern Ireland Cabinet Committee. The mass of conflicting stories and theories that emerged boiled down to the soldiers' accounts against those of survivors and eyewitnesses. To a man, the soldiers insisted that every one of those shot was in the act of attacking a soldier. Widgery concluded that if the soldiers were parties to a lying conspiracy it would have come to light in the rigorous cross-examination to which they were subjected. He added: 'Those accustomed to listening to witnesses could not fail to be impressed by the demeanour of the soldiers of 1 Para. They gave their evidence with confidence and without hesitation or prevarication and withstood a rigorous cross-examination without contradicting themselves or each other.'

Many on both sides of the Irish Sea were aghast at Widgery's findings and made no bones about it. It did not take long for someone to point out that he had been a lieutenant colonel in the Royal Artillery and a brigadier in the Territorial Army. His landed background also made him appear – in the eyes of every Irish Republican – a member of the British establishment they loathed. They needed no convincing at all that Widgery's task was to get the inquiry over and buried as soon as possible because this had been a politically motivated operation rather than a military one. It was clear even then that there would be protests about a number of crucial issues that remained unvisited and did no one any favours – least of all 1 Para, who now faced years of vilification and threats.

Meanwhile the RUC presented a very substantial file on its own inquiries into the events of Bloody Sunday to the Director of Public Prosecutions for Northern Ireland, who, after considering all the evidence, announced there was insufficient evidence to warrant the prosecution of any member of the security forces.

The inquest into the 13 deaths was held in August 1973. The Coroner, Major Hubert O'Neill, was more outspoken than anyone in public office up to that point:

This Sunday became known as Bloody Sunday and bloody it was. It was quite unnecessary. It strikes me that the Army ran amok that day and shot without thinking what they were doing. They were shooting innocent people. These people may have been taking part in a march that was banned but that does not justify the troops coming in and firing live rounds indiscriminately. I would say without hesitation that it was sheer, unadulterated murder. It was murder.

Two days after the shootings demonstrators burned down the British Embassy in Dublin. The Widgery report had come out fast, furious and incomplete in April 1972, by which time the British Prime Minister, Edward Heath, had suspended the Stormont parliament and imposed direct rule from Westminster. A dirtier war was now in progress, encompassing rival factions in British intelligence, competing elements of the security forces and the RUC and a higher echelon of military commanders whose tactics in fighting the bombers relied heavily on their experiences in the colonial wars of the previous two decades. Coupled to this conflict was a political machine distracted and in disarray, which, like its predecessors in the Labour government, showed a complete lack of understanding of Ulster.

Meanwhile both wings of the IRA were preparing to take revenge on the Paras for Bloody Sunday. Both were planning to strike at the headquarters of the 16th Parachute Brigade in Aldershot. The official IRA had already sent a small unit to London to prepare for attacks even before the shootings and now this was to be activated by the Army Council in Dublin to prepare to bomb the Paras. Additional men were sent to London and met up with the unit already there, who were living in a flat in St James's Lane, Muswell Hill, north London. One of the IRA men acquired a British Army uniform to gain access to the Aldershot base and, by simply walking around the site, made a sketch plan of the layout which they all studied back at Muswell Hill. They then drove to Somerset and stole 220 pounds of gelignite and detonators from a quarry. They hired a blue Ford Cortina and the explosives were packed into the boot. In a second car, which had been stolen, they placed a smaller detonating bomb. At 7 a.m. on 22 February the gang drove the two cars to Aldershot. The car bomb was driven close to the officers' mess; the timer was set for midday, when they would all be congregating for lunch. In fact, it had been placed in the wrong position.

The blast hit the kitchens, killing five women who were preparing the meals. Captain Gerry Weston, a Roman Catholic padre who had been awarded an MBE for brave service in Ulster, was walking by the car at the time and was also killed, as was 58-year-old John Hasler, a gardener who was working on the lawn. Two members of the IRA gang were arrested within 24 hours. The others were never caught. One was given a life sentence, the other three and a half years for possessing a firearm. The IRA's Army Council in Dublin was furious because the job had been botched. Although, from the British perspective, the attack was bad enough, not a single soldier had been killed.

The Provos also wanted revenge – an ambition which became more intense in the summer. And after Bloody Sunday came Bloody Friday: 21 July 1972, when the Provisional IRA exploded 22 bombs in Belfast on a single day, killing nine people and wounding dozens more. Ten days later 2 Para was part of a 12,000-strong combined force assembled under Operation Motorman which, supported by tanks and bulldozers, was launched across Belfast and Londonderry to clear the no-go areas.

Thereafter, in the continuing struggle, elements of the Parachute Regiment were in fairly constant attendance in Ulster and, since the Paras were invariably at the sharp end of operations, their casualties mounted as each year of the 1970s passed. By the end of 1976 17 non-commissioned officers and other ranks had been killed on duty during the previous five-year period in Ulster, some shot in the back by snipers, others killed by landmines or, like Sergeant Mike Willetts, bombs. The worst atrocity of all, however, was yet to come. The infamous Warrenpoint Massacre rounded off the decade in a tragically spectacular manner whereby the IRA was adjudged to have finally taken revenge for the Bloody Sunday killings – even though the attack was inflicted not on 1 Para but 2 Para, the historic battalion that could be traced back to Arnhem and Bruneval.

Indeed there was a certain irony in the fact that the man who sent 2 Para's predecessors on the Bruneval raid, Lord Louis Mountbatten, and members of his family were blown up on their boat off County Sligo in the Irish Republic by the IRA on the same day that it carried out one of the most horrific attacks on the British military in the history of the troubles. It was certainly 2 Para's worst day of losses since Arnhem, although the sheer drama of Lord Mountbatten's assassination to some extent overshadowed the horror of Warrenpoint, in which 18 soldiers were killed outright and many more badly wounded in a double bomb attack on a 2 Para convoy. At the time the battalion was one month into another 20-month tour of Northern Ireland.

On the afternoon of 27 August 1979 the victims were caught in an IRA trap which even the Army admitted had been executed with enormous skill. The ambush was set up on the shores of Carlingford Lough, which marks the border between Northern Ireland and the Republic, and followed a pattern that the IRA had perfected over the previous two years. A massive 1000-pound bomb was planted under a stone gateway leading to Narrow Water Castle, a medieval building near a stretch of dual carriageway. The device was made from a mixture of weedkiller and fertilizer, known by Army bomb-disposal officers as 'Co-op mix'. The bomb had a fuse that could be detonated by a signal from the type of equipment used to control model aeroplanes. The site for the bomb had been carefully selected. There was cover against sniper fire and the spot was a natural choice for an Army commander called out to investigate a terrorist incident to make his temporary base. The IRA men could keep the site under observation from a hide across the border, 200 yards away, and detonate the bomb at the required moment.

To create an incident that would lure an Army force to the spot, the terrorists planted a second bomb in a hay trailer. As one of the officers of 2 Para explained: 'At this point, the IRA got lucky. They would have blown up any suitable target that came along the road.

What in fact did come along was a small convoy from 2 Para – about 30 men travelling in two four-ton trucks and a Land Rover, on a routine movement along the coastal road from Ballykinder *en route* for A Company's base at the border town of Newry.'

As the last vehicle of the convoy passed, the IRA detonated the bomb from their hide, completely destroying the second of the trucks. Six soldiers were killed instantly and several others were wounded, two of them very seriously. Ammunition in the blazing vehicle began to explode and, after tending the wounded, the survivors had to take cover to avoid possible sniper fire. The explosion could be heard for miles and a Royal Marines detachment on patrol in Warrenpoint radioed A Company's base at Newry. Two A Company machine-gun patrols, hearing the alert, headed for the explosion site, as did A Company's commander, Major Peter Fursman; he gathered some men and they sped off in two Land Rovers.

At the same time the 1st Battalion the Queen's Own Highlanders, based at Bessbrook, County Armagh, ordered into the air an emergency reaction team of two RAF Wessex helicopters carrying an assault team and three medics. The A Company machine-gunners had set up roadblocks by the time the helicopters landed on the central reservation and began to pick up the wounded for evacuation. A third helicopter, a Gazelle carrying the commanding officer of the 1st Battalion the Queen's Own Highlanders, Lieutenant Colonel David Blair, landed in a field. He disembarked and ran to meet Major Fursman, whose two Land Rovers were parked at the gatehouse – at the very spot where the main IRA bomb had been planted. The IRA ambush team, in their hillside hide, had sat it out for 25 minutes after the first explosion. Now they detonated their second bomb and opened up with rifle fire. This time the carnage was even worse: 12 more soldiers were killed, including Major Peter Fursman, Lieutenant Colonel David Blair and his bodyguard, Lance Corporal Victor MacLeod. Many more were seriously injured. Of the dead, 14 were from 2 Para, which had recently taken a number of newly trained recruits in their late teens or early twenties.

This chapter opened with the story of the first of the Parachute Regiment's wives to become a widow during their husbands' service in Northern Ireland; now this outrage had left eight more widows and seven fatherless children. But even as 2 Para was licking its wounds after this devastating attack, there was a faint cry of developments far away in the South Atlantic that would soon embroil them all – a fresh crisis, greater than anything the regiment had faced since the Second World War.

15

THE FALKLANDS ADVENTURE

The preamble to the Falklands War has been much discussed, but it is worth recalling some of the basic elements since these have become obscured in the fog of other controversies as the years have passed. In the months before the conflict the Conservative government of Margaret Thatcher, and specifically her Defence Secretary, John Nott, were engaged in yet another round of governmental cost-cutting across the whole military establishment. Among those elements on which the axe was about to fall was the Royal Navy's sole bearer of the White Ensign in the southern hemisphere, the ice-patrol vessel *HMS Endurance*. Nott was insisting that it should be withdrawn, thereby saving a miserly £3 million a year from his multi-billion-pound budget, and this opened up a national debate that began with letters to *The Times*. The Argentinians were following this story, and the head of the country's military junta, General Leopold Fortunato Galtieri, took Nott's proposal to mean that Britain no longer cared about its farthest flung outpost, the Falkland Islands.

It was, he decided, an opportune moment for his nation to reclaim what his people believed was their territory and bestow upon the islands their correct title of Las Malvinas. Indeed, there were many in the Falklands who were expecting this to happen; some did not even care, because Britain was something of an absentee landlord to the some 1950 inhabitants of this remote sheep-farming community. A British embassy military attaché in Buenos Aires had been warning for some time that Argentina was planning an invasion and even predicted – almost to the day – when it would happen. No one paid much heed, nor were the appeals to keep the *Endurance* on patrol successful, despite the reports of vastly increased radio traffic monitored by its captain, Nick Barker RN. Captain Barker and others had correctly read the signs, for the pleas to keep the *Endurance* in those waters were turned down by the British government. Minds were changed only at the very last minute, when a group of Argentinian scrap dealers landed on South Georgia – which was not part of the Falklands – and hoisted their national flag. Galtieri's brave lads would surely soon follow.

Whitehall mandarins went into a rapid huddle. What could be done from 8000 miles away? According to one who was there, interviewed by the author for a previous work on the Special Boat Service, the first unit to get ashore, some 'mad, mad schemes were being bandied about … one of them quite astonishing, that the British should make a very loud bang in the South Atlantic by Friday 9 April 1982'. Whatever did he mean? Short of a small A-bomb, there was little possibility of achieving any kind of a loud bang within seven days, but then there were some very foolish people at the helm then. In the words of Denis Healey, who was Labour's Defence Secretary from 1964 to 1970, it was an 'almighty cock-up' – and few could disagree. Lord Carrington took the brunt of the blame, although it was not all his, and resigned as Foreign Secretary. When John Nott offered to stand down, Mrs Thatcher refused to accept his resignation, although he did walk the plank later.

The Prime Minister herself took command and announced that a Falklands task force of 40 ships was being assembled to carry an advance party of SBS, SAS and Royal Marines Commandos, followed by 2 and 3 Para, the Gurkhas, the Blue and Royals, the Scots Guards, the Welsh Guards and other famous elements of the British Army. Major Philip Neame, commander of D Company, 2 Para, was on holiday with his family in Scotland when he read about the invasion. He phoned Aldershot and discovered that the Paras were already being recalled and that Lieutenant Colonel Herbert Jones, commanding officer of 2 Para, was flying back from a skiing holiday in France. In fact, at first it looked as if 2 Para might not be selected for the Falklands, so that it could continue with its already planned six-month semi-operational tour in Belize. Lieutenant Colonel Jones, then 42, was determined that his battalion would not miss the prospect of a scrap. 'H', as everyone knew Jones, who hated his first name, was a tough, no-nonsense, charismatic figure. He was also well known for his thrusting leadership style, always from the front and in the middle of the action. This ability he had demonstrated many times in his career and he was particularly noted for tours in Northern Ireland, when, as a brigade major, he frequently left the safety of his desk to join border patrols as a rifleman in the IRA bandit country of South Armagh. He was awarded an MBE for his work there. Philip Neame recalls:

And so we went haring back to Aldershot expecting to be moving out to the Falklands any day, only to find heaving indecision. 3 Para had already been earmarked to go as the spearhead battalion and perhaps there wasn't a role for us. H wasn't prepared to accept that and, by hook or by crook, he eventually got us stood by as the first tranche of reinforcements for 3 Commando Brigade. It was about a week before we did in fact get confirmation that we were going and things began to happen fairly quickly. I can't help thinking that in the MOD at this stage few people were convinced it was going to end up in a war. At the back of our minds we really wanted to test our mettle, have a little war, get stuck in. The whole battalion was busting a gut to get there, H especially, and put all that training to the test at some stage before we finished our military careers.

Very dominant in our minds also was the Maggie factor. Thatcher said, 'Go' and we were all very much taken by her leadership; from the very first day it grabbed everyone's consciousness in a quite dramatic way. H was always coming out with expressions, if there was something he didn't agree with, like 'I'll get on the phone to Maggie and sort it out.' And we really did set off in that way with the band playing *Don't Cry for Me Argentina* and all this kind of corny stuff, really not that convinced that it was going to end up in a war.

For the journey south, 3 Para went ahead aboard one of the hastily commandeered troop carriers in the first wave of the task force, travelling in some style on the liner SS *Canberra* with the 40th and 42nd Royal Marines Commandos and Zulu Company of the 45th Royal Marines Commando. Meanwhile 2 Para followed on behind aboard the MV *Norland*, a packed-to-the-gills converted car ferry. For the time being our narrative remains with this battalion since this was something of a parting of the ways and the two units would not come together until the final stages of the campaign. The fact was, 2 Para had already been preparing to go overseas, having been assigned to its six-month tour of Belize. The previous autumn the whole battalion had been on an exercise to Kenya for training. Phil Neame was among them:

I was very much the new boy among the company commanders, most of whom had been in their job for about a year. Travelling down on the *Norland*, the rapport with the civilian crew was excellent. They were the unsung heroes of the whole conflict when you consider that the *Norland*, more than any other civilian ship, was right in the thick of it. It was to be effectively used as an amphibious assault ship. It was a bit unfortunate that in the early stages people didn't level with the crew about what would be involved – we were well past Ascension when the order came out that they would be under naval orders. Two minutes later came the news that the *Norland* would be an assault ship and the captain and members of the crew were a bit peeved that it had been done in this way. They were unflattered by this. They didn't need the naval orders because they were going in to do the job anyhow. We had a very warm rapport with them which developed.

The women members of the crew had gone ashore at Freetown [Sierra Leone], leaving only the men. One of them preferred to dress as a woman and behave as a woman and was quickly christened Wendy by the battalion. But Wendy's saving grace was that he was a superb piano player and entertainer with a quick line of wit and for all his penchant for non-heterosexual relationships the battalion took this man under their wing, made him an honorary member and presented him with a battalion tie. It was just an example of how, partly because of the circumstances, prejudices that in other times might have led to different behaviour were pushed aside. The captain, Don Ellerby, a grizzled old sea salt, became a kind of father figure. Before we went ashore at San Carlos Water he came over the ship's PA system and gave a moving, simple speech: have a good trip ashore, come back safely. It was beautifully done and very moving.

Peter Richens, Sergeant Major of 2 Para's B Company, had also been on holiday with his family, in Cornwall, when he heard of the confrontation in the Falklands. He too admits he was hoping that his battalion would be called forward for it, and his colleagues shared this feeling. It was not about saving the Falklands, more to do with getting into a scrap and having a go at some foreign army that had knocked Britain off the top of the pile:

There was great enthusiasm and we trained hard on the way down … but the *Norland* was a bit restricted for space. In spite of that, we managed a lot of sport and exercises. We did a little bit of shooting, firing at sea. We did upset the Royal Navy party very, very badly because we shot an albatross. It was a moving target and someone fired. The Navy chaps, being mariners, were exceedingly angry.

As we neared the islands we began preparations for landings. The *Norland* cargo door measured about 10 [feet] by 10. We had to get a battalion out of that door into landing craft on a very heavy sea. We did a lot of training for that; it was a one-off situation and finally there we were in San Carlos Water, where we were to disembark into landing craft. Before we went, our padre David

Cooper, who is quite a character, both in and out of dog collar, led us in a service which everyone enjoyed and Colonel Jones gave us a pep talk and we went to our different stations. It was supposed to take an hour to get the battalion off the boat and into the landing craft and away to our beach landing. But the sea was very, very rough. When the boat came up on a wave we had to jump into it as it went down again.

This operation took about five hours, which was not what we had expected. B Company was the second company to go into the boats and we had something like a three-hour wait in the water while the whole of the battalion was clear of the *Norland*. We had one accident where one of the soldiers jumped down with an SMG [sub-machine-gun] and it hit some metalwork, cocked itself and went off. It shot him in the thigh. When the whole battalion was off, the commanding officer's boat was going to be the first ashore, but it had a mechanical problem, which displeased him no end; there was a lot of shouting over this.

B Company's was the first landing craft ashore. When I say ashore, that is a bit of an overstatement. The Royal Marines dropped us 150 yards short of the beach. Now I'm six foot and when I stepped off the boat the ice-cold water was up to my chest. My company radio operator, who was with me, was about five feet six and it was a case of grabbing him by his backpack and keeping his head above water as best I could. We remained soaked for days. We didn't know what to expect; we had no briefing on whether the Argentine troops were dug in around San Carlos Water; we didn't know whether they were waiting to see the whites of our eyes before they opened fire. Luckily we hit an unopposed beach for landing. Myself and the company commander, Major John Crosland, saw a light and went forward.

We were approached by British soldiers who said, 'Who are you?' And my Company Commander replied, 'Who are you?'

They said: 'We're the SBS – and we weren't expecting you until tomorrow.'

My company commander said he was sorry about that, lads, but we were staying. We then got ourselves sorted out and had a fairly long approach march to the top of Sussex mountain. We went firm, and dug holes, built sangars using rocks to build up when you can't dig down for protection. B Company was quite lucky. A lot of the Falklands is a peat-like ground and water-sodden. We were on a high feature so that when we dug our trenches and built our sangars we were relatively comfortable. But the likes of D Company, who were down in a kind of a saddle, as they dug their slit trenches they filled up with water. It was also bitterly cold and very wet and for the first ten days we never really dried out from the landing.

When we went ashore we had a total company strength of 94, not including attached arms; between the time we arrived on Sussex mountain and our march to Goose Green, I lost 14 members of the company through trench foot. The procedure was that you had two pairs of socks. One pair of socks would be on and the other pair would be under your armpits drying off, and at nights you changed. At that time the boots the Army issued us with were totally inadequate for that type of terrain. The uppers just let water in and that was our biggest problem. The boots were useless.

In the aftermath, all things considered, it was generally agreed that the Paras had gone ashore overloaded. The least heavy bergen weighed 80 pounds, but many people were carrying 100 pounds or more, which meant a harrowing move across the most appalling terrain up to the top of Sussex mountain, and for a while morale began to slip, as Phil Neame recalls:

For several days on top of Sussex mountain there was a general lack of direction and no one seemed to know what we were doing next. We started to get rumours of political imperatives coming down from London, that something had to be done. We could see the fleet being bombed to bits in San Carlos Water [by 24 May the destroyer HMS *Sheffield*, her sister ship the *Coventry*, the container ship *Atlantic Conveyor* and the British frigate HMS *Antelope* had all been bombed or hit by Exocet missiles] while we were sitting on top of the mountain waiting for orders. And so for the first ten days or so my company were stood by … eventually being assigned to a raid on the area of Port Sussex House, which was a few kilometres south. There was a report of a small Argentine outpost there. I sent 12 Platoon under Jim Barry to take a look, but by the time they got there the Argentines had left. They remained for a couple of days and then we were warned for the first time of a raid on Goose Green and the idea was that I was going to secure Camilla Creek [a key area on the approaches to Goose Green].

We set off and made arrangements to RV with 12 Platoon and just after we met up with them the news came over the radio that the raid had been cancelled and we were to return. So, having got halfway to Goose Green, we walked back. And one must say that all this stop-start business was hardly conducive to confidence and high morale. Also I discovered how tender people's feet had become. No one had had totally dry feet since we came ashore. I started the old-fashioned bit of feet inspections, which I thought had gone out with the ark but had suddenly become important again. This four-mile trek out and four miles back had, in that short time, taken its toll on the feet. I said to H, if we were going to waste our time like this we might have problems – all of which I don't think H took very seriously, but to my mind it was most critical.

We got back that night to be told that the assault was on again and that we were going to be helicoptered down to Camilla Creek the following morning; unbelievable! So stop-start continued and that morning we all bailed out before dawn in stick order all ready for the helicopters, only to be told that there were no helicopters available because of a priority task and the raid was being binned again. We really were beginning to think by this stage, 'What on earth's going on?'

I think it was probably now two days later… Early afternoon, H got hold of me and said the raid's back on; back down to Camilla

Creek; we were to get going as soon as possible and two hours later we were off. We reckoned we'd got about an hour and a half of daylight left and I thought we'd give it a good pasting with the artillery before we went in. It was a very featureless piece of ground as one got off Sussex mountain. I was a bit unsure how far exactly we were from Camilla Creek and decided to call up a fire mission on to Camilla Creek to see where the rounds landed and we could take things from there. We called the fire mission up and waited for what seemed quite a long time. The rounds came down and they landed about 1000 metres behind us. But there was no way I'd overshot Camilla Creek House and we were seriously wondering what had happened. We called the fire mission again, got them to check all their settings and send another load. The rounds came down 1000 metres behind us again. I couldn't understand it and it only became clear later on that they hadn't got all the Met input that they normally have and it was all put down to a change of Met, firing against the wind instead of with the wind, and it was making this sort of difference. That didn't help us very much and we decided to proceed with care to make sure that we didn't just blunder into Camilla Creek.

We got to the point where we could see outbuildings and I sent in one of my platoons to see what was what. They moved in, nothing happened and the whole company followed. The Argentines had left in a hurry and we occupied it without opposition. We made ourselves at home in the house. The battalion was following us down behind and arrived two or three hours later. We were around 120 men, who had settled quite comfortably into the house and the other 500 or so coming up behind us were also intent on sneaking into these buildings and it ended up with the whole battalion crammed into these three buildings like sardines, sheltering from the elements and trying to get some rest that night.

Two interesting things happened. The first was that by now H was talking of an attack on Goose Green, to recover Goose Green and Darwin – as opposed to his earlier briefing to me, which had been a raid. The other thing was that we were listening to the World Service on the radio and there was a report that John Nott had announced in the Commons that afternoon that a Parachute Battalion was within a couple of miles of Darwin and Goose Green. H heard this and threw a complete wobbly. He got [BBC war correspondent] Robert Fox in, berated him and asked what he thought the BBC were up to – although it was quite wrong to blame the BBC at all; they were just reporting what had been said in Parliament. Clearly it was the best possible warning to the Argentines that we were on the way. If they were to do their appreciation, they could easily work out that we were either going to come in from the sea or from the north. It was fairly easy to cover both options and later it became very clear that the Argentines redeployed in response to this information. Thus we undoubtedly met very much tougher opposition as we came down to the settlements than we would have done.

This fact was soon to become very evident to all concerned. News correspondents at the scene all reported that a considerable number of Argentinian reinforcements were moved up from Fitzroy, near Port Stanley, immediately after the broadcast. Colonel Jones, still smarting, told a correspondent from the *Sunday Telegraph* that he intended to sue the BBC for manslaughter when he returned home, although the BBC had already pointed out that it broadcast no information that was not available to other media from official sources in London, including the Ministry of Defence.

Phil Neame resumes the story:

What was of immediate concern to H now was that they would draw rings round our likely assembly areas and bomb them and again – it wasn't too difficult to work out – that is exactly what they did. We spent that day doing our own recces to try to ascertain what we were going to come up against. We were told that there were probably 300–400 in the garrison [at the time of surrender there were in fact more than 1200]. We were getting feedback from the SAS patrols, who had said all you've got to do is knock hard on the front door and the rest will collapse. People were taking it all very relaxed in a way – i.e. that we would go in, hit them hard and we'd go straight through. By the end of that day we'd captured a prisoner, the recce platoon had come up with a certain amount of detail of what was north of Darwin and eventually just before last light we were called in by H for a briefing to attack Darwin and Goose Green. I remember saying to my sergeant major, looking at the map and seeing there wasn't really a great deal of scope for manoeuvring along this narrow isthmus, either we are going to get them by surprise and it's going to be a cakewalk or it's going to be a long bloody day.

Anyhow, we took our orders from H, marked up our maps with all the identified enemy positions and that was just all red from one end of the isthmus to the other. I went back and planted the map down in front of my sergeant major and said, 'I think its going to be the bloody one!' There was no way that this was going to be a piece of piss with all these positions to slog our way through, unless they all collapsed after the first hit – which seemed a bit optimistic.

The attack on Darwin and Goose Green was to be a complicated six-phase operation with every company involved in what was clearly intended to be a fast-moving action that gave little room for error, mishap or miscalculation. At the start line, B Company, under Sergeant Major Peter Richens, was the right forward company. A Company was on the left. At their briefings the two companies had been assured that they would get the support of heavy bombardment of enemy positions from the guns of HMS *Arrow* in Camilla Creek bay. They were promised a few hundred rounds to soften up the targets, to combine with their artillery. Only a dozen or so rounds came over from the ship because a problem developed with the firing mechanism. There were local problems too which affected artillery delivery. The base plates of the mortars were becoming embedded in the soft ground. Later four men suffered broken ankles as they stood on the base plates in an attempt to stabilize them as the weapons were fired. The result was that when they crossed the start line, 2 Para was virtually on its own. The only real firepower was actually that which the battalion itself could muster. They had also been assured that they would have Harrier support at that time, but this also failed to materialize. Peter Richens remembers:

We were on the start line for an hour or so before we got our orders to move. A target appeared to our front; it was a scarecrow, which had a few rounds put in it, which relieved a bit of jumpiness with the lead section. We came across our first trenches, where we took those sections out. It was very difficult and very, very slow. You had to be thorough. Questions have been asked about our particular phase at Goose Green – that we didn't take many prisoners. It's very difficult when you are fighting at night to take prisoners and in the heat of the battle, the screams, the noise and with a lot of fighting going on, taking trench by trench … perhaps someone standing up and throwing their weapon away is all that we could recognize. In pitch-black it is a very difficult situation.

Also, Colonel Jones was very keen to keep us moving. He was getting on to us to get ourselves moving; he was getting very annoyed, very impatient because we weren't making the ground we should have been making. It got to the stage where he said that if we didn't get our arses in gear and get moving, he would pass D Company through us and they would do a better job than us. But in this situation, we just couldn't do it. We could hear that A Company was in a similar situation… We just could not make the pace that was anticipated on the briefing.

Daylight came and the terrain where we were was very open, hilly but no trees, no cover. It was an 'advance to contact', an extended arrowhead formation. We just went through to meet our enemy but unfortunately B Company was totally in the open. We had two platoons up front, Company Headquarters in between and in reserve was our third platoon and reserve Company Headquarters.

As we went on down a slope, the enemy were in very, very well-prepared trenches and we had to double forward into a gully like rats in a hole and our reserve element had to go back up the slope and go for them from the top. The company was split but there was nothing we could do about it. We'd had a lot of fire against us, as well as snipers. We sent a section out to probe, but they had to be brought back. We must have been in there for something like six hours under constant fire. The company commander urged the battalion 2iC to get a Milan [anti-tank missile fired by a team of two] to assist us. It was suggested that it was brought in a bunker-busting role. The Milan eventually got to us, by which time we ourselves were very short of ammunition. The Milan fired into enemy positions and that was the turning point of that particular battle.

Meanwhile Neame's D Company had brought down the wrath of H upon them. Neame had given his orders in the dark: his men were to leave Camilla Creek at midnight and were due to cross the start line at 02.00 hours. His was the reserve company for the first two phases of the attack and then had to move forward with B Company on Phase Three. It was fairly complicated for people to get their heads around, particularly since they hadn't seen the ground:

We got slightly off course, about 500 metres or so, and the net result was we ended up in front of H's tac [tactical party]. He, being a great believer in leading from the front, was most upset that his reserve company was at this stage ahead of him and proceeded to berate me in his usual way; there was no harm done but it was simply an affront to himself that we should be ahead of him. The battle started with A Company on the left and B Company on the right, who took their first objectives without huge opposition. H had gone stomping down the track ahead of us. B Company was reorganizing on the right, and taking a bit of time about it. They should have pushed straight on. I couldn't understand why they were delayed, although it became very clear soon after. H was boiling over with impatience at this delay since he had set himself an extremely tight timetable, six hours to fight through and get to the outside settlements ... seven kilometres of fighting. It was very ambitious, although at the time we didn't think too much of it because we had this sublime view that we'd knock hard and the whole thing would just steamroller on.

So when B Company delayed to reorganize, H came stomping back. He said he could not tolerate this delay and that I was to go forward and attack the enemy position. I said 'Which position?' He pointed: 'Over there... I've just been shot at!' I couldn't see a damn thing in the murk and certainly not enough to launch an attack. So I decided to send one platoon up, advance to contact, and hope for the best. We called down a fire mission from the ship's gun for what I thought was the objective. The ship fired about half a dozen rounds with an illume [illuminating flare] before the gun jammed, so we were back in the dark and in total confusion. However, it did become apparent that we were heading towards a strong enemy position because we were attracting a lot of small-arms fire from a hillock.

In spite of what appeared to be a very great deal of tracer being fired at us, no one got hit and we managed to get on the top of the hill and started to clear it, with 12 Platoon leading at this stage under Jim Barry. Then we were suddenly opened up on by machine-guns on our right flank, sited between where I was and the hill where John Crosland's B Company had already taken. These machine-guns completely pinned down 10 Platoon. They picked up two casualties almost immediately. From where I was I couldn't put down fire on them without hitting B Company, who were just beyond. In fact, we tried that and got an urgent cry from John Crosland, who asked what the hell we thought we were shooting at.

I was caught off balance and with a dilemma which was saved by Chris Waddington, commanding 11 Platoon on my left flank, who on his own initiative did a wheel-round and put in an attack on the machine-guns with no guidance from me at all. He had only been in the battalion a month, straight out of Sandhurst. His attack went in very successfully and we suppressed very quickly, although he picked up two other casualties, one wounded and one killed.

We began to reorganize and I then realized why B Company had been slow themselves. It was pitch-black and the ground was really quite featureless. The whole business of orientation and staying aware of even the direction you were facing, let alone knowing exactly where you were, went completely to the four winds. People were completely disorientated. It was impossible to get a bearing in these conditions. I had to try to pull the company together and get some semblance of order. This was complicated by the fact that 10 Platoon had taken two casualties, potentially two people missing until they were found. So obviously we went through the business of trying to locate them; they may have been injured and needed assistance or they may have been killed – in fact it was the latter but we had no way of knowing. At what point do we say, forget it, we must crack on and abandon them? There is always a reluctance to do that. When you are going into attack you stop for no one; we are all clear about that. But when you stop and reorganize, how long do you spend trying to find these people?

The disorientation of the rest of the company was already a problem. The only way I could resolve it in the end was to put up a flare, which was not the tactical teaching you'd have at Warminster, and say reorganize on me and hope for the best, otherwise we'd be wandering around looking for each other all night. We eventually got back together but we still hadn't found the two missing people. I had to say that we were going to have to leave them and push off. Their bodies were eventually picked up by Battalion Headquarters during daylight. Interestingly, an NCO had been shot first and his buddy, Fletcher, was found lying on top of him with a shell dressing in his hand, the deduction being that he was shot while trying to render first aid.

We took half an hour or more to reorganize. H was tearing his hair out by now because he could see his times going out of the window. A and B Companies had passed us then and we went back into reserve and we carried on. As daylight came up, I was on a little knoll short of Darwin Hill. A Company had already started the battle for Darwin Hill, clearly with a great deal of difficulty. B Company had been brought to a standstill just as daylight was coming up on the extension of Darwin Hill, confronted by the Bocca House Hill feature, with a big open valley like a snooker table in front of them, and they couldn't move without coming under heavy fire. So the whole thing had been plugged down. I was told to stay on the knoll, while elsewhere we saw Argentines wandering along the western shoreline, presumably trying to get back to their own positions. We amused ourselves by taking a few long-range potshots at them, but they were out of range, so I put a stop to that. But it did register in my mind and then, shortly after that, incoming artillery seemed to be zoning in on us; it was being adjusted and it seemed that some observer was giving instructions and they were getting closer. I felt that this wasn't a very healthy place to stay and, despite H's orders to stay where we were, I moved us off into the lee, which was just as well because no sooner had we done that than a significant fire mission came down on to the feature, which provided an explanation to H why I wasn't obeying orders, and he accepted that.

I then thought that we are not going anywhere very fast. Seeing the Argentines moving down the western shoreline came back into mind and I thought that if they could move down there, couldn't we? We could, and being concealed from the main enemy positions ahead of us, there could be scope for turning this. I put this up to H on the radio and was told to mind my own business and stay put. Once again we were spotted and once again the artillery came in and I moved further west again, towards the shoreline in a hollow, and was joined shortly after by C Company, who were having the same problems. I now had a good view of the shoreline and was getting convinced that I could see there was a possibility of infiltrating along the shoreline and turning it.

H was clearly having a frantic time up at Darwin Hill and fairly bit my head off and told me not to try to tell him how to fight his battle and couldn't I see that he was busy? So ... the only sensible thing to do was to get a brew on. The chaps seemed to think that was a rather odd thing to do, but I could think of nothing more positive that we could do; getting some energy inside them for later in the night seemed the best alternative.

My bowl of porridge had literally just come to the boil when we got the news that H had been shot and was out of it.

H had taken it as something of a personal mission, pushing to achieve what Major General Jeremy Moore, Commander Land Forces, had set as a target from the moment he arrived in the Falklands: to find an early battle in which to inflict such a decisive defeat that the Argentinians would never believe they could win the war. The battle he chose was Goose Green and Darwin, and H rose to that occasion – to the extent that it cost him his life. He chose personally to dash to the helm of his advancing troops, picking up a Sterling sub-machine-gun as he went, and led a section into the attack. It was an action which some of his senior colleagues heralded as a turning point of the campaign while others were to criticize it as an act of supreme folly, impatience and irresponsibility, putting the lives of his men at unnecessary risk to satisfy his own lust for glory – a charge for which there was certainly no lack of evidence. Nothing but praise was heaped upon H in London, and this was most vividly demonstrated in the citation published in the *London Gazette* when he was subsequently awarded a posthumous Victoria Cross, the highest honour available:

During an attack against an enemy who was well dug in with mutually supporting positions sited in depth, the battalion was held up just south of Darwin by a particularly well-prepared and resilient enemy position of at least 11 trenches on an important ridge. A number of casualties were received. In order to read the battle fully and to ensure that the momentum of his attack was not lost, Colonel Jones took forward his reconnaissance party to the foot of a re-entrant which a section of battalion had just secured. Despite persistent, heavy and accurate fire the reconnaissance party gained the top of the re-entrant at approximately the same height as the enemy position. From here Colonel Jones encouraged the direction of his battalion mortar fire in an effort to neutralize the enemy positions. However, these had been well prepared and continued to pour effective fire onto the battalion advance which by now was held up for over and hour and was in danger of faltering. In an effort to gain a good viewpoint, Col Jones was now at the very front of his battalion. It was clear to him that desperate measures were needed to overcome the enemy position and rekindle the attack and that unless these measures were taken promptly, the battalion would sustain increasing casualties and the attack perhaps even fail. It was time for personal leadership and action; Col Jones immediately seized a sub-machine gun and calling on those around him and with total disregard for his own safety, charged the nearest enemy position. The action exposed him to fire from a number of trenches. As he charged up a short slope at the enemy position, he was seen to fall and roll backwards. He immediately picked himself up and again charged the enemy trench, firing the machine gun and seemingly oblivious to the intense fire directed at him. He was hit by fire from another trench which he outflanked and fell dying only a few feet from the enemy he had assaulted. A short time later, a company of the battalion attacked the enemy who quickly surrendered.

The devastating display of courage by Colonel Jones completely undermined their will to fight further. Thereafter, the momentum of the attack was rapidly regained...

The citation went on to state that the 'dashing leadership and courage' of the commanding officer was an inspiration to those about him and that the ongoing achievements of 2 Para at Goose Green and Darwin 'set the tone for the subsequent land battle on the Falklands'.

While the latter was quite true, the citation lacked some of the more pertinent details, which were not filled in until later. Predictions about Argentinian resistance crumbling were well wide of the mark, certainly at that point of the battle. There was also to be further confirmation of the lack of air support. A Company urgently needed help. Its commander, Major Dair Farrar-Hockley, had called for a Harrier strike but this had been refused owing to bad weather. Yet three enemy Pucaras flew over on their way to their main target, the gun lines at Camilla Creek House. At 11.55 hours they swept in to attack that zone with bombs and cannon and one was shot down. Reluctant to commit his reserve companies, as Phil Neame had discovered, Colonel Jones decided to go forward himself and attempt to get A Company on the move without the air support. What followed was later analysed and described by Major General John Frost, the Second World War 2 Para commander at Arnhem, himself famed for his heroics:

On his arrival after a hazardous journey ... the CO found 2nd Lieutenant Mark Coe with the company commander. H asked the subaltern: 'Can you get up to the gorse-line?'

'Yes, sir, but it will be pretty hairy.'

'Can you get into a position from which mortar fire can be directed on to the enemy positions?'

'Yes, but that will be really hairy.'

'Well, I want you to take the mortar officer up there with you now.'

Dair Farrar-Hockley was most unhappy about this, however. His company had tried such a manoeuvre with no good result, and after the two officers had gone a part of the way they were called back. It was now thought that perhaps a right flanking move might succeed, and while this was being arranged, the CO said to his company commander: 'Dair, you have got to take that ledge,' indicating a well-defended enemy position above them and to their right, perhaps 60 metres from where they stood. A Company had already tried this about an hour earlier, and had sustained casualties in the process but the company commander realized that, with ammunition running low and support from elsewhere uncertain, it was vital to take the nearest enemy trenches.

Major Farrar-Hockley gathered a party and prepared to lead it up and on to the ledge... The company second-in-command, Captain Chris Dent, and the Adjutant, Captain David Wood, who had come forward with the CO's party, were both determined to get in on the act. Really the latter had no business to be in the area but was heard to say, 'Well done, everyone. Let's remember Arnhem.'

The A Company commander [Dair Farrar-Hockley] responding to the colonel's order ... led a group of perhaps 15 or 16 up on to the ledge. Private Dey, a machine-gunner, was in front, Corporal Hardman forward and to the left, Captain Dent; the Adjutant ... joined this group... [their] position on the ledge was short-lived. Chris Dent was killed instantly, and two others had gone down. After attempting to win the firefight they winkled [their] way off the ledge and back into dead ground. The nearest enemy was only 100 metres away, and could not be breached from this point.

Private Dey had been rather perturbed at seeing the officers so determined on business which was not really theirs. 'You will get killed if you go any further,' he warned. As he did so, Captain Dent fell dead in front of him, and the Adjutant was shot and killed very soon afterwards, as was Corporal Hardman. Caught in a storm of fire from the Argentine positions, and with casualties including two officers killed, Major Farrar-Hockley ordered his group back down off the ledge and into the comparative safety of the lee of the slope. 'If you don't fucking get out now, sir, you ain't getting out,' one of his men called. Meanwhile, the Colonel had started off practically on his own, moving round the spur and into the second gully where Corporal Adams and his section had taken cover in the early moments of the battle.

His determination to see for himself lured him further and further forward. Ever a man for being in front, he must have felt that the key to the success of the whole operation was in his grasp, and that it was being denied him. The company commander was still extricating himself and his men from the vain, if gallant, attack upon the ledge, when one of the officers called to him: 'It's the CO. He's gone round the corner on his own.' 2 Para's Colonel seeing the immediate need to exploit a situation … made a valiant attempt to get in among these nearest trenches with a small tactical party and disrupt the enemy.

Obviously H intended to take the Argentines in the flank while they were still distracted by the attack on the ledge. Sergeant Norman and Lance Corporal Beresford usually accompanied the CO wherever he went and they were not far behind him now as he made his way up the slope towards the enemy trenches. He paused in a small re-entrant right among the enemy positions, none of which seemed to have noticed him, and from there he could see one particular post which plainly had been causing a lot of trouble. He took the magazine off his Sterling to check it, then he set off alone for the enemy post. As he did so, Sergeant Norman noticed another position close behind his CO, which H had failed to see but to which he had now been alerted. 'Watch your back!' he shouted as he dived for cover but H, if he heard, took no notice.

The enemy machine-gun behind him fired and he fell. It was only then that the Argentine troops he was making for realized that he was there, apprised by the sound of his fall. One of the sergeants who had gone forward with H sent a brief message over the wireless: 'Sunray is down.' The loss of its leader can have a shattering effect on any battalion, but this was not the case with 2 Para. The battle continued as the gravely wounded colonel lay where he had fallen but now those who had followed him closely, and those who would have done so, seemed to be spurred on to extra effort. Inspired by the CO's action, the company attacked again – up and on was the order of the day and within 15 minutes white flags or their equivalent appeared in the Argentine trenches. The company commander called a warning lest the enemy be trying a ruse but as the firing died down the Argentine soldiers began to come out. They were quickly made prisoner. As the enemy began to surrender Sergeant Norman ran to the CO, who was very badly wounded and unconscious. There was little that could be done for him. His wounds were dressed and a saline drip was applied and he was gently carried up to a place where it would be possible for a helicopter to land. Urgent signals had been sent for a helicopter to pick up the wounded officer, and Dair Farrar-Hockley waited by his colonel's side. Extra clothing was found, but really nothing could be done to save him and after a few minutes Lieutenant Colonel H Jones died. The time was about 13.30 hours.

As Major General Frost surmised, the loss of their leader did not have an immediate or devastating effect on 2 Para, whose soldiers were by now determined to pursue their goal. Jones, by his example and indelible spirit, had shown that 2 Para was unstoppable, as Phil Neame confirms:

The impact wasn't, I suppose, immediate because we were too far away for the potential significance to penetrate. We then got the word that Chris Keeble had started to take command, some way back, and he delegated temporary command to John Crosland, B Company commander, who was in a better position to see what was going on and told me to move up to see what I could do to help him. It was an irritating order because I hadn't eaten my porridge and spooned it in as we got on the move. Anyway, setting these personal details aside, we eventually got up close to John's position and pushed on until we suddenly found ourselves in range of small-arms fire. Very soon afterwards, on John Crosland's initiative, the support weapons were brought forward. To my mind this should have happened a long time earlier and I think it was a reflection on the fact that H had become too absorbed with what was happening with A Company and had lost, perhaps, that perspective.

I'd opened up with my machine-guns and the Milan opened up near John Crosland's position and within a very short space of time white flags started coming out all over the Bocca House Hill position and I remember thinking then that if they were surrendering, we should take them and get on to the position. John Crosland took a slightly different view that he would keep blasting until nothing was moving before he exposed himself. This was going to be expensive in time and ammunition. I put this up to Chris Keeble that I thought we had a surrender situation here and that we should take it, although we should have everything on call and available in case anything went wrong.

Communications down from the coastline were difficult, but eventually we got it all squared away. Chris wanted to make sure that all support weapons were in place and resupplied to cover all eventualities, and time was dragging on. I noticed the tide was coming in; we had been down there for three-quarters of an hour and I came up with this tall story that unless we had permission to move fairly quickly we'd be cut off by the tide. Complete baloney, but it worked and we got the OK to move.

It all went well initially. The two platoons I had with me set off towards the enemy position but then, coming through the valley bottom, there was a minefield and one of the soldiers set off a trip-mine. We then had to detour around the coast itself and finally got up to the Bocca House Hill position to find a totally decimated position and in the distance Argentine soldiers running for their lives ahead of us. A vivid sight, as well, was an officer, who was obviously commanding a section, driving a tractor hell for leather towards Goose Green 1000 yards away, with a dozen or so of his men running behind him trying to jump aboard. There was evidence of carnage all around us. I left one of our sections to sort out the prisoners and set off in pursuit. We were fairly thin on the ground, a platoon and a half, I suppose, and as we started to move to Goose Green the high ground was riddled with trip-mines. We took another route...

Darwin Hill had now also given way to A Company. Life was beginning to get a bit complicated. Twelve Platoon got themselves into a minefield and were reluctant to move forward. Eleven Platoon got into Goose Green... C Company coming down off Darwin Hill had come under fire and lost their company commander... The enemy battery was still shelling us ... and so on.

We were lucky: the soft ground was absorbing a lot of the damage and we only had two casualties at that point. One of my soldiers got hit and eventually died there – it was a very harrowing time. It took about ten or 15 minutes for him to die. We were all quite helpless. First aid being rendered was not doing any good at all. You could see him slowly dying in our midst. We couldn't get him back to the regimental aid post because we were separated by a slope which was being raked by enemy triple-A fire so we were there stuck with him and the lesson I got from that was the paramount importance of getting casualties off your hands as soon as possible. We had picked up casualties already, but because they were dealt with, they were pushed to the back of your mind. But here was an occasion where we couldn't ... here was this poor bloke slowly draining away in front of us and we were helpless ... it was definitely a compelling moment, not just for me but for everyone around him; people – bearing in mind most of them were fairly new to this – were withering under the impact of what they were seeing.

Then about the same time, without my go-ahead, Jim Barry, the commander of 12 Platoon, decided he was going to go forward and take a surrender from this flagpole position where he'd seen the white flags flying. To some extent I blame myself. He'd been listening to me debating with Chris Keeble about a surrender on Bocca House; if we could achieve a surrender without having to fight for every inch of ground, it would save time and save lives. He obviously hoisted this on board, but over-hoisted it, if you like, because before we'd got along to Bocca House, when I'd gone to great lengths to make sure everyone knew what we were doing, Jim Barry had taken it upon himself to go up there with a section and start parleying with these Argentines without anyone being aware. I got a message he was on his way and tried to get him to stop, but my message never got through.

My interpretation of what happened next was that the machine-gun platoon, who tended to fire on anything that moved anyway, and without the best of communications, saw movement around this flagpole position and engaged it. The Argentines – my interpretation again – thought their surrender wasn't being honoured, they had the parley party of Jim Barry and his men straight opposite, and they just wasted them.

There are other interpretations: that the Argentines thought that Barry was going up to surrender to them, which is hardly credible. But whatever, it was total confusion, fog of war ... whatever ... a mishap. Clearly a very critical one. Barry, the platoon commander, and an entire section of that platoon, effectively wiped out: four killed and two others injured and one unhurt. Twelve Platoon's Sergeant Meredith, the platoon sergeant, had very quickly grasped the situation and with his own hands brought machine-gun fire down on to that position where the Argentines who had shot Barry had gone to ground. Not only that, he'd got anti-tank weapons firing in there which had set a bomb dump alight and which made the area untenable for both the Argentines and ourselves. So when I got around to where 12 Platoon were, the situation was under control and stabilized. We could not move on because there was still small-arms fire coming down on us, so we were pinned down. Meanwhile the attack on the schoolhouse at Goose Green went ahead … the school went on fire. There were various reports of the number of Argentines burned inside the schoolhouse – some said 50 or more – but I doubt that there were…

We had about an hour of daylight left by then, and my platoons were in various places, slightly disorganized, I must admit, but we eventually got it together. Chris Keeble came on the radio and said we weren't to attempt to go forward any further – an air attack was coming in. We heard the aircraft coming over; but it wasn't a Harrier at all, it was a Skyhawk coming down towards us cannons blazing and I had an entire company plus bits of C Company neatly lined up on this track like a duck shoot. I said to myself, 'You prat!' It just hadn't dawned on us. To the right of us there was a minefield, to the left of us we started to get engaged by small-arms fire from Goose Green – circumstances which squashed us into this trap.

I hadn't foreseen what a lovely position we were in for any ground-attack pilot and I had to lay there and pray. I could see this cannon fire coming towards us and all I had to do was raise my hand and it would be shot off; in fact someone was smiling on us. We didn't pick up a single casualty, when in fact it could have been very nasty. Our own air strike then did come in and I think did destroy the triple-As in Goose Green. Bob Iveson, the pilot, got shot down and was recovered the next day. A little while later a Pucara came over and dropped a small napalm bomb on us which just missed us. We managed to shoot it down with small-arms fire and in due course captured the pilot. That was quite amusing because as it flew over, everyone opened up with small-arms and down he came. As smoke started to come out of his engine, a great cheer went up, which relieved the tension.

Things went quiet for a while. Nightfall came on. It was bitterly cold, we were out of water, out of food and we had probably three or four rounds of ammunition per man left. We had casualties and bodies we were trying to get back from the white-flag incident; Jim Barry's body had lain out there for three or four hours until we could recover it after dark. Keeble had begun negotiations for a surrender and we sat there through the night wondering what was going to happen. I had a gut feeling at that stage we had won the day. Had I had any idea there were still 1100 soldiers or more in the settlement I do not believe I'd have taken such a relaxed view as I did that night and got some sleep. The fact was that had the enemy counter-attacked right then, there was virtually nothing we could resist with. We had no ammunition left until well into the night when we were resupplied; we were on our chin straps physically and materially.

The same shortages applied to B Company – indeed all the companies – in those long final hours of manoeuvres towards their targets, often under heavy enemy fire. In times of respite the men huddled together for warmth, not daring to take off their sodden boots. The walking wounded were needing treatment. Helicopters coming to collect the casualties for evacuation to the SS *Uganda* were themselves under constant fire, and many hugely heroic flights were made. Peter Richens, with B Company, had to get out and look for ammunition as John Crosland's company made its tortuous journey, a long encircling movement, towards the settlements:

We came out at the bottom end of Goose Green very low on ammunition, starving hungry and very tired. I took two sections on the scavenging party... At that time we saw a lot of Argentines coming into the settlement, which caused us some concern ... although many just wanted to put their hands up and surrender their weapons. It got a bit silly in the end because with two sections I didn't have the facilities to take prisoners. We did hoard them up, separating the officers, NCOs and private soldiers, and all we could do was break their rifles, take their ammunition and tell them to clear off into the settlement. We found lying all over the place thousands and thousands of rounds of 7.62mm ammunition, which was compatible to our weapons, and there was food in abundance. We struggled back with ammunition and food, and when nightfall came the battalion went firm around the settlement. Major Keeble had sent one of the captured Argentine warrant officers down to the commanding officer of Goose Green settlement to suggest they surrendered.

In the meantime Keeble had sought and obtained from his Brigade Headquarters the promise of reinforcements and a heavy bombardment of the settlement if it became necessary, in spite of the presence of a large number of civilians. That night Keeble and his intelligence officer prepared a written ultimatum in Spanish and outlined what was in store for the enemy if they continued to resist. 'If we had had to go in and fight house to house,' recalls Peter Richens, 'there would have been problems about the survival of the civilians. If we'd had to call down air attacks on to the settlement, many people would have been killed and that wasn't our object.'

Keeble, however, insisted that they were prepared to go in fighting if necessary. At first light Harriers came in and gave a short demonstration of their firepower. The Argentinian commanders agreed to talk. Keeble set off with his party, which included two civilian witnesses: the BBC correspondent Robert Fox and David Norris of the *Daily Mail*. Fox had advised Keeble that the Argentinians would have a need to 'save face'. The meeting took place in a corrugated-iron hut with a white flag outside. The Argentinians said they wanted more time to consider. Keeble refused and his interpreter reiterated the dire consequences if they refused. The enemy commanders returned to the settlement, still without a firm answer. But at 13.10 the surrender began, and 2 Para could not believe their eyes. 'It was quite incredible,' says Peter Richens, 'to discover the amount of people in Goose Green... It was an amazing sight... The battalion strength at that time was about 450 people and taking on an enemy of perhaps 1800 was quite a feat for us.'

The surrender sealed, the battalion began to get itself sorted out to confront the aftermath of the battle. Fifteen men had been killed and 30 wounded. The enemy had lost an estimated 250 dead and the same number wounded. 'We now had to go back and clear the battlefield,' Richens recalls:

which was very disturbing for a lot of the younger soldiers. Our own casualties and fatalities ... had been placed at the side of a track leading down to Goose Green and Darwin to be picked up as the battalion rode on. The Argentine dead were left where they fell; parties were organized to go out and collect the bodies. None were to be buried on the battlefield. In the heat of battle, when you see people shot and other gory sights, people dying, a lot of mayhem, a lot of noise, a lot of screaming and crying, you just go on and do your job. But when things settle down and you go back to look for the bodies, it is a totally different situation. Furthermore, because it was very cold, bodies were frozen. Rigor mortis had set in, bodies tended to be in the positions where they fell, distorted and awful, and now they had to be collected.

We commandeered some tractors and trailers and loaded the bodies on to these as best we could and brought them to a field, which was turned into, for want of a better word, a mortuary. It was quite harrowing for both the young soldiers and even some of the older soldiers. Then the Argentine POWs began protesting about where they were being kept – which was in sheep-shearing sheds, which was the only cover we could allocate to them. With the settlement being so small, they were close to a lot of stockpiled ammunition and their argument was that they should not have been housed so near it. We pointed out there was nowhere else and we were near the ammunition too. We decided to use the prisoners to help in the clear-up operation. They had left the houses in the settlement in a disgusting state: rubbish, excrement; they were just animals.

There were some bonuses. The battalion captured a large amount of stores, weapons and ammunition. B Company also found a small boat filled with rations, mostly tinned food, and since all their rations were dry rations, the quartermaster commandeered the find and they ate very well for several days. The padre, David Cooper, held a church service for the battalion's dead, who were buried in a large pit overlooking San Carlos Water. The classic victory during which they had fallen was celebrated quietly and the battalion was already planning its next move, with the expectation that Major Keeble would be appointed commanding officer. 'A few days later,' Richens explains:

we heard differently and that a new commanding officer would be joining us. We were all a bit sick about that; Chris Keeble had done a good job and now his nose was being put out of joint, which we thought was wrong at the time.

We had no idea who it would be and we were preparing to move from Goose Green ... when this apparition came towards me out of the gloom and said, 'Hello, Sergeant Major...'

It turned out to be the new commanding officer, Lieutenant Colonel David Chaundler, whom I knew from my days in Berlin. We were very pleased it was him; he was well known to the battalion.

16

DROPPED RIGHT IN IT

David Chaundler, veteran of 2 Para with memories of Borneo, Northern Ireland and other tours of duty, was actually working with the defence intelligence staff at the time the task force was sent to the Falklands. His was a small department looking at arms trafficking and especially illegal arms trafficking involving the Warsaw Pact countries. Suddenly the interest switched to identifying sources for Argentinian weapons and to see what could be done to halt them. His main priority was Exocet missiles, largely French in origin, which were doing so much damage to British ships. That task was to end abruptly – at least for him. On 29 May the news came through that Goose Green had been taken, with only light casualties, and that everyone in the Ministry of Defence was ecstatic. Because 2 Para was Chaundler's old battalion – he had been adjutant and a company commander – he knew a great number of people who were down there battling it out, and his feelings were tinged with both relief and envy that he was at the wrong end of the world at the time.

But Chaundler had only heard half the news about Goose Green. He knew nothing of Colonel H Jones's demise. Next morning, after preparation of the daily intelligence briefing, he went down to the MOD canteen for breakfast with Mike Jackson, the only other 'spare lieutenant colonel' in the Parachute Regiment at the time, and there they met Colonel Peter Morton from the directorate of military operations. Chaundler said, 'Jolly good news about 2 Para, isn't it?' Morton looked at them sternly and replied, 'Well … if you call having the commanding officer and the adjutant killed good news…' Then he paused and looked at them before saying, 'I think one of you two is going to have to go.' Shocked by the news of H, they finished breakfast and returned to their office. Chaundler recalls:

It was absolute chaos. There was a particular arms deal in which the Argentinians were negotiating with a European country. In the midst of it, Peter Morton rang and said, 'It's you', at which point I lost all interest in arms deals. I picked up my briefcase and went home. I had already planned to go home that day, because ironically we were going to have H's wife, Sara Jones, and her two boys round for supper that evening. It now became very apparent that next of kin had not yet been informed and indeed the decision had been taken that no next of kin would be informed until the full extent of the casualties was known. At one stage it looked as if we were going to have Sara and the two boys around … knowing that her husband had been killed and her not knowing. Fortunately, that particular decision was reversed.

It was the May bank holiday that weekend and I had to get the quartermaster out of the depot to get a uniform and kit because I had not worn one for a year. I got the message on the Sunday morning that I was going that day … and I would be picked up by car at lunch time. The car duly arrived. It was an extremely dilapidated Ford Escort traveller with a WRAC driver. Halfway to Brize Norton, she announced she was feeling ill and so I drove the rest of the way. I was flown to Ascension Island and arrived at Wideawake Airfield at two in the morning – and it wasn't particularly wide awake. But it was a remarkable sight. A field that normally had about one aeroplane a month flying into it was absolutely covered with aircraft of every kind and size. I was somewhat concerned about my onward passage from Ascension. I knew that the only way I was going to get into the Falklands was to parachute into the sea – and one never normally parachutes into water.

Chaundler spent the day on Ascension, assuming that he would be flown on to the Falklands that night. In fact, at 5 p.m.

he learned from an RAF liaison man that they had no aircraft available. Feeling slightly aggrieved, he called his people in England and said, 'Look, you bastards, you got me down here at no notice at all and now I discover they can't fly me on.' Half an hour later they rang back and said he was first priority to go that night. He was placed into the hands of the Army movers, who said he needed to be at the airfield at two in the morning. He was promised he would be picked up, but in fact no one arrived and he wandered out on to the road just when an aircrew happened to come by. They turned out to be the ones flying him down to the Falklands.

We got on to a Hercules. I was introduced to my parachute, a parachute jump instructor and an orange total-immersion suit. It was an interesting journey. I was the only person in the back, apart from two Army dispatchers who were going to push my kit out (and slept for the entire 18-hour journey), the PJI and the crew. The in-flight refuelling was absolutely riveting, particularly as the pilot had never done it for real before. The maximum speed of the Hercules [C130 Hercules transport aircraft] is slower than the minimum speed of a Victor tanker, so the whole thing had to be done going downhill so that the C130 could get up enough speed to get the nozzle in. We had two goes at it and I didn't like to ask what would happen if they couldn't get it in. We refuelled twice and it took three tanking aircraft to get the Hercules down to the Falklands, the third having to retank the second aircraft that tanked us.

It was quite obvious, looking out of the windows, that the weather was appalling. There were white horses on the sea and a high wind. It was going to be dusk before I dropped into a very unpleasant-looking sea. The PJI said he didn't think he could allow me to drop into that because, he said, I was not water-trained, which was entirely true. I said, 'Look, you've just spent 18 hours flying me down here.... I'm not going to spend 18 hours flying straight back again.' So we agreed to differ and I was to drop.

We got to the point of the drop and I could see a frigate down there. It was getting dark and it didn't look too good. It was one of those sights where you can't see the horizon because the sea disappears into the sky. On the first pass the dispatchers threw quite a lot of heavy kit off the tailgate and the second pass I dropped, my first-ever drop into the sea. The problem was that I came down about a mile from the frigate and the only time I could see it was when I came to the top of a wave. I began to think this was a really stupid thing to be doing because I had no form of beacons, not even a torch. It also turned out that the hook on their helicopter wasn't working, so they couldn't haul me out of the sea and would have to send a boat. I had to float around for a good half an hour... My orange suit was also leaking, so I was extremely cold and taking on water.

Eventually a small boat appeared over the waves with three sailors on board. They had some difficulty in getting me on board because I was pretty waterlogged by this stage. I was also concerned that they seemed more interested in recovering my parachute for their own nefarious purposes than me. Anyway, I eventually got on board and was taken to the frigate. Until then, I had never really considered how I was going to get up on to the deck of this frigate; I suppose I thought there was going to be some sort of companionway up. There wasn't. It was just a rope ladder hung over the side. One of the sailors said, 'Right, sir, up you go then.' And I looked at this thing and when you are at sea level in a Force Eight underneath a frigate, one moment it was towering above you like the Empire State building and the next moment it's below you. I clung on to this rope, one moment being dunked into the sea and then hung high in the air and eventually crawled over the top, absolutely exhausted. The Navy, with its usual courtesy, had put on a chap blowing his whistle and the loudspeaker was going, 'Lieutenant Colonel Chaundler aboard, sir.'

I was taken up to the captain's cabin and handed over my soggy suit and said I never wanted to see that thing again. The captain offered me a drink, and I took a gin. He'd also laid out a plate of Penguin biscuits, which I felt was curiously apt. After an hour I was told a Sea King helicopter was coming to collect me and take me to Sandy Woodward's flagship, an hour's journey away. It was pitch-dark by now and myself and my kit were winched off the deck and duly landed on the aircraft carrier and I was told immediately that I was expected in the Ops room. Attempting to find one's way around the heaving deck of a carrier in pitch-black with no lights showing anywhere was a nightmare. I was ricocheting off Harriers and Sea Kings and hoping I didn't fall over the side. I got in there, and Sandy Woodward met me, gave me a briefing on the war, and he explained to me that he was concerned that if he lost another of his capital ships it might change the complexion of this campaign overnight and that's why he was so far over to the east and why, he explained, he could only provide Harrier cover in an arc halfway over the East Falklands.

Another Sea King was then to take me on to HMS *Fearless*, two and a half hours away, and arrived at two in the morning; everything seemed to be happening at two in the morning. There, I was taken to the general, Jeremy Moore, who made it perfectly obvious that (a) they hadn't asked for me and (b) didn't want me! It was not a great arrival but he gave me a whisky, passed me on to Tony Wilson, who was the brigade commander of 5 Brigade, who had arrived only a day or two before and whom 2 Para would now come under.

Chaundler knew Tony Wilson quite well. They'd had adjoining offices in Northern Ireland a few years before. Wilson's attitude was, 'Well, David, it's very nice to see you and all that, but this is a most unfortunate time to arrive. There's 2 Para down there; they've been through this amazing experience, they're closely united behind the 2iC...' In other words: 'Why don't you piss off back home?' They argued about it until four o'clock in the morning, when Chaundler finally said, 'Look, I'm sorry, but it's my problem not yours and now I desperately need some sleep...

I've had 18 hours in a Hercules, three and a half hours in Sea Kings ... parachuted into the sea.' He grabbed just a few hours' sleep before being flown ashore to find the Brigade Headquarters, which was just setting up. He then discovered that the brigade commander did not have the slightest intention of taking him on to 2 Para and so, after several hours of kicking his heels around HQ, he hijacked a helicopter and said, 'Take me to Goose Green.'

This they did, or at least, put it this way: they landed and I hadn't a clue where I was. There were a few soldiers whom we had picked up from the echelon ... and they didn't know either. We didn't have a map between us, although they did have an advantage over me in that they did have rifles. None of us had a compass. In fact, it turned out we had been dropped at Darwin, not at Goose Green, but we didn't know that at the time. We marched on until we came across a Gurkha and I asked him if he spoke English and he said no. But we got to his leader and he confirmed to me where we were. I then that evening walked in to Goose Green, found Chris Keeble and said 'Hello, I'm your new boss.'

He replied: 'You and I had better have a pretty serious talk.'

I agreed and we went into one of the houses there and he told me he thought the honourable thing to do was if I went back to *Fearless* and stayed there for the rest of the campaign. I said, 'You've got to be joking.' That was that, but thereafter our relationship was extremely good and I can well appreciate his disappointment. At that stage the situation with 2 Para was that they had earlier that day mounted a small raid on Swan Inlet House, by Johnny Crosland, commander of B Company, which was found to be empty of Argentinians but there was a telephone link to Fitzroy and Bluff Cove. He had simply rung up and discovered there were no Argentinians there either, so it had been decided that the one and only Chinook would be used to lift the battalion forward, as many as they could, that evening, and soon after I arrived the first lift took off to land at Bluff Cove.

The problem was that 3 Commando Brigade was to our north and indeed I think the force headquarters didn't know that 5 Brigade had given the go-ahead for this particular operation and at one stage all 3 Commando Brigade's guns were laid on to Bluff Cove, thinking that it was an Argentinian helicopter landing there. But for the very sharp eyes of a corporal in the Royal Marines Arctic Mountain cadre, my command could have started pretty disastrously.

Once the battalion was settled at the new location, Chaundler decided that it was time to make himself known to them. He decided to visit all platoon positions, taking the Medical Officer with him. It was already evident that a number of men were beginning to suffer quite seriously from the effects of the weather. It was extremely bleak and very cold, with the temperature hovering around freezing. Furthermore, they had flown forward on light fighting scale, so had left their bergens, rations, sleeping bags and most creature comforts at Goose Green in the hope that they would be flown forward in a day or so. A number of them were still lightly injured from Goose Green and Chaundler decided that all those suffering from wounds or weather should be taken off mountains and put under cover so that medics could look after them. Left to suffer, many would have deteriorated badly and therefore been permanently pulled out of the now depleted rifle companies, and once they were evacuated to SS *Uganda* there was no return to unit. As it was, twenty soldiers were taken off the mountain that day and of those 18 eventually rejoined their companies.

It was also important that they knew what I stood for and that I wasn't some glory-seeking commanding officer determined to make his name. I told them that my main priority was to get this battalion back to England without further casualties. I explained that the battalion was likely to be committed again to battle, but I gave my guarantee that when we were committed we would have the correct amount of fire support. This was a lesson I had already gathered from Goose Green: that the fire support had been wholly inadequate. This was something that was worrying the soldiers.

My next priority was to start getting the battalion to think positively about the future, discussing all the things we were going to have to do. We looked at the options. It was also a very difficult time because our bergens were not helicoptered in for two or three days and the only rations were those they had stuffed in their pockets before we left Goose Green... [One of the local people] went off and slaughtered some sheep, which his wife then cooked on a peat-burning Rayburn stove. I also had a long discussion with Tony Wilson, the brigade commander, because it was quite obvious to me that the Argentinians were not going to debouch from the mountains and attack us. Bearing in mind we were also desperately short of logistics at the time and we'd run out of food, it seemed to me important that before moving any more infantry into that area it was better to get the air defence and logistics up there and then move the infantry battalions in. This is not with the benefit of hindsight. That is what I told him at the time. He did not, in fact, do it that way; we did get our bergens up and the first unit to arrive was the Scots Guards. The intention was that they would go north of us and take up a defensive position.

I sent a patrol down to meet them. The weather was dreadful. Quite appalling. They had spent six hours in open LCUs [Landing Craft Units] with green water coming over the bow. At one stage during the night our Navy had put star shells up over the top of them because they weren't sure whether they were friendly or enemy. The commanding officer wasn't with them; he was away being briefed.

We were using buildings in both the settlements of Bluff Cove and Fitzroy to rotate platoons through, so that they could get dry, have a brew and get at least one decent night's sleep in the warm. I was using as my HQ one end of a small barn, and after about an hour these horrendous exposure cases started coming in from among the

Scots Guards. What the hell was going on? I had never seen such cases before. Our medical staff and the Scots Guards medics were actually keeping some of these people alive. I went outside and the whole battalion was still there. I got hold of the 2iC immediately and said, 'What the bloody hell do you think you are doing? You're going to write this battalion off if you don't get them out into the countryside, get them warmed up and some shelters up.'

To which he replied, 'I can't do anything until my CO arrives.'

Anyway, the CO arrived soon afterwards and by this stage it was quite evident that it would be better if the Scots Guards took over Bluff Cove and the buildings so that they could do what I had done, which was to use the sheep-shearing shed to rotate the soldiers through it. I put it to him and to Tony Wilson when he appeared soon afterwards and this was agreed. I would then take my two companies, which I had forward at Bluff Cove, back to Fitzroy. My motives weren't entirely altruistic. I needed to get the battalion back together as one unit. The trouble was that the LCUs that had taken the Scots Guards around had now put to sea and we couldn't get their radio frequency to call them back and so Chris Keeble took off in the helicopter to turn them round and the two companies boarded the LCUs and headed off. It was about an hour later, the weather still dreadful, when we landed again, but it occurred to me that it looked suspiciously like Bluff Cove again.

I got hold of the bosun and said, 'That looks like Bluff Cove.'

He said, 'Well … yes… I am afraid it is.'

He had gone around in a big circle and I naturally enquired what the bloody hell he thought he was up to. And he said it was the weather and the kelp and so on.

I pressed the point: 'What you mean is, you bloody well got lost, didn't you?'

He had to admit that he had. It was after dark by the time we eventually got to Fitzroy jetty, and Banks Middleton, who was the technical quartermaster, was there with great tureens of stew and tea, which was wonderful. There we settled down in Fitzroy and started to build up our combat supplies. Resupply didn't work too well once you were in contact [with the enemy] and if you didn't have it then you probably weren't going to get it. So we started to build up large quantities of the high-usage rations of ammunition and batteries for the radio and so on.

And then came another tragedy. David Chaundler's men hadn't taken a great deal of notice when the *Sir Galahad* and the *Sir Tristram* had arrived at Fitzroy on the morning of 8 June just after first light, loaded with British troops. It was one of the few sunny days they had experienced and they were getting on with other things, such as re-zeroing the battalion's weapons on a makeshift range when suddenly:

Four Skyhawks just appeared out of the sky... The first one came in at mast-high level; the hatches on the deck of the *Galahad* were open and one just saw this 1000-pound bomb go into the open hatch. And then all these Welsh Guardsmen started to appear. We were absolutely appalled because we hadn't realized that there were troops on these ships. There were horrendous casualties... My soldiers dashed down and were in the sea pulling out lifeboats and giving first aid, putting drips in arms and so on. There was no one else in Fitzroy apart from elements of 5th Brigade Headquarters.

Back in England, the grim news of the air attack on the *Sir Galahad* and *Sir Tristram* confirmed that 42 soldiers had been killed and many more wounded. The men of 2 Para did what they could before additional aid arrived to take the wounded and bodies from this terrible scene. For 2 Para it had been an especially poignant and unhappy time because the Welsh Guards was a battalion they knew well and they had shared barracks in Berlin and Northern Ireland. Elsewhere preparations were being made to call them back into action as the countdown began for the final assault which would lead them on to Port Stanley and victory. David Chaundler learned that 2 Para was to move under the auspices of 3 Commando Brigade under Brigadier Julian Thompson. It was news that he received with 'great joy':

> ...5 Brigade was, not to put too fine a point on it, a shambles, and there were understandable reasons why that was the case – which are outside the scope of this interview. Julian Thompson gave us the orders for the first phase of attacks on the mountains before Port Stanley. I was told we were to be in reserve on the northern flank behind 3 Para and 45 Commando with orders to exploit forward depending on where the break occurred. My concern was that he clearly didn't know where 2 Para was because he was expecting us to walk due north over some pretty awful terrain. I knew that we could not get to where we were meant to be in the time allocated. It turned out he thought we were still at Bluff Cove, which would have reduced the walk – but even so, a formidable hike. He asked where I wanted to be and I put my finger behind Mount Kent. He saw that we would need helicopters to get there and he just said, 'Right' and turned to his brigade major John Chester and said, 'Fix.'
>
> Next day the whole battalion flew up to the lying up position behind Mount Kent. It was an impressive airlift. Not only were we moving all our stores, we had stockpiled a great deal of ammunition. I had flown up with the battery commander and the company commanders because we hadn't seen the northern flank. We went up and could see right across, although not as far as Port Stanley. We could see the three attacks going in, which was very impressive.

17

MARCH OR DIE!

That impressive sight was part of the three-pronged offensive, launched by Julian Thompson's 3 Commando Brigade on the night of 10 June, that would finally provide 3 Para with the opportunity to demonstrate its mettle. The battalion, under Lieutenant Colonel Hew Pike, had been earmarked for the attack on strongly defended enemy positions on Mount Longdon, while 45 Commando RM went for the Twin Sisters feature and 42 Commando RM would hit Mount Harriet. The series of attacks saw some of the fiercest combat of the campaign but, once those objectives were achieved, the way would be opened up for 2 Para to leapfrog on to Wireless Ridge, one of the last hurdles before the final advance on Port Stanley. For 3 Para, it was the start of something big – and the end of ten days of frustrating manoeuvres across the Falklands. This narrative would be incomplete without recalling their activities in the run-up to their deployment to Mount Longdon.

What 3 Para and 45 Commando had done to arrive at their start line for the battle had been, up to this point, short on heavy engagement but a remarkable achievement in itself. They had marched the entire breadth of the Falklands from their beachhead positions at San Carlos because there were simply not enough helicopters or other transport to give them a lift. A telling signal was sent from Julian Thompson to the Divisional Headquarters as early as 4 June as the build-up for the next major onslaught got under way: 'Understand we only have one Sea King and one Wessex helicopter under operational control tomorrow … this allocation totally inadequate for current resupply tasks, e.g. 2100 rounds 105 ammo… No shells, no attack!'

Behind this curt message was a problem facing the war managers and especially the brigade and battalion commanders. It was not just a case of too few helicopters, but vastly too few, and the situation was made worse by atrocious weather that prevented them flying anywhere near safety limits. And so when 3 Para set off from San Carlos they did so on foot, in the dark and at speed to the first task, which was to take the settlement of Teal Inlet on the east coast of the Falklands, halfway to Port Stanley. The only transport Pike could muster for the heavy armaments and stores were a few tractors and trailers volunteered by local farmers. It was a gruelling march, damp under foot and often in blinding snow and seriously biting winds. The whole battalion was on the march, although initially without D (Patrol) Company, which had been pulled out for an eight-day operation to set up two observation posts covering the West Falklands to report on enemy shipping and warn of air strikes. D Company rejoined the battalion at Teal Inlet, which was taken and secured without opposition. Hew Pike's battalion then continued its yomp to reach Mount Estancia, from which patrols were sent out to recce the approaches to Mount Longdon, the eventual objective.

Jonathan Shaw was an Oxford philosophy and politics graduate and had been an accountant before enlisting in the Paras to discover what the 'real world' was all about. At the time of the Falklands conflict he was a 24-year-old lieutenant commanding the 39 soldiers of 6 Platoon, B Company, 3 Para. (Later he was to become one of the successors to the likes of Johnny Frost and Colonel H. Jones as commander of 2 Para.) On his own admission, he was then a virgin soldier in search of three years of enjoyment, excitement and a challenge and, naturally, had never experienced anything like this in his life; but then few around him had either:

In the beginning the whole Falklands thing had an air of unreality about it. We only realized it was going to lead to action when we sailed south from Ascension. It was never a case of dragging people down there; they were clamouring at the camp gates trying to go. As a new boy I drew enormous strength from those around me. I was very impressed by the spirit of the others. There was a glorious naivety about never having done this sort of thing before. There was a sense of anticipation, a sense of the great unknown. In a way, I suppose our naivety echoed that of the young soldiers and young officers of the First World War coming under fire for the first time. Even when we landed on the Falklands it still seemed pretty unreal. Then the helicopters were shot down and with that came the first deaths on land and we began to realize it was serious.

We had to march across the island – the long march. We did it on half rations. We did it at a speed which outstripped our logistic back-up. People broke down with injuries but we couldn't send for vehicles to carry them because there weren't any, so we just left them, to be collected later. That was an absolutely seminal moment when we started realizing it was march or die. People grew up on that march. I grew up. You looked into your soul on that march because you knew there was no way out until you got to the other end of the island. There was no way back. This was the most real thing I had ever done ... and the most fantastic camaraderie, the most fantastic team spirit. The soldiers weren't even bitching. There was no whingeing. Everyone was unified; we all knew there was nothing to do but go on. We could see Mount Longdon from miles away, we knew the enemy was on it and that certainly focused the mind. And when the battle broke it absolutely broke around our ears. All around us...

Hew Pike's plan for the capture of Mount Longdon was, in Julian Thompson's assessment of events, 'quite simple'. To the uninitiated, including this author, this sounds like a gross understatement. On a mountain filled with every possible natural hazard, heavily populated by enemy troops and surrounded by minefields and the most appalling terrain – to be negotiated in pitch-darkness in which the face of a colleague was unrecognizable at five paces – nothing looked simple. For the young soldiers for whom battle itself was a totally new experience, the drama that befell them on the night of 10 June 1982 would remain in the minds of the survivors for life, as Jonathan Shaw explains:

We had got up on to the mountain and we were there in amongst the enemy before they knew we were there. Even so, the ferocity of their response certainly set us back on our heels. I had 39 men in my platoon. Five were killed and eight were wounded that night. That was 30 per cent casualties. We knew there would be a resistance but what surprised us was the reality of it. This was not an exercise. People were not shouting, 'Bang!' People were falling down for real. That was the shock, the reality of it, the reality of the injuries and the firepower coming in at you. The bullets were flying and they were real. They were coming from machine-guns and snipers. The second person to get hit was the medic and he died in our arms. We just watched his life drift away. Another guy who was shot finished up lying in the perfect place to take cover. We finished up sitting on him most of the night. He was dead, but it was a ghastly thing. The fire was such that we could not get up to get him out. We had to stay there and we had to use him as a resting place for the rest of the night.

You had no time to think about whether you were making mistakes or whether you were really in danger. One of the blessings of being a platoon commander is that you are so busy trying to fight the battle you have no time to think about anything else at all. We ground to a halt. We were on top of the mountain. We held it. Other platoons moved through us and A Company swung around on us. I began to think very, very carefully about what we were doing. I began to reassess the battle plan. I regrouped the platoon in a huddle and thought again. The determination was not to lose any more lives. Three of my soldiers sacrificed their lives. They died trying to help wounded people. The impact of that sacrifice had a very profound long-term effect on me. In the short term I decided the wounded were to be left where they lay because people were being killed and wounded going to help them. We had to kill the enemy first, then tend the injured. That was the hardest decision I took all night. I was a short-service commissioned officer, but I decided that as soon as we returned from the Falklands I would make the Army my career. It suddenly made sense. I could understand what was involved, what it was for. The camaraderie and self-sacrifice my soldiers showed that night was the most religious thing I have ever seen.

They were sacrificing their lives for their fellows. I have a respect and admiration for those soldiers which has stayed with me. You are talking about very special people. The dedication of soldiers to each other is humbling. I am very, very proud of them. I joined to see what the Army could give to me. I realized I wanted to belong to this organization whose men had this sort of spirit.

That spirit was nowhere better demonstrated on the night of the Longdon battle than by the selfless actions of 29-year-old Sergeant Ian John McKay, who was platoon sergeant of 4 Platoon, B Company, 3 Para. He was killed in what was a virtual single-handed attack on enemy positions, specifically to save his colleagues. A quiet, family man from Rotherham, Ian had turned his back on the potentially glamorous world of professional football in Yorkshire to follow a military career. He lost his life not in the pursuit of his career or any drive for self-betterment, but in the action of attempting to help his colleagues, an action for which – like H. Jones – he was posthumously awarded the Victoria Cross. The citation for the award read:

4 Platoon, B Company ... after the initial objective had been secured, was ordered to clear the northern side of the long

east/west ridge feature, held by the enemy in depth, with strong, mutually supporting positions. By now the enemy were fully alert and resisting fiercely. As 4 Platoon's advance continued, it came under increasingly heavy fire from a number of well-sited enemy machine gun positions on the ridge and received casualties. Realizing that no further advance was possible, the platoon commander ordered the platoon to move from its exposed position to seek shelter among the rocks of the ridge itself.

Here it met with part of 5 Platoon. Enemy fire was still both heavy and accurate and the positions of the platoons was becoming increasingly hazardous. Taking Sergeant McKay, a corporal and a few others, and covered by supporting machine gun fire, the platoon commander moved forward to reconnoitre the enemy positions but was hit by a bullet in the leg, and the command devolved upon Sergeant McKay. It was clear that instant action was needed if the advance was not to falter and increasing casualties to ensue. Sergeant McKay decided to convert his reconnaissance into an attack in order to eliminate the enemy positions. He was in no doubt as to the strength and deployment of the enemy as he undertook this attack. He issued orders and, taking three men with him, broke cover and charged the enemy. The assault was met by a hail of fire. His corporal was seriously wounded, a private killed and another wounded. Despite these losses Sergeant McKay, with complete disregard for his own safety, continued to charge the enemy position alone. On reaching it he dispatched the enemy with grenades, thereby relieving the position of the beleaguered 4 and 5 Platoons who were now able to redeploy with relative safety. Sergeant McKay, however, was killed at the moment of his victory, his body falling on the bunker [of the enemy who had killed him]… His was a cool and wholly calculated act, the dangers of which must have been only too apparent to him beforehand. Undeterred he performed with outstanding selflessness, perseverance and courage. With a disregard for his own safety he displayed courage and leadership of the highest order and was an inspiration to all those around him.

For 3 Para, such was the heat of the battle that night on Longdon that memories of it would never leave those involved, said Hew Pike, reflecting upon the episode many years later. By then he was a general with a knighthood and high office in the Army Land Command, although he was noted for remaining the frank, open and welcoming man he had been when they all sailed to the South Atlantic. Despite the many years that had passed, his office was littered with photographs of him with the soldiers of 3 Para, as he recalled:

There were some black moments during the battle. None of us had ever before experienced what we were going through that night. It is impossible to replicate on training. There were certainly times when we couldn't outflank them, we couldn't make progress. Their artillery was proving very effective against us, as were their machine-guns and their snipers. It was then that the quality of the soldiers, their morale, courage, will-power and character came through and won the battle. That is what won it. The Falklands humbled me because 23 of my soldiers did not return. A significant number of those who did returned very badly injured. I, as the commanding officer, still now and to the day I die will live with the question: Could I have done this better, could I have saved some or all of those deaths or injuries? That is a very humbling thing to live with.

Like every commander, I made a lot of mistakes. One balances that by the fact that we succeeded. We achieved our mission and I am also confident that nobody who died or was wounded would have wanted to be anywhere else but serving with 3 Para at that time... It was the most intense experience of my 36 years in the Army. It was certainly the most formative experience ... and without any doubt whatsoever it has made me a better-equipped general. I could not have achieved it without those soldiers' qualities, without their skills, without their character. I respect them enormously… I am immensely proud of what they achieved on Mount Longdon, which, like all the other battles of the Falklands, was close-quarter infantry combat. And that makes for a very nasty, brutal, dangerous, exhausting and scarring experience. During that night on Mount Longdon, and particularly in the following two days in the awful aftermath of that battle, I finally came face to face with the reality of war, as we all did, all the soldiers in 3 Para. I did not like what I saw, not at all. But I chose to stay in because the military makes a crucial contribution to the security of the world. I believe we protect people's rights and freedoms.

* * *

And so, as Hew Pike's Paras and the Commandos attacked the three objectives and then, after the terrible battles described above, opened up the final route in to Port Stanley, there was – apart from Stanley itself – only one major objective remaining. This was Wireless Ridge, whose capture Julian Thompson had assigned to David Chaundler and 2 Para. They were going on, as ordered, towards Furze Brook Pass, below Mount Longdon where 3 Para was engaged, and had to cut around the mountain towards Wireless Ridge, avoiding the minefields laid between there and Mount Tumbledown, where the Scots Guards and the Gurkhas were mopping up enemy positions. At first light on 12 June, Chaundler was getting concerned:

The whole battalion was in the open, we still hadn't reached our RV, and I got on the radio to Julian Thompson, explained the position, that we were still several hours from the RV, and asked him if he was happy for us to continue in daylight. He said yes and so we pressed on. We got to the point overlooking Furze Brook Pass somewhere around midday. By then we had been on our feet for 12 hours and the column stopped; Johnny Crosland, with B Company, was leading and I went up to him and we just lay there for about 20 minutes, looking down into the pass, which was a deep valley. There was Argentinian artillery all along the ridge of the valley and quite a bit of it coming down. We identified a place in the reverse slope where no artillery was coming down and we moved the battalion into that position. I asked for orders and none were forthcoming until around 6 p.m. that evening, two hours before last light, when a helicopter arrived and the liaison officer with 3 Commando Brigade jumped out and ran towards me waving his map and shouted, 'Wireless Ridge tonight, chaps.'

Time was desperately short and I'd left my mortars and blowpipes on the reverse slope behind Mount Kent because they were too heavy to move forward on foot, particularly because of the amount of ammunition needed to make them viable. So I hadn't got my mortars with me; I had artillery but I also had at this stage the CVRTs [Combat Vehicle Reconnaissance (Tracked)], which are technically reconnaissance vehicles but in that kind of warfare were really light tanks. This had come about from when we were back in Bluff Cove because two troops of CVRTs came down with the task force, and no one really knew what to do with them. Before we prevailed north, it seemed a good idea that we took one of these troops with us. They welcomed the opportunity to join in.

We had the orders to attack Wireless Ridge, with just two hours before darkness. I hastily made a plan, got the company commanders together and halfway through orders my boundaries were changed and then the attack was postponed for 24 hours. What followed was the coldest night of my life. It was bitterly, bitterly cold, well below freezing. Next morning we resumed preparation and I flew up to Mount Longdon to look at the terrain we were expected to attack. The other 3 Commando Brigade units had had ten days patrolling their terrain, and knew it pretty well. We didn't know ours at all.

Mount Longdon was under pretty heavy fire all that day. When I landed, my helicopter was taken off me to take out some wounded who were being brought in off the mountain. I met Hew Pike, CO of 3 Para, and we went to have a look over Wireless Ridge. It was quite clear that the enemy positions I had been given were not accurate and my plan needed a total revamp. The problem was that communications with 2 Para were virtually non-existent and I needed to get back there. But before I could get my helicopter back, Hew Pike and I were standing on Mount Longdon when these six Skyhawks flew underneath us. They wheeled round and disappeared round Mount Kent and we heard them bomb Brigade Headquarters. Happily, there were no casualties. But all helicopter flights were stopped, so I couldn't get back to the battalion to change orders, and the helicopters flying up our mortars were also halted. I was actually stuck on Longdon for six hours before helicopter flying started again. I then returned to Brigade Headquarters, where Julian Thompson was giving out orders for the next 24 hours – which accounted for the period after we had taken Wireless Ridge and involved the capture of Port Stanley.

By this stage we had been able to get the company commanders on to Longdon and they had detected there were differences in the intelligence picture. I sent them off to get a brew, which is always good strategy in times of stress while I replanned the attacks. I then got them back and gave them new orders, which lasted about ten minutes. The first decision I had to make was at what time I would make H-Hour [Hour-Hour, the time at which operations are to begin]. I needed enough darkness to capture all the objectives and enough time to get to the start lines. I decided upon an H-hour of midnight, which would give us ten hours. Up to that stage all attacks had been silent, relying on secrecy and no shelling until contact had been made. My view was that the Argentinians knew they were going to be attacked. What they did not know was from what direction and what time. I

311

felt, however, that the advantages of shelling comprehensively beforehand would not give away any surprise because that would come out of direction and time, not intent.

My battery commander had managed to get two batteries of guns to support us and a frigate. We also had 3 Para mortars in range and the four light tanks and my own machine-gun platoon – a considerable amount of firepower. As for the attack itself, we had four positions to attack. I came up with a plan to attack each one from a different direction so they would not know which way we were coming in. The attacks depended upon concentrating all available firepower at one point, capturing that and then moving on to do the same again. At 8 p.m. I sent the patrols company forward to secure our routes and generally guide us in.

The artillery registration of targets had been delayed because the FOO [Forward Observations Officer] on Mount Longdon had been injured during the day and so the registration took place after dark, which was a remarkable achievement. In the event, it was quite spectacular moving up. We moved up behind a low ridge. The Argentinians, knowing they were going to be attacked, were shelling, forming up positions. We were shelling their positions as well. It's worth pausing to reflect, because this was the battalion's third night without sleep. We hadn't actually seen a ration pack for 72 hours and all the food we had was what was left from what we had stuffed in our pockets before we left Mount Kent. We fought all that night between blinding flurries of snow showers. It says a great deal for 2 Para, who were the only battalion to carry out two attacks in the entire campaign. The first time you go into the attack you don't know what to expect. The second time you do know, and you've already seen your friends and colleagues killed and maimed and you know exactly what is out there. Again I had the greatest admiration for my soldiers.

Coming up to midnight, H-Hour was delayed. Chris Keeble said they had something I ought to see and was pretty insistent, so I went back and they had a map captured from the Argentinians which showed a minefield straight across our main access of attack. It was too late to do anything about it at that stage… I went back to Johnny Crosland, leading towards the start lines, and told him. We looked at each other and just shrugged. And so we carried on. The first phase was D Company, who were doing a right hook. They launched the first attack and we put a great deal of fire support down on their position. Their attack went remarkably smoothly. They found a great many enemy soldiers who had just got down into their trenches and pulled their sleeping bags over their heads.

The Argentinians' artillery was fearsome. The second phase was A and B Company attacking in line to the Argentinian headquarters and because of the nature of the terrain I didn't need to provide flanking fire. I had also allocated both batteries of artillery to this attack. Part of my rationale for a noisy attack was that being shelled is a thoroughly unpleasant experience: you just have to lie there in the mud and the dark and take it. My thinking was that the Argentinian soldier was not the best and likely to crack. I felt we could achieve minimum casualties with a comprehensive firepower attack – 12 guns firing six rounds per minute, which is an awful amount of firepower and high explosive to withstand. The Argentinians soon demonstrated they weren't very interested in fighting us, which was exactly the situation I set out to achieve.

There was then a pause after we captured this second objective to move the tanks and the machine-guns on to the next objective, with D Company making their second attack, a long, flanking attack all the way down Wireless Ridge. The first position was taken very quickly and they moved on to the second position. The Argentinians had not detected their approach, mainly I think because they were captivated by the demonstration of firepower we were putting on them. It was a terrific amount, particularly from the light tanks, who were very successful with their machine-guns, their 30mm cannons and 76mm guns. They also had the advantage of possessing second-generation night-sights, so that they could see a lot more than we could. D Company were just about to launch their attack on their final phase when Phil Neame called for his artillery and the whole lot came down on top of him.

Phil Neame, quite naturally, was rather put out by this incident, having gone into Wireless Ridge well prepared for a genuine all-arms attack – the only one of the campaign:

We were going to go in having blitzed the place with oodles of fire support first and we had time to get it all ready and in every other way we had the upper hand. All went quite well until the tail end… We moved forward with a rolling barrage of artillery ahead of us. Then we got to a position overlooking the last ridge and I got my FOO to call up the last target to get a few rounds on that. Unfortunately, he called up the wrong target number. I had a signals sergeant from another battery because, good old British Army, it only provided two FOO parties per battalion. So D Company didn't get a proper FOO. This is where things come home to roost. I'd already established this character couldn't read a map. Now he called up the wrong target number. The target number he called up just happened to be the location exactly where we were sitting – five rounds, fire for effect, airburst overhead, which killed one person and injured another. It was very lucky; we could have had a dozen, two dozen injured or killed. Somehow I managed to refrain from shooting this FOO and then got him to call up the right target number, only to discover that this final target hadn't been adjusted and the rounds were landing down near B Company.

So Chaundler then ordered all fire to stop because he was getting bleats from B Company just as I was about to attack, which was a bit aggravating; having once been pasted by our own artillery, got rid of that, all fire ceased and we went through this long rigmarole while the target was adjusted. My FOO had by then completely lost his nerve, but eventually we called down our fire mission on the final objective, got ready to move again and after two rounds, fire ceased again. What now? It appeared that one of the guns had slid out of alignment and this time some rounds were landing near C Company. David Chaundler once again ordered fire to stop. I was tearing my hair out – in the middle of an attack and trying to bring it to a conclusion. Tough, C Company; get down on your hands and knees and pray, but don't fuck me around any more!

Anyway, another long delay while the gunner tries to find out which was the gun out of alignment and God knows what else, in the midst of which Chaundler got on the telephone and said, 'When are you going to attack?'

I said, 'When I get the fire support you promised me!'

Some shirty dialogue ensued because I was not moving until we got fire support on this final objective and the saving grace was that the Scorpions [light tanks] were able to keep the enemy's heads down while all this was going on. Anyway, with only four guns firing on the target instead of six, we went in. It was fairly critical. We had been stuck up there for an hour in the freezing cold and it took a certain amount of encouragement to get people going again. We got to within about 100 metres of the enemy and someone let off an illume. I don't know who did it, but they shouldn't have done, and at that point the enemy realized the attack was coming not from the north but their west. Then all their small-arms fire switched towards us and everyone hit the deck. Another crisis ensued. After the earlier difficulties it was a hell of a job to get the momentum going again: there was a lot of shouting before the adrenalin started to flow. And off we went. As I took off I lost my signaller, the only one left by this stage; I assumed he'd been shot. I still had my own personal company radio, fortunately, but what I didn't have was any real link to the battalion any longer, which was to cause some aggravation later on in the evening. Finally we got into our target position and once we were there the enemy started to run and they kept running… We literally cleared the position on the trot; grenades were coming down like confetti.

We had limited exploitation, because we'd have been out of support of the battalion and were not to go beyond a line of telegraph posts ahead because the SAS were said to be operating in that area. As it happened, the SAS never got ashore but we did not know that; so when we got to that line we stopped; the enemy, who were still running, saw we'd stopped, and half an hour later counter-attacked. Fortunately, it was a half-baked counter-attack and by then we had the artillery more or less back on form and my platoon sergeant called up a fire mission and that discouraged them. All the time we were being harried from small-arms fire because the Scots Guards hadn't yet quelled Tumbledown. Every time you moved you knew you were going to be fired at. It was a fairly harrowing couple of hours while we reorganized, in the middle of which Chaundler was busting a gut demanding to know what was happening. Eventually we got some communications going and I told him we had been a little bit busy, thanks! He wasn't where I was and it was a bit hairy.

As daylight came, things calmed down and I met up with most of my command post. My signaller had not been shot after all. He had fallen into a shell hole full of water; he was a black man from Liverpool and there was no hope of finding him in the dark, so I had to wait until daylight. Things now settled down. The Scots Guards got on to Tumbledown and we could see hundreds of Argentinians walking off Tumbledown into Stanley. At the same time we could see equal numbers of enemy walking out of Stanley on to Sapper Hill, which was obviously going to be the next objective. I was trying to get fire mission down on to these targets but once again was told that the battery was unavailable because of other tasks. I think they had allocated that station to 5 Brigade. I was tearing my hair out with exasperation. We started to try to engage them with long-range fire and as soon as we did that we were shelled by the Argentinians, so we stopped firing.

Chaundler came up to take a look for himself; I don't think he quite believed what I was trying to describe. Literally an army in complete rout; targets galore. Why don't you shoot them with your machine-guns? he said. I had to explain that we had tried that and all we did was get a lot of grief back and they were mostly out of range anyhow. We eventually got the fire missions up, but by then it was absolutely clear that we were fighting an army that was no longer resisting. It crystallized in this period of time – half an hour during which the whole thing had changed.

David Chaundler again:

At first light I had joined Phil Neame on Wireless Ridge, during the very long dawn, and here suddenly was this extraordinary sight of the Argentinians cracking. They were coming down the hills towards Port Stanley, heads down, totally dejected, utterly defeated and withdrawing back to Port Stanley. We were in seventh heaven. The Scouts came up with SS11s [air-to-air or air-to-ground missiles fitted to light helicopters]; the machine-guns were firing, the tanks were up and firing. Tony Rice, the battery commander, was in gunner seventh heaven in that he had … the whole regiment firing into the Moody Brook Valley. Suddenly I realized that you couldn't do this any more. There is a moral dimension in war and we were effectively in danger of crossing over that boundary in that we were slaughtering people for no good cause. I ordered, 'Cease fire!' immediately and this was six hours before the official ceasefire. In fact, we never fired another shot again.

My next realization was that I knew the orders had been given out for the next night's operation, which was the capture of Port Stanley. I realized that Port Stanley was there for the taking now, and there were so many examples in history where the initiative hadn't been taken, and what you could take with a platoon today you would have to take with a division tomorrow. I knew I had to get down into Port Stanley. The problem was that communications back to 3 Brigade were not good, because Mount Longdon was in the way, and I was having to relay everything through my headquarters. I was saying, 'Hello ... it's finished ... they're withdrawing.' And I was getting a message back saying, 'How many Argentinians can you see?'

I was jumping up and down and shouting, 'I can see thousands of them.' By this stage I had A and B Company coming forward on to the ridge line because we had to get down into Port Stanley to follow this up. I was just about to order the leading company down when Julian Thompson arrived by helicopter. It was quite amusing really. I was feeling pretty happy with life at this stage, standing out there on the forward slope surveying this incredible sight, and he, obviously not realizing the full extent of the tactical situation, crawled up on the ridge behind a rock. Obviously, concerned that he had already lost one commanding officer, he rushed forward with a flying rugger tackle to bring me down.

I said, 'It's OK ... it's OK, Brigadier ... look down there ... it's all over. We've got to get into Port Stanley.'

He had a look, agreed and ordered Johnny Crosland's B Company down to Moody Brook and on to high ground on the other side, and Dair Farrar-Hockley's A Company down to Moody Brook on the road into Port Stanley, followed up by Phil Neame's D Company. They were followed with great rapidity by C Company of 3 Para, who had come off Mount Longdon. I think they were trying to race us. We encountered a small amount of small-arms fire; we had covering fire available should we need it from artillery, who were silently marking us and the light tanks. In the event, none of it was necessary ... and we made our entry, the first British troops there since we were chucked out 11 weeks before.

And so it was all over. At 13.30 on 14 June the Paras led the way into Port Stanley and by the end of the day the surrender of the Argentinians was formalized. They began their journey home 11 days later, when both 2 and 3 Para boarded the MV *Norland* to sail up to Ascension and then, in RAF VC10s, on to England and a hero's welcome from Prince Charles, their

Colonel-in-Chief, General Sir Anthony Farrar-Hockley, the Colonel Commandant, and their families. Casualties for 2 Para on Wireless Ridge had been light, reflecting as Phil Neame said, the 'oodles of firepower' lined up in advance. In total the Parachute Regiment lost 40 men killed and 82 wounded; four sappers of 9 Parachute Squadron RE also died. Awards received by the Parachute Regiment included the two posthumous Victoria Crosses already mentioned, two Distinguished Service Orders, five Military Crosses (two posthumously awarded), five Distinguished Conduct Medals (one posthumous), 12 Military Medals (two posthumous), 34 Mentions in Dispatches (four posthumous) and one MBE.

18

BLOODSTAINED HEROES?

After the Falklands War the three regular battalions of the Parachute Regiment continued as an integral part of operations in Northern Ireland, variously deployed on tours usually lasting from four months to two years as resident battalion. Over that time the Paras were used there more than any other unit of the British Army apart from specialist groups. Indeed not a year has passed since the onset of the Troubles when they have not been on duty somewhere in the province, providing the manpower for a diverse range of tasks and in the process suffering more than ten per cent of the Army's total number of casualties.

Up to the 1980s the regiment's approach in Northern Ireland became progressively more sophisticated and organized compared with its early days there, although it continued to carry the burden of Bloody Sunday. IRA propagandists and other activists labelled the Paras the killer battalions and brutes, and the fear of their presence remained in the province.

Well aware of this reputation, Thatcher's ministers continued to present them as the front-line troops, regardless of what had gone before. What was happening in Ulster in the eighties provides a good vantage point from which to look back to those early days and forward to what followed as the deployment of parachute troops continued. None better to give an insight into that period and the men themselves than Brigadier Hamish McGregor, whose 37 years of military service until he retired from the Army in 1998 took him into a variety of roles, including being an officer in the Paras, recruit training and staff jobs. There was something of a family tradition to parachuting too. His father was one of the founder members of the SAS with

David Stirling, winning a DSO as a lieutenant and, like his son years later, a Military Cross.

Hamish McGregor was commissioned into the Parachute Regiment in 1963, having done two years at Sandhurst, and saw action with 1 Para in Cyprus, Aden and the Radfan before joining the legendary Para stalwart Lieutenant Colonel Joe Starling, who was then running the Para Battle School at Brecon, in Wales. He was, at various times during his career, involved in training recruits and took a particular interest in the preparation of troops for Northern Ireland:

Whereas now the troops are trained very carefully before they even get to Northern Ireland, in those early days we had no one to train us because very few units had been there on operations. There was simply no one with any experience of the kind of situations that were to confront us and there could be no overnight solution either. It would, and did, take years to build up our operational expertise. The story goes that when the first units unfurled their banners which said, 'Halt! Halt! or we fire', they were in Arabic. It was quite difficult, to say the least, although even so in those early months 1 Para was a very happy, busy battalion. We were in Northern Ireland with our families, although we did not see an enormous amount of them because we were round and about the place, sometimes away on operations for a week at a time.

We were operating then as a province reserve and would be sent wherever there were problems and so got to know the whole of the Northern Ireland area very well. Training became a desperately important aspect and we faced a very steep learning curve, simply because it was all new. We were dealing with our own people, British people on the streets of the United Kingdom. It really was so very different from Cyprus and Aden. And we were consistently called upon at the most crucial times. In 1969, 1 Para had done a short tour and therefore it was one of the few units which had been there before when it went out as a resident battalion. No one could be classed as 'experienced', although I don't think our behaviour or attitudes were any different.

We trained as well as we could, but the formal training infrastructure as exists today was simply not there. There was no such thing as special moving-target ranges, scenario training aides or for such events as we were to experience in Northern Ireland. Everything in the province in the early days came as a bit of a surprise, quite frankly. I'm not blaming anyone; there just hadn't been time to think it all out and indeed I think the pioneers did pretty well, considering the constraints. They did their best and had to think it out on the run and on their own because there was no model, no established military framework. If you wanted to try this or that procedure, it was up to those troops on the ground to suggest it; quite basic developments came from the ground level up, such as asking for a helmet with a visor because people were throwing stones at us, or please can we have a shield that we can see through so we know what we're looking at? Or can we have something that tells us where a sniper's firing from, and what about a remote probe for suspected bombs – the remote-controlled anti-bomb devices – so that our chaps don't get blown up prodding suspect packages? All of these things, and many others, were invented for us and you changed your tactics to suit them. Wars tend to produce the implements that become necessary and the new technology began to come on stream in a big way in the 1980s.

I think everyone would admit that in the beginning we were very naive. Whether we were heavy-handed or not is another matter. Personally, I don't think we were; we frankly became the object of propaganda. I don't think we have acted very differently from any other regiment. I don't think anyone would dispute that their time in Northern Ireland was a very interesting period; dangerous, true enough, and there had always been this difficult business of training the Parachute Regiment soldier. There has been a theory put forward by those who want to find fault with us that it was not surprising that events on Bloody Sunday went the way they did or that events occurred in the Falklands because of the way soldiers were trained, that they were not trained in the same way as other regiments. Having run recruit training for all that time, I can categorically deny that. We were tougher; of course we were, because we had to be: we had a role which required it. But I also know that we trained to a rigid syllabus which was set by the Army, as it still is. We did not use our own syllabus. The traditions and needs of airborne soldiers were clearly accommodated in that routine, based upon the original foundations of the regiment. The regiment always boasted that it was an élite force ... and everyone was determined to see that those traditions were upheld and that the highest military standards were maintained.

I don't think there is any question that recruits of yesteryear were tougher to start with. They perhaps weren't as well educated as they are today, because the regiment now needs people capable of coping with the technology of modern armies. But by and large, I don't think the guys have changed that much. The basic material is very much the same, although the age profile of recruits has come down by a marked degree. When I first joined there were some 'older' chaps in the platoon who were touching 30 and as a platoon commander I was the youngest of the group. They had been trained by the previous generation of Paras, who had been in the war, at Arnhem and so on, and there was a completely different attitude, a different philosophy.

Now, they can get in from 17½ and because many do not serve for as long, the average age of other ranks in a platoon is probably under 24. Its corny but true: they come in as boys and if they pass the rigorous training procedures they come out of it not just as men, but as highly skilled soldiers, fit and exceedingly well-disciplined soldiers, and as 18-year-olds they can be called upon to take part in peacekeeping or humanitarian operations and be able to cope with very sophisticated weapon systems.

The regular Army very often thought that the Parachute Regiment drew its recruits from the lower intelligence levels.

Actually that was never the case and isn't now. When grades of one to five were given, the Parachute Regiment would take down to grade three only – in spite of our continuing manpower shortages – and they also had to be physically strong. The numbers who fail the parachute selection still remains high. Those who fail to qualify simply could not cope with what we were asking them to do. However, contrary to common belief, every effort is made to get a soldier through his training. Even so, an interesting thought: Are we training them incorrectly? It is something we have to constantly analyze and update. What is important is that Parachute Regiment instructors continue to train Parachute Regiment soldiers as they are very focused and understand what is required. You are expecting and get an enormous amount from what is basically a very ordinary lad – and he *is* a very ordinary lad. So tough, imaginative and disciplined training is everything.

Ordinary lads may bleed and die and many have in years of running battles with the IRA and in collectively larger numbers in the Falklands. Their heroics have been plain to see in these chapters and they would continue to serve in this way. But as Sara Jones has underlined, one of the favourite pastimes of the British is to kick their heroes, and after the Falklands War, in which her husband was killed, a noticeably more virulent stream of criticism began to be directed against the Paras, in part self-inflicted. The fact was that the Paras remained in the front line of Northern Ireland coverage, firstly because they were part of the Army's own rotational manpower plans and secondly because the politicians wanted them there. If the politicians hadn't, or had decided that the Paras were too heavy-handed or brutal to remain in Northern Ireland, they would simply have withdrawn them, and perhaps even reduced their operational strength. Regardless of opinions about Para heavy-handedness, there are always two sides to the story. The other side is highlighted by the Ex-Services

Mental Welfare Society, whose literature in the late eighties focused on activities in Northern Ireland to draw attention to the plight of some of the veterans on its books:

Six-foot-four Sergeant 'Tiny' G-t-r-e DCM was perhaps the bravest man the colonel ever knew. But now, after being booby-trapped and ambushed in Northern Ireland, Sgt Tiny cannot bear to turn a corner for fear of what is on the other side. It is the bravest men and women from the Services who suffer most from mental breakdown – for they have tried to give more than they could in the service of their country.

This side of the reaction to dealing with the situations daily facing the Paras in Northern Ireland, or in the Falklands, was usually hidden from public view. More often, the questions which came to the fore were about how the Paras conducted their operations. Indeed numerous media studies were made in an attempt to support the belief, widely held and propagated in Ireland, that they were brutal and cavalier, opening fire at will, occasionally shooting people dead and generally stamping around the place with an abusive arrogance.

A book published in the early eighties by a former officer of 3 Para, Captain Tony Clarke, certainly gave that impression. *Contact* harked back to the dark days of the early seventies, when the RUC and the military had lost their grip on large sections of the province to parliamentary control and Edward Heath's Conservative government, after studying the worst-case scenarios, signalled tougher policies across the board, including military reaction and intervention. That the Paras were allowed, if not encouraged, to go over the top was denied by the government, the Army's top brass and the regiment itself. Then came Clarke's book, a staccato diary firing words like a machine-gun, with strong passages like this one, describing a Protestant riot in the Shankill Road:

We are getting high on the violence now, the exhilaration of the chase; the feeling of uplift every time an Irishman goes down. We don't bother to take any prisoners. Just zap them with the dick gun [firing rubber bullets] and trample over the prostrate forms ... For the first time in months the shackles of restraint have fallen away and we're doing just what we want.

The book contained many such references. Residents in houses being searched were regular targets and, according to Clarke, everyone was delighted when this met with similar hatred, because it livened up the action. He claimed that once a patrol deliberately delayed a car carrying a wounded IRA suspect to hospital so that he died; disobeyed the 'yellow card' firing instructions; and had buckshee ammunition passed on to them by other battalions which could be fired during a gun battle without being accounted for. Many of the complaints of local residents, about which journalists in Northern Ireland had been writing for years, were confirmed. Clarke himself, on publication of his book, denied that he was trying to justify the troops' behaviour. But it did happen like this, he said, and it had a brutalizing effect on the soldiers as well as the people of Northern Ireland.

Clarke joined the Army on a service commission in 1972 but left after six years following an illness that he claimed was caused by poor diet and stress in Northern Ireland, particularly in South Armagh, which was well known to all soldiers as the most dangerous and frightening and where the yellow card was disregarded by soldiers on the ground 'or you'd be dead'. This, of course, all aligned with the views of those in Northern Ireland who had for years complained that the Paras were the most heavy-handed of all the regiments to serve in the province – a theory that Clarke did not dismiss, instead pointing out that 'we are trained killers'. It might be said that all soldiers fall into that category, but there is no doubt that Parachute Regiment training has always been tougher and indeed is so for a particular purpose. This is because the aim, according to the Army's own published literature on recruitment and training, is to build an élite unit that is based upon 'arguably the toughest and most professional recruit training in the world today ... training is hard but it is really the easy bit; you can always give up in training – you can't give up in the bush ... train hard – fight easy ... all you need is guts and determination and the will to be a paratrooper!'

Those are the slogans. The clear intention is, and always has been, to produce a bunch of hard men who can carry the British Army forward in whatever kind of situation that may confront it. Historically, this ability has been demonstrated time and again, and perhaps, in such circumstances, it must be expected that difficult situations that draw headlines such as 'War heroes or murderers?' will arise. In fact, that very headline was provoked by another book, which followed Clarke's, this time an ex-soldier's account of his experiences with 3 Para during the battle for Mount Longdon in the Falklands conflict. The author, Lance Corporal Vincent Bramley, alleged that his erstwhile colleagues committed serious war crimes such as shooting prisoners and desecrating bodies. He alleged also that ears were cut from dead Argentinians as trophies.

Wars provoke such incidents, and the British more than most nations generally expect their soldiers to behave within the law – a fact which, it may be recalled, occurred to David Chaundler, for example, as he realized that the prospect of shooting retreating Argentinians after 2 Para's final battle was against all the conventions. Two Scotland Yard officers, Detective Superintendent Alec Edwards and Detective Inspector David Shipperlee, were sent to the Falkland Islands to investigate the allegations of war crimes against members of 3 Para and after a thorough investigation by both military and civil police it was found that there was no case to answer.

Even so, the cold facts, almost bland in their recital to the general public by the media, recording a battle won and casualties lost, give no clue as to the horrors and emotions of war in the style of the Falklands conflict or the stark realities of urban warfare as in Northern Ireland. On the one hand, the battle for Mount Longdon was a fast, furious engagement, frightening, noisy, bloody, in pitch-darkness and bitter cold, with grown men screaming in terrible, almost hand-to-hand fighting, dying where they fell. In Northern Ireland, conversely, it was an intermittent struggle spanning 30 years in which the Paras suffered heavily, although their casualty figures – bad enough – were minuscule compared with the total of almost 3300 deaths and 30,000 wounded among both civilian and service personnel in the province since 1969.

The IRA and the Republican movement had long made allegations of 'war crimes' against the British military, and the Paras in particular, thus accusing them of acts which represent the suspension of all basic values of a humane society. Such a suspension has always been denied, but battlefields – either in urban warfare, or the Falklands or the Gulf – have always been a confusing and challenging place, especially for young men only a year or so out of school, who may be experiencing for the first time a real sense of fear. Their thoughts and senses may be swirling from the sheer drama of the activity all about them, adrenalin rushing through their bodies, heads throbbing from relentless gunfire, attention diverted by the need to dodge the thwack, thwack of bullets hitting the ground around them. They may themselves be shot or find themselves surrounded by the blood-covered bodies of friend and foe alike.

In the cold light of dawn, when a comrade is found cut to pieces by gunfire or mines, anger rises. And while there have been many studies of the actions of the Paras, there have been few on their own reaction to their experiences, other than those largely conducted by service charities. The line between legitimate and possibly criminal acts is so blurred as to be barely definable, especially in the heat of the moment, as poignantly demonstrated by the recollections of former Colour Sergeant Brian Faulkner. He was with 3 Para and under fire in both Northern Ireland and the Falklands. As a medic, he saw it all – the battles, the deaths, the appalling injuries – and observed and noted the reaction of the men around him. Armchair judges anger him. How can they know what goes through a soldier's mind as he runs the gamut of artillery and machine-gun fire in an infantry attack, or the sniper fire on the streets of Derry, or the real prospect of landmines blowing you sky-high while driving through the country lanes of South Armagh? Soldiers, he points out, are humans trained to perform inhuman tasks; those who have not been through the experience cannot begin to appreciate their feelings.

Faulkner, like generations before him, trod a well-worn path to the Army recruiting office. For many a young man from South Yorkshire the Services were the only escape from a life of drudgery at the coal face. In December 1962 he signed up for his local unit, the York and Lancaster Regiment. He had spent the previous four years, between the ages of 12 and 16, in an Army Cadet unit attached to the King's Own Yorkshire Light Infantry. While their neighbours had traditions of sons following fathers down the pit or into apprenticeships in the mills and foundries, the Faulkners had always fought for their country. His grandfather fought in the Royal Navy in the First World War and saw service in the Battle of Jutland. He was involved in the operation to help the Russian royal family flee their homeland during the Revolution. His father was a regular soldier – a lance bombardier in the Royal Artillery – who saw service in India and in the North African campaign in the Second World War; captured at Tobruk, he spent the rest of the war in POW camps in Italy and Germany. His mother worked long shifts in the munitions factories. In other words, the family had given as good as most to the British cause, and Brian Faulkner himself now followed suit:

One day a group of paratroopers arrived at my camp in Chester. They looked terrific. Not just because of their distinctive red berets. Everything about them was different. The way they conducted themselves, the way they went about their business with an air of confidence bordering on the arrogant. They looked professional, they really looked the part. I decided there and then I wanted to be a paratrooper. I wanted to be a part of their organization. Early in 1965 I did P Company and transferred over and joined 3 Para in what was then British Guyana. After three years in a normal line regiment, not really doing a lot, I was ecstatic about getting into the Paras. I was part of an élite, part or something really special, I was a soldier in the 16th Independent Parachute Brigade. Technically, I should only have been with the Paras for two or three years and then returned to my old unit. Although I wore the red beret and Para cap badge, I still wore the collar dogs of the Yorks and Lancs. During the defence cuts of the sixties my regiment was disbanded so I stayed on with the Paras. It was just as well because I never had any intention of leaving them.

In the ranks of the Parachute Regiment at that time were many men from a similar background. They had a common bond. Many had never been outside their home region, let alone abroad. After a two-year tour in the sunshine of Malta Brian Faulkner's battalion returned to Britain and were put on immediate standby for deployment to Northern Ireland. In 1970 the men of 3 Para were pitched into West Belfast, where the divided communities were at each other's throats. It was the first of the five tours in the province that Faulkner was to undertake. And it was the first time he was to come under fire for real. In the first such incident, several IRA men with automatic weapons engaged the men of 3 Para:

It lasted for easily an hour and a half and, incredibly, there were no casualties on either side, except for a young lad who was driving through. He was hit in the back. It was a real tragedy. To this day I honestly believe it was the IRA who hit him, not us. The locals claimed it was us but I am convinced we did not do it. I was under fire again in Northern Ireland when I was a corporal, but nothing I had experienced there really prepared me for the fire I was to see in the Falklands. We had all seen and experienced gunfire and we had seen and heard artillery, but nobody had undergone a severe artillery bombardment since Korea. The people who went to the Falklands were the first since then. When you have sustained machine-gun fire, light artillery guns, big howitzers and everything else banging away at you it is something else ... quite unnerving. You don't know how you are going to react or how the others are going to react. It is, quite simply, a situation you can handle or you can't. Luckily for us, we could handle it. We didn't like it, but we got on with it. That is what British soldiers do whether they are paratroopers, Royal Marines, Guardsmen or anything else. They get on with it because that is what their history and traditions have taught them.

When we sailed off to the Falklands I was a colour sergeant, married, with three children aged between three and 11, sailing off into the unknown and travelling the length of the globe to get there. I will be honest and say there were times when I wondered if I would be killed and how my family would survive without me. And I don't think I was the only one who had those thoughts. But I was determined to survive and come home again. We had trained mainly to fight in the European theatre and here we were sailing 8000 miles to fight an enemy we knew nothing about in a place we knew even less about.

We did the long march from Port San Carlos across to Teal Inlet. It was hard. Very hard. The march hurt. People were exhausted. It came down to the will of the individual to succeed, the sheer will to keep on putting one foot in front of the other and keep going despite the appalling weather and awful terrain. On exercises you know how long things are going to take. You know the exercise will last a week, two weeks or three weeks and then there is the cut-off point. But on this you didn't know whether the march and then the fighting was going to last a week, a fortnight, a month, three months or six months. That was unnerving a bit. We were marching in howling wind, driving rain, freezing cold and without adequate bad-weather clothing and without sleeping bags ... and that was just on the way to battle. We were going to have to fight after all this. The conditions were affecting people, some of them pretty badly. Some people dropped out. They simply keeled over. They had frostbite, trench foot, or exhaustion or a combination of all three. It was not their fault. There was nothing they could do. No one wanted to give up.

By the end of the march every part of your body ached. You were cold, tired, hungry, sick and exhausted and you knew that you would still have to fight. For every one of us who was there it was a totally new experience. No one had ever experienced it. It was an experience new to the modern-day British Army. We did not have air superiority, which we always believed we would have. We did not have anything like the helicopter support or artillery support the text books said we should have to fight a modern battle. In the end it was going to be down to each individual, his training, will-power and the teams he fought with to overcome it all.

I'll tell you how bad it was on that march: throughout all the time I had spent in the Army I had never come across cases of frostbite and trench foot. All of a sudden we were swamped by them. No sooner had we treated the guys for these ailments than they were off again, squelching through the cold and water again. It was hopeless. They should have been flown out, dried out and rested and then come back to us, but that just couldn't happen. We had to press on. Some of the guys were also carrying incredible loads. I was carrying my rifle with six extra magazines, two belts of ammunition each containing 200 rounds, four grenades and my bergen rucksack crammed with medical equipment. It weighed 90–100 pounds. All the medics were the same. The only way to get the stuff there was to carry it. There is no point in being a medic and going without your kit. Although we were medics in the Paras we were soldiers first and medics second. We were there to fight as well as to help casualties. Fighting was our foremost occupation.

At Teal Inlet we met up with the Royal Marines, who had just completed their long march, and they too were in a terrible state. Totally knackered and their feet were awful. When the battle for Mount Longdon began our boots were rotting on our feet. As it started the medics were split into two groups and began running ammunition to the machine-guns and the Milan anti-tank missile posts. We were about 1000 metres from the assaulting rifle companies when Corporal Brian Milne stepped on a mine and that was it. The Argentines opened up with everything they had on B Company, the lead company in the assault. They began taking casualties immediately and as I was in the lead medical team we were called forward right away. We didn't know it but immediately in front of us was a minefield which we had to cross in the dark and under fire to get to our comrades. The first casualties we found were one of our own medics and a Royal Engineers corporal who had been killed. We set up a first-aid post – the doctor, Captain John Burgess, our padre Captain Derek Heaver, another medic and myself – and then we began supporting the assault. We had decided to set up a regimental aid post as close to the fighting companies as possible. That meant we didn't have to exhaust ourselves too much going for the casualties and bringing them back and that we would have a position we could defend if the Argentines tried to break out. We would be able to protect the casualties and still support our friends on the assault.

As we crossed the minefield to get to B Company the Argentines saw us coming and opened up on us with machine-gun and rifle fire. The mountainside had erupted. It was all red and green tracer, grenade flashes and lit up by flares. The fire was coming from every angle it could conceivably come from and all we knew was that we had to get through, we had to get to the hill to get to our guys who were dying and being severely wounded. I was afraid, but I don't know how to define it. I don't know how to put into words what fear is. It is a knotted feeling that is in your guts, coupled with the feeling that the next one to get hit could be me. Once we got on the mountain we could hear the crack and thump of the weapons even more clearly and the sound of guys being hit. We had rounded up cooks and other guys attached to us who were not part of the fighting force and turned them into stretcher-bearers. It was bayonets on for them to fight their way up the hill to the casualties and then return with them.

There were four of us, all senior NCOs – me, Sergeant Dex Allen, Sergeant Pete Marshall, who was our cook sergeant, and our orderly room sergeant, Keith Hopper – and we would fight our way through the battle to locate the casualties, then we would withdraw, get the stretcher-bearers and fight out way back again to get the dead and wounded. We would fight our way in and our way out and when we got the stretchers back we would treat the wounded and get them evacuated as soon as possible. All through the night we worked and during the day we came under heavy and sustained shellfire. At one stage there was a lull and one of the guys from 9 Squadron Royal Engineers who was helping guard our flank noticed a large group of Argentines approaching our area from an angle which was outflanking one of the fighting companies. I rallied everyone I could find – cooks, bottle washers, engineers – and we attacked them. They broke and ran. So we dispersed and got back as quick as we could to tend the wounded.

It was all a very strange sensation being there. I had seen dead people before, but they had always been on the other side like in Northern Ireland. But now it was different. I was dealing with people I knew very well, men I had served with in the sixties and the seventies, men I had travelled the world with, men who had been alive a few minutes before and were now lying in front of me lifeless. That was really very distressing. There were young soldiers I had known since they joined the battalion and then there was Sergeant Ian McKay, who was posthumously awarded the Victoria

Cross. I had seen him about two hours before the battle started. Mac and I had shared a cabin on the *Canberra* on the way to the Falklands. We parted with the words 'See you later in Stanley when it is over' and now a few hours later I was recovering his body.

His body had lain where it fell for several hours because we couldn't get to him. There was also Doc Murdoch, the B Company storeman, with whom I had soldiered. He was a lovely guy, a brilliant guy, a tender guy, a loving guy, full of life, very fit and a first-rate soldier. Poor Doc was shot out on the mountainside and he wouldn't allow anybody to go forward to recover him in case they, too, got shot. Several of the boys were wounded and killed going to the assistance of wounded comrades. Doc knew if anybody had gone to help him they would have been killed, so he wouldn't let anyone help him. He was a very, very brave man. The Argentines had some incredibly efficient snipers there and they were picking off guys at random. There was nothing anyone could do. Our medical team was only seven people and two of them were killed and one wounded by snipers trying to get to wounded guys. In percentage terms, if you think of our medical casualties it was a very high percentage. Pete Marshall, who was mentioned in dispatches afterwards, was actually blown up twice carrying a casualty back. He just picked himself up, shook himself and carried on with his team bringing the casualty back.

At that stage I did not believe we had sufficient manpower to carry on to Port Stanley. I knew the soldiers would try to do it and probably did, but I did not think we had enough supplies to take Port Stanley. The greatest fear we had was that a lot more people would die or be wounded and be left in the unpleasant conditions on Mount Longdon. All the stretcher-bearers were carrying their allotted amount of ammunition plus extras so they could resupply the machine-gun positions or use it themselves if needed. They were there first and foremost as fighting soldiers. They fought their way in with the stretchers, passed on supplies to the guys in the front and then made their way back with the dead and wounded.

Because of our position with regard to supplies I did not think we would go on to finish the war. Simply because our next obstacle after Longdon was to have been Port Stanley itself and I just did not think we had enough supplies or back-up to get us through the capital. Even worse, it could have degenerated into a stalemate on the edge of town. If the momentum had become bogged down we could have been sitting there on the edge of Stanley in those atrocious weather conditions for weeks. There were still civilians in Stanley, the very people we had come to free, and they would have been in a terrible situation if we had had to fight through. But suddenly the white flags went up over Port Stanley and I was ecstatic.

Seeing our casualties shocked me. I don't know why because there are always casualties in war. I don't think I had ever anticipated that our battalion could take so many. It was as simple as that. I was also shocked by the number of Argentine casualties. As a human being I felt for them, too. I have never seen anything as gruesome, such a violation of human life, as I saw on that mountain. We did not differentiate between British and Argentine wounded. We brought them all back to be treated. They were all human beings. In their situation I would like to think the Argentines would have treated me as I treated them. We lined their stretchers up to one side, but we did not put *them* to one side. We only had them separated for security and identification purposes. If an Argentine was more seriously wounded that one of our guys and his life needed saving there and then, we did that.

We had gone through Hell itself and when it was over there was a great sense of relief. But my next priority was my family back home. I wanted to be sure that they knew I had survived unharmed, that they would not be sitting there waiting for a knock on the door and the telegram or a padre to tell them the worst. Having said everything I have said, I am still extremely proud that we went to the Falklands, ever so proud that the people back home supported us to the hilt and that at long last somebody in government had the balls to stand up to what was right even though the population of the Falklands is very small.

Afterwards I was awarded the Distinguished Conduct Medal. I am not a hero. The way I see it, I had a God-given right to save those people. I believe you are given a task in life and the one I was given was to try to save those lives. And I believe that in nine cases out of ten we stopped soldiers dying and got them on the way back home to their families. Lieutenant Colonel Hew Pike called me into his office and said, 'Congratulations, you have won the DCM.' I was absolutely stunned. I hadn't the slightest inkling I was going to get anything. Towards the end of the year Sergeant John Pettinger, who also won the DCM, and I went to Buckingham Palace to receive our awards from the Queen. Brigadier Julian Thompson, who was our brigade commander, was also there. He chatted away to us as if rank didn't exist. He was a very fine man and a great commander. We went in style: Colonel Pike sent us up there in his staff car with his driver. The Queen pinned the award on me and spoke quite a bit to us, but to this day I cannot remember what she said. I was so overawed by the whole occasion I can't remember a thing. But I can tell you it was one of the greatest days of my life, which I shall remember for ever … what finer accolade can a soldier have than to be decorated for gallantry and have the Sovereign pin it on your chest?

In 1987, with the rank of sergeant major, Brian Faulkner left the Army after almost 25 years. He then began the round of job-seeking, but even with a DCM and Falklands and Northern Ireland to his name, police forces did not want to employ him. A succession of jobs followed until he met one of his former officers, who offered him a job as an officer with the Army Cadet Force. When Brian Faulkner left the Army he invested his end-of-term gratuity in stocks and shares, but when the market crashed he lost the lot:

We had nothing left and I decided the DCM had to go. A medal collector gave me £7000 for it and we got back on our feet. I never told my wife, Kath. I simply bought a replica. Eventually someone else got the medal and decided to auction it – the story was about to break in the newspapers so I had to come clean. Kath was very understanding, if bemused, about it. As far as I am concerned it had to be done. To this day I bitterly regret having to get rid of it because I treasured it, but needs must. However, I am delighted to say someone bought it and donated it to the National Army Museum in London. If I won the Lottery I would buy it back tomorrow and then give it back to the National Army Museum, but at least I would know it was wholly mine again.

17. Suez: the first light assault on the control tower at El Gamil Airport, 5 November 1956 (Airborne Forces Museum)

18. A leisurely stroll through the shelling at El Gamil: Lieutenant Colonel Paul Crook, Commanding Officer of 3 Para, with his RSM still putting his beret on (Airborne Forces Museum)

19. Images of the colonial wars. The Radfan, Aden, 1964: 3 Para toughs it out on the extraordinary terrain of the 'Arnold S' spur (Airborne Forces Museum)

20, 21. *Below*: Borneo, 1965–7: 3 Para on patrol in the jungle (Airborne Forces Museum)

Daily Mirror

BRITAIN'S BIGGEST DAILY SALE

ULSTER'S BLOODY SUNDAY

From Joe Gorman to Londonderry

THIRTEEN men were killed yesterday as Army paratroopers broke up a banned Civil Rights march in Londonderry.

13 die.. Army accused of 'massacre'

'SOLDIERS DIDN'T FIRE FIRST SHOT'

THE LAST RITES

22. Northern Ireland, 1972 – and still the controversy rages. Was it a 'massacre', as claimed by the relatives of the dead; or were the Paras fired on first, as suggested by the *Daily Mirror*? The new Bloody Sunday Inquiry, under the chairmanship of Lord Saville, was set up in 1998 to make a further attempt, following the Widgery Report, to unravel the conflicting evidence

23. No controversy here: the charred remains after the infamous IRA attack at Warrenpoint in August 1979: first a bomb attack on a Para patrol and then, as rescuers arrive, a second explosion. Of the 18 soldiers killed in the attack, 14 were from 2 Para (*Daily Mail*)

24. The Falklands, 8 June 1982: 2 Para, leaving Fitzroy for the next stage of their battle after a harrowing experience earlier that day. The troop carriers the *Sir Galahad* and *Sir Tristam* arrived in the bay loaded with British soldiers when four Argentinian Skyhawks appeared out of the morning sun and attacked the two ships. The *Galahad*, still burning in the background of this picture, took a direct hit from a 1000-pound bomb which went through an open hatch into the hold, packed with Welsh Guardsmen. Forty-two soldiers were killed and many more injured (Airborne Forces Museum)

25. Lieutenant Colonel 'H' Jones, Commanding Officer of 2 Para, who was killed leading an attack during the battle for Goose Green, for which he was awarded a posthumous Victoria Cross

26. Lieutenant Colonel David Chaundler, who was parachuted into the South Atlantic to take over after the death of 'H'

27. Men of 3 Para, bloodstained and weary after a 'March or Die' trek across the Falklands and into battle on Mount Longdon

28. At the final hurdle before Port Stanley: Brigadier Julian Thompson (*left*) and Lieutenant Hew Pike, Commanding Officer of 3 Para

29. The dreaded P Company: the preliminary tests that confront all new recruits (Airborne Forces Museum)

30. The log-carrying race, in deep mud: a severe test of stamina (Airborne Forces Museum)

31. *Above:* High-wire acts on the P Company aerial obstacle course (Airborne Forces Museum)

32. *Left:* Down to earth and into the mire during the assault course (Airborne Forces Museum)

33. *Above:* Macedonia, 1999: the men of 1 Para dash to board their helicopters, and become the first British troops into Kosovo after the NATO bombing campaign (Press Association)

34. *Left:* Securing the road to Pristina while colleagues check for mines (Press Association)

19

NOTES FROM A SMALL IRELAND

The activities of the Parachute Battalions over a period of many years, reflected in regimental logs and in the journal of the airborne forces, *Pegasus*, cover a vast array of exercises and deployments to various parts of the world, including Belize, Kenya, Germany, Canada, the USA, Botswana, Egypt, Jordan, France and Cyprus in the 1990s alone. Always, however, they returned to Northern Ireland, which continued to demand a presence of one of the three battalions, on either two-year residential tours with their families or short rotational engagements of six months.

The Army's own operational policy remained, in theory at least, the same as it had been since the Troubles began, which was to assist the RUC to return Northern Ireland to normality through what its own internal literature described as the 'three pillars of attrition, deterrence and reassurance'. Attrition covered a multitude of operational possibilities and was aimed primarily at hitting the capability of the terror gangs by arresting suspects and seizing weapons and explosives. Permitted levels of interrogation, once carried out by the regular military units, were restricted by the 1980s and, according to the Army handbook, terrorists were – by law – to be handed over to the police within four hours of being taken into custody. The yellow card governing the use of force and weapons was amended on numerous occasions over the years, but the message remained basically the same: that armed force could only be used as a last resort, that it had to be within the law and if those guidelines were breached the perpetrators faced being charged and brought before a civil court.

Deterrence was the second avenue of attack on the IRA and other paramilitary gangs, and was to be achieved through constant patrolling throughout the province, stop-and-search, cordon-and-search and an extensive pattern of vehicle checks, all of which measures were aimed at 'introducing doubt and uncertainty into terrorist planning'. The final avenue of operations on the list was reassurance, a kind of hearts and minds programme which was supposed to demonstrate to the whole community of Northern Ireland that the British Army was there only to protect them against the 'threat and actions of the terrorist, whilst causing the minimum disruption to their day to day lives'.

To cover all of those areas, the Parachute Battalions were, as Hamish McGregor pointed out, required to undergo fresh training. This would allow them to keep up with intelligence information and known patterns of terrorist operations; familiarize themselves with sophisticated new aids ranging from communications to night sights; and deal with the computerization of the vast amount of data now being collected on personalities, weapon supplies, funding, vehicles and every aspect of life in Northern Ireland that might help them make inroads into terrorist activity. Intelligence had improved dramatically, and by now was being gleaned from a raft of agencies operating in the province, including the RUC Special Branch, MI5 and MI6, Military Intelligence and the Army's own and expanding Special Duties units, among which were the SAS and the 14th Intelligence Company, the latter created especially for work in Northern Ireland. Foot patrols, mobile patrols and patrols inserted by helicopter, aerial observation, snap vehicle checkpoints, patrol bases, observation posts and close surveillance work were among the many tasks that were allotted to the Paras, and indeed all of the regiments who were part of the rotational deployments. Other duties carried out in support of the RUC included large-scale operations providing back-up for that force's anti-racketeering squad, providing protection for refurbishment work on police stations and Army bases, as well as more mundane tasks such as community policing and serving summonses.

In addition to the patrols by foot and helicopter, the Army maintained patrol bases close to the border. These formed another strand in the policy of 'deterring or apprehending' the terrorist. In order to observe the movements of suspected terrorists, a large number of tall observation posts and towers were built throughout the province, high enough to conduct surveillance over a wide area using new aids such as image-intensifiers and infrared night-for-day and night-observation capability. In all of these activities the Paras figured prominently through the years. Latterly one of their former commanders, Lieutenant General Sir Hew Pike (formerly commanding officer of 3 Para), took over as General Officer Commanding the armed forces in Northern Ireland. Based in Lisburn, County Antrim, 10 miles from Belfast city centre, he was in charge of three Brigade Headquarters: the 3rd Infantry Brigade in Portadown, the 8th Infantry Brigade in Londonderry and the 39th Infantry Brigade in Lisburn. At any one time in Northern Ireland there were six resident and six rotational battalions, as well as the six Home Service battalions of the Royal Irish Regiment, plus engineering, communications, logistical, administrative and other support troops – a total of approximately 15,500 Army men and women, in addition to whom there were 1500 Royal Navy and Royal Air Force personnel.

Residential tours, which for most of the eighties and nineties engaged one or other of the three Para battalions, last two years and are 'accompanied' – that is, they deploy 'complete' with their families and their full unit infrastructure. There are also *roulement* units for 'emergency' tours, which last a period of six months. These are unaccompanied tours and tend to be in areas of high threat. Until the ceasefires of the mid-nineties, terrorist groups matched the increased efficiency of the Army, and acquired their own sophisticated range of weaponry from a variety of sources over the years. Weapons found in both the United Kingdom and the Republic of Ireland included heavy and general-purpose machine-guns, high-velocity rifles, rocket-propelled grenades, flame-throwers and commercial explosives. In addition, the IRA and other paramilitary groups had developed a range of lethal improvised weapons. These included mortars, anti-armour grenades and rockets, under-car booby-traps, vehicle bombs and landmines, all of which were capable of detonation by timers, command wires or by remote control. The Paras' battalion logs are filled with references to their encounters with 'the enemy'.

For 1989, 2 Para's note-writer recorded: 'We left our Tern Hill Barracks gently smouldering after the IRA bombing in February...' And commencing in that same month, 3 Para's log records:

The battalion began a two-year residential tour of Northern Ireland where the work has been hard and we have had to mourn the tragic loss of four soldiers from within our own ranks (with four others wounded in 14 separate terrorist attacks during that tour). Nonetheless, the battalion remained in good heart ... we certainly consider ourselves fortunate to be stationed in Palace Barracks, situated close to the town of Holywood, County Down, which is widely recognized as the best barracks in Northern Ireland. It has some excellent recreational and sporting facilities, both for soldiers and their dependants ... this is a small, predominantly Protestant town which offers excellent shopping facilities for wives as well as providing several restaurants and pubs which can be used for off-duty soldiers. Despite restrictions imposed on soldiers while off duty, many have taken the opportunity to visit the surrounding areas of County Down and County Antrim, a further advantage is that Belfast is only 15 minutes away by car...

At all times, the battalion has a company deployed in south west Belfast in support of the RUC. The company is responsible for a lively estate comprising mainly Catholics. There are very few highrise flats, the estates are open and attractively designed to include neighbourhood terraces and cul-de-sacs ... yet despite the benefit of planning, the local population endures chronic unemployment and the threat of terrorist attack against soldiers and police alike is constant ... in short the process of relocation away from the ghettos of the Lower Falls and Divis Flats has merely allowed the terrorist to expand his domain, bringing with him a toll of knee-cappings, beatings, command wire initiated devices and the risk of attacks on vehicles...

Tragically, it was during a tour of Rathfriland in County Down that A Company had three soldiers killed when an IRA bomb was detonated beside their Land Rover... L/Cpl Steven Wilson, Pte Matthew 'Tex' Marshall and Pte Donald MacAulay were killed instantly. Miraculously, Pte Lee Manning survived (though seriously injured) ... it is remarkable how strong the immediate relatives were. The mother of Donald MacAulay said to assembled media, 'It's the badge he lived for and the badge he died for.' It was also A Company which lost Pte Robert Spikins, when he was killed by a hit and run driver on the Falls Road.

In February 1990 2 Para was deployed to Northern Ireland for its tenth tour since 1969. It was tasked as the Fermanagh Roulement Battalion, with responsibility for 120 miles of remote border, commonly referred to in the media as 'bandit country'. The battalion's tactical headquarters shared its base with 4 UDR in Enniskillen, new premises called Grosvenor Barracks, described by the battalion's log as:

this blastproof edifice ... best described as a cross between a factory and a U-boat pen ... meanwhile B Company and Support Company, along with the battalion's Echelon, was based at St Angelo, an old wartime airfield ... in a selection of portacabins located at the end of a disused runway while A Company was crammed into shared accommodation with the RUC at Lisnaskea... Throughout the tour, the threat of attack was exceptionally high and required high levels of motivation and alertness ... additional contact with the general public had to be maintained to give reassurance and gain low level intelligence. ... diplomacy was well tried by the end of the tour ... as men became well adapted at dealing with irate inhabitants...

3 Para continued its residential tour in 1991:

Our main concerns remain the pursuance of successful operations against the Provisional IRA and security duty against terrorist attack. In both respects we have accumulated considerable experience in the three key facets of deterrence ... in terms of munitions found and arrests made. Regrettably, as yet, we have not been fortunate to have claimed any kills but there have been a number of occasions when prompt and accurate return of fire has undoubtedly dissuaded further attack.

Later in 1991, 1 Para took over from 3 Para as resident battalion:

On an operational front, the Regiment is now into a continuous period of four years service in Northern Ireland ... we had on occasions two battalions here, and for a brief period, all three. It has been extremely busy coming at a time of cutbacks and redundancies throughout the army [as a result of the Options for Change programme] ... and we learn that this period is to be extended for several more years making it quite unique and a record unlikely to be beaten by another regiment. One key aspect of our overall effort is to isolate the terrorists from communities within which they operate ... community relations are vital...

And in the midst of it all the wives and children on the two-year tour carry on regardless:

The Palace Barracks Ladies Club continues to be a thriving success with many functions and events through the year. Themed dinner nights have proved very popular, the latest of which was a barbecue and beachwear night that proved swimmingly successful. The Playschool has also been hard at work raising funds to equip the Creche...

The log-writer was quick to add in the final instalment of his notes that the relative calm in the Palace Barracks tended to give a false impression to visitors, offering no hint of the 'insidious pressures which are brought to bear on all ranks ... the constant mental switching on and switching off eventually takes its toll. Nowhere else in the army are soldiers held under such conditions for so long...'

And so it went on: year after year through the eighties and on into the ceasefires and peace negotiations of the latter half of the nineties, which continued on a knife-edge of hope. Throughout all this time, and indeed since the early seventies, something had been dogging the veterans of 1 Para: Bloody Sunday, which, as the nineties ended, was about to become a big issue again. As part of the peripheral deals – which some have termed appeasement of the IRA – in the discussions surrounding the Good Friday peace agreement, a new inquiry, under the chairmanship of Lord Saville, was ordered by Tony Blair in 1998. Its task was to conduct a 'thorough and comprehensive re-examination of the events of that day' and to follow up some of the mass of complaints and fresh evidence accumulated by campaigners, families of the dead and civil-rights activists.

Much had been published in the intervening years under the auspices of those various groups, to which was added a damning reassessment by the Irish government. Bloody Sunday had become a major component in Northern Ireland's long-established mess of suspicion and hate among Catholics, Nationalists and Republicans towards British forces and successive governments. It rested at the top of the long list of British political and military mishaps in the province which had provided the IRA with such an abundance of propaganda material. And there was to be a divisive and uncomfortable conflict arising from the refusal of Lord Saville to guarantee the anonymity of 17 of the soldiers of 1 Para involved in Bloody Sunday, who were to be called to give evidence. This fact had already been announced to past and present members of the regiment in a circular and a full-page statement in the June 1999 issue of *Pegasus* calling for witnesses, published as the battalion was heading towards Kosovo:

Key members of 1 Para and other Regiments and Corps are now coming forward and others are being contacted by the Inquiry to provide evidence. There are others, some who were directly involved and others who may be able to contribute vital information who have not yet made contact. In order that the new Inquiry can achieve its objective – to establish the truth – it is vital that all potential witnesses come forward. If you are a potential witness then you may have concerns about the issues of:

a.   The cost and provision of legal advice.
b.   Anonymity and your personal security.
c.   Immunity – in the case of those who believe their evidence might lead to prosecution of themselves or former comrades.

These issues are regarded as relevant and valid concerns and the MOD has made provision to offer legal advice and representation as appropriate. This is strongly recommended for all serving and retired members of the Army who present themselves as witnesses or who are contacted by the Inquiry. The powers of the new Tribunal granted under the Tribunals of Inquiry (Evidence) Act, 1921 are wide ranging and it does have the power to subpoena persons who are believed to be material witnesses. In layman's language this means that the Civil Police have the power to arrest and enforce the attendance of witnesses if ordered by the Tribunal. It is, therefore, of vital importance that all members of The Parachute Regiment and other servicemen and women who were present in Londonderry on 30 January 1972, who have factual and verifiable evidence, come forward without delay.

Once again the Paras were facing a painful and indeed awkward rekindling of an event in British history in which accountability was, in truth, as much the issue as the deed itself. Those foot soldiers who were in the front line when 13 civilians were shot could in theory, if the inquiry found against them, now be arrested and charged with murder. Even if that extreme was not reached, it could be argued that Lord Saville's avowed intention of naming names, putting faces to those soldiers who fired on the civil-rights crowd and revealing the identities of others who may not have fired but were there anyhow, was as good as sentencing them to some misfortune at the hands of IRA avengers. Saville disagreed and it was only one of several misconceptions that his lordship held on his road to reviewing the incident. He had clearly taken no heed of the aftermath of the Widgery report, and merely seemed intent at the outset on swinging the pendulum in the opposite direction. Several newspapers immediately picked up on the central issue of identification of the soldiers, notably the *Daily Mail*, which launched a campaign demanding that their anonymity be maintained, under the banner: 'Don't betray the Paras.' Thousands of people voiced their support, among them some very high-profile names from many walks of life, including the military. Among the latter was General Sir Peter de la Billière, a former SAS boss and Britain's commander in the Gulf War, who was at the time giving a daily commentary in the *Mail* on events in the Kosovo crisis. He was unequivocal in his view that:

it should be remembered at the time that civil society had almost broken down in much of the province which was close to anarchy or civil war. In the following May alone, 28 soldiers were killed and 110 wounded. Our soldiers feared for their lives while their senior officers feared a collapse of law and order. It is small wonder that events in Londonderry were chaotic on that day.

Sir Peter also mentioned that the new Bloody Sunday inquiry appeared to have been brokered in response to the IRA's agreement to point out the location of the bodies of Northern Ireland's 'disappeared' – those members of the community, mostly Catholic and dissident to the IRA cause (and including Special Forces liaison officer Captain Robert Nairac), who had been murdered in the intervening years. In the event, with the exception of perhaps three sets of remains recovered, the 'disappeared' are still exactly that, but the IRA had achieved its goal of a fresh inquiry into Bloody Sunday. The nature of the deals-on-the-side that Blair and his ministers threw on the table in order to achieve the ceasefire and peace agreement soon became very obvious to all. The 'disappeared in exchange for a Bloody Sunday inquiry' was one of the shoddier adjuncts to the peace agreement and Peter de la Billière, among many, was forthright in his denouncement of it: 'As far as I can see, the reopening of this inquiry now is a political exercise, the effect of which will be to appease the IRA and humiliate and embarrass the armed forces.'

That is certainly true. This author has, in over 30 years of other writings and journalistic enterprises, been highly critical of both the military and central and local government (as then existed) for the oft-times shambolic handling of the Northern Ireland crisis.

What was overlooked in this whole debacle was the fact that Bloody Sunday, used as a chess piece in this political game, was also the result of a political decision – not a military one. All decisions to move 1 Para into position on that day were taken not in Belfast, at Brigade Headquarters, but in London, approved by ministers and ultimately sanctioned by the then Home Secretary, Reginald Maudling. Without that sanction, those troops – the majority of whom were, as was well known, only youngsters, kids almost – would not have been confronted with the decision which they themselves, each one of them individually, had to make: to open fire with live rounds.

The anonymity debate therefore was blown out of proportion. There is no denying that it was important to both the soldiers involved and to the campaigners and the families of the dead. I know from personal contact that many wives and families – quite apart from former soldiers themselves – have lived with that fear throughout, some suffering nervous breakdowns or broken marriages as a direct result. However, the fundamental issues went far deeper and ought long ago to have been pursued through the higher echelons of the military command and ultimately back to the government of the day itself. The soldiers involved in the shootings were themselves pawns. They may have fired the shots; but who was it that placed them in that position, gave them live ammunition and a little yellow card explaining under what circumstances they might open fire, which was utterly useless in such a dramatic, nerve-racking, fast-moving crisis? Why was that decision, in the end, left to a bunch of frightened young men confronted by a mob?

Well-disciplined soldiers they may have been, but, as has become abundantly clear in these pages, at that time there had been *no* specific training of soldiers for such eventualities. It was simply asking too much to require them to handle the responsibility of making a decision to open fire, possibly to kill fellow countrymen.

Saville himself began his task with unseemly enthusiasm for an adjudicator of such an important inquiry and proceeded to put the new inquiry in danger of ridicule from the outset by focusing on the names of the individual soldiers concerned, perhaps because he had been briefed to do so as that was what the

Nationalists, the IRA and Sinn Fein wanted to hear. A cynic might be inclined to assume that this was one of the things that needed to be ticked off on their shopping list of goodies in order to ensure their continued involvement in the peace process.

In reality, identification was a red herring, and it was a ridiculous notion to imagine that, once informed of the situation, mainland Britain would stand for it. To focus on which Para fired when, where and at whom was to miss the point: accountability should begin at the top, not the bottom, and deal firmly and openly with the process of government control over the placing of what was known to be the toughest unit in the British Army – apart from the SAS – in a position where its men may have had to fire on what was, ostensibly at least, a political demonstration. That truth was never pursued, but swept away to become one more of the many unsatisfactory and unsavoury resolutions in Northern Ireland which helped to undermine confidence in the British political, judicial and military establishment.

Across the Irish Sea in mainland Britain, Bloody Sunday could never arouse the same passions as it did among the civil-rights activists, the Nationalist population and Sinn Fein. In simple terms, it was catalogued as one more atrocity, no more appalling than the dozens of IRA attacks on both sides of the water in the past three decades in which innocent citizens and hundreds of soldiers were slaughtered and horrifically maimed year in and year out and whose perpetrators – or at least those who were caught, tried and sentenced – were in the process of being freed from prison sentences under the early-release scheme which was another part of the Good Friday agreement. This at the very time of the row over the Paras' identities. It was truly a disturbing scenario, frighteningly naive, and made all the more incredible by Saville's opening gambit: Name the killer Paras.

Accountability was the real issue, and if it was to be judiciously pursued in this alleged arena of peace-making, were there others who should be brought to book as well? For a start, British politicians who were part of the original decision-making process, followed perhaps by some of the leading figures in such organizations as Sinn Fein, the Ulster Unionists and supposed reformed former terrorists from the IRA and Protestant paramilitaries now residing in a glow of respectability, who in fact might know more about certain killings than has so far been admitted. If, as in South Africa, the truth was to come out, how far up the line should this process go? Or is it that reconciliation and peace could be achieved only by grilling a handful of soldiers who, back in 1972, were very young and who now, as these words were being written, might well have worn a cap with 'Scapegoat!' emblazoned upon the peak.

The tragedy of Bloody Sunday can never be erased, nor can the straightforward fact that members of the Parachute Regiment killed people, some of whom were probably innocent. Indeed, Widgery went further and recorded that none of the deceased or wounded was proved to have been shot while handling a firearm or a bomb. It remained a lasting epitaph to the dead, and an indelible stain on the record of 1 Para, that the soldiers there at that time should be branded killers. And yet there was one more curiosity in this succession of counter-arguments: that at the very time of Saville's insistence on naming names, convicted IRA terrorists, perpetrators of so many horrific murders on the mainland and on the island of Ireland, were being freed from prison.

In adopting this course, the Blair government was, in fact, agreeing to recast those prisoners not as murderers but as men who were acting as soldiers in the Irish Republican Army (or the Provisional version) and as such were prisoners of war, not prisoners of justice.

It was not difficult to understand the horror and disgust felt by the relatives of the thousands of victims of IRA and Loyalist atrocities on both sides of the water at the sight and the arrogance of those terrorists as they walked free. And to that we can also add the other element that entered this discussion sideways on: the shootings in Kosovo (see Chapter 20) – that hot, riot-torn, frightening confrontation. In the air was the wider issue of NATO bombing the Serbs into submission and urging the community as a whole to force Slobodan Milosevic into resignation so that he could be brought to account for sending his minions out into that province to kill, maim and expel innocent members of the community. It was a combination of all these images that took the debate about anonymity to a point of open ridicule, and unfortunately, at the time of writing, it seems unlikely that Saville will fare any better than Widgery with his inquiry into Bloody Sunday. Nor perhaps would he consider it relevant that the memorial to members of the Parachute Regiment who died on active service in Ulster between 1971 and 1997 contains 52 names. Or that across the British Army as a whole, 448 men have been killed in the same period and 5544 wounded, many of them seriously (figures which exclude the horrendous tally suffered by the Ulster Defence Regiment and the Royal Ulster Constabulary).

Throughout those years lives were wrecked in other ways. Derek Wilford, the then commanding officer of 1 Para, and several who were identifiable members of the unit, were hounded and under threat. Wilford was 38 at that time, a young and ambitious officer who had been awarded the Order of the British Empire. His career stalled, however, and he grew disenchanted with the Army. Although exonerated by the Widgery report, Wilford was certain that he and his men were scapegoated. He left the Army ten years later, took an arts course in London and became a painter. He blamed Bloody Sunday for the disintegration of his 22-year marriage to Janet. The collapse of his marriage also saw him estranged from his son, Jamie, who nonetheless followed his father into the Parachute Regiment and at the time of writing has reached the rank of major.

Wilford has throughout this time remained firm in the defence of his men. He insisted with table-thumping emphasis that they came under fire first, and that the response of the unit which opened fire was in pursuit of 'orders from the top'. He is adamant also that 'the whole thing has been a whitewash. My name has not been cleared. I could see I was going to be the scapegoat. They all walked away and left me to carry the can.' One of Wilford's young officers there on that day concurred and at the time of writing expects to be called to give evidence to the Saville inquiry. He told this author:

It would be interesting to work it through ... to discover if, for example, the Lancashire Regiment had been put in the same position and created the same number of casualties, whether we'd still be hearing about it. I wonder...

Wilford and the rest have been dogged by this all of their lives and it is not surprising that some of them have snapped. Everyone there that day, in the service of the Queen, felt we were doing the right thing... Wilford may not have asked, 'What happens if [the IRA open fire]...?' but in a way that was irrelevant. The situation was the same in all operations in Northern Ireland at that time, and since, which were governed by the general rule that if someone fires at you, you fire back. The yellow card was available. It has been changed over the years – but then you don't whip out a card and look at it when you're facing the wrong end of a sniper's rifle or a mob charging down. You know roughly that in defence of yourself, people or property you should fire back. And in those days, the troops did not have automatic rifles and so it was not some spur of the moment situation...

But the point is, those soldiers were ambushed. I saw it. I was there. It was a fearful affair. Rossville Flats was the scene of it ... an out-and-out ambush. I have every sympathy with people who got fired at. You don't wait to see if you're going to get hit, you try to defend yourself, and in my mind there is absolutely no doubt that this is what happened on that day. Derek Wilford was very concerned that events were overtaking themselves, and moving too quickly. He came to the conclusion that the sooner he moved the company in and blocked them, the problem would be minimized ... get in there early rather than wait for the whole thing to bubble up.

20

BLOODY HOT!

There was never any doubt that the Paras would become involved in Kosovo. Their experience in three decades of urban warfare in Northern Ireland was enough to secure them a leading place, quite apart from their past role as spearhead battalion – the leading unit in an operational movement – and a tough reputation which, as ever, preceded them into their areas of deployment. In any event, a unit such as 1 Para was quite clearly in demand both by the military planners and the politicians, who needed to get this particular genie back into the bottle as soon as possible. The Paras weren't chosen for their humanitarian tendencies, but to secure the route into Kosovo for those who would fulfil that role and help establish some semblance of order to a country ripped apart at every level. They were also the choice, naturally, of Lieutenant General Sir Mike Jackson, commander of NATO ground forces, himself a former Para and at the time also Colonel Commandant of the Parachute Regiment.

Sir Mike, then 55, had served as commander of NATO's ACE Rapid Reaction Corps since 1997 and his craggy, tanned features had earned him a variety of media nicknames (most of which he loathes), including the Prince of Darkness, Britain's toughest-looking soldier and Macho Jacko. Those who served with him in a long career with the Paras – notably in Northern Ireland and Berlin – knew him as a quick-witted man with a good sense of humour, yet in spite of his lanky appearance he was never really classed as a robust officer. Born to a Service family, he began his military career at 19 in the Intelligence Corps, studying Russian before transferring to the Parachute Regiment in 1970, where he rose to command 1 Para between 1984 and 1986. He remained in close touch as he progressed and members of the regiment had been seconded to his personal staff during peacekeeping operations in the Balkans in the mid-1990s, when he was commander of the UN implementation force in Bosnia .

Another of the senior commanders during the Kosovo crisis was also an ex-Para officer of some renown, Brigadier Adrian Freer, a former commanding officer of 2 Para, who was by then running the 5th Airborne Brigade, which comprised a Headquarters Company, 1 Para, 1 Royal Gurkha Rifles, elements of the 7th Regiment the Royal Horse Artillery, elements of the 21st Explosive Ordnance Disposal Squadron RE and CSS (Combat Service Support). Behind the call to 1 Para to prepare for deployment to Kosovo with the 5th Airborne Brigade there was an internal drama, panic stations almost, although this was not generally known. At that time 2 Para was considerably short of its full establishment, which, in these days of shortfalls in recruitment and retention of trained soldiers, is not an unusual occurrence. In fact, it has become the norm. Commanding officer Lieutenant Colonel Paul Gibson had to rush around borrowing men from other units to get the battalion up to fighting strength.

In the past this situation had been eased by calling upon the 4th, 10th and 15th Volunteer Battalions, the Parachute Regiment's Territorial Army reserve, whose soldiers traditionally made up any shortfalls by moving men around the units to fulfil various roles. The Volunteer, or V, Battalions, whose pedigree stemmed from some of the great Second World War formations, were themselves in the throes of serious reorganization and swingeing cuts demanded under the government's Strategic Defence Review. The 15th (Scottish) Volunteer Battalion had already been disbanded as a result of the Options for Change study.

Much to the very great anger of TA Paras and their branches throughout the country, hundreds of volunteers and the historic 10th Volunteer Battalion were being axed. TA soldiers had remained a very useful source of manpower to fill in the gaps during crises and manpower shortages but, with cuts in their own ranks, this facility was no longer available. When the order came to prepare for deployment in Kosovo, 1 Para needed 180 men to bring the battalion to fighting strength and the only solution was to borrow men from other units. In fact, 2 Para was unable to help, being currently fully deployed in Northern Ireland, and so the entire burden fell upon 3 Para, then stationed in Dover, which was asked to supply 120 men to form a rifle company plus another group as an Assault Pioneer platoon. Other soldiers from 3 Para were seconded to a mortar section and three anti-tank detachments. These temporary postings meant that 3 Para was itself critically short of men to the point that it would be almost impossible for it to be deployed as a fighting unit if the need arose. The seconded soldiers were rushed into training in Scotland in a desperate effort to prepare them in time to join 1 Para in Macedonia.

There, as NATO war planes screamed overhead and nations around the world watched those final scenes in the horrific process of ethnic cleansing become ever more tragic by the hour, the ground forces massed at a discreet distance, waiting for the word to move in, either in a full-blown invasion or, more likely, as part of a peace deal, this being the preferred option and the solution more or less demanded by the majority. The former option was never entirely ruled out, however. British Army elements had spent weeks in training exercises for that possibility. Quite early on in the NATO campaign there was a plan 'on the table' in Whitehall which amounted to nothing short of an invasion of Serbia itself, and would have entailed the SAS and British Paras dropping on airports within territory of the former Yugoslavia – possibly including Belgrade itself – capturing the administrative buildings and securing the perimeters. Thereafter they would have been joined by rapidly deployed air-landed troops, including their good friends the 1st Battalion the Royal Gurkha Rifles, to establish a forward base to which a strong

NATO force could be delivered. This proposal was one of many which never actually got off the drawing board. Nor could it have, because of the reluctance of the Americans and several of Britain's European partners in the project to enter into manpower-costly ground combat which entailed the likelihood of body bags by the score and a resultant political disaster for President Clinton, then in the final throes of his sex scandal. While all of the possible options were being considered in London, a key meeting between US defence chiefs and their European counterparts to discuss sending in ground troops ended in stalemate.

The hawks among the British officials, including Foreign Secretary Robin Cook, were privately asserting that a ground-force invasion might eventually be necessary but continued to insist publicly that there was no immediate likelihood of it happening. Ministry of Defence sources acknowledged, however, that the contingency plans for such a move had to remain active, especially if the bombing campaign dragged on through the summer. Time was running out and a deadline was set for the middle of July if a successful operation was to be launched before the winter set in. British Defence Secretary George Robertson was among those lobbying strongly for a state of readiness for a full-scale invasion. Although talk of this measure was played down, contingency plans were well in hand for Britain to send 50,000 troops as part of a 150,000-strong NATO army to move into Kosovo if it became necessary. The Americans, however, were prepared to consider only the formation of a KFOR peacekeeping force of around 50,000 personnel.

The detractors who opposed a forced entry into Kosovo – and there were plenty – preferred to continue the NATO bombardment of key Serbian installation and troop positions until submission was achieved, although there were waverers against that, too. The bombardment simply went on and on, until a diplomatic effort finally brought an agreement from the Serbian president, Slobodan Milosevic, on 10 June 1999 to pull his troops out of Kosovo, to make way for KFOR ground forces under the command of General Jackson. And so began the West's most ambitious military deployment since the Gulf War, with heavy contingents of British, German, French, Italian and American troops preparing to cross the border from Macedonia and Albania. Britain alone had close on 2500 tanks, self-propelled artillery pieces, armoured troop carriers, trucks, Land Rovers and other vehicles waiting in the wings for the move up country and into villages, towns and cities devastated by both the NATO bombing campaign and months of ruthless ethnic cleansing, wanton destruction and murder by the most brutal regime in that region since the Nazis.

The Paras, coming up from their training area at Petrovec near Skopje's international airport, prepared for the initial movement into Kosovo by helicopter while the Gurkhas marched and drove in full combat order with hefty bergens and a large assortment of weaponry, including mortars, Milan anti-tank missiles and small arms. Both units would take their place at the head of the 11,000 British troops waiting on the Macedonian border. Surrounded by a tough bodyguard of Paras and Gurkhas, Brigadier Adrian Freer stood at the top of the first contingent of the massive force drawn up behind him to begin the thrust towards Pristina and, hopefully, a resolution to the Kosovan nightmare as soon as he received the Go! signal.

Initially two options for the move into Kosovo were considered, and training for both had been carried out in the run-up to the final signal for entry. One was to fly the British airborne forces to Pristina airport, ahead of the rest as soon as the military agreement was signed. Some commanders of the individual NATO countries supplying peacekeeping troops, including Germany and France, had proposed a high-profile parachute drop into their designated zones. The British commanders opted for a helicopter-borne deployment, or tactical airlanding operation, which would allow rapid deployment under controlled conditions. Politicians in London would have preferred a more spectacular arrival for its obvious media benefits, with troops parachuting direct on to Pristina airport. But 1 Para, going in first, was not in the business of providing spectacles at the cost of its men. It would be flying into the face of the unknown: no one could really say with any certainty that the Serbs would have vacated by then, or that there were enough well-armed civilians to cause them bother and attempt to shoot them out of the sky.

There were certainly no guarantees about anything, least of all the Serbs' promised withdrawal from Kosovo, which was by no means even half completed at the time the Paras were due to move out. Furthermore, safe and mine-free DZs were not easy to come by in the most difficult terrain, for which there had been no opportunity of a close inspection. And so, using Chinook and Puma helicopters, the Paras flew in to make a rapid deployment, first into the hills immediately inside Kosovo and then, crucially, to secure a pass lying towards Kacanik and a mile from the Macedonian border with Kosovo, banked by steep, mountainous terrain that could hide 1000 snipers and plenty of machine-gun nests or rocket launchers with no problem.

The route also contained two tunnels, four large bridges and about ten smaller ones which were obvious targets for booby-traps, mines and ambush situations for any remaining Serbian paramilitaries who might want to make life difficult for the oncoming troops. Since the whole of 4th Armoured Brigade, with its vast column of men and machines, would have to negotiate the pass, a trouble-free passage was imperative both for safety's sake and the speed of the operation itself. For speed was of the essence in this most volatile of situations, not merely to secure their positions but to ensure there was no outbreak of bloodletting and revenge killings. The routes through to Pristina had to be cleared of all potential hazards, including thousands of pieces of unexploded NATO ordnance which littered the countryside and, sadly, killed two Gurkha soldiers in the very early stages of the advance. The push forward by the British contingent would signal the start of the overall movement of the 50,000 NATO troops who made up KFOR into their own designated areas of protection – a movement which Adrian Freer had to delay for several hours because several nations, including the Americans, were not ready; some angry exchanges ensued.

The Americans were particularly reluctant to move their troops into Macedonia, apparently under orders from Washington not to advance if there was a real threat of confrontation with the Serbian Army or strong paramilitary forces. They kept their 2200 marines stacked up in ships parked in the Adriatic until the all-clear was sounded, this resulting in part from assurances to be received at the border from Serbian military commanders and from the initial reconnoitre by British troops. At dawn on 13 June the second part of this proposal was under way as the Paras swept into southern Kosovo in spectacular style – and certainly flash enough to please the politicians in London as they viewed the movement along with the rest of the nation on their television screens. All looked good for the dash to Pristina.

As the 1 Para units took off for the mission in their Chinooks and Pumas from the Macedonian border, the huge, noisy, snaking convoys of wheeled and tracked vehicles headed for the frontier flanked by Gurkhas with heavy backpacks. By then the remaining Serbs at the border had scooted and only three customs men remained, along with a few military policemen of the dreaded MUP, who were immediately arrested by the Gurkhas. Lieutenant Colonel Paul Gibson, commanding 1 Para, who was to have met Serbian military people at the border for discussions, was clearly getting fed up hanging around and decided he couldn't wait any longer: 'The Yugoslav Army were supposed to show up and I was supposed to meet the local boss, Colonel Jelic, but he hasn't showed and that's not entirely unexpected. So, I decided to go forward by helicopter.' At the raise of an arm from one of his men, a Puma came from nowhere and landed beside him in a cloud of dust. Off they flew, low and fast, along the dangerously narrow gorge to Kacanik, sometimes almost touching the rocks and shrubbery of the steep sides.

At the LZ, the helicopter blades whirred noisily and kicked up a swirling down-draught that was like a twister to the disembarking paratroopers in the confined space. One of them accidentally discovered the dangers that completely surrounded the company. Hit by a sudden gust, the anti-tank rocket he was unloading rolled out of his hands down a bank. He jumped down to retrieve it and then heard the shout from one of his colleagues: 'Mine! FREEZE!' He then spent almost an hour prodding around with his bayonet to find a safe path back.

The Paras found the town of Kacanik empty except for a few people too old or infirm to take refuge in the hills. The once charming little houses had been ethnically gutted inside and sappers found many booby-traps. Slowly, people began to move out of the hills where they had been hiding for three months, desperate for food and many in need of medical aid.

At midday and in scorching heat, the Paras received orders for the second stage of their deployment, which was to leapfrog ahead of the British motor train heading up country for what became a quite dramatic dash towards the southern entrance to Pristina airport. On their arrival, there was a problem. A Russian paratroop unit, responding to Moscow's desperate wish not to be left out of the peacekeeping party the Russians had helped negotiate, made its own overnight run for the airport, coming from the opposite direction, and for a while a diplomatic incident seemed on the cards. Indeed the Americans were beginning to get quite threatening in their body language and Moscow dug its heels in about its troops in Pristina. Adrian Freer, tough and uncompromising, warned the Russians not to mess him about. They just stared back in icy silence, ignoring his threatening tone.

Even General Jackson, who flew into Pristina Airport by helicopter expecting to set up his base there, was ordered to the edge of the area by a Russian general who outranked him by a couple of stars.

The sight of Russian armoured personnel carriers tearing around the airstrips did not impress the British, and while diplomatic efforts dragged on in Washington, London and Moscow, Jackson himself took the heat out of the situation locally. He knew that 1 Para and other British Army troops at the entrance to the airfield were in an exposed position, lightly armed and facing potential dangers, especially as the column of vehicles coming up through the Allied corridor from Macedonia was delayed by the political posturing and a huge logistical traffic jam south of the capital.

Inspired by the arrival of the Russian troops, whom they regarded as their friends, the Serbs noticeably slowed their withdrawal. Additionally, the French had been halted by serious minefields and the Italians had been moving at a snail's pace from Albania. The Paras were thus exposed to some danger in a forward position while the move north descended into a compelling scenario which embraced the extremes of high drama, spectacle and, to some extent, farce. There was jubilation as the Paras approached Pristina: crowds began coming to the roadside to greet them in scenes quite similar to those that met the liberators at the end of the Second World War. As the first troops in, the Paras saw for themselves the incredible sights of destruction, caused in part by the NATO bombers and, of course, there was still the Serbian section of the population to deal with. In the end, General Jackson saved the great dash forward by the British forces from potential disaster by arranging a local agreement with the commander of the Russian paratroopers for the shared occupation of the airbase until the issue over a Russian 'zone' was resolved.

Meanwhile the remainder of 1 Para moved into Pristina itself to strengthen the KFOR presence in an exceedingly tense city in which the atmosphere of hate could almost be cut with a knife. The *Daily Telegraph* reported the scene:

Carrying a general purpose machine gun, Private Stuart Gardiner, 22, of Warminster, Wiltshire, said: 'There are some guns going off but we're not too bothered about that. As far as I am concerned it's all part of doing my job.' Lance Corporal Phil Finch, 26, of Maidstone, Kent, said: 'We're ready for anything. As far as we know we're not getting anything fired at us but it's just a case of staying vigilant and keeping your eyes peeled.' With an anti-tank rocket system strapped to his back, Private Nick Hollis, 18, from Walsall, said: 'There are a lot of people coming out being friendly to us, giving us chocolate, flowers and things like that. It just makes it feel great to be here.'

Within hours of arriving, however, 1 Para was plunged into controversy when one of its soldiers shot dead a Serb militiaman. The Serb had been among a group talking to eight Paras beside a modern block of flats when he suddenly drew a gun. Lieutenant Colonel Nick Clissitt explained that the man was told repeatedly to put the gun down and when he refused he was shot four times 'in self-defence'. It was an immediate lesson in the Paras' toughness and news of their preparedness to shoot if necessary travelled like wildfire around the city.

Serb civilians were spitting their hostility towards the British soldiers in scenes not unlike the early days of confrontation in Northern Ireland. Their mood became altogether more sombre as members of the War Crimes Commission began digging up the suspected sites of mass graves, and soon they were even more wary of insulting the British soldiers as the ethnic Albanian Kosovars began returning in droves to reverse the ethnic cleansing process. Indeed it was to the Paras that a group of Serbs turned for protection a couple of weeks later. With Pristina in a state of chaos, high-spirited members of the Kosovo Liberation

Army were joyriding around the city, firing their guns into the air and threatening to do nasty things to any Serbs they encountered. The result of this escapade was another shooting incident involving 1 Para. The paratroopers were accused a firing recklessly into a carload of young Albanian men who had been firing AK47s into the air and pointing their weapons menacingly towards the crowd of Serbs. Two KLA fighters were killed and two Albanian civilians wounded by the group of paras.

According to 1 Para's account, a patrol opened fire because they believed their lives were being endangered by the men firing their guns, and in particular by a man on the car roof. The Paras were, at the time, protecting a group of Serbian civilians sheltering in a nearby building. The *Independent on Sunday*, owned by the Irish-based Independent Newspapers group, and a regular critic of the Parachute Regiment's robust style of soldiering, claimed that the soldiers actively pursued the car, which was moving away from both them and the Serbian civilians when the shots were fired. The newspaper produced witnesses who said that the man on the car roof was firing vertically at the time and it was nothing more than 'happy firing' of the kind that had been going on for some hours with the acquiescence and even encouragement of British soldiers on patrol. Rather than simply taking out the single man firing the weapon, the soldiers sprayed the car, the paper claimed. 'They were shot in the back without knowing what hit them,' said an Albanian woman who saw the killings. 'No question about it: this was an execution.' The young Kosovars' only crime had been to celebrate a key anniversary in their fight for independence.

In fact, the constant rattle of automatic fire had been heard for hours as the KLA youths fired their deadly AK47s into the air in breach of the disarmament agreement between KFOR troops and the KLA. For a while the Paras involved had the prospect of a murder charge hanging over their heads. This was dropped on 14 July after an investigation by the SIB supported the Paras' story that they shouted warnings and fired shots into the air to further warn the young Kosovars. They opened fire under the terms of engagement set by the Army: at the point when they believed their lives were in danger. There were, however, no further fatal incidents during the Paras' stay in the troubled province and, at the end of August, 1 Para was able to return to home base after four months in the region. At the height of the Balkans summer, in a place where tensions were running to extremes, exacerbated by the noise, dust and diesel fumes from thousands of military vehicles, it had been, one of their number told me, 'bloody hot'.

Even as the Paras were deploying to Kosovo great changes in the regiment's place in the future of Britain's airborne forces were under way. The Government's Strategic Review had outlined proposals for a new airborne assault force and in September 1999 the implications of this became clear. The 5th Airborne Brigade, of which the Parachute Regiment was part, was merged into the new 16th Air Assault Brigade (see Epilogue) and at the same time the regiment's long association with Aldershot would finally end with its relocation to a new base at Colchester.

The 16th Air Assault Brigade (16 AAB) will provide a high-tech-led air-assault capability in the Airborne Battlegroup role (ABBG), based on the awesome firepower of the Apache attack helicopter. Supported by parachute artillery, engineers, signallers, logisticians and medics, the formation has been designed, according to Army specifications, 'to move rapidly over strategic, operational and tactical distances, deploying the most modern technology with the traditionally aggressive and determined ethos of Airborne Forces'.

However, the story of this regrouping had a sting in the tail. The 5th Airborne Brigade was to lose its famous Pegasus symbol. The historic flying-horse emblem – adopted by all airborne forces, not just the Paras – in the Second World War was replaced by a new Striking Eagle badge in September 1999, although the Paras would retain their distinctive maroon berets and 'wing' badges.

Lieutenant General Sir Michael Gray, a former Colonel Commandant of the Paras, was among the many critics of the move. He told *The Times*: 'I am very pleased about the new airborne brigade. But I am very, very sad that they will do away with Pegasus. It was a very emotive and macho symbol.'

That and the demise of the 10th Volunteer Battalion, whose history went back to Arnhem, cut two more links with the past traditions and those far-off days of heroics by thousands of men of Britain's airborne forces, spurred and inspired by the determination of Winston Churchill. The days of mass parachute drops and airborne landings of troops were, in effect, also being consigned to history. What remains is a Parachute Regiment, hand in glove with the very latest airborne technology, entering the twenty-first century at the cutting edge of military capability.

Epilogue

DO YOU WANT TO ... ?

An oft-quoted assessment of the British Paras was made by their former Colonel Commandant, Field Marshal Viscount Montgomery. They had shown themselves, he said, to be as tenacious and determined in defence as they were courageous in attack, and added: 'They are in fact men apart – every man an Emperor.' Times may have changed and technology now rules the military front lines, but the basic premise remains the same and is still drummed into new recruits with the same ardour and strong language as ever. There is one problem, however. New recruits are not queuing up outside the regimental headquarters in the same numbers as before. Indeed, right across the British Army there are manpower shortages – as demonstrated by 1 Para, who had to borrow men from other battalions to get its numbers up to strength for Kosovo. From the early 1990s the Gurkhas – the only British regiment to be heavily oversubscribed with recruits, with 300 men applying for every vacancy – have been supplying reserve companies to the Paras and other regiments to fill the operational gaps.

While refusing to lower standards, the regiment insists, in its latest literature to encourage young men to come forward, that they do not have to be supermen. However, it does make the point that:

Para recruit training is arguably the best, toughest, and most professional in the world today. Soldiers finish training and are ready to take their place in an operational parachute battalion on 72-hrs notice to enplane. That is very achievable. There are many people out there who would like to be paratroopers but are afraid of failure ... there is the myth that one can't join unless you're already super fit and hard as nails.

To prove the point, the regiment began offering a free weekend for potential recruits to see what it was like, aimed at both those considering immediate enlistment and teenagers still at school and thinking about a career in the military. Applicants will receive free travel warrants and take part in a weekend course 'without obligation or commitment' that will provide an introduction to fitness training, presentations on all aspects of the regiment, simulated parachute training, equipment and weapons demonstrations, firepower demonstrations with live firing on a range, and thorough briefings of what to expect in training.

All new recruits pass through a series of interviews and aptitude tests, after which they move into the two-phase basic training programme, which lasts up to eight months. The first phase follows the Army's Common Military Syllabus, with some add-ons which are specific to the Parachute Regiment's requirements and are run by its own training company. The course comprises fieldcraft, fitness (which progresses gradually as the course develops), drill, discipline and turnout, military knowledge and basic weapon handling and marksmanship. Recruits have the right to leave the Army during the first 12 weeks of training, but after that they are contracted to stay for three years. The recruits then move to Catterick, North Yorkshire, for phase two, a 19-week course constructed as follows:

Weeks 1–9: A gradual but intense fitness programme, including endurance marches, speed marches, numerous fieldcraft exercises covering all phases of war; marksmanship training, moving up from static ranges to field firing (movement) exercises. All infantry weapons are loaded and fired.

Week 10: This includes the dreaded Pre-Para Selection, better known as P-Company, a tough knockabout with much strong language which all recruits must pass before they can continue their training. It is a major stepping stone and those who pass earn the coveted maroon beret and are qualified to go on to parachute training.

Week 11: This is the field-firing week. Recruits will fire all the infantry weapons including grenades, anti-tank missiles and medium machine-guns, using only live ammunition. They progress from individual close-quarter battle exercises to full-blown platoon attacks. It is arguably one of the most adrenalin-pumping – and hardest – weeks in training. Recruits must pass this week to continue.

Weeks 12–13: The final hurdle to acceptance is Exercise Dynamite Mole, ten tough days of digging trenches from which the recruits live and fight, firing live ammunition by day and night. Only the Paras use this training procedure, incorporating live firing platoon attacks.

Weeks 14–17: The basic parachute course run by the RAF at Brize Norton, Oxfordshire. The recruits learn all aspects of military parachuting. They complete eight jumps in all, one from a Skyvan and seven from a C130 Hercules, including one at night. On completion of the 'jumps' course recruits earn their 'wings', and their pay increases to include Paras' pay.

Week 18–19: The recruits' final two weeks in training before their passing-out parade as trained parachute soldiers: a five-day airborne exercise, usually involving live firing, two parachute jumps and FIBUA (Fighting In Built Up Areas) exercise.

Now for the postings. The Regiment is made up of three regular Battalions, 1, 2 and 3 Para, and, from June 1999, one Territorial Army Battalion, 4 (V) Para. Each battalion has a total strength of 750 men. Jobs are wide and varied and include linguists, drivers, dog handlers, regimental policeman, physical training instructors, snipers and demolition experts. Many further courses are available, providing additional qualifications – HGV driving, first aid, health and safety, leadership training, management and computer skills – and there is an extensive programme of adventure training and sport.

A number of sub-units are attached to the battalions and there is a stand-alone Pathfinder Platoon which operates on similar lines to activities described in earlier pages, conducting advance operations prior to airborne assaults. These operations include covert reconnaissance, and location and marking of DZs, tactical LZs and helicopter LZs. They may also include target reconnaissance and limited high-value Offensive Action in support of the main-force insertions. The Pathfinder Platoon may be inserted up to seven days before the arrival of the main force. Once the main force has landed, the Pathfinder Platoon conducts brigade-level intelligence, surveillance, target acquisition and reconnaissance operations to provide tactical intelligence vital to decision-making within the Brigade Headquarters.

The Pathfinder Platoon specializes in air insertion and all members are capable of being inserted and resupplied by all in-service parachutes, including High Altitude Low Opening (HALO), High Altitude High Opening (HAHO) and by fixed- and rotary-wing techniques. Additionally, all personnel must be fully conversant and regularly practised in support helicopter operations, including Special Forces procedures. Because of the extensive range of operations in all anticipated phases of war, platoon members must be trained in specialist skills, including the following: Resistance to interrogation training, combat survival, jungle warfare skills, medical aids, abseiling from a hovering helicopter, explosives and demolitions and mountain warfare.

The essence of airborne operations remains much the same as in the past, although updated with the use of modern weaponry and transport, such as the Apache helicopter. Today airborne assaults come as a package deal, with advance operations to protect the insertion of an assault force through hostile airspace. Referred to as Composite Air Operations, these packages use the full range of RAF aircraft to punch a hole in the enemy's air defences to protect a stream of aircraft carrying the assault force, to and from the target. This force attacks from the air using either parachute, support helicopter or a Tactical Airland Operation (TALO) assault. TALO allows the use of up to four C130 aircraft in a main-force assault to seize a target, but it does require a single runway length of at least 1500 metres. The use of massed support helicopters (SH) for an assault is an area which the 5th Airborne Brigade and the RAF's Support Helicopter Force have greatly refined over recent years and the former became the leading user of massed SH, an approach which proved to have the advantage of inserting forces more accurately.

The landmark reorganization of Britain's airborne forces came into effect in September 1999 with the closure of the 24th Airmobile Brigade and its merger with elements of the 5th Airborne Brigade, including the Paras, to form the 16th Air Assault Brigade. In addition to delivering the existing Aviation and Airborne Battlegroups at high readiness, 16 AAB was to be the lead organization in developing the British military's strategy for rapidly deployable forces in the first decade of the new millennium. It will operate as a specialist brigade, manned by selected soldiers from all arms and services. It will be used in every aspect of conflict once the Apache force is fully fielded by the year 2005, a unique formation in the UK, with tremendous firepower. It was aimed at rapid deployment on a scale previously only dreamed of by airborne forces and designed to secure or open points of entry for other land or air elements with an exceedingly high combat power.

The brigade's combined armed elements will meet a wide variety of threats, and undertake a range of missions and tasks, well into the twenty-first century, first under the overall control of the newly formed Joint Helicopter Command from 1 October 1999 and then under Operational Command from 1 April 2000. Its primary war fighting role would be strike operations within a divisional or corps offensive battle, with the strength to cross the forward line of its own troops or drop into a war theatre with airlanding or helicopter-borne support for seize-and-hold operations, large-scale raids and support to Special Forces. A great deal of emphasis and training will also be focused on operations other than war, using a combination of strategically deployable aviation and ground elements for peace support (as in Kosovo), humanitarian relief and evacuation or extraction operations. The new brigade will also maintain a pool of high-readiness forces for the Joint Rapid Reaction Force, capable of delivering an airborne battle group at two to five days' notice, a lead battle group at five to ten days' notice, and a squadron to support amphibious operations with the 3rd Commando Brigade while being able to deploy the remainder of the brigade within 30 days.

The high-tech development of modern airborne troops, however, has brought some casualties within the Parachute Regiment. After the Second World War, 12 TA Parachute Battalions came into being as the wartime Para regiments and independent companies were signed off or merged. A lively membership was reflected in TA units across the country, usually reflecting the regional flavour of many of the wartime battalions (for example, the Scottish, the Welsh and the Eastern and Home Counties Battalions). Gradually these were reduced by successive Ministry of Defence cuts in TA requirements until finally there were two, the 4th and 10th Battalions. And then there was one…

As 1 Para led the advance into Kosovo, 10 Para marched into oblivion with a last parade in London in June 1999. Lieutenant Colonel Paul Gibson, commanding officer of 1 Para, sent a message of condolence from Kosovo: 'It is a sad day for the Parachute Regiment.' Although Defence Secretary George Robertson had promised that 'almost no one' would be sacked in the TA cuts, 250 were signed off and the remaining 150 found places in other TA units. However, although 10 Para was axed from the Parachute Regiment's TA establishment, the number of the battalion was commemorated by the formation of the new

10th Company 4 Para. Space does not permit a more detailed excursion into the activities of the TA or Volunteer battalions, but in fact they can be summed up by a brief sortie through the life of just one man: Tex Banwell, who at 81 had been one of the stalwarts of the 10th Battalion since its formation in 1942. He was there at the London parade in his wheelchair to see the 10th off, having made his last parachute jump just four years earlier.

Keith Dember 'Tex' Banwell was one of the all-time great characters of the Parachute Regiment and it is perhaps fitting that we should end these pages with one last wartime story: an account of his incredible list of achievements, which included being an official impersonator of General Montgomery in North Africa, being taken prisoner (and escaping) five times, once from a German guard named Max Schmeling – who was the heavyweight boxing champion of the world from 1930 to 1932 – and making more than 1000 parachute drops 'for fun'.

Banwell began his military career with the Coldstream Guards, later transferring to the Royal Hampshire Regiment (1st Battalion) on India's North-West Frontier. In 1938 the Hampshires moved to Palestine, where they were engaged in counter-terrorist duties, and then in 1939 to Egypt, where he answered the cross-regimental call for volunteers for special duties. Banwell ended up in the Long Range Desert Group, which operated very closely with the SAS.

He was first captured in a raid on Tobruk, but with a friend managed to steal a German vehicle and escape. During a subsequent raid on Crete, he was taken prisoner at Heraklion and put under the personal supervision of Max Schmeling, who unfortunately nodded off and allowed his captors to borrow a landing craft and slip quietly away. Unfortunately, the craft ran out of fuel and was adrift for nine days before coming up on the sands of the North African coast. Banwell was in hospital for 12 weeks. When he had recovered, and having lost a considerable amount of weight, it was noticed that he now looked uncommonly like General Montgomery – certainly the resemblance was strong enough to fool the Germans. He was sent to Cairo to meet Montgomery, provided with suitable attire, insignia and badges, and was sent on trips around the Middle East, causing great confusion among the enemy's surveillance teams. There was only one problem – he was much taller than Monty, and was instructed that on no account should he get out of the car. He soon found this assignment somewhat tedious and, having put in for an RTU, was sent to the 10th Battalion of the Parachute Regiment to become a paratrooper.

In September 1944 he was heading for Arnhem. His Dakota was hit by anti-aircraft fire as it came towards the DZ and six of the 15 Paras on board were killed as they came out. Banwell was among those who landed safely; he fought with his battalion until it was virtually wiped out, was wounded and captured again by the Germans. He jumped from the train taking the prisoners to Germany just as it crossed the border and managed to reach the Dutch resistance, for whom he became an instructor in weapons and explosives. He led one of their most successful raids, but while escorting a small party of escaping prisoners he was again taken by the Germans.

They considered that because Banwell was living with the Dutch resistance he had forfeited his military status and, after a court martial, he was sentenced to death. He was told, however, that if he disclosed the names of his resistance contacts he would be reprieved. When he refused, he was placed in front of a firing squad, stood to attention as all the orders but the last one were barked out and then returned to his cell. The next day he suffered the same fate, this time with the squad being told to 'Fire!'– except that the shells were blanks. He still refused to talk and was carted off to Auschwitz, where he remained until the camp was liberated by the Russians. But Tex Banwell's story of narrow escapes was not yet over.

After the war, by then with the 10th Battalion TA, he had had a bad landing and lay motionless on the ground. He was declared dead and taken to the mortuary and would have been boxed up if the attendant hadn't noticed a flutter of an eyelid and resuscitated him. In his time, Banwell was also a second-Dan black belt at judo, held the record for the 10th Battalion road walk from Birmingham to London, marched from London to Brighton in ten and a half hours and from John O'Groats to Land's End in full army kit, wearing standard-issue leather boots with no socks in them. He also represented 10 Para five times in the Westminster to Devizes canoe race. In 1969 he was awarded a BEM and the Netherlands Silver Cross for his services to the Dutch resistance movement. Banwell made his thousandth jump at Arnhem in 1984 at the fortieth anniversary of the battle. He made a repeat performance ten years later, on the fiftieth anniversary.

Sergeant K. D. Banwell BEM died at the end of August 1999, just a few weeks after laying his battalion to rest. Tex had been, like the Paras themselves, Ready for Anything.

SELECT BIBLIOGRAPHY

Allen, Charles, *The Savage Wars of Peace*, Michael Joseph, 1990.

Arthur, Max, *Men of the Red Beret*, Hutchinson, 1990.

Bridson, Rory, *The Making of a Para*, Sidgwick & Jackson, 1989.

Cavenagh, Sandy, *Airborne to Suez*, William Kimber, 1965.

Frost, Major General John, *A Drop Too Many*, Cassell, 1980.

2 PARA Falklands: The Battalion At War, Buchan & Enright, 1983.

Harclerode, Peter, *Go To It! The Illustrated History of the 6th Airborne Division*, Bloomsbury Publishing, 1990.

Para! Fifty Years of the Parachute Regiment, Cassell, 1992.

Hastings, Max, and Jenkins, Simon, *The Battle for the Falklands*, Michael Joseph, 1983.

Montgomery, Field Marshal the Viscount, *The Memoirs of Field Marshal Montgomery*, Collins, 1958.

Norton, G. G., *The Red Devils*, Leo Cooper, 1971.

Parker, John, *The Gurkhas*, Headline, 1999.

Death of a Hero: Captain Robert Nairac and the Undercover War in Northern Ireland, Metro Books, 1999.

Inside The Foreign Legion, Piatkus Books, 1998.

SBS: The Inside Story of the Special Boat Service, Headline, 1997.

Pocock, Tom, *Fighting General*, Collins, 1973.

Saunders, Hilary St George, *The Red Beret*, Michael Joseph, 1950.

Thompson, Julian, *No Picnic – 3 Commando Brigade in the South Atlantic 1982*, Leo Cooper, 1985.

Ready For Anything, Weidenfeld & Nicolson, 1989.

War Behind Enemy Lines, Sidgwick & Jackson, 1998.

Weldon, Sir Hugh, *Red Berets Into Normandy*, Jarrold Publishing, 1982.

Ziegler, Philip, *Mountbatten*, Collins, 1985.

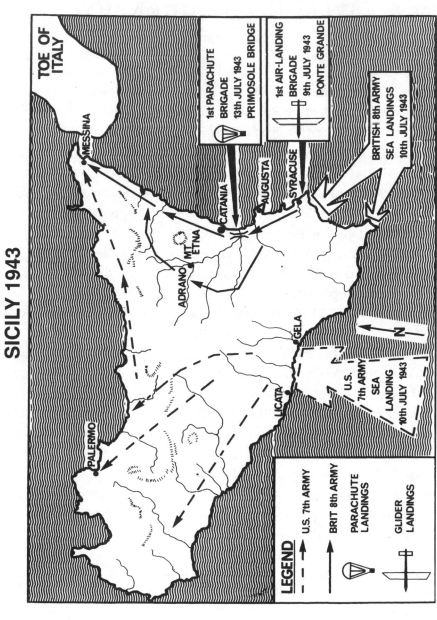

SICILY 1943

TOE OF ITALY

MESSINA

CATANIA

AUGUSTA

SYRACUSE

MT. ETNA

ADRANO

GELA

LICATA

PALERMO

1st PARACHUTE BRIGADE
13th JULY 1943
PRIMOSOLE BRIDGE

1st AIR-LANDING BRIGADE
9th JULY 1943
PONTE GRANDE

BRITISH 8th ARMY
SEA LANDINGS
10th JULY 1943

U.S. 7th ARMY
SEA LANDING
10th JULY 1943

N

LEGEND

U.S. 7th ARMY

BRIT 8th ARMY

PARACHUTE LANDINGS

GLIDER LANDINGS

(Reproduced courtesy of the Airborne Forces Museum)

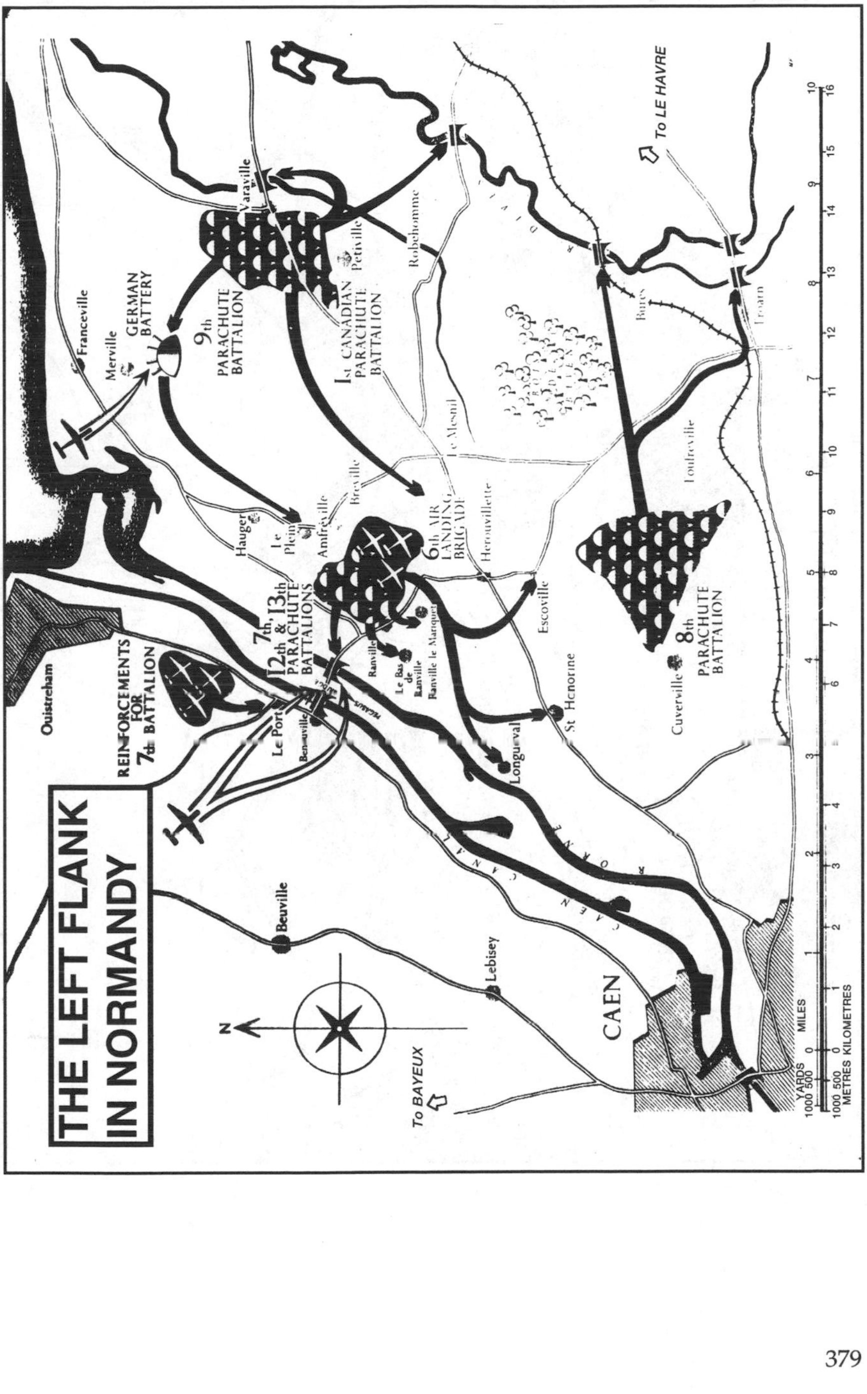
THE LEFT FLANK
IN NORMANDY
N
To BAYEUX
CAEN
Lebisey
Beuville
Ouistreham
REINFORCEMENTS
FOR
7th BATTALION
Le Port
Benouville
7th, 12th & 13th
PARACHUTE
BATTALIONS
Ranville
Le Bas de Ranville
Ranville le Mariquet
Longueval
St Honorine
Escoville
Herouvillette
6th AIR
LANDING
BRIGADE
Amfréville
Le Plein
Hauger
Bréville
Le Mesnil
Merville
Franceville
GERMAN
BATTERY
9th
PARACHUTE
BATTALION
1st CANADIAN
PARACHUTE
BATTALION
Petiville
Varaville
Robehomme
Bures
Troarn
Toufreville
Cuverville
8th
PARACHUTE
BATTALION
To LE HAVRE
CAEN CANAL
ORNE R
DIVES R
YARDS 1000 500 0
MILES
METRES 1000 500 0 KILOMETRES

(Reproduced courtesy of the Airborne Forces Museum)

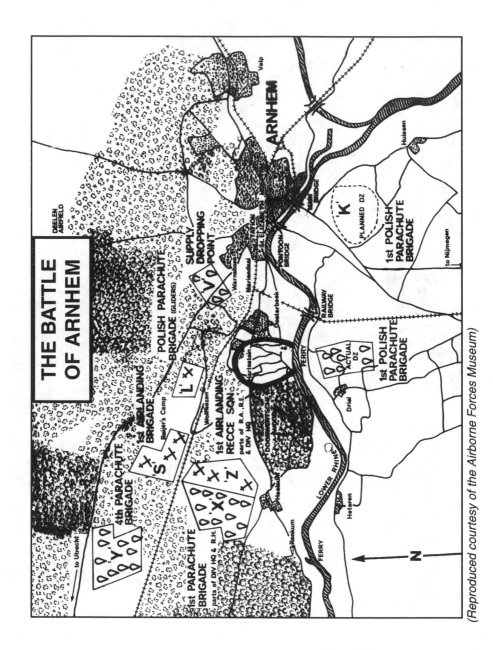

THE BATTLE OF ARNHEM

DEELEN AIRFELD

4th PARACHUTE BRIGADE

1st AIRLANDING BRIGADE

POLISH PARACHUTE BRIGADE (GLIDERS)

SUPPLY DROPPING POINT

1st PARACHUTE BRIGADE

parts of DIV HQ & R.H.

1st AIRLANDING RECCE SQN.

parts of R.A., R.E. & DIV HQ

ARNHEM

1st POLISH PARACHUTE BRIGADE

1st POLISH PARACHUTE BRIGADE

'K' PLANNED DZ

ACTUAL DZ

RAILWAY BRIDGE

LOWER RHINE

FERRY

to Utrecht

to Nijmegen

Velp

Huissen

Driel

Heteren

Renkum

N

(Reproduced courtesy of the Airborne Forces Museum)

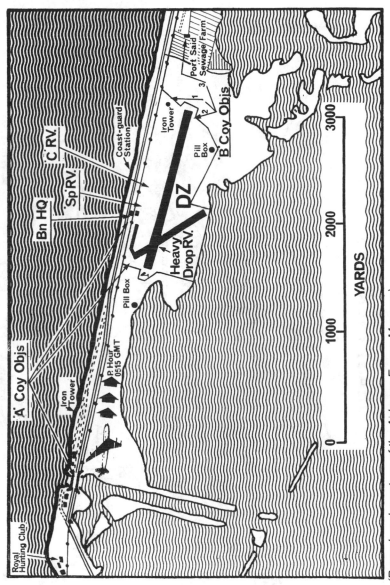

CAPTURE OF EL GAMIL AIRFIELD
5 November 1956, 3 Para Group

Royal Hunting Club

'A' Coy Objs

Iron Tower

P Hour 0515 GMT

Pill Box

Bn HQ

Sp RV.

C RV.

Coast-guard Station

Iron Tower

Pill Box

Heavy Drop RV.

DZ

'B' Coy Objs

1

2

3

Port Said Sewage Farm

YARDS

0   1000   2000   3000

(Reproduced courtesy of the Airborne Forces Museum)

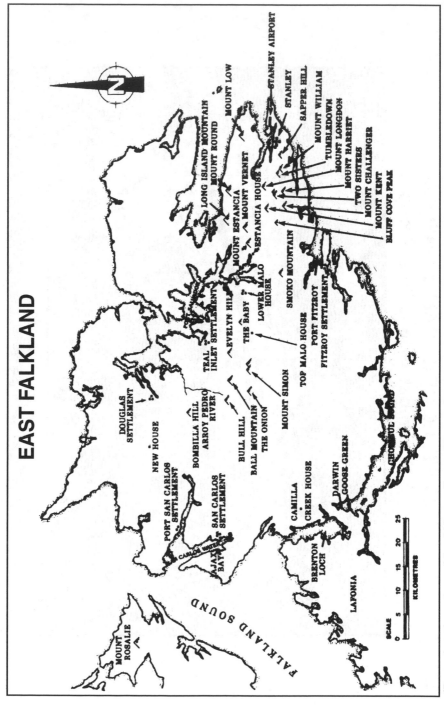

(Reproduced courtesy of the Airborne Forces Museum)

INDEX